Why Innovations Live or Die
South Africa's innovation system

EDITED BY

Zamanzima Mazibuko-Makena
and Thomas Pogue

MAPUNGUBWE
INSTITUTE FOR STRATEGIC REFLECTION (MISTRA)

First published by the Mapungubwe Institute for Strategic Reflection (MISTRA) in 2024

142 Western Service Road
Woodmead
Johannesburg

ISBN 978-1-920690-45-8

© MISTRA, 2024

Production and design by Jacana Media, 2024
Cover design: Hothouse Design
Text editor: Terry Shakinovsky
Copy editor: Lara Jacob
Proofreader: Megan Mance
Indexer: Rita Sephton
Designer: Sam van Straaten
Set in Stempel Garamond 10.5/15pt

Please cite this publication as follows:
MISTRA. 2024. *Why Innovations Live or Die: South Africa's innovation system.*
Johannesburg: Mapungubwe Institute for Strategic Reflection.

Contents

Acknowledgements. vii

Acronyms and abbreviations ix

Contributors xiv

Preface xxiii

Chapter 1:   Introduction: South African technologies and
commercialisation

– Thomas Pogue and Zamanzima Mazibuko-Makena . . 1

PART ONE
TRANSFORMATIONAL ORIENTATION OF SOUTH AFRICA'S NATIONAL SYSTEM OF INNOVATION SINCE DEMOCRATISATION

Chapter 2:   Where innovations may come to life: A new policy mix
to build firm capabilities across the national system of
innovation

– Glenda Kruss, Amy Kahn and Il-haam Petersen . . . 34

Chapter 3:   Reorienting technology transfer in South African
universities and science councils towards public
value outcomes

– Nazeem Mustapha and Gerard Ralphs 75

PART TWO
TECHNOLOGIES' JOURNEYS

Chapter 4:   The role of intermediaries in overcoming systemic failure in the South African economy: A case study of policy interventions in the furniture industry in the southern Cape

– Andre Kraak 112

Chapter 5:   Frugal and reverse innovation in the medical devices industry in South Africa

– Zamanzima Mazibuko-Makena 139

Chapter 6:   Life and death in the NSI: The role of public sector innovation

– Geci Karuri-Sebina, Mjumo Mzyece, Pierre Schoonraad, Nsizwa Dlamini 160

Chapter 7:   Government-led technological missions: An assessment of the PBMR, SKA and HySA projects

– Nqobile Xaba and Xolile Fuku 186

Chapter 8:   Structural change and innovation in the mineral resource finance network

– Thomas Pogue 216

PART THREE
PUBLIC POLICY AND INNOVATION SYSTEM NAVIGATION

Chapter 9:   Death by centralisation: Exploring disjunctures and opportunities for city-driven innovation systems in South Africa

– Stacey-Leigh Joseph and Geci Karuri-Sebina 244

Chapter 10: Moving beyond national systems of innovation:
Insights from antiretroviral localisation

– *David Walwyn* 281

Chapter 11: Chasms of understanding: Testing the innovation
chasm construct

– *Michael Kahn* 315

Chapter 12: Conclusions and policy recommendations

– *Thomas Pogue and Zamanzima
Mazibuko-Makena* 341

Index 364

Acknowledgements

The Mapungubwe Institute for Strategic Reflection (MISTRA) would like to express its earnest gratitude to the editors of this volume, Thomas Pogue and Zamanzima Mazibuko-Makena, who provided oversight of, and editorial contributions to, this book. Thanks are also extended to Nqobile Xaba, the project coordinator, assisted by Anelile Gibixego, for providing valuable support. MISTRA is honoured to have worked with the high calibre of authors who dedicated their time and energy to producing these chapters. Appreciation is also extended to the subject specialists who reviewed these chapters and provided invaluable comments.

Gratitude goes to the MISTRA staff who contributed to the successful completion of this project: the fundraising, operations and project management teams; Terry Shakinovsky, who copy-edited the book and managed the publication process; Professor Susan Booysen for her efforts to ensure that this publication meets the highest standards, and Joel Netshitenzhe for his thorough reading of the manuscript. Final thanks go to the Jacana Media publishing team.

MISTRA Funders
Intellectual endeavours of this magnitude are not possible without financial resources. The Department of Science and Innovation (DSI) deserve our special thanks for its support of this project. MISTRA also thanks the following corporate donors who support the Institute and make its work possible. They include:

Anglo American Platinum
Anglo American Head Office

Batho Batho Trust
Discovery Central Services
Friedrich-Ebert-Stiftung (FES)
Harith Partners
National Institute for Humanities and Social Sciences (NIHSS)
Oppenheimer Memorial Trust (OMT)
Royal Bafokeng
Shell South Africa
Simeka Capital Holdings
Standard Bank
Transnet
Yellowwoods

Acronyms and abbreviations

4IR	Fourth Industrial Revolution
AAA	Astronomy Advantage Area
AGA	Astronomy Geographic Advantage
AIDS	acquired immunodeficiency syndrome
AMSP	Africa Medical Supplies Platform
API	active pharmaceutical ingredient
ARC	Agricultural Research Council
ART	ARV treatment
ARV	antiretroviral
ASSAF	Academy of Science of South Africa
AU	Africa Union
BEE	Black Economic Empowerment
CCs	competency centres
CERN	European Council for Nuclear Research
CESTII	Centre for Science, Technology and Innovation Indicators
CHAI	Clinton Health AIDS Initiative
CHE	Council on Higher Education
COMRO	Chamber of Mines Research Organisation
COMSA	Chamber of Mines of South Africa
COVID-19	Coronavirus disease 2019
CPSI	Centre for Public Service Innovation
CSIR	Council for Scientific and Industrial Research
CUT	Central University of Technology
DACST	Department of Arts, Culture, Science and Technology
DEFF	Department of Environment, Forestry and Fisheries
DoE	Department of Energy
DP	Decadal Plan
DPSA	Department of Public Service Administration

DSI	Department of Science and Innovation
DST	Department of Science and Technology
DTI	Department of Trade and Industry
DTIC	Department of Trade, Industry and Competition
DUI	Doing, Using and Interacting
EPWP	Expanded Public Works Programme
ESA	European Space Agency
ESFRI	European Strategy Forum of Research Infrastructures
ESI	Essential Science Indicator
ESO	European Southern Observatory
EU	European Union
EUROSTAT	European Statistics
FURNTECH	Furniture Technology Centre Trust
FWR	Far West Rand
GDP	Gross Domestic Product
GOV	Government Agency or State-Owned Enterprise
HBDI	Historically Black and Disadvantaged Institutions
HCD	Human Capital Development
HESTIL	Higher Education, Science, Technology and Innovation Landscape
HIV	Human Immunodeficiency Virus
HSRC	Human Sciences Research Council
HTR	High temperature Reactor
HTR-PM	High-Temperature Gas-Cooled Modular Pebble Bed
HWPI	Historically White and Privileged Institutions
HySA	Hydrogen South Africa
IAP	invasive alien plant
IDC	Industrial Development Corporation
IDP	Integrated Development Plans
IDRC	International Development Research Centre
IEEE	Institute of Electrical and Electronic Engineers
IP	Intellectual Property
IP&TT	Intellectual Property and Technology Transfer
IPHE	International Partnership for Hydrogen and Fuel Cells and the Economy
IPR-PFRD	Intellectual Property Rights from Publicly Financed Research and Development

IST	Integrated Systems Technology
IT	Industrial Technology
KAT	Karoo Array Telescope
LMIC	low- and middle-income countries
LSI	local systems of innovation
MEA	membrane electrode assembly
MIMI	Municipal Innovation Maturity Index
MINTEK	Council for Mineral Technology
MIT	Massachusetts Institute of Technology
MLP	multi-level perspective
MRC	Medical Research Council
MRFN	mineral resource finance network
MW	mega watts
NACI	National Advisory Council on Innovation
NBESR	National Bureau of Educational and Social Research
NCOA	Natal Coal Owners' Association
NDP	National Development Plan
NECSA	Nuclear Energy Corporation of South Africa
NEMBA	National Environment Management Biodiversity Act
NEPAD	New Partnership for Africa's Development
NGO	non-governmental organisation
NIMPO	National Intellectual Property Management Office
NIPMO	Intellectual Property Management Office
NP	National Party
NPC	National Planning Commission
NRC	Nuclear Regulatory Commission
NRF	National Research Foundation
NSI	national systems of innovation
OECD	Organisation for Economic Cooperation and Development
OFS	Orange Free State
OTTs	Offices of Technology Transfer
PBMR	Pebble Bed Modular Reactor
PEM	Proton Exchange Membrane
PGM	Platinum Group Metal
PLHIV	people living with HIV
PRO	public research organisation

PSI	public sector innovation
PV	photo voltaic
PWR	pressurised water reactor
R&D	research and development
RC	Research Councils or Science Councils
RDI	Research and Development and Innovation
RSA	Republic of South Africa
SA	South Africa
SADC	Southern African Development Community
SAHPRA	South African Health Products Regulatory Authority
SAIAMC	South African Institute for Advanced Materials Chemistry
SAIMM	Southern African Institute of Mining and Metallurgy
SAMERDI	South African Mining Extraction Research, Development & Innovation
SAMRC	South African Medical Research Council
SANParks	South African National Parks
SARIMA	Southern African Research & Innovation Management Association
SARS	South African Revenue Service
SATCAP	Successful Application of Technology Centred Around People
SDCI	School Desks and Conservation Initiative
SDF	Spatial Development Framework
SDG	Sustainable Development Goals
SEDA	Small Enterprise Development Agency
SET	science, engineering and technology
SETA	Sector Education and Training Authority
SKA	Square Kilometre Array
SME	small and micro enterprise
SMME	small, medium and micro-enterprises
SMR	small modular reactor
SPII	Support Programme for Industrial Innovation
SPLUMA	Spatial Planning and Land Use Management Act
STI	science, technology and innovation
TCOA	Transvaal Coal Owners' Association
THRIP	Technology and Human Resources for Innovation programme

TIA	Technology Innovation Agency
TIPC	Transformative Innovation Policy Consortium
TLD	Tenofovir, Lamivudine and Dolutegravir
TRIPS	Trade-Related Aspects of Intellectual Property
UCT	University of Cape Town
UK	United Kingdom
UN	United Nations
US	United States
USA	United States of America
UTF	University Technology Fund
WHO	World Health Organization
WP	White Paper

Contributors

Zamanzima Mazibuko-Makena, co-editor of this volume, is the senior researcher in the Knowledge Economy and Scientific Advancement Faculty at the Mapungubwe Institute for Strategic Reflection (MISTRA). She obtained her MSc (Med) in Pharmaceutics (cum laude) from the University of the Witwatersrand. Mazibuko-Makena has authored journal articles on nano-enabled drug delivery technologies and the Fourth Industrial Revolution (4IR) and has a pending patent filed with Wits Enterprise for a nano-enabled drug delivery system. Mazibuko-Makena is the editor of and contributing author to the MISTRA volumes *Beyond Imagination: The Ethics and Applications of Nanotechnology and Bio-Economics in South Africa, Epidemics and the Health of African Nations* and most recently co-edited *Leap 4.0: African Perspectives of the Fourth Industrial Revolution.* Her research interests include healthcare systems in Africa, nanomedicine, systems of innovation, the low-carbon economy, and the beneficiation of strategic minerals in South Africa (particularly platinum group metals).

Thomas Pogue, co-editor of this volume, is an executive director of the Center for Business and Policy Research (CBPR) at the University of the Pacific in the United States of America. At the CBPR since 2010, he has led its efforts to assess changing socio-economic relationships across northern California. While building CBPR's expertise on skills ecosystems and equitable economic development, he has also continued work monitoring and evaluating innovation systems at various levels in South Africa. Thomas has amassed extensive experience with research institutes in the United States, Europe and South Africa, including Tshwane University of Technology's Institute for Economic Research on Innovation (IERI), the Council for Scientific and Industrial Research (CSIR) and the University of Cape Town's Development Policy Research Unit. That work began with an initial concern about sustainable development policy and evolved to include the economics of technological change, human capital development and regional economic transitions.

Amy Kahn (PhD) is a research specialist at the Centre for the Science, Technology and Innovation Indicators (CeSTII) at the Human Sciences Research Council (HSRC). She project leads the South African Business Innovation Survey, one of CeSTII's flagship surveys. Prior to joining the HSCR in February 2020, Kahn completed her doctorate in Economics at the University of Cape Town. She also worked for several years in the design and implementation of large-scale socio-economic surveys in East Africa and South Africa. Her current and previous research has focused on R&D and innovation in the South African business sector, skills development, basic and higher education, labour markets and survey methodology.

Andre Kraak (PhD) is currently a consultant on post-school education and training and the economy. He has worked at two South African universities (UWC and Wits), the Human Sciences Research Council (HSRC) and for a consultancy firm on Skills Development, Mzabalaso Advisory Services (MAS). He has a PhD in Education Policy and has recently submitted a second PhD in the Economics of Innovation at the University of Johannesburg. Dr Kraak has been involved in several education and training policy development initiatives including the comprehensive 2018 review of the third National Skills Development Strategy for the National Skills Authority. Dr Kraak's interests span further and higher education, skills development, science and technology policy studies and evolutionary economics.

David Walwyn (PhD) is a Professor in the Graduate School of Technology Management at the University of Pretoria. His research interests cover sustainability transitions (particularly with respect to the socio-technical systems of energy and mobility), science and innovation policy, research management and industry localisation, the latter focused mainly on health technologies (vaccines and pharmaceuticals), renewable energy technologies and chemicals. In the broadest sense, his work lies at the interface between techno-economics, innovation/industrial policy and socio-technical transitions. He currently teaches courses on engineering economics, project economics, circular economy and energy value chains. He supervises at least 15 Master's students each year on the Management of Technology and Innovation programme offered by the University of Pretoria and has three PhD students. He has published widely in the area of science and technology policy, research management, health sciences and biotechnology (1 patent, 45 articles in peer-reviewed journals, six book chapters, 58 conference papers and many articles in the press on sites such as *The Conversation* and *Engineering News*). He has also consulted on multiple policy projects relating to innovation policy and supported university technology transfer through techno-economic feasibility studies (25 policy papers). Dr Walwyn has a BSc in Chemical Engineering from the University of Cape Town and a PhD in Organic Chemistry from the University of Cambridge. He is a member of the Academy of Sciences of South Africa and an Associate Editor of *International Journal of Innovation and Technology Management*.

Geci Karuri-Sebina (PhD) is a scholar-practitioner based in Johannesburg working in the intersection between people, place and technological change. She is an associate professor at the Wits School of Governance where she hosts the Civic Tech Innovation Network and coordinates the establishment of a new African Centre of Excellence in Digital Governance. She is also Adjunct Professor at the University of Cape Town's African Centre for Cities, associate of South African Cities Network and a global faculty member with Singularity University on the future of cities and governance. Karuri-Sebina also currently serves as a board member of PlanAct, is a founding director of the Southern African Node of the Millennium Project, and as the Vice-Chairperson of AfricaLICS (the community of innovation scholars in Africa). Karuri-Sebina is recognised and published in the fields of development planning, policy, foresight and innovation and is involved in editorial roles in several leading journals in the fields of futures and innovation. She previously held positions at the Council for Scientific and Industrial Research, the Human Sciences Research Council and South Africa's National Treasury. Karuri-Sebina holds bachelor's degrees in Computer Science and Sociology (Iowa); master's degrees in Urban Planning and Architecture from UCLA (Los Angeles); and a PhD from the University of the Witwatersrand (Johannesburg).

Gerard Ralphs is Policy Analyst and Programme Manager, Centre for Science, Technology and Innovation Indicators, Human Sciences Research Council, where he leads a project on Centre advocacy. He is also a doctoral candidate in public management and governance with a specialisation in innovation at the University of Johannesburg's Trilateral Chair on Transformative Innovation, 4IR and Sustainable Development.

Glenda Kruss (PhD) is the Executive Head of the Centre for Science, Technology and Innovation Indicators (CeSTII) unit at the Human Sciences Research Council. Over the past twenty years, she has worked in the field of innovation studies, to understand the role of universities and public research institutes in economic and social development, and the determinants of skills and knowledge flows within sectoral, national and global systems of innovation. Her current research focus is oriented towards contextually appropriate datasets, measures and indicators of Science, Technology and Innovation for inclusive and sustainable development in South Africa and sub-Saharan Africa. She has collaborated widely on comparative research projects in Africa, Latin America, Asia and Europe, and has led large scale projects for national government, building alliances and networks between researchers, policy makers and practitioners in South Africa and the global South.

Il-haam Petersen (PhD) is Chief Research Specialist at the Centre for the Science, Technology and Innovation Indicators (CeSTII) at the Human Sciences Research Council (HSRC). She holds a DPhil in Sociology from Trinity College Dublin. Prior to joining CeSTII in 2017, she completed a post-doctoral fellowship in the Education and Skills Development programme at the HSRC. Il-haam's research focuses on inter-organisational innovation networks, particularly the micro-foundations of innovation, and experimentation with new methodologies for understanding and measuring innovation in informal settings.

Mjumo Mzyece (PhD) is an associate professor of Technology and Operations Management at the Wits Business School in Johannesburg, South Africa. Previously, he led the Smart Industries (ICT and Advanced Manufacturing) unit at The Innovation Hub, the innovation agency of the Gauteng Provincial Government. He has extensive international experience in the global technology industry and has held various operational, management, R&D, academic and consulting roles in leading organisations, including IBM U.S., Econet Group and Agilent Technologies. He has authored or co-authored over 70 peer-reviewed scientific and technical publications, including a significant body of work that has been nationally and internationally influential in the area of dynamic and opportunistic spectrum management. He holds a Bachelor of Engineering (BEng) (Honours) in Electronic and Electrical Engineering from Manchester University, England; a Master of Science (MSc) (Distinction) in Communications Technology and Policy and a PhD in Electronic and Electrical Engineering, both from Strathclyde University, Scotland; and a Master of Business Administration (MBA) from Duke University, USA.

Michael Kahn (PhD) is an independent policy advisor and evaluator of research and innovation. He has served as ministerial advisor, government official, NGO director, academic and researcher, as executive director of the Human Sciences Research Council (HSRC), and international consultant. He is Honorary Professor of Practice in the University of Johannesburg, Research Fellow in the Centre for Research on Evaluation, Science and Technology at Stellenbosch University, and Extraordinary Professor of the University of the

Western Cape. He is a skilled communicator and facilitator with strengths in policy, strategy and planning, measurement, monitoring and evaluation, working with clients in government, universities, the multilateral organisations, development banks and private sector, with wide country experience. He is a frequent keynote speaker at international meetings. His academic studies cover engineering, mathematical physics and education policy, planning and management. He holds the PhD, and DIC of Imperial College, MA of the University of London, and BSc (Hons) of the University of Cape Town. He is the author of more than 110 peer-reviewed journal articles, books and book chapters, and another hundred consultancy reports.

Nazeem Mustapha (PhD) holds a PhD in Applied Mathematics from the University of Cape Town. At UCT he lectured students in the Faculty of Engineering and the Built Environment, before moving on to the government sector as a senior manager in statistical methodology at the national statistical institute of South Africa, known as Stats SA. He currently leads the R&D measurement and analysis programme within the Centre for Science, Technology and Innovation Indicators (CeSTII) of the Human Sciences Research Council (HSRC) in South Africa. Most recently, Dr Mustapha led the development of research into the measurement of innovation in the informal sector at the Centre. Prior to this, he opened up new areas of measurement and research on intellectual property and technology transfer in publicly funded institutions, and on the innovation capabilities of state-owned enterprises. In addition to participation in conferences on innovation, Dr Mustapha regularly interacts with local and global innovation policy makers routinely as part of his work function and also has been invited to advise provincial and national bodies on innovation measurement in his personal capacity.

Nqobile Xaba (PhD) is a researcher in the Knowledge Economy and Scientific Advancement faculty at the Mapungubwe Institute for Strategic Reflection (MISTRA). Her work focuses on the just transition in South Africa, and the broader climate change and environmental issues, and platinum group metals (PGM) beneficiation through hydrogen and fuel cell technologies. Prior to joining MISTRA she was a lecturer at Tshwane University of Technology. She previously worked as a doctoral candidate and postdoctoral fellow at the at the Council of Scientific and Industrial Research (CSIR) focusing on the development of materials for fuel cell electrocatalysts and rechargeable battery applications. She holds a BSc degree in Pure and Applied Chemistry (cum laude) from the University of KwaZulu-Natal (UKZN), a BSc honours degree in Chemistry, an MSc degree in Chemical Engineering Science from the University of North-West (NWU), and a PhD in Chemistry from the University of the Western Cape (UWC). She has published her work in renowned scientific journal articles, has contributed book chapters and editorial opinion articles on leading South African publications. She is the co-editor and contributing author to the MISTRA volume *A Just Transition to a Low Carbon Future in South Africa.*

Nsizwa Dlamini is an innovation researcher at the Centre for Public Service Innovation. He is mainly responsible for innovation-related research and impact assessment work on various initiatives that the organisation embarks on. He also develops case studies on various initiatives that the CPSI has undertaken and has managed some public sector innovation pilot projects. Before joining the CPSI he worked at the Natal Museum as an Anthropology Researcher. He then joined the Department of Public Service and Administration in 2005 where he was responsible for case study writing, managing a publication and supporting its knowledge management initiatives. He has a master's degree from the University of KwaZulu-Natal obtained in 2002. He has contributed two book chapters and a journal article on representations of 'zuluness'. He has also published a range of public sector innovation related articles and case studies in CPSI publications that are not peer reviewed.

Pierre Schoonraad is Chief Director: Research and Development at the Centre for Public Service Innovation (CPSI), a Government Component reporting to the Minister for Public Service and Administration. His responsibilities include the research and development of innovations in support of government's priority outcomes and collaborating with entities of the national system of innovation, social entrepreneurs and innovators to develop new service delivery solutions as part of a sustainable, open innovation system. He is also responsible for anticipatory innovation, thus working towards finding solutions for the problems of tomorrow and building a public service for the next generation. He previously served in the DPSA's Learning, Knowledge Management and Research Unit as Director: Research. Amongst other tasks, he conducted research and capacity assessments to inform Cabinet on the efficacy of policy implementation. Before joining the public service in 2004, Schoonraad spent more than a decade as researcher and project manager in the not-for-profit sector conducting action research in urban informal settlements focusing on finding innovative solutions for poverty-related challenges. He researched and developed solutions for diverse challenges such as energy efficiency in low-cost housing, job creation and combatting air pollution. He contributes internationally to promote public sector innovation and strategic foresight, working closely with development agencies such as the UNDP and other international organisations such as the OECD. He serves as National Contact Point of the OECD's Observatory of Public Sector Innovation (OPSI) and the OECD Government Foresight Practitioners Network. Schoonraad holds BA and BD degrees from the University of Pretoria.

Xolile Fuku (PhD) is a senior lecturer at the University of South Africa's Institute for Nanotechnology and Water Sustainability (iNanoWS). Dr Fuku holds a PhD in Chemistry and a diploma in Business Administration from the University of the Western Cape and the University of the Witwatersrand, respectively. He is a previous member of International Society of Electrochemistry (ISE) and currently a registered member of the South African Chemical Institute (SACI) and the South African Council for Natural Scientific Professions (SACNASP) as well as the Royal Society of Chemistry. Dr Fuku was elected as an African Academy of Science (AAS) affiliate for his significant contribution to the water-energy nexus through technology advancement and innovation. His research interests include electrochemical sensors, energy conversion and storage systems, with emphasis on hydrogen technology, fuel cells and battery materials. He has significantly expanded his research focus to other energy-related fields, such as clean, sustainable energy solutions, with a specific interest in thermal energy, electrolysis and carbon dioxide conversion into sustainable green hydrogen and other valuable chemicals. He has over 40 peer-reviewed scientific papers, four book chapters, and has presented at over 54 local and international conferences. Furthermore, he supervises and mentors early-career researchers as well as MSc and PhD students.

Preface

A vision for South Africa's National System of Innovation (NSI) was articulated some three decades ago in the *White Paper on Science and Technology* (1996). The idealism that inspired a nation in rebirth also found expression in the science and innovation sector, with a better life for all and inclusion in a competitive economy infusing the policy outlook.

Since then, the NSI has been moulded and re-moulded in light of domestic and global experiences. In a book published in 2016 on innovation systems in southern Africa, the Mapungubwe Institute for Strategic Reflection (MISTRA) traced various dimensions of innovation from the pre-colonial period, highlighting the importance of continuous learning which, as a rule, comes with both success and failure.

South Africa has registered many achievements in science and innovation both before and after the attainment of democracy. The fundamental question, though, is about the relevance and utility of innovations to the lived experiences of the country's population. This relates to whether the system promotes economic growth and social inclusion and whether it inspires social agency and initiative across all sectors of the population.

The success of an innovation system should be measured primarily by its impact on the economic, social, governance and safety and security areas of human endeavour. But the process is not linear: even in the wreckage of failure are innumerable positive lessons that can inspire new and valuable pursuits. The capacities that are built and supported; the refinement of the value chain from scientific research through to commercialisation; the ability not only to invent but also to adopt and adapt – all these and other issues are fundamental to building a system that serves the core objective of improving the human condition.

This volume, *Why Innovations Live or Die: South Africa's innovation system*, interrogates these questions. It examines the factors that affect the application and commercialisation of innovations. And there, in the 'valley of death' or 'the innovation chasm', are to be found technologies that succumbed to the gravity of failure. But beyond the valley are inventions that emerged into the sunlight of successful application and commercialisation.

The book examines lessons from some highly promising research endeavours that fell by the wayside. Many of these initiatives floundered in the complexities of a defective value chain; some were abandoned only to be pursued by others beyond the country's borders. Importantly, the book also interrogates the successes of South African innovations which continue to impact positively on people's lives, and the factors that underpin these accomplishments. Authors trace the journeys of undertakings such as the Joule electric car, the Square Kilometre Array, the Pebble Bed Modular Reactor, and transdisciplinary efforts on HIV and Covid-19.

In critiquing standard approaches to evaluating the utility of innovation activities, the authors distinguish between broad and narrow conceptualisations. The former emphasises issues such as networks, breadth of know-how, and the macrosocial environment in which the NSI operates; the latter deals with formal, explicit and technical systems and structures. Authors argue that the philosophical outlook that informs innovation policy; the attitude of mind in both the public and private sectors; and the content and timeframes attached to national development planning, among other factors, are as important as (if not more important than) technical issues related to scientific expertise, training pipelines and resource allocation. In other words, the system of innovation is a holistic domain, straddling a variety of disciplines and spatial issues that include centralisation and decentralisation in planning and application. The book also underlines that, while it is logical to build on existing expertise and associated endeavours, conscious efforts should be made to broaden the vistas of research and avoid path dependency.

It is against the backdrop of these and other insights that the volume proffers policy recommendations that MISTRA hopes will deepen strategic reflections and practical actions on a matter that is fundamental to South Africa's socioeconomic progress.

MISTRA is grateful to the researchers and practitioners who contributed to the conceptualisation and content of this volume. Gratitude also goes to the Department of Science and Innovation (DSI) for its all-round support, and to all of MISTRA's donors for assisting the Institute in its work.

Joel Netshitenzhe
Executive Director

ONE

Introduction
South African technologies and commercialisation

THOMAS POGUE AND ZAMANZIMA
MAZIBUKO-MAKENA

INTRODUCTION

South Africa has made great progress in developing its scientific and technological capabilities and in introducing policies to support economic and social development through science and technology. Despite this progress, there appear to be challenges to the country delivering on the commercialisation of highly promising research, including some world-class research projects. While recognising that innovative activities are inherently unpredictable and unlikely to be linear, improving the commercialisation and success of new products would mean that South Africa would be better able to produce innovations that support economic growth and employment creation, and establish the country as a more competitive innovation destination. Successful development of technologies requires investment, know-

1

ledge of institutional environments, specialised skills and understanding of opportunity niches.

Innovation and entrepreneurship are defined as strategic factors for economic development (Mamabolo, Kerrin and Kele, 2017). Higher education institutions, science councils, public entities and private research institutions are facing growing pressure to contribute towards innovation and entrepreneurship that have commercial value and contribute to economic development. Furthermore, public-funded universities are expected to play a significant role in uplifting social and economic conditions through the direct transfer of innovative knowledge products to industry and the private sector (Bercovitz and Feldman, 2006). Essentially, publicly supported research is expected to provide better and faster answers to South Africa's public-issue concerns.

However, even with efforts to address the commercialisation of research outputs, ground-breaking innovations such as the Joule[1] – detailed in Appendix 1 at the end of this chapter – have not been successful at the commercialisation stage. This was despite the fact that the company that developed the Joule, Optimal Energy, had conducted a rigorous and successful development process; had a solid team of 108 people; substantial in-house technology; and a remarkable network of partners and suppliers. Nonetheless it could not successfully commercialise the technology and had to close (Swart, 2015).

This is but one example of many South African failures to deliver on the commercialisation of highly promising technology. This introductory chapter lays the groundwork for the discussions the authors in this book have on the journeys of various technologies in South Africa and what fundamental, systemic causes contribute to their failure or success. This chapter begins with an overview of the post-apartheid national system of innovation, providing a brief history of science and technology policies introduced after 1994. Subsequently, key technology and innovation concepts are highlighted, thereby

---

1   Joule was an electric, five-seat passenger car conceived by Optimal Energy, a South African company based in Cape Town. It was a concept car that was never released commercially. As mentioned in the text above, please see Appendix 1 for more information and analysis.

establishing a unifying analytical foundation on which the chapters in the book are founded. In the book *The Emergence of Systems of Innovation in South(ern) Africa: Long Histories and Contemporary Debates* by MISTRA (2016), it was found that the relevance and utility of a system of innovation should be measured primarily by the extent to which it helps to solve societal problems and to improve the human condition. Consequently, it is at what we are terming the 'domain level' – a concept discussed later in the chapter – that technologies in this publication are assessed. Therefore, after discussing integrated theoretical and methodological approaches, this introductory chapter reframes the ensuing chapters of this book in this context. The final chapter contains reflections on what will be identified as the primary research questions and on the policy implications of these.

POST-APARTHEID NATIONAL SYSTEM OF INNOVATION: A BRIEF OVERVIEW

South Africa's first democratically elected government of 1994 had the immediate task of either updating or completely reconstructing national policy in different areas. The Reconstruction and Development Programme (RDP) of 1994 – an integrated, coherent socioeconomic policy framework introduced at the onset of democracy – promoted the role of science and technology in innovation and the economy. The processes of democratisation initiated after 1994 provided the opportunity for South Africa to attempt a far-reaching transformation of its science and technology system. At a technical level, the country was building on the foundation of a system that had developed under colonial governments and the apartheid regime. This sought not only to modernise the country's economic base but also, when appropriate, to build a military-industrial complex and attain a level of self-sufficiency against the backdrop of international isolation.

The importance of a more coordinated view of science and technology was immediately identified. As a result, the Department of Arts, Culture, Science and Technology (DACST) was formed in 1994 with the responsibility of developing national science and technology policy, elaborating on the high-level directives contained in the RDP.

However, the combination of science and technology with arts and culture was already an indication that science and technology, as well as innovation, were not given high priority in the first democratic government. Nonetheless, the White Paper on Science and Technology was subsequently produced (DACST, 1996). This was followed by a number of studies in support of the White Paper such as the National Science and Technology Audit (DACST, 1998a), National Research and Technology Foresight (DACST, 1999), and a review of South Africa's Science Councils (Science, Engineering and Technology Institutional Reviews) (DACST, 1998b).

The White Paper was subtitled 'Preparing for the 21st Century' and was an important tool to describe how government planned to launch South Africa into the competitive world economy. Furthermore, it posited a future in which all South Africans could experience a better quality of life while participating in a competitive economy. This was all to be achieved under a system referred to as the national system of innovation (NSI). The framework proposed by the White Paper assumed a set of institutions, organisations and policies that would help to implement the various objectives and functions of the NSI.

The following six goals were deemed essential by the developers of the 1996 White Paper in order to realise South Africa's vision for an improved future (Hart et al., 2013: 11):

1. Establish an efficient, well-coordinated and integrated system of technological and social innovation;
2. Encourage creative and collaborative partnerships for individual and national benefit;
3. Aim at problem-solving and involving the multidisciplinary use of engineering and natural, health, environmental, human and social sciences;
4. Include formerly marginalised stakeholders in science and technology policymaking and resource-allocation activities;
5. Ensure that the advancement of knowledge is valued as important to national development; and
6. Improve support for all types of innovation fundamental to sustainable economic growth, employment creation, and equity achieved through redress and social development.

The NSI approach is subject to an array of definitions. These range from a narrow construct where innovations are restricted to technological innovations, organisations and institutions that are limited to those involved in research and development. At the other end of the spectrum, the definitions extend to a broad construct where innovations include all aspects of how economic activity is organised, institutional set-ups affecting learning as well as research and development (Lundvall, 1992; MISTRA, 2016).

The White Paper defined the NSI as 'a network of institutions in the public and private sectors whose activities and actions initiate, import, modify and diffuse new technologies' (DACST, 1996). This definition was taken directly from Freeman (1991) and in its focus on technology inclines towards the narrow definition of the NSI. This definition was progressive, expanding beyond the pre-1994 limited and exclusionary practices of science and technology research and development (R&D) in South Africa.

A large portion of the White Paper specified the role of government and institutional arrangements in achieving the goals of the NSI. Crucial institutional arrangements included the establishment of the Department of Science and Technology (DST) separate from the Department of Arts and Culture (DAC). The key directive of the DST was to 'develop, manage and coordinate the national system of innovation in order to maximise human capital development, sustainable economic growth and improved quality of life for all as mandated by the *White Paper on Science and Technology* of 1996' (DST, 2002). Additionally, there was the formation of the Ministers Committee on Science and Technology (MCST) and the National Advisory Council on Innovation (NACI) for the development of policy and to ensure the integration of science, technology and innovation (STI) into various sectors of the economy and society.

Some of the institutional and governance proposals of the White Paper were made more explicit when the National Research and Development Strategy was accepted by Cabinet in 2002. The strategies were endorsed in order to improve on the NSI and to address key challenges to the system's vigour and effectiveness. A review of South Africa's innovation policies by the Organisation for Economic Cooperation and Development (OECD, 2007), however, found that many of the proposals were not implemented. The OECD report attributed this to a failure to use research and innovation to support key social and economic objectives of the post-1994 government.

In 2007, the DST introduced the Ten-Year Plan for South Africa, which was a shift towards fostering a knowledge-based economy. Innovation Towards a Knowledge-based Economy: Ten-Year Plan for South Africa (2008–2018) anticipated that prioritising fundamentals such as research, infrastructure and the development of human capital would be key to growing the economy and narrowing the gap between research and socioeconomic outcomes.

By 2019, however, South Africa had not fully benefitted from the potential of STI to advance the objectives of the White Paper and the mandate for the NSI to deliver on its promises had not been fully achieved (DST, 2019). Policy on STI remained fragmented across government, and partnerships with business, academia and civil society still required strengthening. The set target of 1.5 per cent gross expenditure on research and development (GERD), as a percentage of the country's gross domestic product (GDP) target, had not been realised (0.82 per cent in 2016/17) (NACI, 2019), and the participation of black people and women in senior positions was still relatively low (DST, 2019). Black women and men made up less than 5 per cent and 20 per cent of professors respectively (NACI, 2019).

Subsequently, a 2019 White Paper on Science, Technology and Innovation, based on extensive reviews of the NSI, was released (DST, 2019). This White Paper is centred around South Africa using STI to take advantage of developments such as the Fourth Industrial Revolution (4IR) and geopolitical and demographic shifts. The 2019 White Paper highlights the core themes of inclusivity, transformation and partnerships. It puts forward suggestions on addressing policy coherence, developing human capabilities and local innovation systems, knowledge expansion and increased investment (DST, 2019).

A further development in 2019 was the formation of the Ministry of Higher Education, Science and Innovation. This meant that the Department of Higher Education and the now Department of Science and Innovation were housed under one ministry. However, the two departments still operate separately and have their own objectives and mandates. According to the DSI, the shift from the Department of Science and Technology to the Department of Science and Innovation puts greater emphasis on driving the innovation agenda (DSI, 2021). It remains to be seen, however, whether these changes will result in the NSI enabling exceptional innovations to be commercialised, thus facilitating the growth of the economy and the optimisation of public services or if innovations will still face limiting barriers with the NSI reproducing an inherited political economy (Maharajh, 2016).

Bearing this brief overview of South African innovation and commercialisation policy in mind, we turn next to the theoretical framing of the book.

THEORETICAL APPROACH: COMPLEXITY ECONOMICS

The individual chapters of this volume employ diverse theoretical perspectives. However, we believe that their focus on the journeys of technologies towards innovation allows them each to be framed within Arthur's (2009) conceptualisation, which takes into account that applied improvements may come in several forms. This conceptualisation is theoretically rooted in complexity economics. As explained by Arthur (2021), complexity economics views technologies as means to human purposes which are put together – combined – from parts, assemblies and sub-assemblies. As such, new technologies form by combinations of existing technologies, which lead to a recurring (algorithmic) sequence of events whereby the economy continually creates itself from itself. This involves the appearance of a new technology that replaces existing technologies; calls forth new ones to satisfy its needs; becomes a component available for the creation of further new technologies; and causes the economy, society and their institutions to rearrange themselves.

Complexity economics thereby looks at the process of formation and economic change over time. It also takes explicit consideration of the difficulties in distributing technologies in an environment where some may benefit, and some may lose. These are critical issues to be considered given the book's focus on the dynamics of technological development and technologies' impacts on realising transformative change. Arthur's (2009) approach also incorporates the existence of positive feedback (increasing returns), which may lead to situations where the winning technology may not be the best because of dynamic processes with random events and natural positive feedbacks. We further describe the key concepts of this approach in the next section.

KEY TECHNOLOGY AND INNOVATION CONCEPTS

Products of processes

Standard engineering is a design process that provides a key source of innovation and technological evolution. It involves the planning and construction of a new version of a known technology. This takes place within design projects that may involve the application of customary practices and standard components, or the application of experimental practices and parts. The projects begin with a new problem or set of problems and are solved or concluded when solutions or sets of solutions are identified. Individually the design solutions may contain little that is novel or innovative, but collectively incremental solutions steadily accumulate and improve over time, creating a distinct process of innovation.

Novel technologies use either new principles or established principles for a different purpose with exploitable effects or sets of effects. They may be need-driven or phenomenon-driven. Perceived needs that give rise to technologies may be produced by outside stimuli, such as social or economic needs, or may arise from internal technical problems. Alternatively, technologies that originate from a phenomenon or effect will entail some applications of their principles. Regardless of the process, novel technologies are part of discontinuous or 'step' change that is distinct from existing practices.

Structural deepening occurs as new versions of the technology emerge through a process of evolutionary selection, but also through two deliberate processes. In the first, components of a technology are replaced by improved versions. As the new components improve the technology's performance, they may necessitate changes in other parts of the technology, and thereby facilitate increased complexity. In the second, an existing technology's components are retained but additional components/assemblies are added to work around a technology's limitations. Through this process of adding additional assemblies, the technology's performance improves and the technology's structure becomes more complicated.

Constellation of technologies that creates and is created by wealth and power

A domain is any cluster of components forming devices or methods, along with an associated collection of practices and knowledge, rules of combination and associated ways of thinking. In contrast to the first three types of innovation, which involve a product or a process, a domain is a constellation of technologies that creates and is created by wealth and power. In this sense domains are not just a process of technology adoption, but a process of market change and technology adaptation mediated by finance, institutions, management, public policy and the availability of human capital.

Innovation as applied improvements of a technology

Technologies' successful introduction and adoption depend on putting together parts and assemblies to 'supply' new technologies such that they match opportunity niches.[2] As elements add to or disappear from the active collection of technologies, the collection of opportunity niches changes too. A co-evolution occurs between the set of arrangements and activities by which a society satisfies its needs and the collection of technologies available to fulfil them.

In this context, when considering the challenges to and opportunities for an innovation's successful adoption, we are presented with an array of factors which include:

- the need to design product/process improvements;
- the need to apply a novel phenomenon or effect;
- the need to replace components or add solutions; and

---

2 While opportunity niches are akin to 'demand' in the context of technologies, they are distinct as technologies can create needs as well as respond to them.

- the need to find solutions to a perceived need.

Significantly, though, it is also necessary to recognise technologies' interdependence on their social and economic environments. While it may appear that outputs from South Africa's science and technology system are unable to be adopted, which has been referred to as the innovation chasm (UNISA, 2020), the context in which there is demand, or opportunity niches, for the technologies is also shaped by the social and economic environment. Attempts to address the innovation chasm have included the establishment of institutions such as the National Intellectual Property Management Office (NIPMO) and the Technology Innovation Agency (TIA). However, only limited progress has been made in terms of tangible outputs such as technology firms, employment, patents and commercialisation revenues. It is therefore necessary to not only analyse South Africa's minimal success in commercialising its science and technological innovations but to also interrogate the nature of the processes that lead from technology and product development to eventual commercialisation. Essentially, domain change, or lack thereof, is a necessary component of analysis when examining the chasms and successes of commercialisation in South Africa's innovation system.

RESEARCH METHODOLOGY

We apply Arthur's (2009) conceptualisation of technology to a multidimensional analytical framework proposed by Weber and Rohracher (2012). This framework combines multi-level perspective and innovation systems as well as considerations of neoclassical market optimisation to analyse the factors affecting technologies' journeys from exploratory principles to innovations exploiting opportunity niches. This approach allows for an emphasis on the demandside (opportunity niches) and integration with other issue-centred policy areas such as development policy, as well as emphasis on the supply-side (principles creation) capabilities of innovation system constituents. The framework thereby allows for a three-dimensional conceptualisation of a technology's commercialisation as well as processes of transformative technological, social and economic change.

Those dimensions, and their component barriers to a technology's commercialisation, consist of the following elements:

1. *Market system failures*, which may result in sub-optimal investment in knowledge development because of:

    a) Information asymmetries when a short time horizon applied by market actors leads to the underfunding of relevant research and development;

    b) Knowledge spillovers, which arise because the public good character of certain types of knowledge can lead to socially sub-optimal investment in (basic) research and development;

    c) Externalisation of costs may be a problem with innovations-generated social costs, which are not borne by the producer and/or the consumer; or

    d) Exploitation of public resources leads to underinvestment in knowledge development.

2. *Structural system failures*, which may create mechanisms that contribute to weak system performance because of:

    a) Infrastructural failure, which results from under-investment in research and innovation due to deficits in existing physical and knowledge infrastructures;

    b) Institutional failures when there is a need for new institution-building as well as removal or modification of existing institutions. It is possible to make a distinction here between hard and soft failures:

        i) Hard institutional failures, which occur when there is an absence, excess or shortcoming of formal institutional mechanisms (laws/legislation, regulations, and standards);

        ii) Soft institutional failures, which occur when there are failures in political and socioeconomic cultures, social norms and values interactions or networks;

    c) Network failures, which occur when interactions are too dense to allow for novel insights, or when network inadequacies limit exchanges with third parties, thus inhibiting interactive learning and ultimately innovation;

    d) Capabilities failure, which occurs when the absence of the capabilities necessary for adapting to new and changing circumstances and (technological) opportunities leads to an inability to switch from an old to a new technological trajectory:

    i)   An element of under-investment in research (i.e. of market failure);

    ii)   A systemic problem of firms exhibiting path dependency due to their inability to absorb new knowledge.

3. *Transformational system failures*, which occur when there is a failure to induce strategic processes of change because of:

    a)   Directionality failure, not just to generate innovations as effectively and efficiently as possible, but also to contribute to a particular direction of transformation;

    b)   Demand articulation failures associated with the influence of demand during the incremental exploitation stage when failures due to insufficient complementary social, organisational or institutional innovation (domain technology) may prevent the uptake of socially desirable innovations by users and consumers;

    c)   Policy coordination failures, which occur when there is either a lack of vertical coherence between the activities of national, regional, sectoral and technological institutions and/or horizontal coordination across STI-policy, sectoral policies (e.g., transport, energy, health, industrial sector policies) and cross-cutting policies (e.g., tax policy, economic policy, regional policy); or

    d)   Reflexive failures: these occur when there is not enough ongoing monitoring of whether policies are contributing towards transformation goals. They are also a result of policies intended to create transformative change, which do not take sufficient account of the distributed nature of decision-making and intelligence. Policymakers also fail to take cognisance of relevant informal societal discourse, and more formal discussion in government spheres.

This book analyses the journeys of South African technologies and their technology domains. It describes the movement from exploratory principles to exploitation in opportunity niches as well as established opportunity niches feeding back into different combinations and exploratory principles. Through its consideration of these experiences, it seeks to advance understanding about the determinants of commercialisation and the extent to which technologies that are successfully commercialised contribute to South Africa's development goals. Further, the volume also examines what can be done to improve the impact of commercialised technologies on national socioeconomic priorities.

THE BOOK'S OBJECTIVES AND SUMMARY OF THE CHAPTERS

Research design

The book focuses on a series of technology case studies and policy assessments. These include cases of publicly and privately funded technologies as well as public–private partnerships. The analysis also takes cognisance of technology-related surveys and databases to augment insights from the other research. A transdisciplinary approach (MISTRA, 2013), which transcends the confines of conventional disciplines, is used to provide a deeper understanding of South Africa's commercialisation processes and their impact on the achievement of the country's developmental goals. This project brings together researchers in innovation studies, economic history, technological sciences and political economy to produce evidence-based, inclusive research outcomes.

The book's objectives can be framed through three primary research questions:

1. What impact is South Africa's commercialised research having on the achievement of its development goals?
2. Why are some technologies successfully commercialised, and others not?
3. Which policy changes could increase the socioeconomic impact of South African technology?

In addressing the first question, it is necessary to distinguish between broad and narrow conceptualisations of the national system of innovation. As a narrow concept, the national system of innovation consists of formal, explicit and defined structures. In contrast, the broad concept of a national system of innovation adds networks, capabilities and know-how as well as other informal features.[3] This distinction allows one to differentiate between the success, or lack thereof, of the narrow national system of innovation (formal institutions) and the broad national system of innovation (formal and informal institutions) in solving society's problems and advancing South Africa's development goals. Similarly, consideration is given to the extent to which contemporary technology domains are facilitating or impeding socially impactful technological development. There is also consideration of which technology domains are currently driving technological, social and economic change.

The second question addresses the key characteristics of technologies' journeys to commercialisation and how, if at all, successfully commercialised technologies feed back into the development of additional technologies. Exploring this question requires consideration of which factors tend to be associated with success and which tend to be associated with the failure to commercialise a technology. It is also important to reflect on whether it is possible to discern factors affecting the manner or rate at which technologies commercialise. The concept of the so-called 'innovation chasm' often comes up in this context. Given the significance attached to the idea of an innovation chasm in many South African discussions, the usefulness – or lack thereof – of this concept in commercialisation must also be considered. The principal narrative is that technologies can fall into a chasm in the journey from the basic ideation, research, development and piloting – all illustrated on the left-hand side of Figure 1.1 – to commercialisation. The innovation chasm then is the area where this linear path to commercialisation – achieved through a scaling-up of the initial technology for the market – stalls (depicted on the right side of Figure 1.1), and an otherwise viable technology fails to reach commercialisation.

---

3   Our distinction similarly follows the narrow and broad differentiation of Cassiolato and Lastres (2008) as well as that by MISTRA (2016).

In Chapter 11, however, Kahn critiques the usefulness of this concept, and its use and history in South African science and technology discussions.[4] For the most part the innovation chasm has not played a central role in the analyses in this volume. We contend that the fundamentally linear approach to a technology's development in the innovation chasm paradigm limits its insights and effectiveness. To illustrate these limitations, in Appendix 1 at the end of this chapter, we compare the failure to successfully commercialise the Joule electric vehicle (EV) with the journey of another EV, Tesla. This comparison of the routes taken by these two technologies is also illustrative of the limitation of the innovation chasm concept, and of the insights offered in the broader analytical framework used throughout this volume.

Figure 1.1: A conceptualisation of the innovation chasm

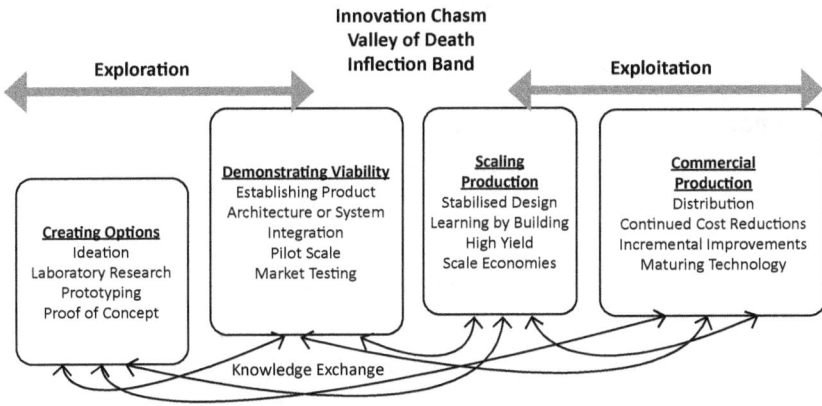

Source: Authors' illustrative summary of innovation chasm and innovation system literature

Lastly, the third question raised the issue of which policy changes can be made to improve the impact that successfully commercialised technologies have on South Africa's socio-economic needs. Particular

---

4   As Kahn points out in Chapter 11, the concept of an innovation chasm appears in several South African policy documents, including the National R&D Strategy (DST, 2002) and the Ten-Year Innovation Plan (DST, 2008) as well as the Presidential Commission of the 4th Industrial Revolution (Presidency, 2020: 33).

emphasis is given to what can be done to improve the impact of South Africa's publicly supported technologies on the country's development goals and related issues of public concern.

BOOK CHAPTERS AND THEIR CONTRIBUTIONS

The chapters in this volume are organised into three sections, each addressing one of our three primary research questions. This overview of these sections frames the chapters in relation to the unifying theoretical approach and research design described above. We return to this overview of the chapters in the Conclusion, which focuses on each chapter's relationship to the research questions and the policy implications thereof.

The first section of the book examines how South Africa's national system of innovation has been orientated towards transformation since the advent of democracy. Both chapters in Section One focus on aspects of South Africa's technological domains and the extent to which there are failures in the country's system aimed at transformation. In Chapter 2, the authors take South Africa's limited success in achieving its development goals as their starting point. They also identify an orientation towards technology-push in the post-1994 government, which did not take sufficient account of the realities of the broader national system of innovation. They contend that there is a need for investment in science and technology capacity that better aligns with South Africa's directionality. In order to address this directionality failure, the authors analyse available national datasets describing innovation at the firm level. They examine middle- and low-income countries that give a more central role to innovative activities resulting from what is termed 'doing, using, and interacting' as well as opportunity niches and capabilities. They use this analysis to identify distinct characteristics of innovation by South African firms. Their analysis shows that most innovation in South African firms occurred in the exploitation space, where standard engineering characterises the process. They show a pattern of evidence from the innovation surveys, which suggests that connections to opportunity niches are strong drivers of innovation. Given this evidence, the authors contend that the limited impact of exploration-focused, supply-side policies since democratisation is not surprising. The authors map out a top-down taxonomy of firm innovative inputs and outputs, with the aim of beginning to redress the inadequate attention given to innovation emerging through an exploitation orientation. Through this, the chapter details the capabilities and opportunity niche orientation of various types of firms. They identify the areas in which groups of firms lag in technological intensity as well as innovation capabilities. A policy conclusion from their analysis is that building capabilities at the firm level can strengthen innovation across economic sectors. However, they recognise that this is only a starting point, and a bottom-up analysis needs to complement their top-down perspective.

In Chapter 3, Mustapha and Ralphs consider the performance of the South African innovation system's infrastructure. They examine the generation of intellectual property by the nation's public research institutions. The authors note that South Africa has adopted several innovation system policies to shepherd publicly supported research towards commercialisation. The authors explore whether these policies are leading to transformative demand articulation. They conclude that there is a need to increase the directionality of the national innovation system to focus better on key developmental challenges. Further, the authors reflect on how inherited capabilities, or lack thereof, have been perpetuated since democratisation. Finding limited change, the authors propose a differentiated conception of publicly financed research institutions in order to address this perpetuation of disadvantage. The authors' analysis also finds an 'insufficiency of the technology transfer process' whereby the path-dependent process of linear interest group focus has limited the broader economic benefits of the narrow national system of innovation. They contend that public value rather than strict commercial value needs to be considered. This is particularly urgent in South Africa where technology transfer functions are perpetuating pre-democracy technology domains and hindering the commercialisation of South Africa's research to achieve the country's development goals.

The second section of the book focuses on technologies' journeys as they attempt to reach commercialisation. The section begins with three chapters that emphasise the role played by opportunity niches in these journeys. In the final two chapters of this section, attention turns to descriptions of the products and the processes of innovation behind the technologies.

Kraak in Chapter 4 explores the effectiveness of state interventions to transform and create new market opportunities through two case studies in South Africa's Western Cape furniture cluster. The analysis identifies the need for network facilitation in an innovation ecosystem characterised by infrastructural and institutional failures. In that context, the author details significant policy coordination failures in the state's interventions as well as inadequate capabilities in these programmes, which resulted in the imposition of additional regulatory and administrative burdens, rather than the addressing of needs. Describing the trajectories and systemic challenges facing the cluster, the author suggests that third-party intermediaries offer significant opportunities to address these challenges. Accordingly, it is suggested that intermediaries could provide capabilities to link industry with transformative training opportunities and to build social capital that would facilitate the development of collaborative capabilities across the cluster.

In Chapter 5, Mazibuko-Makena explores the concepts of frugal innovation and reverse innovation through three medical technologies developed in South Africa, two of which have also been successfully commercialised internationally. In describing these technologies' journeys to commercialisation, the author highlights the technologies' roles in meeting South Africa's socioeconomic needs and development goals, particularly in healthcare. The author discusses a South African chest drainage system, a Covid-19 antigen test, and a whole-body rapid scanner, detailing their development and usage in a relatively less economically developed country with an overburdened healthcare system. These frugal medical devices offer a more affordable opportunity niche for the South African healthcare system; moreover, their value is also realised in more economically developed countries, evident in the use of the Lodox scanner and the Sinapi chest drains case studies. The development of these medical devices was driven by socioeconomic needs and their commercialisation was supported through partnerships with established entities. The case studies also reveal the sparseness of government support in the development of these technologies.

Karuri-Sebina et al., in Chapter 6, consider the journey of two technologies developed with a focus on opportunity niches in the public sector. The authors review two examples of public sector innovation, and reflect on the contextual conditions that support such innovation. The first case raises the issue of capabilities for scaling a government delivery model for roll-out in communities. The second case, which is on a community-developed security system, identifies policy coordination challenges as being critical to the successful commercialisation of the technology, which addresses a socioeconomic need. The authors frame the case studies within a critique of government's capacity to enable innovation. They argue against a narrow focus on the supply-side generation of formal science, engineering and technology in favour of opportunity niches, fostering needs and providing enabling conditions to solve societal problems.

In Chapter 7, Xaba and Fuku analyse three large technology programmes developed with significant public sector support. They consider the nature of the technologies and the applied improvements developed in these programmes as the technologies matured from the exploration phase to exploitation. As an example of a case study in which learning is facilitated through failure, the authors examine the Pebble Bed Modular Reactor (PBMR). Given indications of the technology's successful development in China and significant progress in its development in Russia, the United States and Japan, the authors' analysis suggests that market system failures may not have been adequately addressed in South Africa, despite the significant quantity of state resources invested. The analysis also points to the country's current challenges with electricity supply as likely to mean that the programme will lack the capabilities needed for its success. The case study also suggests that infrastructural failures might have led to underinvestment in commercialising the technology.

The challenges of the PBMR are contrasted with the opportunities that seem to be emerging around the development of the Square Kilometre Array (SKA). An analysis of this case describes the important human capital infrastructure that has been developed to support the technology, significant local and international network construction, and other ways in which the programme has fostered capabilities. The active role the government has played in supporting these efforts also suggests significant policy coordination and ongoing reflection and adjustment to the programme. Lastly, the authors' examination of Hydrogen South Africa (HySA) technology describes a more ambivalent experience. While also identifying some success in building human capital infrastructure and fostering capabilities, there seems to be doubt as to whether there is adequate facilitation of networks that will promote development. Given the transformative nature of this technology, perhaps of even greater import are the failures the authors describe in policy coordination and potential directionality efforts to get the technology adopted.

Pogue in Chapter 8 compares successes and failures in the journeys of two technologies developed within South Africa's Mineral Resource Finance Network (MRFN). The first case describes the development of South Africa's export market for coal, which entails a complex process of demand articulation. The distributed dynamic capabilities of the MRFN in this case are held to have facilitated a transition to a new technological trajectory, coordinated policies to enable that transition, and the overcoming of potential market failures. That experience is contrasted with the second case, which reviews water-based hydraulic technology developed for use in South Africa's deep-level mines. In that case, the author describes an apparent lack of capabilities to leverage the base technology to broader applications. The transformation of the MRFN infrastructure and institutional mechanisms are identified as contributing factors to this inability to access seemingly broader opportunity niches. The author concludes the chapter with an assessment of which capabilities remain in the South African MRFN and how those can be leveraged to deliver socially impactful transformative change.

The third section considers ways that public policy could better facilitate alignment with national socioeconomic needs. Returning to the need to address the transformational system failures also raised in Section One, the contributions in this section concentrate on demand articulation failures and reflexivity failures.

Joseph and Karuri-Sebina in Chapter 9 draw attention to the question of why publicly supported research is not providing answers to South Africa's issues of public concern. They do so through an examination of policy coordination failures resulting from limited vertical coherence between national and local innovation policies. They argue that local government is structurally better positioned to identify and address social concerns than national government. They present evidence that local innovation systems are also better at fostering networks that address soft institutional failures. The authors argue that the need to address this disjuncture between national and local policies is particularly acute for African cities because the cities are under resourced. They identify the informal economy as an important feature of local innovation systems in African countries, as well as in other developing nations. This means that policies focused on local innovation systems have the potential to significantly impact on growth and development in some of the most disadvantaged communities. However, the authors argue that there has been systemic neglect of local innovation system capacity, which has been compounded by under- or un-funded, devolved development mandates. The authors make the case that these mandates should rather be elevated to being an important component of broader national innovation system policies. Detailing the development of innovation policy in the City of Tshwane, the authors identify several dimensions of local innovation system challenges. These include ad hoc funding streams from the Department of Science and Innovation at national level; challenges – if not outright hostility – to innovations in the delivery of local government services; and barriers, constructed by central government to the creation of joined-up initiatives that build on local synergies.

In Chapter 10 Walwyn looks critically at the national systems of innovation approach in a case study of the attempt to establish antiretroviral (ARV) manufacturing in South Africa. He argues that the systems of innovation approach led to a neglect of the transformative technological, social and economic change that South Africa has needed since the advent of democracy. Following a brief discussion of the nation's innovation system to achieve its development goals, the author turns to his case study on antiretroviral treatment (ART).

A discussion of the costs of antiretroviral treatment establishes a case for domestic manufacturing, which is then contextualised with a description of the internationally highly contested nature of pharmaceutical manufacturing. The process through which ARV manufacturing capacity was then pursued is then detailed. However, despite the socioeconomic need for domestic ART manufacturing, the author describes a failure within the innovation systems framework to address that demand.

Walwyn then reviews four distinct analytical approaches and the method through which they address strategic transformational change. It is in this context that the author identifies the predominance of the national system of innovation approach in South African innovation policy. He goes on to highlight a seeming structural disconnect between this approach and the country's development goals. That shortfall is contrasted with transformational systems approaches such as the multi-level perspective (MLP). With these frameworks in mind, efforts to establish ARV manufacturing are further described, including the government's failure to support the initiatives through its procurement policies, despite contradictory policies intended to do just that. This proved a critical barrier as, without an offtake agreement, no capital was available for the construction of the manufacturing facility. The author explains how even when a foreign pharmaceutical manufacturer was willing to make an outward technology transfer, narrow government calculation of benefits from the endeavour relative to risk led to the failure of that opportunity as well. The author concludes that, given this inability to realise domestic ARV manufacturing, an alternative framework is required for a national system of innovation – one that avoids the current focus on structural systems. Given the failures discussed, the author makes the case for transformational systems perspectives like the MLP to be adopted as a guiding innovation framework.

Kahn in Chapter 11 critiques the conceptualisation of an innovation chasm. He notes that this conceptualisation tends to support notions of innovation as a linear process, rather than as the more complicated and dynamic one we understand it to be. He contends that the space between exploration and exploitation (see Figure 1.1), in which the innovation chasm is conceptualised to exist, is a natural feature of the innovation process. He argues therefore that South Africa's 'challenges' to produce successful and transformative commercialised technologies should be seen as aberrations. Using an informal review of several technologies developed since democratisation, Kahn contends that there has been limited transformation of the national system of innovation. He argues however that this failure is a product of inadequate articulation between national development and transformation policies rather than science and technology. Kahn contends that national science, technology and innovation (STI) policy has suffered from a lack of directionality and that there is a need to articulate a vision for that policy to follow rather than the other way around. He contends that another problem associated with the paradigm is its failure to adequately consider the path dependence inherent in the system and the resulting need for associated technological domain shifts to realise a different result.

The last chapter, Chapter 12, begins with a summary of the integrated analytical framework that was discussed in this chapter. Attention then turns to reviewing each chapter's contributions to the project's framing research questions, and to policy issues raised. The second section of the chapter reviews key policy recommendations arising out of authors' analyses and case studies. Chapter 12 then concludes with a brief discussion of areas for further analysis.

Facilitating a technology's commercial viability is a complex process that involves a multitude of issues and considerations. These range from market viability to socioeconomic impacts as well as scalability, integration and capital resources to mention just a few. This volume is unique in bringing together a wide range of experiences of commercialisation of technologies in South Africa. In presenting these experiences, the authors have endeavoured to draw out clear implications and policy recommendations throughout. The analyses have the potential to mark the beginning of an important, if to date neglected, conversation around the complex issues associated with commercialisation.

While this discussion is important as South Africa aspires to leverage science and technology to advance socioeconomic development, it also relates to broader conversations about the costs and benefits of new technologies. While the issue of the commercialisation of technologies in South Africa has been addressed elsewhere, we believe this volume is unique in its focus on the evolution of the country's national system of innovation, and the ramifications of how this system has evolved. As such, the book forms an important contribution to the literature on the commercialisation of technologies in South Africa.

REFERENCES

Arthur, W.B. 2009. *The Nature of Technology: What It Is and How It Evolves*. New York: Allen Lane.

Arthur, W.B. 2021. 'Foundations of complexity economics'. *Nature Reviews Physics*, 3, 136–145. https://doi.org/10.1038/S42254-020-00273-3, accessed 7 September 2022.

Bercovitz, J. and Feldman, M. 2006. 'Entrepreneurial universities and technology transfer: A conceptual framework for understanding knowledge-based economic development'. *The Journal of Technology Transfer*, 31(1), 175–188.

Cassiolato, J. and Lastres, H. 2008. 'Discussing innovation and development: Converging points between the Latin American school and the Innovation Systems perspective?' GLOBELICS Working Paper Series. Aalborg, Denmark, http://www.globelics.org/wp-content/uploads/2016/06/GWP2008-02.pdf, accessed 27 March 2023.

Department of Arts, Culture, Science and Technology (DACST). 1996. 'White Paper on Science and Technology: Preparing for the 21st Century'. Department of Arts, Culture, Science and Technology, Pretoria.

Department of Arts, Culture, Science and Technology (DACST). 1998a. 'National Research and Technology Audit: Scientific and Technological Infrastructure'. Foundation for Research Development, Pretoria.

Department of Arts, Culture, Science and Technology (DACST). 1998b. 'Report of the System-wide Review of Public-sector Science, Engineering and Technology Institutions'. https://www.dst.gov.za/images/pdfs/sw_review1.pdf, accessed 12 February 2023.

Department of Arts, Culture, Science and Technology (DACST). 1999. 'National Research and Technology Foresight'. Department of Arts, Culture, Science and Technology, Pretoria.

Department of Science and Innovation (DSI). 2021. 'Making sure it is possible with science, technology and innovation at the new Department of Science and Innovation'. DSI, https://www.dst.gov.za/index.php/about-us/new-dsi, accessed 28 April 2023.

Department of Science and Technology (DST). 2002. 'South Africa's National Research and Development Strategy'. Department of Science and Technology, Pretoria.

Department of Science and Technology (DST). 2007. 'South Africa's 10-Year Innovation Plan: Innovation Towards a Knowledge-based Economy'. Department of Science and Technology, Pretoria.

Department of Science and Technology (DST). 2008. 'Innovation Towards a Knowledge-Based Economy: Ten-Year Plan for South Africa (2008–2018)'. Department of Science and Technology, Pretoria.

Department of Science and Technology (DST). 2019. 'White Paper on Science, Technology and Innovation'. Department of Science and Technology, Pretoria.

Freeman, C. 1991. 'Networks of innovators: A synthesis of research issues'. *Research Policy*, 20, 499–514.

Hart, T., Jacobs, P. and Mhula, A. 2013. 'Review of South African Innovation Policy and Strategy 1994–2012: Innovation for Rural Development', Rural Innovation Assessement Tool (RIAT) Concept Paper Series No. 3, Department of Science and Technology (DST) and Human Sciences Research Council.

Hussain, M. 2019. 'How South Africa lost its electric Joule'. *City Press*, 18 October. https://www.news24.com/citypress/business/how-south-africa-lost-its-electric-joule-20191011, accessed April 2023.

Lundvall, B-Å. 1992. *National Systems of Innovation: Towards a Theory of Innovation and Interactive Learning*. UK: Pinter Publishers.

Maharajh, R. 2016. 'Racial capitalism, apartheid, and the negotiated post-apartheid constitutional democracy', in MISTRA, Scerri (ed.). The *Emergence of Systems of Innovation in South(ern) Africa: Long Histories and Current Debates*. Johannesburg: Mapungubwe Institute for Strategic Reflection (MISTRA), chapter 8.

Mamabolo, M.A., Kerrin, M. and Kele, T. 2017. 'Entrepreneurship management skills requirements in an emerging economy: A South African outlook'. *Southern African Journal of Entrepreneurship and Small Business Management,* 9(1), a111. https://doi.org/10.4102/, accessed 12 August 2022.

Mapungubwe Institute for Strategic Reflection (MISTRA). 2013. *The Concept and Application of Transdisciplinarity in Intellectual Discourse and Research*. Johannesburg: MISTRA.

Mapungubwe Institute for Strategic Reflection (MISTRA), Scerri, M. (ed.). 2016. *The Emergence of Systems of Innovation in South(ern) Africa: Long Histories and Contemporary Debates*. Johannesburg: Mapungubwe Institute for Strategic Reflection (MISTRA).

National Advisory Council on Innovation (NACI). 2019. 'The South African Science, Technology and Innovation Indicators Report'. Department of Science and Technology, https://www.naci.org.za/wp-content/uploads/2022/07/South-African-Science-Technology-Indicators-Report-2019.pdf, accessed April 2023.

Organisation for Economic Co-operation and Development (OECD). 2007. *OECD Reviews of Innovation Policy*. Paris: Organisation for Economic Co-operation and Development.

Presidency. 2020. 'Report of the National Commission for the Fourth Industrial Revolution'. The Presidency, Pretoria.

Swart, G. 2015. 'Innovation lessons learned from the Joule EV development'. *International Association for Management of Technology: IAMOT 2015 Conference Proceedings*, 3, 1743–1769.

University of South Africa (UNISA). 2020. 'Considering the innovation chasm'. https://www.unisa.ac.za/sites/corporate/default/Colleges/College-of-Graduate-Studies/Media-&-events/Articles/Considering-the-innovation-chasm, accessed 21 July 2021.

Weber, K.M. and Rohracher, H. 2012. 'Legitimizing research, technology and innovation policies for transformative change: Combining insights from innovation systems and multi-level perspective in a comprehensive 'failures' framework'. *Research Policy*, 41(6), 1037–1047. https://doi.org/10.1016/j.respol.2011.10.015, accessed 3 March 2023.

APPENDIX 1: THE JOULE EV AND THE INNOVATION CHASM

In 2004 a new start-up, Optimal Energy, emerged with the aim of developing a South African Electric Vehicle (EV). According to Swart (2015), in December 2005, after 18 months of consideration, the Innovation Fund approved an initial three-year R15 million investment to create a prototype EV.

Importantly, Optimal Energy's mission was not to just build an EV prototype. Rather, it was envisioned that it would create a South African EV industry with global exports. This scope required that the prototype would eventually be produced at viable market cost, meet all road safety requirements, and have support for distribution and sales.

Optimal Energy's progress on the prototype, what would become the Joule EV, led to the Industrial Development Corporation (IDC) purchasing a significant stake in Optimal Energy in 2007 to assist in commercialisation activities. By late 2008 the first-generation prototype Joule EV was unveiled and was well received at the 2008 Paris Auto Show. Further refinements were highlighted in a second-generation prototype at the 2010 Geneva Motor Show and by early 2011 four roadworthy, third-generation Joule EV prototypes were being tested. That point had been reached through several partnerships with Optimal Energy, and a R250 million investment. Further significant investment was required, however, to establish a 50,000-vehicle-a-year production and distribution network: the scale deemed necessary for successful commercialisation. In Swart's telling, several factors associated with the South African innovation chasm combined to prevent Optimal Energy from securing the estimated R9.5 billion in funding needed. In June 2012 Optimal Energy was liquidated (Swart, 2015). As government funds had been invested in Optimal Energy, the EV technology developed under its stewardship was transferred to the uYilo eMobility Programme at the Nelson Mandela University in Port Elizabeth. Since 2013, the university has been leading development of South Africa's electric mobility ecosystem.[5]

The innovation chasm appears to capture part of Optimal Energy's relatively linear journey to establish a South African EV industry. According to this narrative, the small number of Joule EV prototypes fell into the "innovation chasm" – or the so-called "valley of death". This occurs when the process of development offers no "bridge" for a potential product to move from the exploration of new technology to exploitation or small-scale commercial production (see Figure 1.1).

In his application of the innovation chasm, Swart (2015) seems to follow a typical South African conceptualisation. Arguing that the South African government needs to do more to develop its domestic manufacturing abilities, he contends that the innovation chasm is an area of limited South African innovation activity outside large corporations and the defence/aerospace industry where greater system engineering skills could be used.[6] However, Khan in Chapter 11 of this book critiques the notion, saying that the innovation chasm concept does not offer much guidance beyond providing a paradigmatic, techno-nationalist rally call for change and greater commercialisation of domestic technologies.

Swart identifies a disjuncture between the then Department of

---

5   See Hussain (2019) and the uYilo eMobility website (https://www.uyilo. org.za/) for further details.
6   See in particular Figure 12 of Swart (2015: 15).

Science and Technology's Technology Innovation Agency (TIA) and the Department of Trade and Industry's (DTI) IDC. Alignment of those two department's funding of the next phase of the South African EV industry's development was critical to securing international investment and start-up loans (Swart, 2015: 4). That lack of alignment is then returned to in the concluding section of Swart's analysis where that funding alignment is attributed to being the cause of Optimal Energy's death in the innovation chasm (Swart, 2015: 16).

It is interesting to contrast Optimal Energy's Joule's journey with Tesla's Roadster, given that there was some overlap in the times at which the two EVs were being developed. In 2003 Tesla was established to manufacture EVs for a mass market (Perkins and Murmann, 2018: 472). Three years later in July 2006, it unveiled its first prototype, the Tesla Roadster (Tesla, 2010). While the Joule and Roadster shared innovative battery cooling technologies, Optimal Energy preceded Tesla with its horizontal battery installation. There were differences too in target markets: the Roadster was a niche sportscar focused on performance and ride experience, while from the outset the Joule sought to be a mass-market everyday commuter. Seven years after it was established, Tesla had managed to produce 1,000 Roadsters with a total investment of US$ 185 million (Perkins and Murmann, 2018: 475). Starting a year later, seven years after launch, Optimal Energy had managed to produce four Joule prototypes from an equivalent dollar investment of US$33 million.[7] Having established production capabilities for the Roadster, in 2008 and 2009 Tesla secured funding to manufacture its second vehicle, the Model S. The first Model S was ready for retail delivery 20 months later in June 2012 (Boudreau, 2012), with Tesla having secured a former Toyota Northern California production facility in 2010 on very favourable terms, and some US$465 million in loans from the US Department of Energy.

Perkins and Murmann (2018), in their analysis of the Tesla experience, conclude that other companies could develop a niche luxury EV from scratch in three to five years with an investment

---

7   A 2011 Rand/Dollar exchange rate of R7.57 is applied to convert Optimal Energy's R250 million investment.

between US$1 to US$2 billion. Interestingly, these estimated costs are in line with the US$1.4 billion (R9.5b) that Optimal Energy believed was necessary to produce the Joule EV at scale. As the numerous case studies in this book have shown successful commercialisation of a technology is fraught with challenges, particularly ones like Optimal Energy's envisioned reshaping of the automobile industry. Teece (2018) describes Tesla (and by implication Optimal Energy) as facing deep uncertainty in its endeavours. In this context, uncertainty involves unknown and unknowable risks which make predictions fraught but a structured approach such as the dynamics capabilities framework can assist management when uncertainty is ubiquitous.[8]

Teece (2018) further contends Tesla developed strong dynamic capabilities that allowed it to realise the commercialisation envisioned for its products. The extent to which a lack of dynamic capabilities contributed to Optimal Energy's failure to realise commercialisation is not clear. However, it is also important to recognise the supportive institutional environment that Tesla operated in. As an American firm it had the benefit of a large consumer market with associated sales to cover the costs of research and development, and a deep capital market from which to raise finance. Furthermore, Tesla emerged from Silicon Valley in Northern California, an area with renowned venture capital resources and a leading information technology cluster, both of which Tesla leveraged in its development (Perkins and Murmann, 2018: 474). In addition, Tesla was a direct beneficiary of the US Department of Energy's large-scale loan-funding scheme, which was designed to facilitate the commercialisation of this type of disruptive, environmentally impactful technology.[9] Significantly, federal legislative efforts to promote alternative fuel and fuel economy began decades before Tesla and included the 1976 Electric and Hybrid Vehicle Research

---

8   For further details of the dynamic capabilities framework see Teece et al. (2016) and Leih et al. (2015).

9   The Department of Energy (DoE) loans were part of the Advanced Technology Vehicle Manufacturing Program, which provides incentives to new and established automakers to build more fuel-efficient vehicles. For further details see the DoE's Loan Programs Office website at: https://www.energy.gov/lpo/about-us-home.

Development Act.[10] That federal support of EV technology continued over subsequent years,[11] and at the same time, Tesla was also supported by incentives from the state of California. These incentives, along with federal programmes, provide demand-side impetus for the purchase of EVs. Federal support of the infrastructure needed to charge electric vehicles, beginning with the American Recovery and Reinvestment Act of 2009,[12] provided yet another important dimension of broader institutional backing for the adoption of Tesla's EV technology.

Although Optimal Energy and Tesla originated around the same time and faced deep uncertainties, their technologies' journeys occurred in very different environments. Even a brief comparison of these two experiences highlights the multitude of factors that can influence the success or failure of a technology's commercialisation. The innovation chasm paradigm, however, reduces these complex and multi-dimensional factors to a linear, technology-orientated, supply-focused narrative. Critically, it also completely ignores the key role played by dynamic capabilities in a technology's commercialisation. Careful consideration of this broader context is required if we are to learn meaningful lessons from the failure of the Joule. To limit the story of its journey to the innovation chasm is to ignore critical questions around the adequacy of management's dynamic capabilities, the consistency of state support for technology commercialisation, and the capacity of South Africa's technology finance system.

REFERENCES

Boudreau, J. 2012. 'Tesla Motors begins delivering Model S electric cars in a Silicon Valley milestone.' *The Mercury News*, 22 June 2012. https://www.mercurynews.com/2012/06/22/tesla-motors-begins-delivering-model-s-electric-cars-in-a-silicon-valley-milestone-2/, accessed April 2023.

---

10 https://www.congress.gov/bill/94th-congress/house-bill/8800.

11 For a summary of federal legislation see the US Department of Energy's Alternative Fuels Data Center at: https://afdc.energy.gov/laws/key_legislation.

12 The Recovery Act alone supported installation of over 18,000 residential, commercial and public charges across the U.S. (U.S. Department of Energy, 2023).

Hussain, M. 2019. 'How South Africa lost its electric Joule.' *City Press*, 18 October 2019. https://www.news24.com/citypress/business/how-south-africa-lost-its-electric-joule-20191011, accessed April 2023.

Leih, S., Linden, G., Teece, D.J. 2015. 'Business model innovation and organizational design: A dynamic capabilities perspective', in N.J. Foss, and T. Saebi (eds). *Business model innovation: The organizational dimension*. Oxford, UK: Oxford University Press, pp. 24–42.

Perkins, G. andMurmann,, J.P. 2018. 'What Does the Success of Tesla Mean for the Future Dynamics in the Global Automobile Sector?'. *Management and Organization Review*, 14(3), September 2018: 471–480. https://doi.org/10.1017/mor.2018.31, accessed April 2023.

Swart, G. 2015. 'Innovation Lessons Learned from the Joule EV Development.' *IAMOT 2015 Conference Proceedings*, International Association for Management of Technology, https://www.researchgate.net/publication/280221310, accessed April 2023.

Teece, D. 2018. 'Tesla and the Reshaping of the Auto Industry'. *Management and Organization Review*, 14(3): 501–512. https://doi.org/10.1017/mor.2018.33, accessed April 2023.

Teece, D., Peteraf, M. and Leih, S. 2016. Dynamic capabilities and organizational agility: Risk, uncertainty, and strategy in the innovation economy. *California Management Review*, 58(4), 13–35.

Tesla, 2010. 'Tesla Motors Begins Regular Production of 2008 Tesla Roadster'. *Tesla Blog*. 20 April 2010. https://www.tesla.com/blog/tesla-motors-begins-regular-production-2008-tesla-roadster, accessed April 2023.

US Department of Energy. 2023. 'Energy Saver 101 History Timeline: The Electric Car'. United States Department of Energy Website. https://www.energy.gov/energysaver/energy-saver-101-history-timeline-electric-car, accessed 22 April 2023.

Part One

*Transformational orientation of
South Africa's national system of
innovation since democratisation*

TWO

Where innovations may come to life: A new policy mix to build firm capabilities across the national system of innovation

Glenda Kruss, Amy Kahn and
Il-haam Petersen

INTRODUCTION

This chapter contributes to the growing recognition that bringing innovations to life in South Africa requires a different, contextually appropriate policy mix. We need to balance interventions to build firms' technological capabilities with the current emphasis on growing science and technology capabilities. There is only a very limited understanding of how firms innovate across sectors in the national system of innovation. A stronger evidence base is needed to inform policy design and implementation processes. This chapter experiments with analysing available, firm-level innovation data in new ways in order to identify distinct modes of innovation capabilities. It aims to contribute to building new indicators that can provide the kinds of evidence needed to inform a shifting policy mix. This introduction elaborates on these claims. An old problem, not unique to South Africa, is the long dominance of science, technology and innovation (STI) policy mix that has been overly focused on supply-side interventions to grow scientific institutions, research and development (R&D) and knowledge production. The most recent innovation policy frameworks (DSI, 2019; 2022) have shifted to prioritise the need to grow capabilities for localisation and commercialisation of technology in priority sectors such as agriculture, mining and manufacturing. The complexity of current growth and development challenges makes it difficult, but more imperative than ever, to analyse the types of STI policy mix – both demand and supply-driven – that can work better in specific contexts. In order to translate development objectives into policy instruments, it is necessary to identify and specify the nature of innovation problems to be addressed (Boon and Edler, 2018; Borrás and Edquist, 2013; Cocos and Lepori, 2020).

More than a decade ago, Lorentzen (2009: 33) highlighted a gap in South African STI policy models, arguing that they were not sufficiently informed by context-specific evidence on the determinants of technological learning and upgrading in local firms (Edler, 2009; Lall, 1993). Lorentezen (2009: 33) said this lack 'made for a veritable black box hiding the engines of innovation'; he was highlighting that we need to understand South African firms' technological capabilities, which span both their production capabilities (their ability to operate effectively in local and global value chains – and their innovation capabilities – their ability to develop new and improved products and processes.

This chapter begins with the assumption that an STI policy) mix[1] capable of fostering innovation capabilities requires stronger evidence of how innovation occurs at firm level. For instance, in South Africa, as in many other middle-income countries, few firms report modes of innovation that are R&D-led or require novel, locally developed technologies (CeSTII, 2020: 29–31). Firms are more likely to report

---

1   An STI policy mix cuts across the spheres of government, and requires coordination and alignment between industrial, innovation and sector-specific policy frameworks and instruments.

innovation activities that entail the adoption of new ICTs, machinery and equipment acquired from elsewhere, and to report training or the acquisition of new equipment and IT technologies as their most frequent innovation activity. Such modes of innovation equally require learning, knowledge and technology transfer, particularly given that much of the new technology is acquired from global innovation and production networks. To use newly adopted, adapted or invented technologies to best effect requires capabilities in firm technological, management and workforce skills. An absence of these skills may hinder learning and the ability to make further modifications which would increase productivity and help to grow markets (Marcelle, 2004). Relatively low technological capabilities are a key obstacle to strengthening South African firms' productivity and competitiveness in domestic or international markets, though not the only one (NACI, n.d; Walwyn and Cloete, 2018). Baker and Sovacool (2017), for example, show that low technological capabilities raise the risk profile of South African firms, hindering access to finance, which is a crucial factor for the localisation of technologies for renewable energy. Similarly, Bell et al. (2019) highlight the importance of building local technological capabilities to enable firms to become more competitive by taking advantage of industry 4.0 advanced technologies. They base their argument on their study of plastics as a root industry in which South Africa lags in comparison to other upper-middle-income countries. There is growing recognition that a South African policy mix should foreground firms' capacities for learning, in particular the capacity to access and adapt new technologies to South Africa's technological pathways.

This chapter will contribute to building new evidence of firms' innovation capabilities at a national level through analysis of existing firm-level innovation data (Gregersen and Johnson, 2021). The aim is to identify firm-level modes of innovation across the South African system, which reflect both production and innovation capabilities. These make it possible to map patterns of innovation capabilities across sectors and size classes. Profiles of innovation capabilities can contribute to the selection of contextually informed policy mixes that focus on learning and competence building.

The first section of this chapter draws on recent analyses of the need for structural transformation of the South African economy and the challenges to this transformation. This is in order to provide a foundation for an analysis of the main innovation problem and key policy directions in our context as a middle-income country (Andreoni et al., 2021a, 2021b; Bhorat et al., 2014; Kruss, 2021).

The second section consults the global literature on designing and classifying modes of firm-level innovation, including from comparative middle-income countries aiming to grow firm technological capabilities (Crespi and Dutrenit, 2014; Cassiolato and Vitorino, 2011; Dutrenit et al., 2013). While data on firm innovation activities has been collected since the early 2000s, there is little analysis to reveal the patterns of modes of innovation found empirically in South Africa. One analytical framework developed to enhance the value of formal business innovation data is described and adopted (Arundel and Hollanders, 2008; OECD, 2009).

In the third section, the main empirical focus of the chapter, existing patterns of modes of innovation are analysed and profiled, using the South African national Business Innovation Survey 2014–16 dataset of formal manufacturing and services enterprises (CeSTII, 2020). Distinct types of firm innovation capabilities are identified using a multi-dimensional classification system, based on the nature of the firms' markets, their in-house innovation capabilities, and the novelty of their innovations.

The fourth section aims to extract insights for a more context-appropriate policy mix. It is proposed that in order to bring innovations to life, government needs to articulate and implement differentiated types of strategies and interventions oriented to building the full range of firm innovation capabilities.

THE SOUTH AFRICAN INNOVATION PROBLEM

The demand for technological upgrading to break the middle-income trap

South Africa has experienced decelerated economic growth and stagnation (Bhorat et al., 2014, 2016; Chipkin and Swilling, 2018) since the global economic crisis of 2009. However, in that South Africa has struggled for decades to transition to a high-income economy, it can be argued that this is the most recent negative cycle of the lock-in to a classic middle-income trap (Luiz, 2016; Bhorat et al., 2014; 2016; Chipkin and Swilling, 2018; Kruss, 2020; Lee, 2019). There is widespread agreement that the economy requires structural transformation to break the lock-in, and to combat the inordinately high levels of poverty, unemployment and inequality experienced by the majority of citizens. Analysts question the ongoing dominance of upstream, capital-intensive resource sectors, rather than downstream, labour-intensive economic sectors (Mondliwa and Roberts, 2021).

In the context of globalisation, three structural factors are typically promoted for increased technological sophistication: breaking into globally concentrated systems of industrial production; linking into global value chains in ways that link back into local production systems to drive structural transformation; and keeping pace with technological change. Technological upgrading is promoted as one means of shifting the ongoing reliance on mineral resources, the premature deindustrialisation and decline of manufacturing sectors, and the growth of services sectors, many of which are non-tradeable (Andreoni and Tregenna, 2021; Fine and Rustomjee, 1996; Oqubay et al., 2021). For technological upgrading and competitiveness, firms require dynamic capabilities that enable them to constantly scan rapidly shifting technology environments and change their operations to take advantage of new opportunities in global and local markets (Teece et al., 2020).

The challenge is that South Africa is also constrained by a 'middle-income *technology* trap', in that there are 'specific structural and institutional configurations that are not conducive to increasing domestic value-add and sustained industrial and technological upgrading' (Andreoni and Tregenna, 2020: 324). The conclusion is that South Africa has not kept pace with technological change globally, and lags both in 'inputs' to technological upgrading, and in the 'outputs' of technological intensity (Andreoni and Tregenna 2021). These conditions raise critical questions about the ideal development path for South Africa, which in turn, shapes understanding of the specific innovation problem in our context. It therefore becomes vital to develop STI policy mixes for technological upgrading that can drive R&D, learning and innovation capabilities across the system of innovation, and articulate with industrial and priority sectoral policy mixes.

Borrowed innovation policy mixes a constraint

The White Paper on Science, Technology and Innovation (DSI, 2019) sets a new transformative vision and objectives, with implementation to be informed by a new Decadal Plan (DSI, 2022). From 1994, the STI policy framework promoted strengthening the national system of innovation inherited from the apartheid era and re-orienting it to economic growth and equitable development goals. The policy mix was heavily influenced by global STI frameworks, through the Organisation for Economic Cooperation and Development (OECD) and World Bank advisers and reviews (ASSAF, 2013; DST, 2012; OECD, 2007; Walwyn and Boraine, 2006). Support from global STI bodies enabled the basic design of strategies, funding and policy mechanisms, with an emphasis on supply-side strategies such as incentivising the commercialisation and technology transfer of research funded and conducted by public entities. The provision of evidence to monitor progress was based on OECD standard STI indicators, using national R&D and innovation surveys that allow for global comparability (Kruss and Ralphs, 2021). Such an STI policy mix is not sufficient to drive and promote change in a context that requires structural, systemic and sustained firm technological upgrading (Boon and Edler, 2018).

From the outset, analysts have noted low levels of firm demand for, and capabilities in, innovation or commercialisation of local technologies (Kaplan, 2008; Kruss and Lorentzen, 2011; Malele et al., 2019; NACI, 2022), and there is a gap in the capabilities for locally learned policy design (see Borrás, 2011). In this regard, Walwyn and Naidoo (2020) found that whereas we might expect South Africa to have an innovation policy mix more akin to India, a lower-middle-income economy, the policy mix is more similar to Canada, a high-income economy. Specifically, their analysis shows that the South African policy mix for the manufacturing sector is characterised more by generic than sector-specific instruments and is dominated by supply-side instruments and non-competitively awarded financial instruments, with stronger support for early-stage research interventions. These may not be addressing the full range of capabilities for innovation at firm level. The solution is seen to be a greater articulation between demand-side, competitive and sector-specific instruments.

In contrast, India has adopted a larger set of complementary demand-side, competitive and sector-specific instruments, aimed at stimulating markets and creating environments conducive to firm-level innovation (NACI, n.d.; see also Walwyn and Naidoo, 2018). In a similar vein, the recent review of the Higher Education, Science and Technology Landscape (HESTIL, 2022) was very critical of past STI investment in high technology domains, underpinned by a linear model of innovation and a technology push approach. The review supports the claim that the policy mix should be informed by the specific innovation and economic development problems in South Africa, and the existing innovation capabilities of firms, alongside vital investment in science and technology development capacity.

The need to create better evidence for policy learning

Policy mixes based on analyses of firm innovation patterns in high-income contexts will likely lead to incorrect interpretations, which might steer a policy mix aimed at breaking the lock-in to a middle-income trap in the wrong direction (Borrás and Edquist, 2013). There may be attempts to grow innovation activity and systems where they do not yet exist, but local conditions may not yet be optimal to achieve such a policy goal. Or there may be contextually important emergent forms of innovation that are not typically measured or supported in high-income countries, but which should be grown and nurtured in a middle-income context. And, in a context in which multinationals control global innovation networks, firms in middle-income contexts may not have the capabilities required to access and absorb new technologies. As Lall (1993) highlights, to do so requires complex learning processes which are not guaranteed success, and which vary, depending on the types of technology, market efficiencies and technology competencies at play. Such heterogeneous modes of innovation exist at the same time in a country, requiring a range of well-designed and distinctive interventions. It is vital to map the patterns of innovation found across local firms, to identify clusters ready for growth in different kinds of innovation activity and clusters where innovation capabilities may first need to be improved. Information on the relative spread, importance and intensity of innovation capabilities in specific clusters of firms can be of great value for policy learning.

The next section will consider how to define a set of innovation modes that capture firm behaviour, using appropriate analytical lenses. The national Survey of Business Innovation (CeSTII, 2020) datasets include nationally representative samples of firms and can provide data for a high-level mapping exercise (see Appendix 2A at the end of this chapter). It is important to bear in mind that this is only one possible methodological approach to creating evidence of firm-level innovation capabilities. For example, a set of in-depth sectoral case studies would be another vital source of evidence in the future.

ANALYSING MODES OF INNOVATION AT FIRM LEVEL

This section interrogates the innovation studies literature that aims to distinguish between modes of innovation and identify key firm-level drivers to identify analytical tools.

An evolving literature defining modes of innovation

In the late 1990s and early 2000s in the literature on innovation research and policy, the definitions of innovation modes were very simple, based on binary distinctions between degrees of novelty (radical or incremental) or high-level types of activity (product or process). Disaggregated analyses could examine the drivers and outcomes of, and barriers to, types of innovation, across and between industrial sectors. These simple indicators have been adopted in South Africa so that we typically compare differences between product and process innovation, or technological and non-technological innovation (CeSTII, 2020). These indicators can be used for benchmarking progress over time, and to compare national progress relative to other countries. They have limited value, however, as policy evidence to understand distinctive national, sectoral or regional patterns that reflect local innovation capabilities.

Over time, more nuanced and complex distinctions emerged in the literature, as understanding grew of innovation activity in different sectors, types of firms, and regional and national systems (Arundel and Hollanders, 2008; Roud, 2018; Vargas, 2022). Researchers critically interrogated the application and value of different taxonomies and analytical models to provide a means to understand innovation processes in a national system of innovation (Arundel and Hollanders, 2005; Bogliacino and Pianta, 2016; Huang et al., 2010). Some identified patterns of innovation by categorising firms in terms of science intensity – R&D, non-R&D and technologically driven innovation (Huang et al., 2010). Other researchers questioned the dominant trend of focusing policy and analysis on R&D-led innovation (Arundel et al., 2007a). Some of these studies focused on illuminating 'hidden' forms of innovation that were under-studied, such as external innovation investments (O'Brien, 2016) or design-led innovation (Filipetti, 2010; Townson et al., 2016) or doing, using and interacting modes (Jensen et al., 2016; Lukhele and Soumonni, 2021; Parrilli and Heras, 2016; Parrilli and Radcic, 2021). Such modes of innovation, which are typically neglected, may have great policy significance in middle-income countries' contexts.

Multi-dimensional classification systems to assess firm innovation capabilities

The design of indicators of *how firms innovate* can be of greater policy value if they are informed by innovation challenges in the specific, relevant context (Arundel, 2006; Hollanders and Arundel 2007). This approach enables the task of 'constructing new categories that are viable as the target of next-generation innovation policies' (Roud, 2018: 249). Binary classifications are not suitable for this purpose. The classification system used to define indicators needs to be able to capture complexity along multiple dimensions.

In a high-income economy like Australia, for example, the development challenge is to grow the innovation capabilities of businesses in key high-technology sectors to drive greater global competitiveness (Arundel and O'Brien, 2009; O'Brien, 2016). Hence, the core dimensions used to define modes of innovation assess novelty, market reach and the people or institutions responsible for innovation. This yields a taxonomy with directionality determined by the proportion of firms that can be classified as the ideal of 'new to market international innovators' – able to operate on international markets and develop their own in-house innovations in the form of new-to-world product innovations – at the one end of the scale. At the other, are firms that are 'adopters' of innovations developed elsewhere. The policy goal is to support more firms to evolve towards the category of 'new to market international innovators'.

The Latin American focus on processes of learning and technological capability building as determinants of economic development provides insights that are potentially important for defining modes of innovation in middle-income countries (Dutrenit et al., 2013). One volume (Crespi and Dutrenit, 2014) on Latin American countries traced the evolution of STI policy mixes. These have mutated from a supply-side, top-down orientation with little vertical and horizontal coordination and interaction to a more bottom-up, demand-led orientation, with weak coordination and emerging interaction. Furthermore, since the 2000s, these policy mixes have tended towards a systemic orientation with growing support for vertical policies, and top-down/bottom-up policy coordination (Crespi and Dutrenit, 2014). This policy evolution is based on extensive conceptual and empirical work across Latin America (Crespi and Dutrenit, 2014; Dutrenit et al., 2013; Vargas, 2022) investigating the distinctive nature and dynamics of technological change, learning and innovation capability building.

Much of the Latin American analysis was informed by the work of Katz, based on the identification of two broad phases of technological upgrading (Dutrenit et al., 2013; Vera-Cruz and Vargas, 2013). In the acquisition phase, firms in a middle-income country identify, select and acquire technologies, developed by global firms closer to the technology frontier, which can be purchased, transferred and used locally in production. In the assimilation and learning phase, technologies evolve as local firms adapt, adjust or modify the technologies to local conditions and markets. Subsequent work builds on and refines these distinctions, reinforcing the need for policy to promote firm-level technological learning and capability building to grow national capabilities to an economy-wide level (Vargas, 2022).

In countries like China, India and Brazil, local firms have leveraged global innovation networks to successfully modify or develop new technologies that allow them to enter global value chains more competitively (Gastrow and Kruss, 2017). Analysis of the South African economy in the previous section revealed a pattern of firms that are technological 'laggards', lacking the innovation capabilities to operate near the technology frontier. Technology localisation has been foregrounded as a policy priority, but many South African firms lack the dynamic capabilities for innovation (Aterido et al., 2019; Teece, et al., 2020). The drivers of innovation may not be strong enough, as firms may benefit enough from short-term incremental changes and strengthened operational efficiencies to remain competitive in their local markets. Firm investments in strategies to strengthen their dynamic innovation capabilities may not be sufficiently economically viable to be adopted widely, but they are vital to learning and upgrading across a specific sector, and to embedding innovation across the national economy (Teece et al., 2020). To promote the desired direction towards more localisation, STI policy design and implementation will need to be informed by information about the specific spread of firms. For example, if funding mechanisms primarily incentivise R&D collaboration with firms, but evidence shows that most firms do not have such innovation capabilities, the policy mix will need to be refined.

The implication is that indicators for modes of innovation in middle-income countries should be able to capture activity across the full spectrum of innovation capabilities. In particular, they should be fine-grained at the adoption, imitation and modification end of the spectrum.

Defining modes of innovation using standard innovation survey data

Although originating in high-income countries, there is a useful stream of research initiated by the OECD (2009) on modes of innovation. These are defined using multiple dimensions including novelty, markets and firms' internal capabilities (Arundel et al., 2007a, 2007b; Arundel and Hollanders, 2008; Hollanders and Arundel, 2007). They improve upon simple binary indicators by classifying firms in a more fine-grained manner. A strand in the literature builds on these taxonomies and attempts to define, both conceptually and empirically, contextually specific classifications of modes of innovation, to track changes over time (Gokhberg and Roud, 2016) or in specific countries (Hagen, 2014; Peneder, 2007, 2010) or regions (Frenz and Lambert, 2012; Vargas, 2022). Frenz and Lambert (2012) used this model to include both input and output measures, using exploratory factor analysis to identify and compare core modes between a range of countries, including South Africa, and within the same sectors across these countries. More recently, the European Union (Eurostat, 2020) launched an ambitious project, which is gaining wide traction, to measure, map and track a common set of indicators of innovation modes across all member countries.

Such taxonomies have value in illuminating critical dimensions. Understanding the key factors shaping heterogeneous modes of innovation can allow causal relationships to be investigated (Bogliacino and Pianta, 2016; Gokhberg and Roud, 2016; Vargas, 2022). The advantage is that these taxonomies are built on readily available innovation survey datasets, following the global standard *Oslo Manual*. They therefore provide a good starting point for analysing how South African firms display diverse modes of innovation capabilities.

A first classification system for analysis of South African firm innovation

Much of the research uses the taxonomical principles elaborated by Peneder (2003) to define modes in one or more of three ways:

- a 'cut-off' approach using a single variable, like many of the binary indicators described above;
- data-driven taxonomies using a range of dimensions; and
- top-down mixed classifications using multiple variables.

The analysis in the next section uses a top-down, mixed classification, as a first analytical phase,[2] adapting the distinctions elaborated by Arundel and O'Brien (2009) (see also Hollanders and Arundel, 2007; Eurostat, 2020; O'Brien 2016). Their work in the Australian context elaborates a model to operationalise simple composite indicators using standard business innovation survey datasets based on the *Oslo Manual* design, with a high degree of comparability (Arundel and O'Brien, 2009).

FIRM INNOVATION CAPABILITY TRENDS IN SOUTH AFRICA

A descriptive analysis of the most recently available Business Innovation Survey 2014–2016 data[3] provides evidence of the scale and nature of firm innovation capabilities in South Africa. Appendix 2A provides a description of the *Oslo Manual*-aligned (OECD, 2005) design and methodology of the survey[4]. Table 2.1 presents the sectoral and size class distributions of the full sample of firms, split by innovation and non-innovation-active firms. Virtually 70 per cent of firms reported they were innovation-active, while the remaining 30 per cent reported no innovation activities during the survey reference period. Overall, most firms surveyed (63 per cent) fell within the services sector; a lower proportion (36 per cent) were in the manufacturing sector. Very few firms were from the mining, quarrying and utilities sectors. The sectoral distribution of firms in the innovation-active and the non-innovation-active groups is very similar to the overall picture.[5]

A large portion of firms (45 per cent) in the Business Innovation

---

2   A second analytical phase will be to conduct Principle Component Analysis to determine the underlying relationships that identify context-specific modes of innovation in South Africa.

3   The next survey cycle, 2019–2021, is currently in field.

4   The BIS sample was stratified by sector and firm size class. Although size class was based on turnover according to the national business register of Statistics South Africa (Stats SA), in this analysis firms are classified according to their number of employees, as per the data collected in the survey.

5   Using a weighting calculation, survey data has been statistically adjusted to be representative of the entire South African business population within the chosen sectors.

Survey 2014-2016 data were categorised as small (10–49 employees); 28 per cent were micro (0–9 employees); 22 per cent were medium (50–249 employees), and only 6 per cent were large (250+ employees). The size-class spread of firms in the innovation and non-innovation active groups is also similar, although innovation-active firms are slightly more concentrated in the medium and large class sizes (24 per cent and 7 per cent respectively) compared to non-innovation active firms (16 per cent and 3 per cent respectively).

Table 2.1: Sectoral and size class spread of firms in the South African Business Innovation Survey 2014–2016

		Total	Innovation active	Non-innovation active
		(n=41,507)	(69.90%)	(30.10%)
Sector	Manufacturing	36.23%	36.84%	34.81%
	Services	62.67%	62.19%	63.78%
	Mining & quarrying	0.82%	0.82%	1.20%
	Electricity, gas & water supply	0.17%	0.16%	0.20%
		100%	100%	100%

		Total	Innovation active	Non-innovation active
Firm size*	Micro (0–9 employees)	27.90%	24.94%	34.68%
	Small (10–49 employees)	45.10%	44.71%	45.97%
	Medium (50–249 employees)	21.50%	23.71%	16.29%
	Large (250+ employees)	5.60%	6.64%	3.06%
		100%	100%	100%

* Survey weights have been used such that the data are representative of the South African business population.

Source: Author extraction and calculations from CeSTII, 2020. South African Business Innovation Survey 2014–2016.

Table 2.2 provides a summary of key indicators describing the nature of innovation: types, novelty, access to markets and collaboration. Nearly all (96 per cent) of the innovation-active firms introduced an innovation to the firm or market, and almost half (48 per cent) of these innovative businesses introduced a product innovation. Most of these product innovations were incremental, with low degrees of novelty. Only 12 per cent and 16 per cent of product innovators indicated that they had new-to-the-world or new-to-the-country innovations respectively. In addition, the data indicate that 80 per cent of turnover for these product innovators was generated by innovative products that were unchanged or marginally modified. Nevertheless, innovation-active firms were more likely to access national and global markets (64 per cent), while non-innovation-active firms were more likely to access provincial markets. Firm innovation was not strongly based on connections and linkages across the national system of innovation, with only about a fifth of innovation-active firms reporting collaboration to support their innovation activities. These collaborations were more likely with other firms or customers, while non-innovation active firms tended to rely on their customers and suppliers as their main sources of information for innovation. A higher percentage of firms in the services sector reported collaborations compared to firms in manufacturing (24 per cent versus 16 per cent respectively).

These trends confirm that supply-side STI policy interventions since 1996 have not had significant impact in terms of driving firm innovation capabilities to become more STI-led in collaboration with actors in the science system, or to operate at the technology frontier to create new globally competitive industries. Interaction and technology transfer across the national system of innovation is weak. Firms neither collaborate nor rely on external sources of information, and commercialisation of new-to-the-world innovation does not occur on a significant scale. This descriptive analysis in effect largely identifies absences of and weaknesses in desirable innovation activities or capabilities. It provides limited evidence for the design and implementation of alternative policy mixes, however.

MAPPING MODES OF INNOVATION

Evidence is required to illuminate a wider range of actual firm capabilities for uptake and the employment of new knowledge and technology. Analysing innovation modes can suggest where there are emergent firm strengths to be nurtured, or major gaps that require more systemic interventions to address market failures. In this way,

Table 2.2: Indicators of the nature of innovation in innovation-active firms in the South African Business Innovation Survey 2014–2016

% of innovation-active businesses with an innovation		96.0%
	Businesses with product innovations	48.2%
Innovative businesses	Businesses with process innovations	34.6%
	Businesses with organisational innovations	42.0%
	Businesses with marketing innovations	41.7%
	New-to-the-world	12.3%
Novelty of product innovations	New-to-the-country	15.6%
	New-to-the-industry	22.6%
	New-to-the-market	46.4%
	New-to-the-firm	56.4%
Access to markets	Innovation-active businesses operating on global or national markets	63.6%
	Non-innovation-active businesses operating on global or national markets	43.3%
Collabora-tion among innovation-active businesses	Businesses with collaborations	20.8%
	% Industry businesses with collaborations	16.2%
	% Services businesses with collaborations	23.6%

Source: Author extraction from CeSTII, 2020. South African Business Innovation Survey 2014–2016. Survey weights have been used such that the data are representative of the South African business population.

analysis of modes of innovation enables critical consideration of the likely reach of well-established policy instruments and also highlights potential points for policy leverage towards shifting and new STI policy intents.

The analysis in this section begins by implementing a top-down taxonomy, and then identifies patterns of characteristics such as sector or firm size, to profile sets of firms with similar innovation capabilities. The distribution of firms across modes yields a map of the spectrum of innovation capabilities at a specific point in time in the South African context.

Predominantly adoption and modification modes of innovation
Mapping modes using output data that reflect innovation capabilities is only possible using the relatively small subset of product innovators in South Africa: 48 per cent of the total sample. Appendix 2B at the end of this chapter sets out the definitions and technical models used to classify firms. The analysis reflected in Figure 2.1 confirms a distinctive spread of five modes of product innovation, skewed to the modification and adoption ends of the spectrum (see Figure 2.1).

The set of South African product innovators with cutting-edge innovation capabilities ('new-to-market international innovators') who operate on international markets, develop innovations in-house and implement new-to-world product innovations is relatively small (13 per cent), and the group of 'new-to-market domestic innovators' (7 per cent) is even smaller. Just over a quarter (28 per cent) of product innovators are classified as 'adopters', with low innovation capabilities whose innovations are developed by external organisations. Interventions with this relatively significant group would need to support the building of capabilities to access and modify innovations developed by other actors.

Of policy interest is the significant set of firms with some internal innovation capabilities. 'International modifiers' (34 per cent) are firms that operate on international markets and are able to develop innovations in-house, but the resulting products have low degrees of novelty, being new to domestic markets or to the firm itself. Interventions to support these firms to engage in global value chains in ways that link back into and drive technological upgrading in local production systems could be important to the process of structural transformation. 'Domestic modifiers' (19 per cent) operate at national or local levels only, and develop innovations in-house, but the resulting products are new to the firm only. Interventions to strengthen learning and capabilities for adapting, adjusting and modifying technologies in this set of firms may also strengthen the capacity for domestic value-add and employment generation. With the opportunities opened up by the African Continental Free Trade Agreement, developing innovation capabilities to operate on regional markets may also be significant.

Figure 2.1: Modes of innovation capabilities of product innovators

New-to-market international innovators | n=14 742

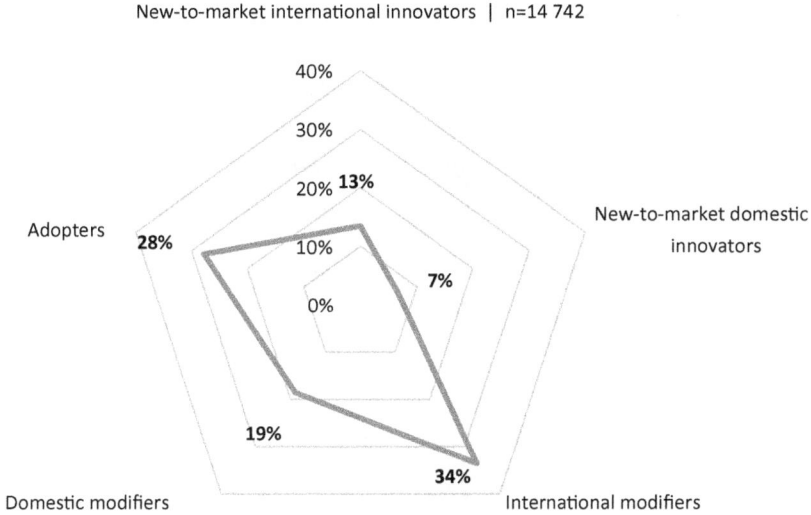

Source: Authors' calculation from CeSTII, 2020: South African Business Innovation Survey 2014–2016. Survey weights have been used such that the data are representative of the South African business population.

The following sections profile the product-innovative firms classified in each of the five modes, in terms of their technology intensity, sectors, size and perceptions of innovation barriers.

Technological intensity of firms with specific modes of innovation

Figure 2.2 shows that 'new-to-market international innovators' were most likely to develop or use four to six advanced technologies.[6] 'Adopters' were most likely to develop or use no advanced

---

6 The list of technologies included in the BIS 2014–2016 instrument was informed by consultation with local stakeholders: biotechnologies/ bioproducts, nanotechnology, geomatics, advanced processing technologies, advanced information control technologies, green technologies, business intelligence technologies, computerised design and engineering and supply chain/logistics technologies.

technologies, suggesting low technology intensity of the innovations they adopt, for example, purchase of standard software, hardware or equipment that is only new to the firm. A degree of technology intensity was evident in the use of one to three advanced technologies by 'new-to-market domestic innovators' (57 per cent), 'domestic' (59 per cent) and 'international' (62 per cent) modifiers. Note that the top three advanced technologies that all innovation-active firms were most likely to develop or use are: computerised design and engineering (44 per cent), supply chain and logistics technologies (32 per cent) and business intelligence technologies (25 per cent) (CeSTII, 2020: 41).

Figure 2.2: Number of advanced technologies developed or used by firms with a mode of innovation

n=14,622

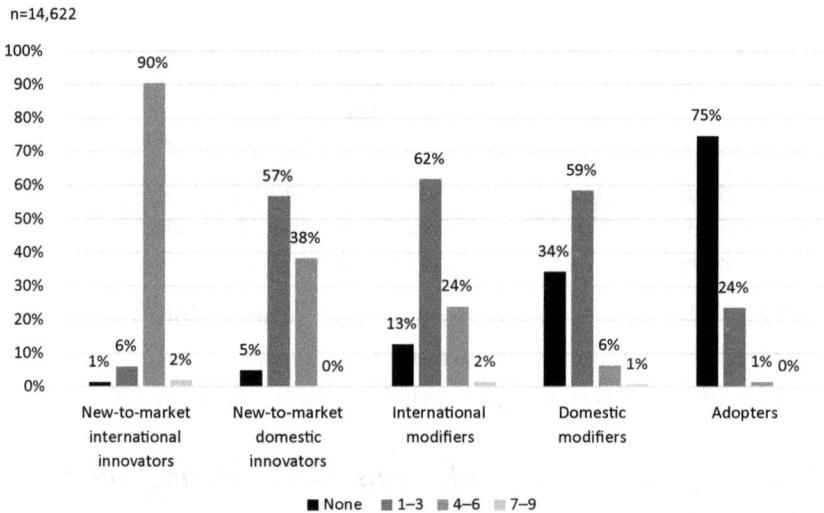

Survey weights have been used such that the data are representative of the South African business population.

Source: Authors' calculation from CeSTII, 2020: South African Business Innovation Survey 2014–2016.

Coordinated innovation, sectoral and industrial policy interventions are required to nurture the development and use of these advanced technologies by more 'domestic modifier', 'domestic innovator' and 'adopter' firms, as they are enablers for firms to absorb and modify a wider range of advanced technologies to local conditions. Significant groups of innovation-active firms will be missing from economic change interventions if the policy focus is primarily on firms that use advanced technologies to build export capabilities or are able to operate at the technological frontier.

Sectoral patterns of modes of innovation

The White Paper (DST, 2019) proposes a stronger focus on sectoral innovation strategies and structural arrangements to implement sectoral linkages (see also NACI, 2019b). Figure 2.3 reflects a high-level disaggregation, indicating distinctive patterns for firms in the manufacturing and services sectors. The two sectors are relatively similar in the proportions of 'adopters', 'international modifiers' and 'new-to-market international innovators'. They differ in the patterns of 'new-to-market domestic innovators' (13 per cent of manufacturing firms as compared to 1 per cent of services firms); and 'domestic modifiers' (11 per cent of manufacturing firms as compared to 22 per cent of services firms). Firms in the services sector have stronger capabilities for innovation at the international level, evident in the slightly larger proportion of 'new-to-market international innovators' in this sector (15 per cent). Additionally, manufacturing firms (36 per cent) are more likely than services firms (29 per cent) to be 'international modifiers', rather than innovators.

Modes of innovation across firms of different sizes

Mapping patterns of innovation modes across firm size class (categorised in terms of number of employees), Table 2.3 shows that 'new-to-market international innovators' are most likely to be small firms (88 per cent of firms with this mode of innovation). 'Domestic modifiers' are most likely to be micro-firms (70 per cent). 'Adopters' are spread over micro, medium and small firms, in that order. 'International modifiers' are also more spread out, but over small, medium, large and micro firms, in that order. One policy insight from these trends is to align current interventions and programmes across government departments aimed at supporting SMMEs (Booyens, 2011), particularly small enterprises, or the need to create opportunities and stimulate technological change in sectors where markets are highly concentrated and dominated by

Figure 2.3: Modes of innovation in manufacturing and services sectors

New-to-market international innovators | n=14,622

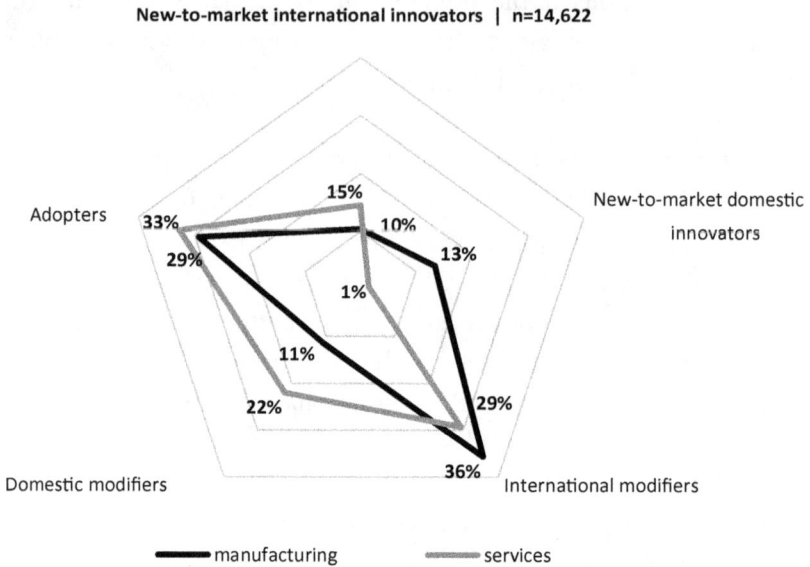

manufacturing — services

Source: Authors' calculation from CeSTII, 2020: South African Business Innovation Survey 2014–2016. Survey weights have been used such that the data are representative of the South African business population.

large firms. Interventions that build capabilities to strengthen or grow emergent innovation modes may have maximum effect when strategies are targeted at a specific class of firm size, for example, to increase the capabilities of medium-sized 'domestic modifiers'.

Barriers to innovation point to spaces for intervention

Analysing data on barriers to innovation activity provides insights into the contextual and systemic conditions that constrain firms' innovation capabilities. Figure 2.4 shows that the most important barriers to innovation reported across all output modes were cost and market factors. 'Cost factors' refer to situations in which the costs of innovation are too high, and firms lack access to credit, private equity or funds from outside sources or public sector grants to meet these costs. 'Market factors' refer to the fact that markets are dominated by established enterprises or are too competitive, combined with uncertain customer demand – not only for innovation goods or services but for

Table 2.3: Modes of innovation by firm size class

	Firm size (no. employees) Total number = 14 036				
	Micro (0–9)	Small (10–49)	Medium (50–249)	Large (250+)	Total
New-to-market international innovators	0%	88%	6%	6%	100%
New-to-market domestic innovators	0%	56%	32%	12%	100%
International modifiers	16%	39%	26%	19%	100%
Domestic modifiers	70%	5%	23%	1%	100%
Adopters	46%	22%	30%	2%	100%
Total	**31%**	**36%**	**25%**	**9%**	**100%**

Source: Authors' calculation from CeSTII, 2020: South African Business Innovation Survey 2014–2016. Survey weights have been used such that the data are representative of the South African business population.

all outputs by a firm. 'Adopter' firms are particularly likely to identify these barriers as blockages.

Knowledge factors (lack of managerial and engineering skills, lack of technicians, lack of information on technology, markets or partners – and institutional factors – lack of infrastructure, weak IP rights, legislation, regulations, standards and taxation) tended to be rated with lower levels of importance, particularly by 'domestic modifiers' and 'adopters'. These are most important for 'international modifiers', pointing to a set of firms that could benefit strongly from institutional- and knowledge-support types of policy intervention. Of note is that knowledge and institutional barriers were the same for both 'domestic' and 'international' innovators.

Mapping patterns in this way points to spaces for multi-faceted targeted interventions in a context-appropriate policy mix (see Table 2.4 and discussion in the next section).

Figure 2.4: Average importance of barriers to innovation activities

Importance of factor impeding innovation activities:

0 = Not experienced; Low = 1; Medium = 2; High = 3; n=14,622

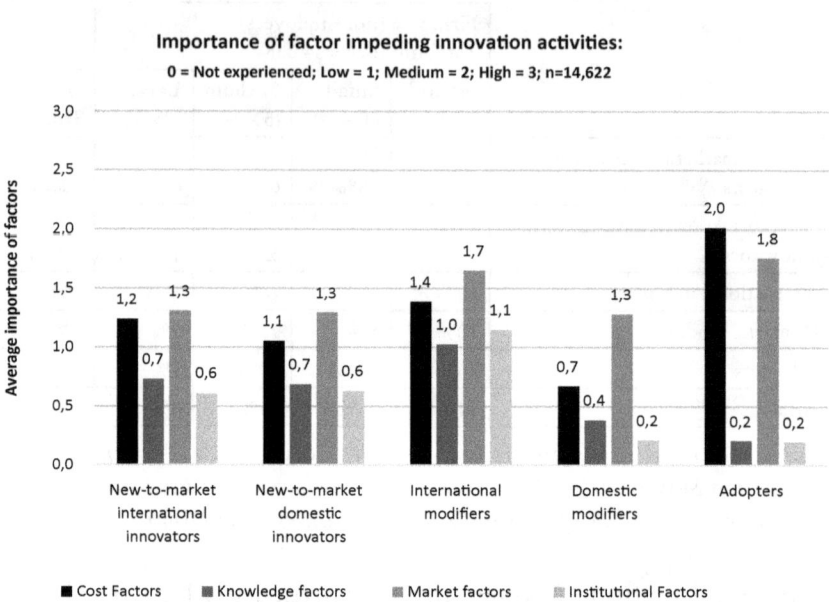

Survey weights have been used such that the data are representative of the South African business population.

Source: Authors' calculation from CeSTII, 2020: South African Business Innovation Survey 2014–2016.

WHERE INNOVATIONS CAN BE BROUGHT TO LIFE

Policy insights from mapping patterns of firm modes of innovation in South Africa

The innovation problem in South Africa centres on building firm-level capabilities for driving inclusive and sustainable re-industrialisation and structural change in the economy; this should drive our innovation policy mix. It is important not to assume a development model of 'catch-up' to the technology frontier, nor that the focus is for all firms to evolve towards becoming 'new-to-market international' innovators. As Lee (2019) highlights, middle-income countries need to design their own technological development pathways based on building dynamic innovation capabilities in key sectors, technologies or niches in which they can have comparative advantage. The role of government is critical: traditionally it's been seen as there to 'fix' market and other failures but increasingly it's required to shape more conducive conditions for strengthening innovation and production capabilities (NACI, n.d; see also Walwyn and Cloete, 2018). Policy interventions require a wide range of different patterns and implementations, given the complex processes of learning and innovation entailed (Lall, 1993). Implementing a policy mix in ways that ignore the current modes of innovation capabilities can lead to mismatches and misalignment. Across a range of Latin American countries, distinctive practices (such as exploring, protecting, partnering or modernising processes) were classified to yield four very different main innovation modes: product-orientated; production-improvement; management and opportunistic modes (Vargas, 2022). A context-specific, distinctive Latin American mode of 'open management' was identified, where innovation relied on introducing new business practices in an open way, informed by external knowledge. Similarly, Gokhberg and Roud (2016) analysed different modes that provided significant policy insights for the Russian system of innovation: modernisation in line with regulation; new products for market demand; innovation for quality, flexibility and efficiency; product-driven expansion; and synergic effects of innovation.

Table 2.4 summarises our empirical analysis of how South African firms innovate, as a model that can begin to provide evidence for the design and implementation of a contextually specific policy mix. It identifies three main policy priorities to build firms' innovation capabilities and the modes of innovation and firm profiles associated with each. A policy mix centred on driving structural transformation and inclusive development should make provision for interventions addressing all three priorities. The right-hand column provides examples of different kinds of STI policy interventions most pertinent for each mode of innovation capabilities for illustrative purposes only, drawing on recent research on policy mixes and choices of instruments (Borrás, 2011; Borrás and Edler, 2020; Boon and Edler, 2018; Borrás and Edquist, 2013; Cocos and Lepori, 2020).

First, there is a priority to strengthen the dynamic innovation capabilities of firms that can operate on global or domestic markets, oriented to the sets of 'new-to-market international/domestic innovators'. Here, interventions could focus on addressing the wide range of barriers firms experience. In addition to horizontal policy instruments to make the environment more conducive for firms' productive capabilities, such as skilled workers or a competitive environment with IPR or export regulations, a range of vertical interventions are required, including incentivising knowledge networks. Table 2.4 provides examples of the kinds of policy interventions that are typically used to strengthen the capabilities of the sets of 'innovator' firms, such as those dealing with competitive research funds, tax incentives or technology transfer support. These firms are more likely to have the capabilities to access currently available commercialisation and localisation funding instruments.

There is a second policy priority: to build the innovation capabilities of firms for technology modification on global or domestic markets; such policy would be oriented to the demands of the 'international/ domestic modifiers'. Here, additional interventions are required to stimulate innovation capabilities at sectoral levels, particularly those levels identified as critical to economic growth. Policy instruments to support and drive collaboration amongst firms within a specific sector to share the costs and benefits of new technologies could be of value in promoting technological acquisition and learning. To address the significant market barriers reported by these firms requires coordination between innovation, trade and industry and competition policies, and/ or partnerships with industry and sectoral associations. Examples include collaboration around setting quality standards, digital services or incentive and support services to regulate market interactions. Market barriers can also be addressed by programmes to build firms' capabilities to search for suitable technologies and adaptations for use inside the firm (Teece et al., 2020). Knowledge barriers were identified as more significant for the 'international modifiers', and interventions for this set of firms could include investment in the development of technical, engineering and managerial skills and research. Strengthening capabilities for learning at firm level is also required.

The third policy priority has not been a strong focus thus far in South Africa: to broaden the innovation capabilities of firms to access and absorb technologies for productive efficiency. Building capabilities and stimulating demand from 'adopters', and from the large set of firms that do not innovate at all, can strengthen a national system of innovation. The aim is not for all firms to develop capabilities to operate in global markets, or at the technological frontier through R&D and science-driven modes of innovation. Rather, firms need to be able to innovate in ways that can stimulate market demand within existing economic conditions, and with varying levels of technological intensity. This may require voluntary, non-coercive 'soft' policy tools, such as sectoral innovation campaigns, codes of conduct or facilitation of information exchange. To broaden the capabilities of additional firms requires addressing barriers to market entry and offering different kinds of funding incentives. Public procurement and public–private partnerships including innovation conditionalities are typically used for this purpose, for example.

The analysis points to the potential value of new kinds of STI public funding mechanisms aimed at strengthening the adoption and modification of innovation modes more widely across the system of innovation. Based on emergent trends in other countries, Teece et al. (2020: 10) recommended the establishment of a funding pool in South Africa, to build firm-level productivity 'through a programme aimed at identifying, acquiring and widely diffusing existing best-practice ordinary capabilities and technologies'.

The analysis summarised in Table 2.4 therefore highlights the need to build technological capabilities across the full range of firms, including those displaying no or minimal innovation capabilities. Defining modes can provide more nuanced information to inform policy interventions than is possible to extract from the binary indicators that are typically used. The multi-dimensional taxonomy can equally be used to track change over time towards desired policy goals. The challenge for the design of an STI policy mix is to shift the patterns of modes of innovation in multiple directions over time towards the development goal of breaking the middle-income trap. For innovation to come to life across the national system of innovation requires a policy mix with both demand- and supply-led orientation, together with top-down and bottom-up policy coordination (Crespi

Table 2.4: Mapping modes of innovation in South Africa 2014–2016

Policy priority to inform the mix of strategies and interventions	Mode of innovation capabilities	Technology intensity	Sectoral spread	Firm size class	Barriers	Examples of policy interventions to build innovation capabilities*
Broaden the capabilities of additional firms to access and absorb new technologies	Adopters	Low technology intensity	Similar proportion of manufacturing and services	Spread over micro, medium and small firms	Cost and market barriers are more strongly important; knowledge and institutional factors less important	Voluntary, non-coercive 'soft' tools: • campaigns • codes of conduct, • Information exchange • global/sectoral/HE/PRIs • public procurement • public–private partnerships with innovation conditions • SME incentives/support services/legal advice • Skills, education and training to build competencies
Build stronger capabilities for technology modification and upgrading to operate on global or domestic markets	International modifiers	Moderate technology intensity	Similar proportion of manufacturing and services	Spread over small, medium, large and micro firms	Cost and market barriers important Knowledge and institutional factors are more important	• Sector-specific financial and other incentives, positive or negative • Regulatory social and market interactions • Quality standards • Public support to HE and PRIs
	Domestic modifiers	Moderate technology intensity	More services than manufacturing	More likely to be micro firms	Knowledge and institutional factors are less important	• SME incentives and support services • Digital services
Strengthen dynamic innovation capabilities of groups of firms that can operate in global or domestic markets	New-to-market international innovators	High technology intensity	Similar proportion of manufacturing and services	More likely to be small firms	Cost and market barriers important	• Competition/IPR policy regulation • Competitive research funds/tax incentives/tech transfer/support/incubators • Venture/seed capital • Sector-specific interventions
	New-to-market domestic innovators	Moderate technology intensity	More manufacturing than services	Spread over small, medium, large firms	Cost and market barriers important	

* *Types of policy intervention interpreted and aligned drawing on Borrás and Edquist (2013).*

Source: Authors' compilation.

and Dutrenit, 2014), targeted to and informed by the range of firm-level capabilities and needs.

Mapping innovation modes identifies spaces for coordination and alignment between policy actors

Drawing on lessons from East Asian countries, Mamphiswana (2022) proposed a policy framework for South Africa with a two-fold orientation, based on a distinction between two types of innovation. The first promotes disruptive technologies and can create new industries, which are at higher risk; hence, government plays a key role in investing to stimulate new markets. This kind of strategy is more likely to be oriented to our categories of 'new-to-market international and domestic innovator' modes. An example in South Africa is DSI investment and network building in the hydrogen economy, through the HySA programme, over the past decade. Mazzucato's concept of mission-driven innovation potentially provides direction here, in proposing that government should 'actively shape markets, rather than simply fixing failures' (Mazzucato et al., 2021: 12). The second orientation focuses on sustainable innovations that will enable higher prices and/or improve efficiency to reduce operating costs. These are more likely to be oriented to 'domestic modifiers', 'adopters' and 'non-innovators'. Disruptive innovations are to target new industries and are to be driven by DSI policy instruments (such as incubators, international technology transfers and R&D investments), while sustaining and efficiency innovations are to be supported by DTIC policy interventions, targeting existing industries.

For some decades, the Strategic Management Model (2004) for the alignment between DSI and other STI-intensive line departments was predicated on a two-fold distinction: that DSI would take the lead in emerging sectors and might be involved in sector-specific initiatives led by other sector-based departments but would not play an active role in mature industries (DSI, 2022). Our analysis illustrated that such a framework is too binary, and there is value in defining a more complex spectrum of modes of innovation capabilities. Informed by NACI (2020) reviews, such a shift is evident in the Decadal Plan (2022), which conceptualises more integrated sets of alignments on a 'co-creation continuum' that mandates DSI to support all types of research, development and innovation (RDI), through the elaboration of sector-specific RDI strategies that support line department strategies (DSI, 2022).

If government is increasingly recognised as a major actor shaping the directionality of innovation, this requires a strong articulation of demand and demand conditions, whether for general innovation, or sector-specific or challenge-oriented policy (Boon and Edler, 2018). The patterns of innovation capabilities mapped out here provide an articulation of demand, pointing to the significance of reconceptualising a differentiated policy mix, which aligns innovation, industrialisation and specific sectoral[7] policies in mutually reinforcing and coordinated ways. It reinforces the proposed policy shift to a new strategic management model, supported by different government departments, which overcomes binaries between disruptive and sustaining innovations, and can potentially address failures in innovation and industrial policy coordination.

Table 2. 4 provides examples of the kinds of policy interventions that may deepen the innovation capabilities of the main clusters of firms. DSI funding of local technology development in universities or research institutes must be balanced with demand-side measures that open up product markets – this would provide incentives for collaborative firm-level innovation. Firm learning and capacity building are cumulative over time so interventions oriented to supporting more widespread upgrading in the form of 'technology adoption' may strengthen the foundations for innovation within a sector. The extension of public support interventions to groups of 'non-innovator', 'adopter' and 'modifier' firms, on the part of both DSI and DTIC, is vital to developing innovation and production capabilities for technological upgrading.

---

7   Bear in mind though that the analysis mapped modes of innovation and firm profiles in the formal manufacturing and services sectors only. It did not provide much-needed insight into other historically significant resource sectors such as mining and agriculture, identified as key foci for 'modernisation' through STI.

CONCLUSION

This chapter argues that analysis of firms' existing innovation capabilities should inform context-specific policy mixes (Edler, 2009) aimed at breaking the middle-income country technology trap and driving the structural changes desired in South Africa. A well-designed STI policy mix does not automatically guarantee that desired changes and learnings will occur, but it does provide a vital framework for directionality and coordination. We showed the value of moving beyond the traditional focus on binary distinctions such as those between product and process innovation, technological and non-technological innovation, or STI- and DUI- (doing, using and interacting) driven innovation strategies. These binary distinctions provide limited policy direction and can lead to misalignment and gaps. The analysis points to a way to create firm-level evidence that can be used to inform and monitor the implementation of an emerging, contextually appropriate balance of demand and supply side interventions. Profiling firm innovation modes provides evidence for a better understanding of national and sectoral patterns of capabilities. The resulting taxonomy proposes directionality, categorising South African product innovators into groups: new-to-market international innovators, new-to-market domestic innovators, international modifiers, domestic modifiers, adopters and non-innovators. To grow the innovation capabilities of each category of firms across the national system of innovation requires systematic articulation of a differentiated spread of interventions. These include regulatory, financial and 'soft' policy interventions that tackle market and system failures in a way that actively shapes and changes barriers at firm level.

REFERENCES

Academy of Science of South Africa (ASSAF). 2013. 'Review of the State of the Science, Technology and Innovation (STI) System in South Africa'. http://hdl.handle.net/20.500.11911/79, accessed 27 July 2022.

Andreoni, A., Mondliwa, P., Roberts, S. and Tregenna, F. (eds). 2021a. *Structural Transformation in South Africa: The Challenges of Inclusive Industrial Development in a Middle-Income Country*. Oxford Scholarship Online.

DOI:10.1093/oso/9780192894311.001.0001, accessed 19 August 2022.

Andreoni, A., Mondliwa, P., Roberts, S. and Tregenna, F. 2021b. 'Towards a new industrial policy for structural transformation', in Andreoni, A., Mondliwa, P., Roberts, S. and Tregenna, F. (eds). *Structural Transformation in South Africa: The Challenges of Inclusive Industrial Development in a Middle-Income Country*. Oxford Scholarship Online. DOI:10.1093/oso/9780192894311.001.0001, accessed 19 August 2022.

Andreoni, A. and Tregenna, F. 2020. 'Escaping the middle-income technology trap: A comparative analysis of industrial policies, China, Brazil and South Africa', *Structural Change and Economic Dynamics*, 54, 323 –40.

Andreoni, A. and Tregenna, F. 2021. 'The middle-income trap and premature deindustrialization in South Africa', in Andreoni, A., Mondliwa, P., Roberts, S. and Tregenna, F. (eds). *Structural Transformation in South Africa: The Challenges of Inclusive Industrial Development in a Middle-Income Country*. Oxford Scholarship Online. DOI:10.1093/oso/9780192894311.001.0001, accessed 20 August 2022.

Arundel, A. 2006. 'Innovation survey indicators: Any progress since 1996'. Paper for the G20 at the Leader's Level Workshop (L20 Workshop), Maastricht, The Netherlands.

Arundel, A. and Hollanders, H. 2005. 'Policy, indicators and targets: Measuring the impacts of innovation policies', *European Trend Chart on Innovation*. MERIT, Maastricht.

Arundel A. and Hollanders, H. 2008. 'Innovation scoreboards: Indicators and policy use', in Nauwelaers C. and Wintjes R. (eds). *Innovation Policy in Europe: Measurement and Strategy*. Cheltenham: Edward Elgar Publishing, 29–51.

Arundel, A., Bordoy, C. and Kanerva, M. 2007a. 'Neglected innovators: How do innovative firms that do not perform R&D innovate? Results of an analysis of the Innobarometer 2007 Survey No. 215', INNO-Metrics Thematic Paper. MERIT, Maastricht.

Arundel, A., Kanerva, M., Van Cruysen, A. and Hollanders, H. 2007b. *Innovation Statistics for the European Service Sector*. Brussels: European Commission.

Arundel, A. and O'Brien, K. 2009. 'Innovation Metrics Framework Project'. Department of Innovation Industry, Science and Research: Australian Government. https://www.researchgate.net/publication/279661153_Innovation_metrics_for_Australia, accessed 28 March 2023.

Arundel, A., Casali, L. and Hollanders, H. 2015. 'How European public sector agencies innovate: The use of bottom-up, policy-dependent and knowledge-scanning innovation methods'. *Research Policy*, 44(7), 1271–1282.

Arundel, A., Bloch, C. and Ferguson, B. 2019. 'Advancing innovation in the public sector: Aligning innovation measurement with policy goals'. *Research Policy*, 48(3), 789–798.

Aterido, R., Hlatshwayo, A., Pieterse, D. and Steenkamp, A. 2019. 'Firm dynamics, job outcomes and productivity: South African Formal Businesses, 2010–14'. Policy Research Working Paper No 8788, World Bank Group.

Bell, J.F., Mondliwa, P. and Nyamwena, J. 2019. 'Technological change and productive capabilities in the plastics industry'. CCRED Working Paper Series 2019/11. https://www.competition.org.za/working-papers, accessed 15 June 2023.

Baker, L. and Sovacool, B.K. 2017. 'The political economy of technological capabilities and global production networks in South Africa's wind and solar photovoltaic (PV) industries'. *Political Geography*, 60, 1–12.

Bhorat, H., Cassim, A. and Hirsch, A. 2014. 'Policy coordination and growth traps in a middle-income country setting: The case of South Africa'. WIDER Working Paper, No, 2014/155. https://www.wider.unu.edu/publication/policy-co-ordination-and-growth-traps-middle-income-country-setting, accessed 17 June 2023.

Bhorat, H., Naidoo, K., Oosthuizen, M. and Pillay, K. 2016. 'Demographic, employment, and wage trends in South Africa', Understanding the African Lions – Growth Traps and Opportunities in Six Dominant African Economies, https://www.brookings.edu/wp-content/uploads/2016/07/06-demographic-employment-wage-trends-south-africa.pdf, accessed 13 July 2023.

Bogliacino, F, and Pianta. M. 2016. 'Innovation and employment: A reinvestigation using revised Pavitt classes'. *Research Policy* 39(6), 799–809.

Boon, W. and Edler, J. 2018. 'Demand, challenges and innovation: Making sense of new trends in innovation policy'. *Science and Public Policy*, 45(4), 435–447.

Borrás, S. 2011. 'Policy learning and organisational capacities in innovation policies'. *Science and Public Policy*, 38(9), 725–734.

Borrás, S. and Edler, J. 2020. 'The roles of the state in the governance of socio-technical systems' transformation'. *Research Policy*, 49(5), 103971.

Borrás, S. and Edquist, C. 2013. 'The choice of innovation policy instruments'. *Technological Forecasting and Social* Change, 80(8), 1513–1522.

Booyens, I. 2011. 'Are small, medium-and micro-sized enterprises engines of innovation? The reality in South Africa', *Science and Public Policy*, 38(1), 67–78.

Chipkin, I. and Swilling, M. 2018. *Shadow State: The Politics of State Capture*. New York: NYU Press.

Cassiolato, J. and Vitorino, V. (eds). 2011. *BRICS and Development Alternatives: Innovation Systems and Policies*. London: Anthem Press.

Centre for Science, Technology and Innovation Indicators (CeSTII). 2020. 'Innovation performance in South African businesses 2014–2016:

Activities, outcomes, enablers, constraints'. Cape Town: Human Sciences Research Council. https://hsrc.ac.za/uploads/pageContent/11943/SA%20 BUSINESS%20INNOVATION%20SURVEY%202014-2016%20 PUBLIC%20REPORT.pdf, accessed 19 June 2022.

Cocos, M. and Lepori, B. 2020. 'What we know about the research policy mix'. *Science and Public Policy*, 47(2), 235–245.

Crespi, G. and Dutrenit, G. (eds). 2014. *Science, Technology and Innovation for Development: The Latin American Experience*. New York: Springer International Publishing.

Dutrenit, G., Lee, K., Nelson, R., Soete, L. and Vera-Cruz, A. (eds). 2013. *Learning, Capability Building and Innovation for Development*. Basingstoke: Palgrave-MacMillan.

Department of Science and Innovation (DSI). 2022. 'South Africa's Science, Technology and Innovation Decadal Plan: An Instrument for Enabling Africa's Reawakening and Inclusive and Sustainable Development'. https://www.naci.org.za/wp-content/uploads/2022/09/DDG-Daan-du-Toit-220909-NACI-Africa-Decadal-Plan.pdf, accessed 17 January 2023.

Department of Science and Innovation (DSI). 2019. 'White Paper on Science, Technology and Innovation'. https://www.dst.gov.za/index.php/legal-statutory/white-papers/2775-white-paper-on-science-technology-and-innovation, accessed 26 January 2023.

Department of Science and Technology (DST). 2012. *Ministerial Review Committee on Science, Technology and Innovation Landscape in South Africa: Final Report*. Pretoria: Department of Science and Technology.

Edler, J. 2009. 'Demand policies for innovation in EU CEE countries'. Manchester Business School Working Paper No. 579, Manchester Business School, The University of Manchester.

Eurostat. 2020. 'Innovation profiling – first results. Working Group on Statistics on Science, Technology and Innovation', Eurostat/G4/STI/WG/2020/Document 10, European Commission, https://circabc.europa.eu/w/browse/3f884f3e-f596-43a9-bde7-b93d87972984, accessed 17 July 2022.

Filippetti, A. 2010. 'The role of design in firms' innovation activity: A micro-level analysis'. *SSRN Electronic Journal*, https://doi.org/10.2139/SSRN.1623345, accessed 11 Jul 2022.

Fine, B. and Rustomjee, Z. 1996. *The Political Economy of South Africa: From Minerals-Energy Complex to Industrialisation*. New York: Routledge.

Frenz, M. and Lambert, R. 2012. 'Mixed modes of innovation: an empiric approach to capturing firms' innovation behaviour'. OECD Science, Technology and Industry Working Papers No. 2012/06, OECD Publishing, https://doi.org/10.1787/5k8x6l0bp3bp-en, accessed 11 July 2022.

Gastrow, M. and Kruss, G. 2017. *Capability Building and Global Innovation Networks*. London: Routledge.

Gokhberg, L., and Roud, V. 2016. 'Structural changes in the national innovation system: Longitudinal study of innovation modes in the Russian industry'. *Economic Change and Restructuring*, 49(2), 269–288.

Gregersen, B. and Johnson, B. 2021. 'The measurement and performance of the Danish innovation system in relation to sustainable development', in Christensen, J., Gergersen, B., Holm, R. and Lorenz, E. (eds), *Globalisation, New and Emerging Technologies, and Sustainable Development*. London: Routledge, 252–266.

Hagen, H.O. 2014. 'Innovators and firm developers'. Statistics Sweden. IFI/ ES/Statistics Sweden 2014-12-01.

Higher Education, Science, Technology, Innovation and Information Landscape (HESTIIL). 2022. 'A New Pathway 2030: Catalysing South Africa's NSI for Urgent Scaled Social and Economic Impact. A Review of South Africa's Higher Education, Science, Technology and Innovation Institutional Landscape (HESTIIL)'. Report by the HESTIIL Ministerial Committee, https://www.dst.gov.za/images/2021/Higher%20 Education,%20Science,%20Technology%20and%20Innovation%20 Institutional%20Landscape%20Review%20Report.pdf, accessed 23 March 2023.

Huang, C., Arundel, A. and Hollanders, H. 2010. 'How firms innovate: R&D, non-R&D, and technology adoption'. UNU-Merit Working Paper series-2020-027, United Nations University, Netherlands.

Hollanders, H. and Arundel, A. 2007. 'Differences in socio-economic conditions and regulatory environments: Explanatory variations in national innovation performance and policy implications'. Inno Metrics Thematic Paper, *Inno Metrics*, MERIT, Maastricht University, Netherlands.

Jensen, M.B., Johnson, B., Lorenz, E., Lundvall, B.Å. and Lundvall, B.A. 2016. 'Forms of knowledge and modes of innovation,' in Lundvall, B. (ed.). *The Learning Economy and the Economics of Hope*. UK, London; USA, New York: Anthem Press.

Kaplan, D. 2008. 'Science and technology policy in South Africa: Past performance and proposals for the future'. *Science, Technology and Society* 13(1),95–122.

Kruss, G. 2020. 'Catching up, falling behind: The need for political coalitions for innovation and inclusive development in South Africa'. *Nova Economia*, 30, 1115–1144.

Kruss, G. and Lorentzen, J. 2011. 'The South African innovation policies: Potential and constraint', in Cassiolato, J. and Vitorino, V. (eds). *BRICS and Development Alternatives: Innovation Systems and Policies*. New York: Anthem Press, 163–189.

Kruss, G. and Ralphs, G. 2021. 'The value of a 'fixed' mandate for the knowledge commons: A history of the HSRC's role in R&D and innovation measurement (1966–2018)', in Soudien, C., Swartz, S. and Houston, G.F.

(eds). *Society, Research and Power: A History of the Human Sciences Research Council from 1929 to 2019*. Cape Town: HSRC Press.

Lall, S. 1993. 'Understanding technology development'. *Development and Change*, 24(4), 719–753.

Lee, K. 2019. *The Art of Economic Catch-up: Barriers, Detours and Leapfrogging in Innovation Systems*. Cambridge: Cambridge University Press.

Lorentzen, J. 2009. 'Learning by firms: The black box of South Africa's innovation system'. *Science and Public Policy*, 36(1), 33–45.

Luiz, J.M. 2016. 'The political economy of middle-income traps: Is South Africa in a long-run growth trap? The path to "bounded populism"'. *South African Journal of Economics*, 84(1), 3–19.

Lukhele, N. and Soumonni, O. 2021. 'Modes of innovation used by SMMEs to tackle social challenges in South Africa'. *African Journal of Science, Technology, Innovation and Development*, 13(7), 829–837.

Malele, V., Mpofu, K. and Muchie, M. 2019. 'Bridging the innovation chasm: Measuring awareness of entrepreneurship and innovation policies and platforms at the universities of technology in South Africa'. *African Journal of Science, Technology, Innovation and Development*, 11(7), 783–793.

Mamphiswana, R. 2022. 'Positioning the South African economy for new industries: Policy lessons from East Asia'. SARChI Industrial Development Policy Brief Series PB 2202-02', University of Johannesburg, https://www.uj.ac.za/wp-content/uploads/2021/10/sarchi-wp-2022-05-mamphiswana-march-2022.pdf, accessed 9 March 2023.

Marcelle, G.M. 2004. *Technological Learning: A Strategic Imperative for Firms in the Developing World*. Cheltenham: Edward Elgar Publishing.

Mondliwa, P. and Roberts, S. 2021. 'The political economy of structural transformation: Political settlements and industrial policy', in Andreoni, A., Mondliwa, P., Roberts, S. and Tregenna, F. (eds). *Structural Transformation in South Africa: The Challenges of Inclusive Industrial Development in a Middle-Income Country*. Oxford Scholarship Online. DOI:10.1093/oso/9780192894311.001.0001, accessed 5 March 2023.

Mazzucato, M., Qobo, M. and Kattel, R. 2021. 'Building state capacities and dynamic capabilities to drive social and economic development: The case of South Africa'. UCL Institute for Innovation and Public Purpose Working paper series IIPP WP 22-09.

Mustapha, N., Petersen, I.H., Jegede, O., Bortagaray, I. and Kruss, G. 2021. 'Measurement of innovation in the informal sector in Africa: the importance to industrial policy'. *Innovation and Development*, DOI: 10.1080/2157930X.2021.1887614, accessed 28 August 2022.

National Advisory Council on Innovation (NACI). No Date. *Review of the White Paper on Science and Technology*. Pretoria: National Advisory Council on Innovation. http://www.naci.org.za/wp-content/uploads/2010/01/Review-of-the-White-Paper-on-Science-and-

Technology.pdf, accessed 28 August 2022.

National Advisory Council on Innovation (NACI). 2019a. 'South Africa Foresight Exercise for Science, Technology and Innovation 2030. Synthesis Report'. https://edhe.co.za/wp-content/uploads/South_African_Foresight_Exercise_for_STI_2019.pdf, accessed 28 August 2022.

National Advisory Council on Innovation (NACI). 2019b. 'Design and implementation evaluation of the Sector Innovation Fund programme', National Advisory Council on Innovation, Pretoria.

National Advisory Council on Innovation (NACI). 2020. 'A review of the national Research and Development Plan and the Ten Year Innovation Strategy', National Advisory Council on Innovation, Pretoria.

National Advisory Council on Innovation (NACI). 2022. *The State Of Science, Technology And Innovation Indicators Report 2022*. Pretoria: National Advisory Council on Innovation.

O'Brien, K. 2016. 'Revealing hidden innovation: Patterns of external innovation investment in Australian businesses'. *Technology Innovation Management Review*, 6(6), 41–48.

Organisation for Economic Cooperation and Development (OECD). 2005. *Oslo Manual: Guidelines for Collecting and Interpreting Innovation Data*. 3rd edition. Paris: Organisation for Economic Cooperation and Development.

Organisation for Economic Cooperation and Development (OECD). 2007. *Reviews of Innovation Policy: South Africa 2007*. Paris: Organisation for Economic Cooperation and Development.

Organisation for Economic Cooperation and Development (OECD). 2009. *Innovation in Firms: A Microeconomic Perspective*. Paris: Organisation for Economic Cooperation and Development.

Oqubay, A., Minister, E.S., Tregenna, F. and Valodia, I. (eds). 2021. *The Oxford Handbook of the South African Economy*. UK: Oxford University Press.

Parrilli, M.D. and Heras, H.A. 2016. 'STI and DUI innovation modes: Scientific-technological and context-specific nuances'. *Research Policy*, 45(4), 747–756.

Parrilli, M.D. and Radicic, D. 2021. 'STI and DUI innovation modes in micro-, small-, medium-and large-sized firms: Distinctive patterns across Europe and the US'. *European Planning Studies*, 29(2), 346–368.

Peneder, M. 2003. 'Industry classifications: Aim, scope and techniques'. *Journal of Industry, Competition and Trade*, 3(1), 109–129.

Peneder, M. 2007. 'Sectoral taxonomies: Identifying competitive regimes by statistical cluster analysis', in *The Elgar Companion to Neo-Schumpeterian Economics*. Cheltenham: Edward Elgar Publishing, 525–543.

Peneder, M. 2010. 'Technological regimes and the variety of innovation behaviour: Creating integrated taxonomies of firms and sectors'. *Research Policy*, 39(3), 323–334.

Roud, V. 2018. 'Understanding the heterogeneity of innovation modes: Performance effects, barriers, and demand for state support'. *Technological Forecasting and Social Change*, 133, 238–253.

Teece, D., Brown, K., Alves, P., Mthombeni, M. and Mondliwa, P. 2020. 'Firm-level capabilities: The missing link in South African industrial growth strategy. BRG Institute', Gordon Institute of Business University of Pretoria. https://repository.up.ac.za/bitstream/handle/2263/82700/Teece_Firm_2020.pdf?sequence=1, accessed 19 August 2022.

Townson, P., Matthews, J. and Wrigley, C. 2016. 'Outcomes from applying design-led innovation in an Australian manufacturing firm'. *Technology Innovation Management Review*, 6(6), 49–58.

Vargas, F. 2022. 'How do firms innovate in Latin America? Identification of innovation strategies and their main adoption determinants'. UNU-Merit Working Paper series No 2022-018, United Nations University, Netherlands.

Vera-Cruz, A. and Vargas. A. 2013. 'The significance of Jorge Katz's work for the understanding of learning and technological capability building in developing countries', in Dutrenit, G., Lee, K., Nelson, R., Soete, L. and Vera-Cruz, A. (eds). 2013. *Learning, Capability Building and iInovation for Development*. Basingstoke: Palgrave-MacMillan.

Walwyn, D. and Boraine, H. 2006. *The South African National System of Innovation: Structures, Policies and Performance: Background Report to the OECD Country Review of South Africa's National System on Innovation*. Pretoria: National Advisory Council on Innovation.

Walwyn, D. and Cloete, L. 2018. 'Draft White Paper on Science, Technology and Innovation neglects to prioritise issues of performance and human capability'. *South African Journal of Science*, 114(11/12), 1–6.

Walwyn, D. and Naidoo, S. 2020. 'Policy mixes and overcoming challenges to innovation in developing countries: Insights from South Africa's manufacturing sector'. *African Journal of Science, Technology, Innovation and Development*, 12, 33–46.

APPENDIX 2A: BUSINESS INNOVATION SURVEY METHODOLOGY

The South African Business Innovation Surveys are based on the guidelines of the Organisation for Economic Co-operation and Development's (OECD) *Oslo Manual* (2005).[8] More specifically, these

---

8 The 2014–2016 survey was based on the methodological guidelines outlined in the third edition of the *Oslo Manual*, published in 2005. The *Oslo Manual* has since been revised, and its fourth edition was published in 2018.

surveys use the methodological recommendations for the Community Innovation Survey (CIS) series of the European Union (EU) countries, as provided by Eurostat, the Statistical Office of the European Commission. Indicators that are relevant for both South Africa and other countries are produced using these guidelines.[9]

The survey design is informed by the structure of the National Business Register of Statistics South Africa (Stats SA) and is intended to provide a template for a suitable, stratified, random sample. The *Oslo Manual* recommends size cut-offs that are based on employment, including only businesses with ten or more employees. The Stats SA business register has insufficient information on employment, and hence the size classes are of necessity based on turnover. The relationship between turnover and the number of full-time employees is prescribed by a schedule contained in the National Small Business Amendment Act (Act No. 26 of 2003). Businesses are divided into four size classes. The criteria used to differentiate between the four size classes are sector specific.

The final sample frame for the 2014–2016 survey had 30 Standard Industrial Classification (SIC) codes and four size classes, which gave a total of 120 strata. The SIC codes covered industry sectors (mining, manufacturing, and electricity, gas and water supply) as well as services sectors (wholesale and retail trade, transport, storage and communication, financial intermediation, and computer and related activities).

Probability weights were created to project the survey results to the target population of South African businesses in the sectors. These weights were also adjusted to correct for bias due to non-response as well as invalid businesses (businesses that were found to have merged or been liquidated). The analysis in this chapter applies these weights to all calculations.

---

9   To access previous South African innovation survey reports and datasets, go to http://www.hsrc.ac.za/en/departments/CeSTii/reports-cestii.

APPENDIX 2B: CONSTRUCTION OF OUTPUT MODES
OF INNOVATION CAPABILITIES FROM THE SOUTH
AFRICAN BUSINESS INNOVATION SURVEY 2014–2016

The analysis was restricted to firms who were product innovators, i.e. had introduced a new or significantly improved product (good or service) during the period 2014–2016.[10] This group of firms constituted 48% of the sample.[11]

These firms were then categorised according to a combination of the following three elements:

1. Capabilities: *By whom were these product (goods and services) innovations developed?*
In-house developers:
Mainly your enterprise
OR
Your enterprise together with other enterprises or institutions
OR
Your enterprise by adapting or modifying goods or services originally developed by other enterprises or institutions

Adopters:
Other enterprises in your enterprise group
OR
Mainly other enterprises or institutions

2. Novelty: *Were any of your product innovations (goods and services) during the three years, 2014 to 2016...*
New to international markets:
New to the world? = Yes

---

10 Only product innovators were included because there was no novelty information for process innovators.
11 Note, some of these firms got removed from the subsequent analysis due to missing, don't know or inconsistent responses to the relevant questions pertaining to the categories/groups.

New to domestic markets:
New to the world? = No
AND
A first in South Africa but not the world? = Yes
OR
A first in your industry within South Africa but not new to South Africa or to the world? = Yes
OR
New to your market? = Yes

New to firm:
New to the world? = No
AND
A first in South Africa but not the world? = No
AND
A first in your industry within South Africa but not new to South Africa or to the world? = No
AND
New to your market? = No
AND
Only new to your firm? = Yes

3. Markets of operation: *In which geographic markets did your enterprise sell goods or services during the three years 2014 to 2016?*
Operates on international markets:
Rest of Africa = Yes
OR
Europe = Yes
OR
United States = Yes
OR
Asia = Yes
OR
Other countries = Yes

Operates on domestic markets only:
Rest of Africa = No
AND
Europe = No
AND
United States = No
AND
Asia = No
AND
Other countries = No

THREE

Reorienting technology transfer in South African universities and science councils towards public value outcomes

Nazeem Mustapha and Gerard Ralphs

INTRODUCTION

A key area of South African science and innovation policy receiving substantial attention is the stewardship of intellectual property outputs from publicly financed research and development (R&D). Drawing on the experiences of the US Bayh-Dole Act (1980), which was implemented during a period of stagflation in the US economy, legislation pertaining to intellectual property rights was enacted in South Africa under similar economic conditions. The Intellectual Property Rights from Publicly Financed Research and Development (Act No. 51, 2008) (IPR-PFRD) institutionalised the stewardship process so that '... intellectual property emanating from publicly financed research and development is identified, protected, utilised and commercialised for the benefit of the people of the Republic' (IPR Act of 2008: 4). Central to the realisation of these objectives was the establishment of the National Intellectual Property Management Office (NIPMO) and Offices of Technology Transfer (OTTs) within publicly financed research institutions ('public research institutions').

In effect, NIPMO represents the key 'policy lever' of the Department of Science and Innovation (DSI) to give effect to the IPR-PFRD Act's intent by enhancing the impact of OTTs. This is a goal of the new White Paper on Science, Technology and Innovation 2019 (DST, 2019), supported by its accompanying Decadal Plan (South African Government News Agency, 2022). Next to the OTTs and the NIPMO/ DSI nexus, the public–private South African SME Fund, established by President Cyril Ramaphosa in 2019, has come to form part of this nascent 'public technology transfer system'. It provides additional targeted venture capital, expertise and partnering opportunities through the activities of its University Technology Fund (UTF). Two national surveys tracking the performance of these OTTs, from 2008 to 2018, reflect important progress but also some stumbling blocks (DSI/ SARIMA/NIPMO/KISCH-UP, 2021; Mustapha et al., 2017a).

Critically addressing this specific context, with the express intention of surfacing more questions than answers, this chapter has two goals. First, it aims to locate the practice of technology transfer by South Africa's universities and science councils within the larger systemic challenges facing the country and, more specifically, those confronting its national system of innovation. We reinforce a broader policy position that a differentiated conception of public research institutions, based on their racialised histories and, by extension, histories of disadvantage or relative privilege accumulation, is vital to an appreciation of the current state of institutional development, not least the practice of technology transfer.[1] Using discourse analysis, we undertake a macro-

---

1   As the South African National Development Plan 2030 (NPC, 2013: 326) admits: 'The distribution of research capacity in higher education institutions is skewed in favour of historically white institutions. Under apartheid, the development of research capacity in black universities was severely limited, and they have only recently integrated research into their core functions. A research mandate has only recently been included in the institutional missions of universities of technology.'

level diagnosis of divergent ideas and practices within South African science and innovation policy circles. These practices, with different epistemic drivers, aim to redress historical legacies and, in so doing, shift system directionality towards more inclusive outcomes in line with both policy and legislated objectives.

The second goal of this chapter is diagnostic at the meso level (the level of institutional histories and capabilities). We appeal to the source data of South Africa's first survey of IP and technology transfer in public research institutions. In particular, we use cluster analysis – arranging public research institutions according to their levels of high, medium or low R&D expenditure – to examine key survey indicators of organisational capacity, such as the age of OTTs or the level and types of skills required by OTTs, *inter alia*. We compare and contrast survey indicators from historically white and privileged institutions, and historically black and disadvantaged institutions and merged institutions. The overarching research question that frames this chapter is: how can the practice of technology transfer in South African publicly financed research institutions be reoriented to public value outcomes in line with South Africa's priorities?

By way of chapter structure, there are three sections. The first section examines historical, contextual and discursive elements of publicly financed research with a focus on the directionality of funding, forms of institutional advantage and current policy approaches. Reinforcing this analysis, in the second section we present data on IP and technology transfer in the public arena, utilising a lens that focuses on inequities within the system. Before some concluding remarks, in a third section we provide a critical assessment of the publicly financed technology transfer system and its potential to add public value.

WHY DIRECTIONALITY OF PUBLICLY FINANCED RESEARCH OUTCOMES MATTERS

As a middle-income country, South Africa needs to use its knowledge and innovative products to compete (South Africa's National Development Plan 2030: NPC, 2013: 33).

The overlapping challenges of high unemployment, gross inequality and stifling levels of poverty (Soudien et al., 2019) intersect with the urgency, long identified in the National Development Plan (NDP), for South Africa to use its knowledge and products to compete in the global economy. Indeed, the years that followed the economic surges of the mid-2000s have been characterised by relatively low economic growth in South Africa, moving into and out of recession. This pattern, coupled with state capture (Zondo Commission, 2023), Covid-19 lockdown impacts and protracted electricity blackouts, has placed additional pressure on communities, businesses and livelihoods. Government has a substantial, immediate challenge to rapidly grow the economy, transition to a new energy mix, and provide decent jobs in the context of fiscal constraints. Even with a recent boom in commodities, and President Ramaphosa's laudable drive to market Brand SA to international investors, interest from overseas in sustainable investments across the industrial landscape remains muted. Economically, South Africa risks languishing in a middle-income trap (Kruss, 2020).

These profound and persistent socioeconomic challenges, coupled with intensifying anthropogenic climate change, the effects of the war in Ukraine on energy, global trade and security, and the uncertain effects of rapid technological advancements require novel policy mixes, new configurations of implementation actors, and transformative or at the very least, responsive, approaches. South Africa's public research institutions, whether science councils, universities or state-owned enterprises, are considered among the essential role players to be addressing these intersecting local and global developmental challenges. Alongside private actors, the human capabilities, research infrastructures, networks and technological capabilities of these institutions, in effect, constitute both the substantive and generative qualities of South Africa's national system of innovation (NSI). However, findings of the recently publicised 'Rensburg Review', sanctioned by the Minister of Higher Education, Science and Innovation in 2020, point to an NSI far from optimised in its levels of integration and agility (DSI, 2022; Nordling, 2022). Squarely in the crosshairs of South Africa's governance and public management actors, therefore, is the system's current status – outputs and outcomes it produces and reproduces – and its movement in alignment to or away from the country's stated planning objectives 'to eliminate poverty and reduce inequality by 2030' (NPC, 2013: 1).

Encouragingly, through parliamentary review and other forms of critical reflection, it is the regular evidence-informed 'returns' to system directionality – and the set of vectors that point to where it came from and where it is headed – that remain a notable feature of the South African science and innovation policy community (NACI, 2020, 2021). Within this context, the fairly recent institutionalisation of technology transfer in public research institutions has sharpened attention in the science and innovation policy and scholarly community to any 'system effects'[2] arising from the activities of OTTs.

The formation of a national innovation system in historical perspective

From the middle of the twentieth century onwards the apartheid state's predominant scientific and economic outlook approximated the so-called linear model of R&D-led innovation. The state was building on more than 300 years of imperial/colonial expansion, which from the early 1900s included the formation of the country's first universities (Dubow, 2006; Phillips, 1993) and the emergence of local forms of disciplinary practice (Shepherd, 2002, 2003). However, in the 20th century the apartheid state adopted the linear model, which had started to become more common among both developed and emerging economies (Schot and Steinmueller, 2018) influenced by thought about post-Second World War reconstruction and development in the global North (Godin, 2002). South Africa's version of racial capitalism (Maharajh, 2011), which included mainstream, state-backed R&D under apartheid, was geared towards reinforcing racial hierarchies and segregationist policies in the case of the social sciences and humanities. In the case of the natural sciences and engineering, it was aimed at mitigating the risk of international political and economic isolation through advancing mineral, military and energy industrial capabilities

---

2   The authors are grateful to Juan Rogers from the Georgia Institute of Technology for the formulation 'system effects' in the context of policy analysis and, in particular, policy evaluation.

through state-owned enterprises. Until the late 20th century then, science, technology and innovation in South Africa had been, to all intents and purposes, co-opted by political economies of exclusion.

In the immediate post-apartheid transitional period, a new STI policy began to be expressed in early ANC-led policy reformulation efforts. These were supported by Canada's International Development Research Centre (IDRC) (Muirhead and Harpelle, 2010), and later the 1996 White Paper on Science and Technology, and subsequently the country's first R&D strategy and innovation plan. This policy and planning was, in its early implementation steps, chiefly concerned with redressing the past imbalances in the production of knowledge and human capabilities for the country's development, and, latterly, in marketing the country's comparative advantage in specific areas of science and technology, such as astronomy (NACI, 2020). A marked discursive shift in the 2000s was the adoption of a national system of innovation (NSI) conceptual framework, to organise activity, manage investment and 'steer' the NSI more efficiently and effectively (DST, 2012; OECD, 2007). In 2019, a new White Paper on Science, Technology and Innovation (DST, 2019) was published under the leadership of then Department of Science and Technology Minister Mmamoloko Kubayi-Ngubane, with the tagline of 'Science, technology and innovation enabling inclusive and sustainable South African development in a changing world'. If earlier policy thinking had focused on system building as an end, the White Paper revision saw greater attention paid to broader-based STI policy and programmatic concepts, such as innovation for inclusive development (Kruss et al., 2017).

Uncovering discourses shaping directionality of public research outcomes

In the post-apartheid period to date, at least four discourses (ways of knowing/practising) (Foucault, 1972) have emerged to shape public management and governance discussions about the roles and responsibilities of public research institutions in the context of their formal or codified mandates. A first discourse has put sustained scholarly emphasis on university–industry and university–community interaction, technological capability building, and engaged scholarship (Kruss, et al., 2012; Kruss and Gastrow, 2015). This discourse emerged from the developmental thinking of, for instance, Manuel Castells (1996) and Amartya Sen (1999) and some of the early innovation systems scholars, such as Christopher Freeman, Richard Nelson and Bengt-Åke Lundvall (see for example Lundvall, 2016; Nelson and Nelson, 2002; Nelson, 2002; Yang, 2021). In the South African context, this discourse has been augmented by more recent, novel conceptual and empirical work on science councils, which emphasises their multiple mandates (Kruss et al., 2016). This work pays greater attention to innovation systems, and the potential of networks and linkages between actors, and recognises particularity and specificity in institutional location and trajectories.

A second, and perhaps the dominant, discourse, arising from public administration theory and, in particular, the school of new public management, has emphasized managerialism as its core mantra. It finds currency in regional forums such as the Southern African Research and Innovation Management Association and, to an extent, is reinforced by global or multinational publishing and technology firms operating within research and higher education. If the second discourse emphasises research impact, global networks, rankings indices, and professionalisation of research management and technology transfer, the first discourse, arguably, challenges narrow notions of the 'entrepreneurial university' based on the triple helix (an idea easily co-opted by the enumerators of the second discourse). The triple helix model of innovation, it is important to explain, represents the convergence of government, academia and industry, with universities at the core of knowledge production, with resource inputs from government but largely servicing the needs of industry (for South African evidence, see for example Patra and Muchie (2018)). Underpinning the triple helix is a notion of trickle-down economics, where the fruits of R&D accrue to society through firms. This notion has been further expanded into notions such as the quadruple helix, which – unlike the triple helix model – takes into account society, citizen groups and communities.

A third discourse emerged powerfully during and in the wake of the

#RhodesMustFall and #FeesMustFall student protests, and concerns decoloniality and decolonisation of knowledge (Adonis and Silinda, 2021; Mbembe, 2016; Nordling, 2018). Entirely missing from the dominant discourse to date, and an implicit feature in the first discourse in some of its theoretical roots (e.g., Sen's notion of development as freedom), the third discourse reflects an impulse towards a reckoning with the deep legacies of colonial/apartheid natural and social science given early expression in publicly funded research institutions before 1994. Reflecting on the history of the Human Sciences Research Council (HSRC), for example, former CEO Crain Soudien (2021) exemplifies this third discourse when he writes (Soudien, 2021: 521):

> Coming out of the discussions in the HSRC, the organisation made important decisions about what it should research and how it should project what it was doing. It had, by 2008, already arrived at the conclusion that the developmental challenge in the country was the question of poverty and inequality. Strikingly, in doing so, it reprised the objectives that were the organisation's birth in 1920. It was the people of South Africa that its commitment sought to serve. In 1929, the people were white. The [National Bureau of Educational and Social Research] NBESR's implicit goal at that point was to solve the 'poor-white' problem. Black people did not feature in that reckoning.

Soudien (2021: 521) continues:

> In the present period, it is to help the people of South Africa – *all* who live in it. This, perforce, foregrounds the unapologetic African-focused orientation of the HSRC. In this sense, it sees itself as part of the wider movement towards decolonisation and decoloniality. Its sense of itself is that of an institution rooted in Africa seeking not only to establish its rightful place in global affairs but also to present itself as an eminent site for beginning to explore what it means to be thinking from the perspective of Africa. This consensus has driven the work of the organisation. Processes of strategic development after 2016 not only affirmed

this commitment but gave it specificity.

On the one hand, in a sceptical reading of the discourse, 'decolonisation' is at risk of losing its explanatory power as it has become the latest buzzword within the science and innovation policy community. On the other hand, oriented to futures thinking (Bourgeois et al., 2022), decolonisation discourse or rather decolonial thinking (Mignolo, 2009) has rich potential to reshape more dominant discourse(s) towards more radically inclusive outcomes.

Finally, a fourth discourse arguably has emerged out of the recent influential work of Johan Schot and Ed Steinmeuller (2018) and is currently given expression through the activities of the Transformative Innovation Policy Consortium (TIPC) and its proponents. 'Framing 3' thinking, as it is known, is characterised by holding in mind the tension between a critique of the 'Creative Destruction' of previous policy paradigms (R&D-led innovation (Framing 1) and national systems of innovation (Framing 2)) while remaining open to their positive valences. Framing 3 is also characterised by a new set of possible options for innovation policy. As Schot and Steinmeuller explain (Schot and Steinmeuler, 2018: 10):

It is important to stress that Framing 3 is not principally a model of science and technology regulation. Instead, it focuses on innovation as a search process on the system level, guided by social and environmental objectives, informed by experience and the learning that accompanies that experience, and a willingness to revisit existing arrangements to de-routinize them in order to address societal challenges. A claim underlying Framing 3 is that the innovation process is likely to be effective in achieving these goals if it is inclusive, experimental and aimed at changing the direction of socio-technical systems in all its dimensions.

They continue (Schot and Steinmeuler, 2018: 10):

Since socio-technical systems will be defended by policymakers, users, industry and civil society groups who benefit from their current shape and hold world views and values which would not require systematic change, transformative innovation policy necessitate engagement in science and technology politics not just policy. The type of politics promoted is one which opens up spaces for experimentation, societal learning, public debate, deliberation and negotiation, as advanced in the earlier concept of constructive technology assessment.

If decolonisation has a conception of social justice as a key concern, Framing 3 thinking is appealing theoretically as a tool to disrupt dominant regimes that produce and reproduce undesirable and unsustainable social and environmental outcomes.

Historically white and privileged institutions (which arguably today form a bedrock of South Africa's national system of innovation) emerged into the post-1994 period with distinct advantages in foundational technology transfer capabilities compared with their counterparts – either historically black and disadvantaged institutions, or merged institutions. Various institutional transformation efforts, both top-down and bottom-up, are underway, proceeding at different paces in relation to 'starting conditions'. It is axiomatic that a differentiated conception of institutional trajectories is retained as a basis for the analysis of progress and stumbling blocks. Furthermore, the orientation of institutional strategies is arguably being formed and informed by prevailing discourses, which interpret codified mandates against particular political, economic and philosophical world views, some of which emphasize networks and specificity (Discourse 1); regional and global competitiveness through research and innovation management (Discourse 2); decoloniality (Discourse 3), and transformative innovation (Discourse 4) or some combination thereof. In our reckoning, the creation of public value should be a central principle of institutional strategy and performance. The next section of the chapter will use empirical data to partly illustrate the disparate perceptions of technology transfer capabilities within the institutions comprising the 'public technology transfer system'.

EXPLORING KEY INDICATORS OF
TECHNOLOGY TRANSFER CAPACITY

The data we use comes from the 2017 baseline survey of intellectual property and technology transfer (IP&TT Survey) (Mustapha et al., 2017a) and the South African national R&D Surveys for the reference periods 2008/09 to 2014/15 (Mustapha et al., 2017b). The reason for this choice is so that we can analyse not only the state of organisational capacities as reflected in the baseline survey, but also look at some simple trends. More recent data from the IP&TT Survey (2021) covering more recent periods will also be used to update or contrast findings and attempt to shed light on their mode of creation with respect to inclusivity or public value outcomes. The IP&TT surveys were conducted by collecting data directly from technology transfer offices at higher education institutions and science councils. The inaugural survey was an ambitious baseline project that sought to identify the broadest set of indicators and, at the same time, historical trend data further than five years back. As a consequence, not all the institutions were able to respond to the survey requirements, lacking either data on IP and technology transfer in the year of surveying and/or historical data. By contrast, the national R&D survey is conducted every year on a well-established set of indicators from a stable respondent group of universities and science councils. However, the latter survey only publishes data at the institutional level and not at the level of the OTTs. The qualitative data analysis was sourced from vignettes provided by OTTs as part of the IP&TT surveys, the gathering of which was facilitated by NIPMO.

Typology of institutions
Our analysis proceeds by categorising institutions according to the groupings in Table 3.1: Grouping institutions.

Table 3.1: Grouping institutions

Code	Type of institution
GOV	Government agency or state-owned enterprise
HBDI	Historically black and disadvantaged institutions
HWPI	Historically white and privileged institutions
Merged	Higher education institutions that were merged
RC	Research councils or science councils

Source: Authors' own data

There are 33 institutions that are publicly funded to do R&D. Of these 33, three do not perform intramural R&D.[3] For these units, there is only data on R&D expenditure and FTEs available from the R&D Survey.

Table 3.2: Types of publicly financed research institutions

Type of institution	Agency	Science council	State-owned enterprise	University	University of Science and Technology	Total
GOV	1	0	1	0	0	2
HBDI	0	0	0	4	3	7
HWPI	0	0	0	7	1	8
Merged	0	0	0	4	4	8
RC	0	8	0	0	0	8
Total	1	8	1	15	8	33

Source: Authors' own compilation

From time to time, we also found it useful to discern between the universities of science and technology (previously known or constituted from technikons) and traditional universities; these distinctions will

---

3 Not surprisingly, the one unit in this latter group that was included in the IP&TT Survey (2017) did not report any substantive information on technology transfer or IP. Furthermore, one unit (Council for Geoscience) was not selected for the IP&TT Survey and three universities did not respond to the survey questionnaire.

be mentioned where relevant. The 'merged' institutions in Table 3.2: Types of publicly financed research institutions were composed of universities of science and technology from either historically black and disadvantaged institutions or historically white and privileged institutions. Furthermore, as an additional analytical tool, we did a simple cluster analysis on the R&D expenditure in 2014 of the sample (*k-means* (MacQueen, 1967) with *k=4* to choose the cluster members). This is because in our exploration it became apparent that there were discernible disparities in the R&D expenditures of the institutions.

The results of the cluster analysis effectively provide three[4] distinct groupings which we have chosen to label according to the level of R&D expenditure: high R&D expenditure (or funding), medium R&D expenditure (or funding) and low R&D expenditure (or funding). We use the term elite interchangeably with high R&D, to the extent that this term denotes institutions endowed with historical privilege.

Table 3.3: Institutions categorised by the level of public funding or annual expenditure on R&D

R&D performance/ expenditure level*	GOV	HBDI	HWPI	Merged	RC	Total
Low R&D	2	6	1	4	2	15
Medium R&D	0	1	3	4	4	12
High R&D	0	0	4	0	2	6
Total	2	7	8	8	8	33

* *Note: Clusters: High R&D = Expenditure of R900 million – R2 billion; Medium R&D = R200 million – R700 million; Low R&D R20 million – R160 million*

Source: Authors' own compilation

It is instructive to group the year in which institutions committed at least 0.5 FTE professionals to technology transfer operations, as recorded in Table 3.4. We have used 2008 as a reference value because

---

4 Due to much higher R&D expenditure compared to the other high-expenditure institutions, the CSIR was combined with the other highly funded institutions and formed a cluster on its own.

that is when the implementation of legislation governing technology transfer from publicly funded institutions was being promulgated, signalling rapid growth in the institutionalisation of tech transfer at these research organisations.

Table 3.4: Age of technology transfer at institutions by level of R&D performance*

R&D perfor-mance level	Pre-2008	2008	2009	2010	2011	2012	2014	2015	Total with TTOs	Total no. of institu-tions
Low R&D	1	2	0	2	0	1	1	0	7	15
Medium R&D	3	1	0	1	4	0	0	1	10	12
High R&D	4	1	1	0	0	0	0	0	6	6
Total	8	4	1	3	4	1	1	1	23	33

* Note: The organisations that did not provide information here were assumed to have no significant technology transfer operations.

Source: Authors' own compilation

There are some observations from Table 3.4 that are worth making before considering the data on capabilities in detail. Less than half (46.7 per cent) of the low-funded institutions had institutionalised technology transfer by 2015, whereas 100 per cent of the highest R&D performers had done so. Moreover, two-thirds of the elite institutions established their technology transfer function long before 2008.

On the one hand, the implication is that the low-funded R&D institutions do not have the prerequisites (one of which is sufficient funding) to allocate resources towards a basic technology transfer function at their institutions. On the other hand, the elite institutions have sufficient resources to the extent that all of them had at least established a technology transfer function by 2015. The mid-funded institutions have mostly started up their technology transfer functions in relatively recent times, perhaps as a positive response to the promulgation of the IPR-PFRD Act, although a fair number of them (25 per cent) had established functions prior to 2008. The rest of the analysis will not consider the three institutions for which there is no data – specifically data on their technology transfer operations.

Enablers of technology transfer

The enablers of technology transfer are rated differently by the three categories of institutions in Figure 3.1: Ranking of TT enablers by R&D performance level as a percentage of responding institutions.

Figure 3.1: Ranking of TT enablers by R&D performance level as a percentage of responding institutions

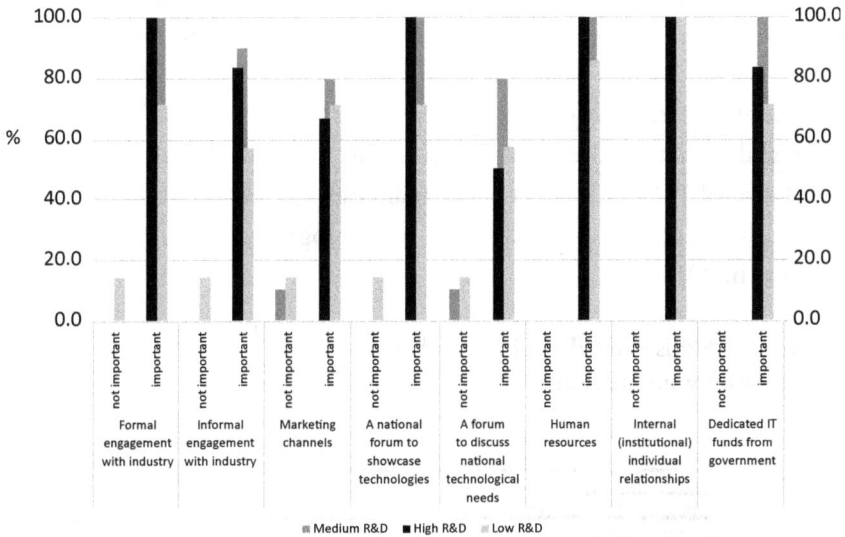

Source: Authors' own compilation

Evidence that institutions are at different stages in terms of their capabilities may be seen from the data on enablers reported in Figure 3.1: Ranking of TT enablers by R&D performance level as a percentage of responding institutions. One expects that the majority of responses would rate these enablers to all be important, given that the respondents are technology transfer specialists, of course. So, it is instructive that some enablers were rated as not so important, depending on the size of the institution. Some of the low-funded R&D institutions did not consider as important engagement with industry (formal or informal), marketing or a national forum to showcase technologies or one to discuss technology needs. This suggests that they see other enablers as much more important, such as internal institutional relationships (perhaps champions for technology transfer). In fact, all the institutions considered internal (institutional) individual relationships as important, and most of them considered human resources and dedicated government funding as also important. We will turn our analysis directly to skills/human resources as the main topic of study, although it is clear that other factors are related to this. For example, the level and proficiency of human resources depends on whether there is dedicated funding for technology transfer, as well as strong relationships inside the organisation that promote such transfers.

Human resource requirements at OTTs

The skills that institutions identified as needed (Figure 3.2: Skills needed as of 2014 by level of performance as a percentage of responding institutions) reflected the stage of technology transfer function they were at in 2014.

Figure 3.2: Skills needed as of 2014 by level of performance as a percentage of responding institutions

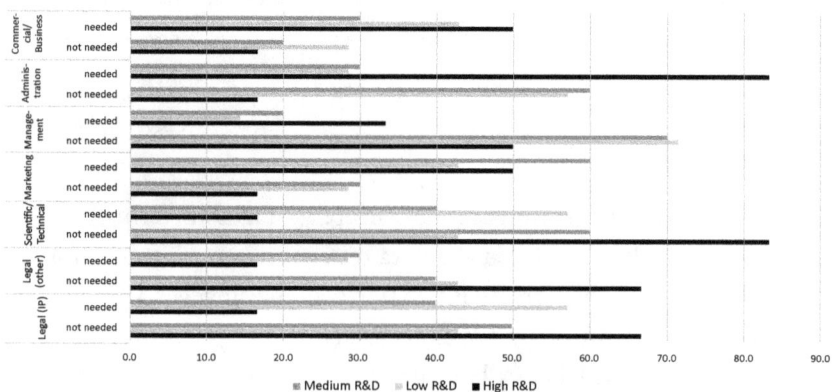

Source: Authors' own compliation

Thus, very few of the highly funded R&D institutions listed the need for core skills such as legal IP skills or other legal skills or scientific/technical skills. Instead, they identified skills required at the 'far end' (downstream) of the technology transfer process such as marketing and commercialisation skills, as well as support resources such as administration skills. This is not unexpected given that these institutions have enjoyed established technology transfer functions for decades. In contrast, the low-funded institutions listed skills needed across all core areas, excluding other legal skills but including business skills. Management and administration skills were not required by these institutions. These responses reinforce the evidence of the low level of technology transfer function at these institutions.

Successful patenting and commercialisation organisations

By far the majority of patents granted (Table 3.5: Patenting success by level of R&D performance between 2008 and 2014) between 2008 and 2014 stem from the high-funded institutions, which is a trend reflected in every year, including the ones not shown. Some interesting observations arise from comparing the local and international patenting behaviour of high-funded and low-funded institutions. The high R&D institutions concentrated their patenting behaviour in overseas patenting offices, with only 35 per cent of their patents held in South Africa. The low R&D institutions show completely the opposite behaviour with 71.4 per cent of their patents held in South Africa.

Table 3.5: Patenting success by level of R&D performance between 2008 and 2014

Patents granted	No. of institutions	Total number of patents granted	SA total	% SA patents granted
High R&D	6	626	219	35,0
Low R&D	12	42	30	71,4
Medium R&D	12	86	40	46,5
Total	30	754	289	38,3

Source: Authors' own compilation

The high R&D institutions have been much more successful at commercialising their IP products than the other two categories of institutions (see Table 3.6: Start-up companies formed by level of R&D performance).

Table 3.6: Start-up companies formed by level of R&D performance

Start-ups formed	No. of institutions	Total number of start-ups formed	BEE enti-ties	% BEE start-ups
High R&D	6	41	1	2,4
Low R&D	12	2	2	100,0
Medium R&D	12	14	3	21,4
Total	30	57	6	10,5

Source: Authors' own compilation

The first thing to note is that there were remarkably few start-ups formed across the whole system, slightly less than two per institution over the seven years between 2008 and 2014. The high R&D institutions have contributed to the majority of start-ups, not surprisingly if we consider the data analysis above. Table 3.6: Start-up companies formed by level of R&D performance also shows that the low R&D and medium R&D institutions tend to promote the growth of BEE start-ups much more than the high R&D institutions. Only 2.4 per cent of the start-ups spun out from the high R&D group were BEE entities, which shows that the high R&D institutions, which are mostly HWPIs, reproduce economic outcomes that advantage the privileged.

The types of successful patenting and commercialisation in evidence

It is informative to view the limited data on successful commercialization from publicly financed IP described in Box 3.1 and Table 3.7 through a lens that recognises success as not having only a commercial (economic) outcome but also broad, public value outcomes. We have chosen Economy, Health, Environment and Inequality as identified outcomes. As we have motivated in earlier sections, it also behoves us to look at how inclusive these processes were.

Box 3.1: Technologies stemming from technology transfer processes and their public value outcomes

The two surveys on intellectual property and technology transfer commissioned by the Department of Science and Innovation (DSI/SARIMA/NIPMO/KISCH-IP, 2021; Mustapha et al., 2017a) provide vignettes or 'case studies' of successful examples of the process. While clearly not exhaustive, these examples are interesting to look at from an analytical perspective that broadly considers the level of inclusivity and public value demonstrated in each example. Details are of course in the reports; we provide a brief summary of the outputs that were developed in this box. It is perhaps also fair and important to say that these vignettes were chosen by the supplying institutions to demonstrate their technology transfer processes in a good light. Secondly, they were provided with limited space to share their stories for deliberate inclusion in the survey reports as exemplars of the practice. While these vignettes do not balance the understanding with stories of failures, they provide an appropriate source for discourse analysis to bring out what the contributors considered important in these successes.

The first thing to note in these vignettes obtained from the OTTs is that institutions find it important to list broader societal outcomes, even though of course their processes are only subjected to measured outcomes of an economic nature and disaggregations thereof. In Table 3.8 the individual vignettes are ranked according to the cases with the highest number of public value outcomes. Interestingly, it is the institutions with low levels of R&D funding that rank highest here (bar one). The second thing that immediately sticks out is that the study with the highest number of public value outcomes is also the one with the highest inclusivity levels, suggesting a link between these two concepts.

Table 3.7: Examples

Technology transfer output	Brief description
VulAmanz water system	A point-of-use water treatment system makes use of a woven fabric microfiltration technology that does not require electricity as a power source; originally developed by a research team at Durban University of Technology and continued at Stellenbosch University after the lead researcher moved there. Maintenance of the system was tested with two models: one community-based and the other municipality-based.
Omega caro-E supplements	A unique high-quality health supplement developed at Cape Peninsula University of Technology.
Encapsulation using supercritical carbon dioxide	A technology that allows for the supply of probiotics that are sufficiently protected in transit and which is produced with a minimum of negative impacts in the environmental or health spheres. The CSIR developed this technology for licensing by external entrepreneurs.
Exatype, a platform for analysing drug resistance in HIV genomes	A cost-effective, web-based platform that analyses sequence data without the need for any specialised bioinformatics expertise; developed by researchers at the University of the Western Cape.
Rugby wheelchair	A locally manufactured wheelchair for disabled rugby players, based on an (expensive) overseas prototype. The project was driven by a disabled athlete, a former Central University of Technology (CUT) student and a member of a disabilities rugby club. Researchers at CUT ran the project with funding from the Technology Innovation Agency. Disabled, unemployed youth were trained to manufacture the wheelchairs.
Lumkani fire detection	Rate-of-rise of temperature technology fire detectors developed at the University of Cape Town for use in informal settlements. 'It utilises low-cost, durable devices that are located within a network of detectors within a 40-metre radius of each other. In the event of a fire, all devices in this range will ring together, enabling a community-wide response to the danger' (Mustapha et al., 2017a).
Mabu casing	Utilises sugar bagasse as a means of growing mushrooms. The initial research project at the University of Pretoria was funded by the South African Mushroom Farmers Association and the Technology and Human Resources for Industry Programme.
Maxhosa by Laduma	High-quality knitwear range inspired by *marsala* (Xhosa initiates) developed by a former Nelson Mandela Metropolitan University student.
Power line inspection robot	An inspection system that does not require helicopters, remotely operated vehicles or inspectors walking the line; developed by researchers at the University of KwaZulu-Natal.
Trade decision support tool	Big data processing and analysis to inform evidence-based decision-making, targeting national tourism bureaus developed by researchers at North-West University.

A 'PUBLIC TECHNOLOGY TRANSFER SYSTEM' ORIENTED TO PUBLIC VALUE OUTCOMES?

> Public investment in science should be redeemed in terms of public value, just as private investment should lead to private benefit to investors and paying customers (Bozeman, 2020: 28).

The discussion that follows is largely speculative, built on the preceding discourse and data analyses. As scholars with a shared interest in matters of systemic and institutional redress, we ask: What are the skills that would be required from OTTs enacting a technology transfer process that seeks to perform an expanded conception of the technology transfer process? One example of this would be an adaptation of Bozeman's public value objective as elucidated in Mustapha and Ralphs (2021). The current policy juncture and discourse is characterised by increasing pressure on state institutions to demonstrate 'return on investment' in terms of public value. Our contention is that this dominant discourse and model of technology transfer, currently practised in public management and innovation governance, should be reappraised. This reappraisal is particularly important in the context of an intensification of the country's key developmental challenges on multiple fronts. One key route to this end, we suggest, is to contemplate the potential for a new matrix of capacities most needed at the institutional level, about which we have four key points to make and some further questions to pose below.

How well are the universities and science councils doing?

> If we were around when the first university got established aeons ago in a town somewhere in Africa, the conversation amongst the elders might have gone something like this: there are some of our people who are very smart. They speak to each other in concepts that none of the rest of us can really understand. But they appear to understand each other; so they must be on to something. Let them go off to the top of the mountain and explore these things, and in a few years when they come down,

Table 3.8: Analysis of technology transfer vignettes incorporating inclusivity and public value outcomes

Size of institutional R&D expenditure	Technology transfer output	Source of knowledge	Provision of technology transfer support
Low R&D	VulAmanz water system	University research	Researchers from the relevant university, municipality and rural community
Low R&D	Omega caro-E supplements	University research	Researchers at the university
High R&D	Encapsulation using supercritical carbon dioxide	Science Council research	Health food entrepreneur
Low R&D	Exatype, a platform for analysing drug resistance in HIV genomes	University research	Researchers at the university
Low R&D	Rugby wheelchair	University research	Researchers at the university, former students and disabled youth
High R&D	Lumkani fire detection	University research	Researchers at the university
High R&D	Mabu casing	University research	Former university researcher (inventor)
Medium R&D	High-quality, Xhosa-inspired knitwear range for *amakrwala* (Xhosa initiates)	Indigenous designs	Individual designer (student) at university
Medium R&D	Power line inspection robot	University research	Researchers at the university
Medium R&D	Trade decision support tool	University research	Former student at the university

Target group of new product	Mode of development: *At what level of inclusivity did the process take place?*	Public value outcome: *Did technology transfer enhance good, broad societally shared values?*			
		Economic	Health	Environment	Inequality
Rural communities with poor access to potable water	Technology pull, consultation with target community, and inclusion of target group in product development	✓	✓	✓	✓
Humanity, local and international	Technology push, no consultation efforts mentioned, and no inclusion of target group at the outset	✓	✓	✓	✗
Probiotic consumers, specifically women and athletes	Technology push, no consultation efforts mentioned, and no inclusion of target group at the outset	✓	✓	✓	✗
HIV patients, local and international	Technology push, no consultation efforts mentioned, and no inclusion of target group at the outset	✓	✓	✗	✓
Disabled athletes	Technology needs arising from the affected community, consultation with the target community, and inclusion of the target group in product manufacturing	✓	✓	✗	✓
Informal settlement dwellers	Technology push, no consultation efforts mentioned, and no inclusion of target group at the outset	✓	✗	✗	✓
Local and Namibian mushroom producers	Technology push, no consultation efforts mentioned, and no inclusion of target group at the outset	✓	✗	✓	✗
High-end consumers	Technology push, no consultation efforts mentioned, and no inclusion of target group at the outset	✓	✗	✗	✗
Power grid companies	Technology push, no consultation efforts mentioned, and no inclusion of target group at the outset	✓	✗	✗	✗
Trade and investment promotion public sector agencies, local and international	Technology push, no consultation efforts mentioned, and no inclusion of target group at the outset	✓	✗	✗	✗

who knows, there may be something that they've discovered that we can put to use (Mustapha, 2022).

In a modern society such as South Africa where there is a perhaps small but discernible surplus, we must create the scope for intellectual pursuits motivated primarily by curiosity or the pursuit of knowledge for its own sake. That pursuit needs to be nurtured and protected from external control. In virtually every field of study, researchers conduct basic research, most of it at universities, and some of it at science councils. In some areas, the basic research South Africa does is at the forefront of world knowledge, perhaps most notably in the space sciences. But, perhaps inevitably, there will also be new knowledge arising from scientific enquiry that is of value to society. This 'useful knowledge' stemming from researchers at universities and science councils needs to be subjected to scrutiny and analysis to direct it towards the greatest benefit of society. The structures that we create to utilise this knowledge must be oriented towards what societal needs are, and cannot simply be left to individual scientists fulfilling their curiosity.

On the face of it, universities and science councils in South Africa are functioning in their role as knowledge producers. These publicly financed institutions, primarily those that are well funded, are also producing knowledge that may ultimately be commercialised. The danger is that if it is mainly the HWPIs that are producing knowledge of utilisable value, and if the focus is mainly on the commercialisation of knowledge, then this will inflate the inequalities that have been 'frozen in' by colonialism and apartheid, notwithstanding post-apartheid reform efforts. To return to the discourse analysis in Section 1, more attention to system integration (Discourse 1) and directionality (Discourse 4) in the context of the decolonisation of knowledge (Discourse 3) may be required.

Technology transfer from public research institutions reflects the history of inequality

As the Section 2 discussion also shows, the survey reports track the numbers of start-ups as a means of assessing the economic benefit of this process. What they do not attempt to assess are the other benefits (social, military or other) from the TTOs that the IPR-PFRD Act lists as the stated objectives of the legislation. Furthermore, since the legislation was passed, the South African government has started putting greater emphasis on promoting the interests of groups that have so far largely been excluded from the benefits of the South African economy. We contend that this insufficiency of the technology transfer process is due to its very limited linear and one-way conception. This conception reflects the way the process is currently perceived to run, which is as an imitation of technology transfer processes – based on the triple helix – in highly developed countries. The process should rather be seen as one that seeks to address the major challenges South Africa currently faces. Could it be that this misplaced objective may also be due to the relative exclusion of historically black and disadvantaged institutions from the technology transfer process?

Thus, the follow-up to the baseline survey included additional data items that bring out challenges at the 'commercialisation end' of this linear process. As we have seen, these are challenges that are mainly of interest to the high R&D institutions, which already have mature technology transfer functionality, at least relative to the less well-funded institutions. In a similar vein, the capacity requirements listed by the high R&D organisations emphasise skills required at the commercialisation end as well. In contrast, the low R&D institutions' capacity needs are related to functionality for technology transfer, as these are barely established, if at all.

The second survey of IP and tech transfer (DSI/SARIMA/NIPMO/KISCH-IP, 2021), which largely followed the framework of the baseline survey (Mustapha et al., 2017a), was modelled on a uni-directional linear conceptualisation of the process of technology transfer. In such a conceptualisation, we have at the one end the knowledge creators who are taken to be at the higher education institutions or science councils. At the other end, once the new knowledge has been commercialised, there is a requirement for those responsible for intellectual property (IP) protection within the process.

In this formulation, research and innovation managerialism (Discourse 2) may have something to offer R&D performers. They can be upskilled through the establishment of research and innovation management communities. These communities can allow for access to global networks of expertise and skills-building.

Is public value a necessary function of technology transfer?

On the one hand, the predominant producers of new knowledge and inventions with social and/or economic benefit are not South Africa's historically black and disadvantaged institutions (HBDIs), but instead historically white and privileged institutions (HWPIs), which benefitted greatly from funding and knowledge flows in the pre-democratic era. Are the former better placed to deliver within a public-value model, rather than the technology push type of transfer process that may be better suited to the institutions with high R&D expenditures? Even so, for the technology transfer offices that are situated within these institutions, '... key skill sets remain lacking' (DSI/SARIMA/NIPMO/KISCH-IP, 2021: 3).

On the other hand, there is a hint that the technology transfer process at HBDIs tends to target a greater number of public value outcomes than the HWPIs. There may also be a greater number of researchers or technology transfer practitioners at the former that are attuned to conducting more inclusive research. Nevertheless, from the vignettes in the survey reports (Table 3.6), it appears that researchers at all institutions appreciate the need for research and outcomes with greater public value. Be that as it may, policymakers utilise evaluation tools that only measure the commercial outcomes of the technology transfer process.

A good example, but not the only one, is the class of knowledge stemming from indigenous knowledge systems (IKS). The benefit of these multi-directional interactions among higher knowledge institutions, government and ordinary citizens may be socio-economic or otherwise, with either local application value or export appeal. Therefore, we argue that the way in which technology transfer is conceptualised needs to be expanded. Indeed, in their development of the revised contingent effectiveness model of technology transfer, Bozeman et al. (2015) have shown that US researchers and evaluators of technology transfer understand effectiveness in a multitude of ways, but that public value is increasingly important as a criterion of effectiveness.[5] Science policymakers will have little chance of achieving the social outcomes they seek unless they take into account the public-value impact of research (Bozeman and Sarewitz, 2011; Bozeman, 2020). Ideas for a new matrix of priority capacities include community engagement skills, incubation skills and indigenous knowledge skills. Even so, it is important to consider not only skills but also to rethink the role of the OTT as an actor in society. The emphasis on directionality in Discourse 4 can help with the creation of policy tools, especially in conjunction with learnings in Discourse 3 on the decolonisation of knowledge.

Inclusivity as a guide to greater public value outcomes

We would like to end this chapter with a provocative question: What does inclusion mean in the context of technology transfer and publicly financed R&D in South Africa? In terms of a systems model or theory of change, one level or part of the system/model includes all key stakeholders as legitimate actors in the innovation *activities* that produce output and outcomes. This model typically consists of an intervention/process with an input, activities and a set of outputs and outcomes. These would range from the training and capability development of R&D personnel to the generation of knowledge and the creation of technology and its applications. Yet another level or part of the system/model attempts to maximise the *output* and *outcomes* to be as inclusive as possible, through, for example, innovation or industrial policy. South Africa's nascent 'public technology transfer system' was the context for the key questions that shaped the reflections in this chapter. Rooted in an understanding that systems are borne in and out of particular contexts – historical, political, economic – all of

---

5 Even though the survey's overall coverage of institutional effectiveness comprises 57 start-up companies and 754 patents attributed technology transfers, in our conceptual framework of public value we would not necessarily want to probe whether the concomitant generation of revenue, job creation and cost savings and productivity gains were of value, particularly economic value. We would want to probe to whom is this value being added (i.e. the public, elites, etc.).

our questions concern the extent to which technology transfer from publicly financed R&D in South Africa is oriented to public value outcomes.

Does the 'public technology transfer system/model' concord with the generation of knowledge and the creation of technology/ applications, which are inclusive of the needs and interests of all South African citizens? Or is it more suited to serving the needs and interests of a narrow section, such as historically white and privileged universities or relatively well-off middle-class citizens? To what extent or in what ways might key stakeholders, such as the recipients of new technology or the custodians of indigenous knowledge, already be included (or excluded) from the technology development process? If the 'public technology transfer system' is not radically inclusive, in the sense of its capacity to substantively redress deep legacies of colonial and apartheid injustice, can it be adapted to be so? Indeed, is this aspiration towards radical inclusion even a consideration for technology transfer communities of practice at publicly financed research institutions? Here, systems integration (Discourse 1), decolonisation of knowledge (Discourse 3) and transformative innovation (Discourse 4) present some potentially useful ideas to be considered.

CONCLUDING REMARKS

It has become a policy maxim that innovation has the potential to spur economic growth. This is, for example, the viewpoint taken in the recent White Paper from the Department of Science and Innovation (DST, 2019), along with an expressed need to focus on including those previously largely left out of the previous economic successes in the economy. Common amongst these viewpoints is a focus on the development of high-technology products at the frontiers of technological innovation from knowledge-intense endeavours such as those located at universities. These have been shown to be successful in improving the export strength of (mostly) developed countries. However, it raises the question of whether such strategies can be implemented successfully in the context of developing countries such as South Africa where the yardsticks of success are sustainable and inclusive economic development. Are the products that stem from such initiatives beneficial to the majority of the South African population who struggle with the challenges of high unemployment, inequality, poverty and muted growth? Are the institutions that generate such products attuned to the needs of the many, and should this matter to them? We have argued that the technology transfer from publicly funded institutions needs to be reconceptualised, and the framework for it broadened to better address the varied scenarios within which IP protection is required. This would be more suited to South Africa than a narrow conception which emphasises the creation of knowledge and IP products at higher education institutions or research centres.

Even viewed from the perspective of the linear model of technology transfer at research institutions, there are challenging questions for policymakers to deal with. What we have shown in this article is that there are two scales at which capacitation of the system needs to be addressed. At the one end there are the needs espoused by mostly the high R&D institutions, which have fairly mature technology transfer systems. The products and outcomes from these elite institutions are far from the levels seen in more developed countries such as the USA. For example, in Cambridge, Massachusetts where Harvard and MIT are based and which houses the innovation district Kendall Square, between 1999 and 2013, 1,400 start-ups created 40,000 jobs and raised close to US$2 billion worth of venture capital. By contrast, all of the elite SA institutions taken together produced 41 start-ups between 2008 and 2014. This appears to have received at least some policy attention, as evidenced by the instrument used to measure the system nationally being adapted to obtain more information on commercialisation, as well as the introduction of targeted venture capital through the SA SME Fund.

What does not appear to have received policy attention is the other big capacitation challenge, which is more systemic in nature. This is the challenge presented by the low R&D institutions, whose capacity problems are at the front end of the linear process, namely the lack of core capacities in legal skills pertaining to intellectual property and scientific or technical skills. These are challenges that stem from historic levels of underfunding and a resulting lack of capacity to do R&D at the level of the institution, not just the technology transfer office. It is interesting to note that these are the institutions that tend to orient their admittedly low levels of commercialisation success towards social outcomes such as black economic empowerment. Viewed in the context of the new White Paper and the National Development Plan, which emphasise concepts such as inclusivity and the developmental state, this creates a conflict in how to address these national imperatives in the arena of arguably essentially elitist activities such as IP protection and the commercialisation of IP. The convergence of newer and older ideas within the public management and governance of the innovation discursive landscape, including subjects such as decolonisation of knowledge and transformative innovation, offer glimpses, at least theoretically, of how to help fill some of these gaps in policy and practice.

RECOMMENDATIONS

The recommendations call for greater funding and a more directed redistribution of funding for technology transfer processes that emphasise public value inputs and outcomes.

Recommendation 1. *The public allocation for research funding of universities and science councils needs to more deliberately take account of apartheid/colonial histories and uneven institutional development trajectories.*

It is quite clear that there is no way that South Africa will meet its targets for a knowledge-centred economy without more pointed funding of research in universities, science councils and other publicly controlled entities. Across these institutions, society should provide the means for basic research that stems from curiosity or the desire to expand humanity's knowledge of the world, and such research should be free from intervention by policymakers.

Recommendation 2. *Researchers in all public research institutions should be stimulated and incentivised to conduct research that is utilisable for public value outcomes.*

There are researchers at universities and science councils who appreciate the need for their efforts to be directed at addressing the requirements of society and the world beyond mere commercial outcomes. Such work needs to be specifically incentivised, and technology transfer offices need to be supported to develop relevant inventions. It should be clear from the outset that public purse R&D must demonstrate public value.

Recommendation 3. *Research that is utilisable for public value outcomes needs to be supported by the technology transfer process, which itself needs new configurations of skills and capacities and stronger enabling conditions.*

Technology transfer processes need to embrace a conception of public value and define outcomes matrices linked to public goals. To achieve this, a reorientation of skills and capacities within OTTs needs to be considered. This shift would be part of the alignment of the 'public technology transfer system' to national priorities as well as those priorities defined at other scales, including global, provincial, district or local levels.

REFERENCES

Adonis, C. and Silinda, F. 2021. 'Institutional culture and transformation in higher education in post-1994 South Africa: A critical race theory analysis'. *Critical African Studies*, 13(1), 73–94.

Bozeman, B. 2020. 'Public value science: Science, the endless frontier at 75', *Issues in Science and Technology*, 34–41.

Bozeman, B. and Sarewitz, D. 2011. 'Public value mapping and science policy evaluation'. *Minerva*, 49(1), 1–23. doi:10.1007/s11024-011-9161-7, accessed 17 September 2022.

Bozeman, B,. Rimes, H. and Youtie, J. 2015. 'The evolving state-of-the-art in technology transfer research: Revisiting the contingent effectiveness model', *Research Policy*, 44, 34–49. doi:10.1016/j.respol.2014.06.008, accessed 17 September 2022.

Bourgeois, G., Karuri-Sebina, G. and Feukeu, K. 2022. 'The future as a public good: Decolonising the future through anticipatory action research'. *Foresight*. https://doi.org/10.1108/FS-11-2021-0225, accessed 26 February 2023.

Castells M. 1996. *The Rise of the Network Society. The Information Age: Economy, Society and Culture, Vol. I*. Oxford: Blackwell.

Department of Science and Innovation (DSI). 2022.'Report on the Review of the Higher Education, Science, Technology and Innovation Institutional Landscape'. *Government Gazette*, 684(46506).

DSI/SARIMA/NIPMO/KISCH-IP. 2021. 'South African National Survey of Intellectual Property and Technology Transfer at Publicly Funded Research Institutions: Second National Survey 2014–2018'. Department of Science and Innovation, Southern African Research & Innovation Management Association, National Intellectual Property Management Office.

Department of Science and Technology (DST). 2012. 'Department of Science and Technology Ministerial Review Committee on the Science, Technology and Innovation Landscape in South Africa: Final Report'. https://www.gov.za/sites/default/files/gcis_document/201409/35392gen425c.pdf, accessed 16 November 2022.

Department of Science and Technology (DST). 2019. 'White Paper on Science, Technology and Innovation 2019'. https://www.dst.gov.za/images/2019/White_paper_web_copyv1.pdf, accessed 5 August 2022.

Dubow, S. 2006. *A Commonwealth of Knowledge: Science, Sensibility and White South Africa 1820–2000*. Oxford: Oxford University Press.

Intellectual Property Rights from Publicly Financed Research and Development Act No. 51 of 2008. https://www.dst.gov.za/images/pdfs/IPR%20Act%20of%202008.pdf, accessed 10 August 2022.

Foucault, M. 1972 [2001]. *The Archaeology of Knowledge*. New York: Harper & Row.

Godin, B. 2000. 'The rise of innovation surveys: Measuring a fuzzy concept', *Canadian Science and Innovation Indicators Consortium, Project on the History and Sociology of S&T Statistics, Paper*, 16(9).

Kruss, G. 2020. 'Catching up, falling behind: The need to build upgrading coalitions for innovation and inclusive development in South Africa', *Nova Economia*, 30, 1115–1144.

Kruss, G. and Gastrow, M. 2015. *Linking Universities and Marginalised Communities: South African Case Studies of Innovation Focused on Livelihoods in Informal Settings*. Cape Town: Human Sciences Research Council and International Development Research Centre.

Kruss, G, Visser, M, Haupt, G. and Aphane, M. 2012. *Academic Interaction with External Social Partners: Investigating the Contribution of Universities to Economic and Social Development*. Cape Town: HSRC

Press, http://hdl.handle.net/20.500.11910/3218, accessed 18 August 2022.

Kruss, G., Haupt, G., Tele, A. and Ranchod, R. 2016. *Balancing Multiple Mandates: The Changing Roles of Science Councils in South Africa.* Cape Town: HSRC Press.

Kruss, G., Petersen, I., Rust, J. and Tele, A. 2017. 'Promoting a science, technology and innovation policy for inclusive development in South Africa'. HSRC Policy Brief, https://www.dst.gov.za/images/2017/2017_pdfs/SAASTA-science-journalism----Policy-brief.pdf, accessed 21 September 2022.

Lundvall, B. 2016. *The Learning Economy and the Economics of Hope.* London & New York: Anthem Press.

MacQueen, J. 1967. 'Some methods for classification and analysis of multivariate observations', in Le Cam, L.M. and Neyman, J. (eds). *Proceedings of the Fifth Berkeley Symposium on Mathematical Statistics and Probability. Volume 1: Statistics.* Berkeley: University of California Press, 281–297.

Maharajh, R. 2011. 'Innovating beyond racial capitalism: A contribution towards the analysis of the political economy of post-apartheid South Africa'. PhD thesis, Lund University, Sweden.

Mbembe, A. 2016. 'Decolonizing the university: New directions'. *Arts and Humanities in Higher Education,* 15(1). https://doi.org/10.1177/1474022215618513, accessed 30 September 2022.

Mignolo, W. 2009. 'Epistemic disobedience, Independent thought and decolonial freedom'. *Theory, Culture & Society,* 26(8), 159–181.

Mustapha, N. 2022. 'Personal communication with Gerard Ralphs'. Human Sciences Research Council, Cape Town.

Mustapha, N., Khan, F., Kondlo, L., Takatshana, S., Ralphs, G., et al. 2017a. 'South African National Survey of Intellectual Property and Technology Transfer at Publicly Funded Research Institutions: Inaugural Baseline Study 2008–2014'. Department of Science and Technology, Southern African Research & Innovation Management Association, National Intellectual Property Management Office & Centre for Science, Technology and Innovation Indicators.

Mustapha, N., Vlotman, N., Parker, S., Clayford, M.A., Saunders, N. et. al. 2017b. 'South African National Survey of Research and Experimental Development: Statistical report 2014/15'. Department of Science and Technology, Pretoria. https://repository.hsrc.ac.za/bitstream/handle/20.500.11910/10871/9725_Confidential.pdf?sequence=1&isAllowed=y, accessed 7 July 2023.

Mustapha, N. and Ralphs, G. 2021. 'Effectiveness of technology transfer in public research institutions in South Africa: A critical review of national indicators and implications for future measurement'. *African Journal of Science, Technology, Innovation and Development,* 14(4), 863–875. doi:

10.1080/20421338.2021.1893467, accessed 17 May 2023.

Muirhead, B. and Harpelle, R.N. 2010. *IDRC: 40 Years of Ideas, Innovation, and Impact*. Waterloo: Wilfrid Laurier University Press.

National Advisory Council on Innovation (NACI). 2020. 'A Review of the National Research and Development Strategy (NRDS) and the Ten-Year Innovation Plan'. https://www.naci.org.za/index.php/new-data-sets-to-support-innovation-policy/, accessed 17 May 2023.

National Advisory Council on Innovation (NACI). 2021. 'National Science, Technology and Innovation Indicators'. https://www.naci.org.za/index.php/studies/, accessed 18 May 2023.

National Advisory Council on Innovation (NACI). No Date. 'Review of the White Paper on Science and Technology'. National Advisory Council on Innovation, Pretoria.

National Planning Commission (NPC). 2013. 'National Development Plan 2030: Our Future - Make It Work'. The Presidency, Pretoria. https://www.gov.za/documents/national-development-plan-2030-our-future-make-it-work, accessed 4 October 2022.

Nelson, R. 2002. 'Erratum to "Technology, institutions and innovation systems", Research Policy 31 (2002) 265–272'. *Research Policy*, 31(8/9), 1509–1509.

Nelson, R. and Nelson, K. 2002. 'Technology, institutions and innovation systems'. *Research Policy*, 31(2), 265–272.

Nordling, L. 2018. 'How decolonization could reshape South African science'. *Nature*, 554, 159–162.

Nordling, L. 2022. 'The Rensburg Review at a glance'. *Research Professional News*, 16 June. https://www.researchprofessionalnews.com/rr-news-africa-south-2022-6-the-rensburg-review-at-a-glance/, accessed 6 April 2023.

Organisation for Economic Co-operation and Development (OECD). 2007. 'OECD Reviews of Innovation Policy: South Africa 2007'. OECD Reviews of Innovation Policy, Paris. https://doi.org/10.1787/9789264038240-en, accessed 27 September 2022.

Patra, S.W. and Muchie, M. 2018. 'Research and innovation in South African universities: From the Triple Helix's Perspective'. *Scientometrics*, 116, 51–76.

Phillips, H. 1993. *The University of Cape Town 1918–1948: The Formative Years*. Cape Town: University of Cape Town.

Shepherd, N. 2002. 'Disciplining archaeology: The invention of South African prehistory, 1923–1953'. *Kronos*, November, 127–145.

Shepherd, N. 2003. 'State of the siscipline: Science, culture and identity in South African archaeology, 1873–2003'. *Journal of Southern African Studies*, 29(4), 823–844.

Sen, A. 1999. *Development as Freedom*. New York: Oxford University Press.

Schot, J. and Steinmueller, W.E. 2018. 'Three frames for innovation policy: R&D, systems of innovation and transformative change'. *Research Policy*, 47(9), 1554–1567. https://doi.org/10.1016/j.respol.2018.08.011, accessed 25 August 2022.

Soudien, C. 2021. 'The HSRC into the future: An afterword', in Soudien, C., Swartz, S. and Houston, G. (eds). *Society, Research and Power: A History of the Human Sciences Research Council from 1929 to 2019*. Pretoria: Human Sciences Research Council Press, 518–522.

Soudien, C., Reddy, V. and Woolard, I. 2019. *Poverty and Inequality: Diagnosis, Prognosis and Response*. Cape Town: HSRC Press.

Soudien, C., Swartz, S. and Houston, G. (eds). 2021. *Society, Research and Power: A History of the Human Sciences Research Council from 1929 to 2019*. Cape Town: HSRC Press.

South African Government News Agency. 2022. 'Cabinet approves Science, Technology and Innovation (STI) Decadal Plan 2022'. https://www.sanews.gov.za/south-africa/cabinet-approves-science-technology-and-innovation-sti-decadal-plan-2022, accessed 7 March 2023.

Yang, K. 2021. 'Innovation, development and sustainability: Inspirations from Freeman's Economics of Hope', *Innovation and Development*, 1–6.

Zondo Commission. 2023. 'Commission of Enquiry Into Allegations of State Capture'. https://www.statecapture.org.za/site/information/reports, accessed 8 August 2023.

Part Two

Technologies' journeys

FOUR

The role of intermediaries in overcoming systemic failure in the South African economy: A case study of policy interventions in the furniture industry in the southern Cape

Andre Kraak

INTRODUCTION

This chapter examines the poor utilisation of intermediation as a mechanism for improving policy outcomes in national system of innovation (NSI) that are characterised by fragmentation and weak interactive capabilities. Intermediation is understood as the collective process of brokerage between multiple actors who are geographically isolated with restricted information flows between them – a communicative and associational void often only resolved through intermediation. The practice of intermediation is about bringing all of these actors to the negotiating table to find solutions to local socio-economic problems. In many developing countries across the globe, including South Africa, the conditions that are required for such intermediation to happen are simply not present. For example, benefitting from collective efficiencies requires that firms interact with other firms such that their collective combination of production practices and knowledge assets can be joined in new combinations to produce incrementally improved products and processes. Therefore, in contexts with poor relational dynamics and a weak NSI, intermediaries are needed to promote actor interactions, assist in crossing boundaries and interfaces, and facilitate access to external knowledge and resources – all key inputs in the innovation process extremely difficult to obtain without assistance from some sort of intermediation (See Szogs et al., 2011; Watkins et al., 2015).

This analysis highlights two potential intermediation interventions in the southern Cape furniture cluster around the coastal towns of George and Knysna. The first potential intermediary is the furniture incubator Furntech in George, funded by the Department of Trade, Industry and Competition (DTIC). The second is the Schools Desks and Conservation Initiative (SDCI), funded by SANParks, an agency of the Department of Environment, Forestry and Fisheries (DEFF). Both had the potential to mediate weak interactive dynamics in the furniture cluster of the southern Cape and build useful networks, but both failed largely because of poor cross-departmental coordination and a bureaucratic and top-down mode of governance with little local buy-in from other economic actors in the furniture cluster. These two examples reflect poorly on South Africa's ability to adopt intermediation as part of its industrial policy armoury.

STRUCTURE OF THIS CHAPTER

The discussion begins with a focus on the theoretical influences shaping the concept of intermediation. The approach is interdisciplinary, borrowing strongly from analytical insights gained in innovation studies, industrial cluster studies and intermediation theory.

The second section focuses on the furniture sector in South Africa.

This is because both intermediation case studies come from this sector, an industry in severe economic decline with problems that could potentially be resolved through intermediation efforts. The third section focuses in detail on two intermediation case studies – the incubator Furntech and the Schools Desks and Conservation Initiative (SDCI), both located in George in the southern Cape furniture cluster. The final section offers concluding observations, the most significant being the poor performance of intermediation efforts in the South African context. Those involved in the two case studies, and in other intermediary bodies referred to in the sector, operate without an explicit understanding of performing intermediary roles. Most of these bodies replicate the 'tick-box compliance' model of the bureaucratic state.

THEORETICAL INFLUENCES

As indicated above, the discussion starts with an outline of the theoretical influences shaping the analysis and arguments developed in this study. The study adopts an inter-disciplinary approach, combining 'highly compatible existing theories in a framework that is incrementally broader than what has come before' (Ponte and Sturgeon, 2014: 2). Ponte and Sturgeon point to a weakness in many theoretical analyses, which seek to remain loyal to one theoretical tradition, in a 'totalizing manner, which can obscure as much as it reveals' (2014: 2). The primary theory utilised in this chapter is that of innovation studies and a sub-body of literature existing within this school focusing on intermediation. The study also utilises theoretical concepts emanating from cluster studies, a sub-field of development theory and economic geography. The discussion now shifts to briefly outline the significance of innovation to our study of the furniture cluster in the southern Cape.

What is innovation?

The national system of innovation (NSI) or innovation studies approach to economic development argues that those firms that prioritise methods of learning from past production practices are likely to be the successful players in the future marketplace – simply because they are most likely to find novel ways of doing things and producing new products (Lundvall, 1985). Much of the extant NSI literature is specifically focused on how firms learn, from whom, and whether this learning is internal or external. Lundvall argues that firm learning occurs best through the interactive processes of actors involved in production. The interaction referred to entails the sharing of production ideas and new knowledge between workers in the same firm; sharing new knowledge across neighbouring firms in the same industry; and seeking knowledge from external actors such as universities, colleges, incubators, consultants and training institutes. Collective inter- and intra-firm learning is a central activity of successful sectors.

Interactive capabilities

Lundvall has defined innovation as an interactive process in which different kinds of knowledge are combined through communication within and across organisational borders (Lundvall, 1985; Lundvall and Borras, 1999). Lundvall stressed the point that firms absorb ideas and new knowledge from their users and suppliers as well as from various external knowledge organisations such as R&D institutes at universities. He then went on to define an innovation system as a social domain encompassing all the organisations and institutions involved in this process of knowledge exchange and transfer (Chaminade et al., 2018: 1; Nelson et al., 2018).

An equally important observation pioneered by the NSI school was that innovation was a process of experience-based 'learning' within and between firms in an industry. This tacit incremental form of learning was as important to the national innovation process as the highly codified formal knowledge that supported formal R&D at universities and in industry laboratories. In 1991, attention was paid to work by Lundvall (1985), which elaborated a broad definition that went beyond the idea of firms interacting largely with research organisations. This expanded definition extended to a wider ensemble including organisations responsible for education and training that played a key role in shaping national competencies. Lundvall also included national specificities such as the structure and patterns of family life, civil society organisations and labour-market dynamics between employers and workers/trade unions: these all have an impact on the quality of experience-based learning in the workplace, which in turn directly shapes national innovation outcomes.

Jensen et al. (2007) developed the concept of learning by *doing, using and interacting* (DUI) to capture this incremental mode of innovation driven by tacit skills and experienced-based learning. They intended this notion to contrast starkly with the science-based learning, which occurs in formal R&D. In their view, innovation has roots in both science and production (Chaminade et al., 2018: 8–9). Jensen et al.'s (2007) observations regarding DUI are now central pillars of the NIS approach. Interactions between economic actors are considered a central driver of innovation and economic growth – primarily because these interactions create a conduit through which useful knowledge can be shared between economic actors. These include users, producers, customers, suppliers, other firms in the cluster or locality, training institutions, incubators, consultants and knowledge networks. In today's globalised economy, those countries that ensure an optimal infrastructure for communication and knowledge sharing and actively cooperate in such knowledge sharing are more likely to see improved performances in their national innovation systems, and more broadly, in their national economies.

Clusters and collective efficiency

Cooperation is clearly key to the requirement for interaction in all NSIs. As powerfully argued by Schmitz in 1999, cooperation in many old manufacturing sectors such as furniture and clothing is required to harness what he termed the 'collective efficiencies' present in these manufacturing processes (Schmitz, 1999: 466). Schmitz defined collective efficiency as the competitive advantage gained by small firms operating in sectors derived from so-called 'external economies' and joint action. External economies arise when the social benefits of an economic activity are higher than private benefits. Classic examples of externalities in clusters are technological spill overs (often 'leaked' from the advanced capabilities of lead firms); a pool of specialised suppliers; shared vocational training services; a sufficient supply of skilled labour, and export advice from public or private marketing agencies, to list only a few examples.

Schmitz argued that externalities on their own were not a sufficient condition for the evolution of successful clusters. He said that consciously pursued joint actions, taken horizontally between cluster firms, are additionally required beyond the involuntary and incidental occurrence of external economies. These joint actions entail individual firms cooperating around the sharing of expensive equipment (often including incubators), joint logistics, marketing or bulk ordering of supplies. Joint actions also entail groups of firms joining forces in business associations and producer consortia with the aim of lowering costs and improving quality and time efficiencies (Schmitz, 1999: 469). Nadvi (2016: 124) warns that such joint outcomes are not easy to achieve and are less common in incipient clusters than in more mature clusters.

Economic geographers Maskell and Lorenzen (2004) followed soon after Schmitz's ground-breaking work with a detailed study of the furniture sectors of several European economies – research which sought to explain why small furniture manufacturers chose to cluster. They focused on the demand conditions that small manufacturers face – particularly those conditions that limit economies of scale and scope. These demand constrictions have to do with the uncertainty pervasive in the furniture industry because of unpredictable volume fluctuations combined with a constantly increasing demand for product variety. To attain competitiveness, furniture producers must manufacture a diverse range of quality products, at speed. According to Maskell and Lorenzen (2004), this is achieved through vertical and horizontal 'relations of flexibility'. Vertical flexibility is achieved through flexible relations with specialised suppliers all located within a cluster environment. By being located close to different suppliers, furniture producers can call on suppliers at very short notice to provide diverse inputs, allowing them to deliver new furniture products at speed and with quality. Horizontal flexible relations entail firms passing on excess orders to each other. To attain this flexibility, firms depend on the market being organised into clusters in which furniture firms use each other regularly, each specialising in a different furniture component or production activity (Maskell and Lorenzen, 2004: 1000).

Intermediation

Intermediation occurs in all spheres of the economy and society; for example, in the NIS, in the labour market and in the triple helix partnerships formed by higher education organisations, government and private actors (Carayannis et al., 2022). Within the NSI, intermediation is largely about the coordination of multiple actors who are geographically isolated with restricted flows of information between them – a communicative and associational void often only resolved through intermediation. In the labour market, intermediation is fundamentally premised on the idea of brokering social compacts around jobs and employment growth. Organisational intermediaries range from non-government organisations (NGOs), small business development agencies and regional economic development organisations (often termed 'quangos'), to employer associations. They undertake a wide array of activities varying from collecting information to advocating policy to orchestrating the coordination of new economic activities – all public goods that are not likely to be undertaken by an organisation operating on its own.

Linking actors across a socially distributed system

Another factor underpinning the need for intermediation is the growth of a far more complex and socially distributed production system than was the case in the past. In the words of Gibbons et al. (1994), production systems are now much more socially distributed, having shifted away from a model where the vertically integrated lead firm dominates production, to a model with many new market and non-market actors. The decline of the vertically integrated corporate firm has contributed to this plurality of actors. Today, large firms keep fewer core competencies in-house, outsourcing the other components of work to external suppliers.

Weaver and Osterman (2014) write that in place of vertically integrated corporates there is now a larger set of smaller firms that provide inputs and services for lead actors in the network. This increase in the number of independent actors poses several problems for the new production regime. The increased numbers of actors are more widely dispersed than before, providing a greater number of moving parts, and therefore posing a potential failure in the market or in coordination within the new production system. If the actors were all to pursue diverse and conflicting strategies, the new system would fail (Weaver and Osterman, 2014: 53). What is required are strategically located network structures that 'glue' these socially distributed systems together. It is often lead firms that play this role. In their absence, intermediaries occupy this gap and perform this function of gluing.

Watkins et al. (2015) outline the well-documented shift in NSI studies. These moved from an initial focus on the macro structures of the national system (which generated criticisms of an overly static picture of the innovation process) and its preoccupation with the triadic interactions between industry, the state and higher education. The focus subsequently shifted to the growth of sub-fields within innovation studies, such as technology innovation systems, regional innovation systems and sectoral innovation systems. These all emphasised the micro-level interactions between firms and multiple other actors, which collectively constituted a dynamic innovation system on the ground. Intermediaries are recognised in this collective as critical additional actors.

Another argument put forward by Watkins et al. (2005) in this review of the historical literature is the role of other actors such as intermediaries became critical once the focus shifted from the institutionally dense national innovation systems of developed economies to the organisationally sparse context of developing economies. These intermediaries became critical in linking actors and organisations who historically had been disconnected (Watkins et al., 2015: 1407–1408). In most instances, it is intermediaries who are called upon to perform the role of bridge-builders, bringing together economic communities who would not otherwise cooperate (Moss et al., 2009: 1481).

A SHORT HISTORY OF THE FURNITURE INDUSTRY

The southern Cape was chosen as the sight for these furniture case studies for several reasons. The first was the region's historical role as the first furniture cluster in the country, which emerged there in the late 1880s. This cluster grew over the next century to become a leading producer of high-end yellowwood furniture for the national market. The southern Cape also housed several nationally competitive mass production plants producing low-cost, standardised pine furniture products.

A second reason for the choice of sector and location is that the industry has faced intense volatility and flux since the late 1990s – what can best be described as the classic economic 'boom and bust' scenario. The boom phase emerged during the mid-1990s up until 2002; it represented a period of growth in South African furniture export market due to a depreciating rand from the mid-1990s until the end of the decade (Morris and Jackson, 2002: 16). The value of furniture exports grew almost tenfold from R54 million in 1990 to R526 million in 1999 (Kaplinsky et al., 2003: 18). However, this expansion was built on fragile legs, resulting mainly from a depreciating rand. These negative conditions worsened when the newly elected democratic government introduced trade liberalisation measures in the late 1990s. These changes led to a massive spike in the importation of cheap furniture goods from East and Southeast Asia (China and Vietnam) as well as from Poland and Indonesia. By the mid-2000s, many mass-producing firms in the southern Cape furniture cluster were forced to close, and most other firms downsized. New industrial policy solutions for the ailing sector were urgently needed. It will be argued that Intermediation offers certain solutions to the problems faced by the sector.

A third reason for interest in the locale and sector is that the state has promoted clusters as a solution to old manufacturing industries such as furniture and clothing. Several proposals for reviving the furniture industry have been drafted in the past two decades (DTI, 2008; Kaplinsky et al., 2003: 22; Kaplinsky and Morris, 2014: 24; DTIC, 2021). These proposals are relevant to the southern Cape as an existing cluster. They have centred on increasing collective efficiencies and harnessing joint actions between actors – tasks best executed with the help of intermediaries (Maskell and Lorenzen, 2004; Schmitz, 1999).

Several problems emerge in the furniture sector

Kaplinsky and Manning characterise the furniture industry in the 1990s as being dominated by large firms and a high degree of concentration in corporate ownership. South African manufacturing in general had a high degree of concentration, with the six largest manufacturing conglomerates in 1992 owning approximately 87 per cent of issued capital on the Johannesburg Stock Exchange (Kaplinsky and Manning, 1998: 142). This dominance of a few large firms over the industry has continued into the present period. Historically, this concentration has affected average plant size, with medium to large firms dominating output from the formal sector. This has meant that South Africa has not been able to follow the historical pathway that evolved in Europe and Southeast Asia, which has led to most furniture sectors currently being run by small family-owned, highly skilled artisanal firms (Kaplinsky et al., 2003).

However, highly concentrated ownership is not the only problem facing the sector. Morris and Jackson (2002: 15, 18) and the DTI (2008: 10–11) argue that productivity and competitiveness in the sector declined in the late 1990s and 2000s. They attribute this to declining investments in new technology and skilled labour, and insufficient design capabilities in the national innovation system, especially in the former technikons (now universities of technology). There was almost none of the research and development (R&D) that was needed to support the revival of the industry.

Several other constraints plagued the industry during this period. For example, flatpack technologies had been evolving since the 1990s and should have assisted global exports. However, South Africa was still too far away from the main export markets to be able to compete effectively with other furniture sectors closer to the main consumer locales: even with the advantages of flatpack containerisation, shipping costs were still too high. Another structural problem that proved difficult to overcome in the sector was the inferior quality of sawn-wood timber going to furniture manufacturers. According to Kaplinsky et al. (2003: 15):

> The saw-milling technology used is old since most new investment has gone into paper and pulp which has higher

profit margins. Consequently, the furniture industry is badly served with respect to input quality and flexibility, and delivery reliability is poor.

Another structural constraint was that although South Africa's middle class had grown significantly since 1994, and incorporated a sizeable black middle class, this resulted in only a limited increase in purchasing power for home ownership and furniture sales. This new middle class, alongside a sizeable salaried working class, aspired to affordable furniture sold at the large chain stores. They did not yet constitute a large market for the higher value-added segments of the furniture market. Moreover, even though South Africa exports to neighbouring countries in Africa, these countries were and remain low-income ones, and the demand from them continues to be for low-cost, standardised furniture.

Sectoral growth has remained flat since the late 2000s. The furniture sector contributed R11.1 billion to gross domestic product (GDP) in 2015, up from R10.8 billion in 2010. This amounts to a contribution of about 1 per cent to manufacturing GDP. It also contributed 1.1 per cent to manufacturing employment (DTI, 2017, 134; DTI, 2018: 136). However, this growth trajectory can be summed up as flat with a slow decline from 2013 onwards (DTI, 2017: 134). Alongside sluggish growth, import penetration has been increasing. It has risen from 21 per cent in 2009 to 32 per cent in 2015. More recent data (See Figure 4.1) shows the rapid changes, which have occurred in South Africa's furniture imports and exports, with the trade gap now significant. In short, exports of both mass production and high-end bespoke products have been declining since 2002, while imports have been increasing steadily since 2002 with a dip in 2008–09, followed by ongoing increases.

This brief economic history makes it clear that the South African furniture industry (including its southern Cape cluster) is in dire straits and is in need of urgent reform and renewal.

Figure 4.1: South African furniture imports and exports

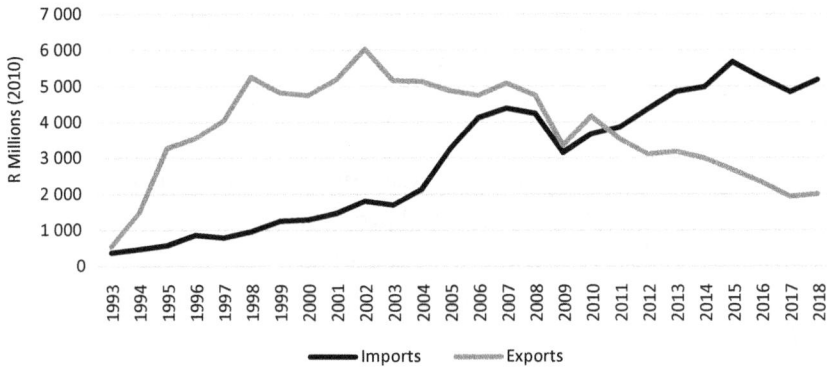

Source: DTIC, 2021

CASE STUDY ONE: THE FURNTECH INCUBATOR

Yusuf (2008: 1170) defines an incubator as an organic intermediary – most often a public agency that offers shared resources, assists with knowledge transfers and provides a variety of other services to small firms and start-ups (for example, joint training, bulk-buying, marketing and shared logistics). Yusuf notes the significance of assisting with the sharing of tacit knowledge in specific industry contexts, where such knowledge is 'sticky' and difficult to transfer to new contexts. It requires cooperation and trust between firms and other actors for such transfers to take place. Incubators, serving as intermediaries, can facilitate such trust and cooperation.

The innovation literature on incubators, drawn largely from the sub-school of researchers writing on entrepreneurial ecosystems, sees the primary role of incubators as that of network systems builders. Hernándes-Chea et al. (2021: 1, 3) argue that incubators have evolved as intermediaries in the past three decades from performing the traditional and basic role of knowledge transfer to the far more complex and advanced role of 'network system builder'. This entails playing a central role in facilitating, orchestrating and coordinating activities within a network of actors. Papia (2006: 31), writing from an innovation perspective, agrees. These networking practices are often informal methods of gaining access to new ideas being talked about in the industry – through attendance at incubator seminars, meetings and expositions. In these fora, networking partners share experiences of successes and failures. Networking also opens up and widens opportunities for access to new markets (Khuzwayo, 2015: 32).

In short, incubators perform a dual function (internal and external) – the first being the traditional role of providing basic resources to start-ups, the second entailing the building of ecosystems that successful start-ups join once they graduate from incubation. To consolidate the second function, incubators often maintain aftercare services, such as mentoring, coaching and the provision of alumni associations, which include other firms that were former incubatees. Such aftercare activities continue the process of interactive learning long after graduation.

This chapter focuses on one of the eight furniture incubators, started by the then-DTI in 2002, located in George, the heart of the southern Cape furniture cluster. The incubators were named Furniture Technology Centre Trust (Furntech) incubators. They were launched in the late 1990s and early 2000s, as an industrial policy initiative of the DTI when furniture manufacturing was considered a priority (CSIR, 2016: 11).

Furntech was launched in 2000. Its first campus was started in George in 2002 at the old Saasveld Forestry College site, and seven other centres were established over the following decade: Cape Town, Nyanga, Durban, White River, Umzimkhulu, Mthatha and Johannesburg. The Furntech campus in George – which is the focus of this case study – received financial and training support from the Swedish International Development Cooperation Agency (SIDA), resulting in the building of a 'state-of-the-art' furniture incubator which opened in 2002 (Chisenga, 2012: 34; Hellström and Hirschsohn, 2007: 14). Training support came from the Tibro furniture cluster in Sweden – one of the leading furniture clusters globally. Most importantly, it provides products for the IKEA global furniture chain.

Furntech offers a two-year incubation process to recruits who are competitively selected based on their experience in manufacturing furniture. Craftspeople with some woodwork skills and experience in running their own small firms are specifically sought. Within the two-year period the performance of the incubatees is monitored and evaluated. The incubatee signs a contract at the beginning, which binds their start-up company to pay 10 per cent of its monthly turnover to Furntech (Chisenga, 2012: 38). The main activity of Furntech in George has been training and providing business and technology services. Courses offered have included ones on cabinet making, wood polishing and supervision, as well as training in computer-aided design (CAD) and computer numerically controlled (CNC) machining (Hellström and Hirschsohn, 2007: 16–17).

A critique of Furntech

The published reviews of the economic impact of the Furntech model over the past two decades have not been very complimentary. Furntech's performance nationally over the past two decades has been mixed. In its annual report of 2020, Furntech reports that 422 small-firm incubatees had graduated through the scheme between 2006 and 2020. This disaggregates into 31 SMEs supported per year across seven Furntech incubator campuses nationally – not a very high output according to Furntech's annual report (Furntech, 2020: 3). Also, new job creation has been low – only 71 jobs were directly created by the SMEs that graduated between 2006 and 2011. And lastly, income from the operating activities of Furntech's tenants has only been able to cover 17 per cent of total costs. These are all indicators of relatively poor performance (Chisenga, 2012: 36–42). Masutha (2012: 97) provides some reasons for these poor outcomes. Firstly, about 20 per cent of Furntech's incubatees drop out before graduating. Secondly, external and internal factors which contribute to the failure rate include lack of commitment, lack of discipline and non-compliance from incubatees.

The George incubator was closed by the DTI in 2014 after having run for more than a decade. The Department then commissioned the CSIR, in 2016, to review the remaining seven Furntech incubators. The review indicated that Furntech was not meeting its incubator objectives to assist SMEs in the sector to overcome the key constraints on trade. The report argued that many stakeholders in the sector indicated that

'Furntech graduates and incubatees were unable to independently source adequate work and income-generating opportunities'. The perception is that 'incubatees depend too heavily on Furntech for marketing their products and businesses, and graduates function sub-optimally once they graduate from the incubation programme' (CSIR, 2016: 2).

Employers in the southern Cape have levelled significant criticism at Furntech, particularly around its prioritisation of the training of unemployed people as semi-skilled workers rather than the production of skilled artisans – who are in short supply. This is an instance of the call to prioritise the training of unemployed youth at the Growth and Development Summit of 2003 impacting negatively on several organisations – including Furntech – that were originally geared to upskilling experienced workers ready to launch their own start-up firms. The task of assisting unemployed people, although a major issue in South African society, is a very different challenge requiring different policy interventions. Jeanne le Roux, owner of bespoke firm Creative Designs, is highly critical of Furntech's mission to incubate start-up firms alongside the training of unskilled workers (Interview with Ms Jeanne le Roux, owner of Creative Design, George, 6 May 2016):

It's a completely confusing model, you can't do training of the unskilled and business incubation in one organisation. That's why Furntech died. I think Furntech completely missed the point, which is that we are always looking for skilled artisans. Here was a fantastic opportunity to supply the industry and for the industry to give feedback on the system so that our existing staff could be upskilled – and then they went and focused on unemployed youth – which is a completely different goal.

Paul Cloete, a lecturer at Nelson Mandela University's wood technology programme (formerly the Saasveld Forestry College), is critical of the lack of support from established firms in the George-Knysna furniture hub (Interview with Paul Cloete, forestry lecturer at Nelson Mandela University, 6 May 2016):

I think given that George and Kynsna became such a strong furniture manufacturing area in the 1980s and earlier, it came to be dominated by certain existing companies that were very successful. Some of these same family businesses are still dominant and there isn't much scope for the entry of new firms. I believe Furntech and its graduates didn't get all the backup they needed from these companies. Countrycraft was supportive because its founder, Luke Martin, is on the Furntech Board – but not so much from other firms. So, it was a difficult task for Furntech to get up and running in the area. And that's why it was eventually closed.

Why Furntech failed in George

The literature on incubators is replete with advice on factors that contribute to the success or failure of incubation processes. Writers such as Altenburg (2009: 1) warn that industrial policies such as science parks and incubators often 'have limited outreach, benefiting relatively small groups of firms' (Altenburg, 2009: 14). This seems to have been the case with the Furntech incubators, which have limited their contribution to that of a traditional incubator – knowledge transfer and information sharing, delivered mainly through an extensive training and incubation programme. The Furntech model (based on its online publications, brochures and an interview with the CEO) gave no indication at all that they built networks of start-up firms either internally, or, more importantly, externally. There is no aftercare programme for graduated incubatees, and most struggle to survive on their own. Furntech chose to be the sole player in the incubation process, seeking no alliances with other actors such as TVET colleges and universities of technology or lead firms. Furthermore, Furntech had no conception of a collective ecosystem structure such as a cluster or local innovation system to which an incubatee's start-up firm was inextricably linked. It treated each incubatee as an individual client who must learn how to run his/her own business. Hence it did no external work to build linkages with the Southern Cape furniture cluster. It certainly could not be described as an orchestrator of key interactive dynamics in the cluster. Most neglected of all inter-dependencies within the cluster were advice and training on acquiring funding to consolidate and grow start-up enterprises; knowledge and contacts about acquiring access to markets; and linkages to formal knowledge producers like colleges and Universities of Technology that teach design and digitalisation. Although Furntech in George was located at the former Saasveld Forestry College (now a campus of Nelson Mandela University), cooperation between Furntech and Saasveld appears to have been episodic.

Another problem identified by Papia is the dependency created in tenants receiving government support, which can include low rent, access to modern technology and assisted access to markets and training. Tenants face difficulty in continuing after incubation without these forms of support (2006: 21). In the case of Furntech in George, the entire campus was closed in 2014 in large part because incubatees failed to stand on their own feet after they graduated. Furntech was clearly an incubator with limited impact on the launching of successful start-up firms. The organisation remained stuck in the role of a traditional incubator and did not progress to more advanced intermediation activities such as building networks and giving direction within the ecosystem. The discussion now shifts to the second intermediation case study.

CASE STUDY TWO: SCHOOL DESKS AND CONSERVATION INITIATIVE (SDCI)

The School Desks and Conservation Initiative (SDCI) project is not a cluster. Rather, it is a state-led experiment with a cooperative structure aimed at creating economies of scale for the participating collective of small firms. The SDCI has three overarching goals, namely:

- To add value to invasive alien plant (IAP) biomass with which to subsidise the clearing of IAPs;
- To create sustainable jobs (including the development of skills); and
- To alleviate poverty through the provision of short-term employment (Ward et al., 2018: 12).

The SDCI's main objective is to establish viable furniture factories making products needed by government. In addition, these factories should use wood from invasive plants, create jobs for 3,025 beneficiaries, work at competitive Expanded Public Works Programme rates, and produce high-quality products at prices lower than if government were to buy them on the open market (Ward, et al., 2018: 2).

The SDCI has seven factories nationally, with one located in George. The SDCI is a relevant case study of collective efficiency and intermediation aimed at better managing the complex challenges of the cross-departmental coordination entailed in large government projects, and of building competencies in furniture manufacturing amongst previously unemployed workers. It is an initiative run out of the offices of SANParks, an agency within the DEFF that has a mandate to protect and manage the national parks of South Africa. It was launched in 2010 after a successful application to the Jobs Fund. Desks created would be manufactured from timber extracted after the removal of invasive trees. The income derived from the sale of these desks to government was then intended to fund the further removal of alien biomass.

Problems emerge around governance
Although a bold initiative on many fronts, the project's management and governance soon became a major problem. Ideally, the SDCI should have been handed over to an appropriate intermediary to run (what the project proposal termed an 'independent trading entity' such as a Section 21 company) given that the manufacture of school desks was not SANParks's core business. In fact, it was a condition of the Jobs Fund that such an organisational arrangement be set up. This did not happen, leaving the SDCI in the very vulnerable position of needing in many ways to behave like a commercial entity but constrained by the bureaucracy and slowness of the state.

The location of the SDCI within SANParks meant it was slotted into the modus operandi of other SANParks programmes such as the Expanded Public Works Programme (EPWP), in which previously unemployed recruits were paid an internship wage significantly lower than the wage stipulated by the Bargaining Council for the furniture industry. Private sector contractors were encouraged to employ EPWP staff, and SANParks would then employ the contractors. The responsibilities of the contractors included training, tree harvesting, planking and factory production. But this model didn't really work in a factory in a commercial environment because it was founded on arms-length employment through the contractor and was impermanent. Neither of these conditions created the ownership of the production process necessary for an economically viable furniture enterprise in the medium to long term (Ward et al., 2018).

The project goes to scale

A second problem was that when the project went to scale to produce 250,000 desks it needed nationally consistent administrative standards and systems. Yet none were developed independently of the very bureaucratic systems applicable to the national parks. The SDCI also never received any help from professional consultants to put these systems in place. National coordination fell under a chief director in Pretoria who was also responsible for administering *Working for Water* and *Working for Fire*. In short, national coordination was thinly spread. The project got big very quickly, and backup administration and systems were simply too slow to provide the necessary support (Ward et al., 2018).

Access to feedstock

A third problem that emerged was difficulties in accessing and harvesting the alien trees, which were most often located on private property belonging to farmers and foresters. Access to the IAPs was supposed to have been facilitated by the passing of legislation – the National Environment Management Biodiversity Act (NEMBA) – which required landowners to clear certain categories of alien plants from their land. However, there have been big challenges implementing NEMBA and in many instances, according to the managers of the SDCI interviewed, access to biomass relies on personal relationships. A private contractor that was sourcing timber for the SDCI factory noted (Ward et al., 2018: 53):

There is plenty of feedstock for the next ten years but the challenge is getting access to it. Government has all the legislation in place but it is just not being implemented at all. Timber is thus being sourced through personal relationships but it is difficult. We are being forced to work from hand-to-mouth with many farmers refusing to allow us access to the timber unless we pay them. But the timber would have zero value if it wasn't for the SDCI.

In the southern Cape, government privatised many forestry plantations with the agreement that the new landowners would remove alien plants and leave the timber at the roadside. This arrangement was supposed to yield 400 cubic metres a month. However, no clearing took place, and no timber was forthcoming from the landowners who benefitted from the privatisation of the government plantations. Without the enforcement of current legislation, access to this timber has proved to be difficult (Interview with Michael de Beer, senior official at the SDCI factory, 7 June 2017, cited in Ward et al., 2018: 43–44):

> We haven't received one log out of the entire landowner initiative in the Garden Route. We're supposed to be getting like four hundred cubes in a month, every month – but nothing has come. Nothing is happening on this front – no clearing is taking place.

Spiralling costs

A fourth problem has been the spiralling costs of the desks, which have shifted way past the commercial price if bought on an open market. It became clear that the programme was costing a substantial amount of money and the intention to generate a surplus or at least break even was not being realised. In a review of the project, Ward et al. (2018) concluded that the programme was not financially sustainable.

Another problem associated with costs was that the Department of Basic Education (DBE) did not pay up on time. At one point, the DBE owed R30 million. If it wasn't for SANParks being able to carry the factories financially, the factories would have closed a long time ago. Late payment is a systemic problem across the whole of government and severely constrains the work of initiatives such as the SDCI. The debts became debilitating and SANParks was forced to scale down quite dramatically. They were even locked out of the factory in George by the landlord because of a failure to pay rent and electricity. Perhaps the biggest blow to this public sector-led project was that it had to eventually recruit private sector help to produce the number of desks required by government using commercially grown timbers and not the alien wood the project was intended to clear.

Attitudes of the private furniture sector

Relationships between the SDCI and the furniture manufacturers in the southern Cape have turned sour. In part this is because the project was started without consulting private sector stakeholders to get them on board and inform them about what was going to be done. Interviewees from furniture firms have accused the SDCI of competing unfairly with the private sector – for example, paying an EPWP wage, which is significantly lower than the minimum wage employers in the sector are required to pay unskilled workers. The SDCI has also been accused of poaching skilled artisans, kiln workers and management personnel to run the project in George. Local manufacturers believe they have been unfairly forced out of the school desks market.

Some of these accusations are true. However, management of the SDCI maintains that the local furniture industry doesn't see the collective production benefits the initiative has brought to George. The managers say local manufacturers have profited significantly from by-products of SDCI business, namely the hiring of their kilns and transport. Previously their kilns were standing empty. In addition, management of the SDCI point out the irony of the furniture manufacturers in the region complaining about unfair subsidies (Interview with Michael de Beer, senior official at the George SDCI factory, 7 June 2017):

> We must not forget that the George-Knysna timber industry was subsidised by the old apartheid government, so the entire industry was born through subsidies on wood, land and electricity. So now, they're saying that we're subsidised. This is a bit disingenuous. A nice irony.

Michael de Beer, a senior official at the George SDCI factory, maintains that the private sector is exploiting the project. For example, they've had an advantage over the SDCI in the past because the SDCI does not have its own drying facilities, so they must use the kilns of their landlords – who charge a huge fee to dry timber when the going market rate is much lower. According to the manager, this is all part of this 'mafioza' mentality (Interview with Michael de Beer, senior official at the George SDCI factory, June 2017):

> They have forced us to get our own drying facilities which we are doing which is basically cutting their throats now, so once we put up our own kilns, they're not going to have that income anymore which would be of their own doing.

There are significant differences of opinion between and across the various cluster actors on the role that government should play in supporting the SDCI. The low labour costs and investment in capital equipment enabled by the EPWP programme and Jobs Fund create certain advantages for the SDCI relative to the private sector. However, in the view of the managers interviewed, this advantage is more than cancelled out by the fact that the SDCI is using alien invasive plants with all the challenges that this introduces into the value chain. It must also be noted that the labour-intensive methods used by the SDCI create many more jobs than the private sector would create commercially for the same product output (Ward et al., 2018: 53).

The SDCI is the kind of project that South Africa needs; it promotes labour-intensive, low-skill employment for those who are unemployed. It intervenes in resolving a major environmental problem of invasive alien plants, and it engages with government procurement as a lever for getting new actors into the wider furniture value chain. However, it hit a major obstacle in the form of government's poor record of ceding governance functions to an intermediary; government rather preferred to rely on its own ineffectual cross-departmental coordination capabilities. This approach has limited the ability of the SDCI to function optimally. Government appears unwilling to let go of its flagship project to a third-party intermediary even though it is failing to achieve most of its stated objectives.

CONCLUSION

In assessing two potential intermediation case studies, the Schools Desk and Conservation Initiative, essentially a cooperative, scores highly on several counts. These include strategic thinking and leadership; impacting on several government priorities in one project; conservation and the clearing of alien trees; training unemployed workers; and the localisation of production (the manufacture of desks and chairs for South African schools). The project failed, however, because of the inefficiency and reluctance of government in not establishing an effective external intermediary to lead and manage the project. Instead, the already overstretched SANParks agency within the DEFF was burdened with its management. SANParks performed poorly, with the unit costs of their school desks significantly higher than similar desks sold in the private market. The state's role was bureaucratic regulation of the process, not intermediation.

With regard to Furntech, the incubator chose to operate as a training organisation and did not transition to the intermediation (networking) roles performed by successful incubators globally. In both case studies, the strong potential for intermediation was lost.

In short, South Africa faces a major intermediation problem given that it has created a huge number of quangos (semi-independent bodies funded by the fiscus but operating at arms-length from direct government control) across all sectors of society and the economy. Kraak (2023), for example, reviews the Sectoral Education and Training Agencies (SETAs) and the South African Furniture Initiative (SAFI) and their failure to perform intermediation functions. Other examples of quangos that perform poorly as intermediaries include the many regional offices and incubators of the Small Enterprise Development Agency (SEDA) and several craft hubs run by provincial governments. There are few examples of quangos functioning with an explicit understanding of the need for performing intermediary roles. Most of these bodies replicate the 'tick-box compliance' model of the bureaucratic state.

A major problem is the fact that there is no understanding of nor support for collective, interactive processes in industry and government, at least in the furniture sector. The dominance of neo-liberal positions regarding the economy amongst private sector leaders and the economists who advise government means that innovation frameworks are ignored (see Kahn, 2013 for additional discussion on this). This is the case even when these frameworks are adopted at national and provincial levels. This lack of understanding of innovation and intermediation as alternative economic policy frameworks for government is problematic because it leads to ignoring one of the strengths of the innovation systems approach – its emphasis on ecosystems and the interdependence of variables shaping the economy. This neglect has led to the predominance of single-factor policy instruments being formulated and implemented by government in its public policies. As we saw earlier, establishing an incubator to simply train and not to interact dynamically with its neighbouring industrial districts and all their component parts (the ecosystem) robs the incubator of its networking and intermediation potential. Secondly, government's top-down, short-termist and underfunded approach to many of its industrial policy initiatives, such as clusters, incubators and cooperatives, has rendered most of these initiatives unsuccessful, with little private sector buy-in. And lastly, the individualism of industry players provides major obstacles to building cooperation, trust and the collective production of goods. In such an environment, intermediation cannot easily emerge and flourish.

However, the strengths of intermediation, if properly conceptualised and implemented, should not be underestimated. Intermediation, coupled with the role of quangos, should be encouraged and refined, using the evidence gathered from experiences such as those outlined in this chapter. This would allow for these organisations to be oriented away from their passive, at arm's length, bureaucratic and siloed modus operandi towards cross-departmental coordination, actor interaction, capability building and the sharing of knowledge resources within sectors such as the furniture one.

REFERENCES

Altenburg, T. 2009. 'Building inclusive innovation systems in developing countries: Challenges for IS research' in Lundvall, B.Å., Joseph, K.J., Chaminade, C. and Vang, J. (eds). *Handbook of Innovation Systems and Developing Countries: Building Domestic Capabilities in a Global Setting.* Cheltenham: Edward Elgar Publishing.

Carayannis, E.G., Campbell, D.F.J. and Grigoroudis, E. 2022. 'Helix trilogy: The triple, quadruple, and quintuple innovation helices from a theory, policy, and practice set of perspectives'. *Journal of the Knowledge Economy,* 13, 2272–2301.

Chaminade, C., Lundvall, B.A. and Haneef, S. 2018. *Advanced Introduction to National Innovation Systems.* Cheltenham: Edward Elgar Publishing.

Chisenga, D.C. 2012. 'Clustering and incubation in Africa's small business development: Some experiences and lessons'. Master's in Economics thesis, University of the Western Cape.

Council for Scientific and Industrial Research (CSIR). 2016. *Inception Report: Furntech Graduates and Small Furniture Manufacturers Productivity and Competitiveness Improvement Project.* Pretoria: CSIR.

Department of Trade and Industry (DTI). 2008. 'Draft Strategy for the Development of the Furniture Industry'. https://pmg.org.za/files/docs/081107furniturestrategy.pdf, accessed 21 February 2023.

Department of Trade and Industry (DTI). 2017. '2017/18–2019/20 Industrial Policy Action Plan: Economic Sectors, Employment and Infrastructure Development Cluster'. https://www.gov.za/sites/default/files/gcis_document/201705/ipap17181920.pdf, accessed 16 November 2022.

Department of Trade and Industry (DTI). 2018. '2018/19–2020/21 Industrial Policy Action Plan: Economic Sectors, Employment and Infrastructure Development Cluster'. https://www.gov.za/sites/default/files/gcis_document/201805/industrial-policy-action-plan.pdf, accessed 13 November 2022.

Department of Trade, Industry and Competition (DTIC). 2021. 'Masterplan for the South African Furniture Industry Master Plan'. http://www.thedtic.gov.za/wp-content/uploads/Master-Plan-South_African_Furniture_Industry.pdf, accessed 24 April 2023.

Furntech. 2020. 'Annual Report 2020'. https://furntech.org.za/wp-content/uploads/2020/09/Furntech-Annual-Report-2020_compressed-1.pdf, accessed 7 November 2022.

Gibbons, M., Limoges, C., Nowotny, H., Schwartzman, S., Scott, P. and Trow, M. 1994. *The New Production of Knowledge: The Dynamics of Science and Research in Contemporary Societies.* Parbhoo: Sage Publications.

Hellström, P. and Hirschsohn, P. 2007. 'Institutional cooperation between Furniture Technology Centre, South Africa and Tibro Training Centre,

Sweden: Evaluation Report Number 41', Swedish International Development Aid (SIDA), Department for Africa. http://www.sida.se/publications, accessed 3 October 2022.

Hernándes-Chea, R., Mahdad, M., Minh, T. and Hjortsø, C. 2021. 'Moving beyond Intermediation: How intermediary organizations shape collaboration dynamics in entrepreneurial ecosystems'. *Technovation*, 108, 1–15.

Jensen, M.B., Johnson, B., Lorenz, E. and Lundvall, B.Å. 2007. 'Forms of knowledge and modes of innovation'. *Research Policy*, 36, 680–693.

Kahn, M.J. 2013. 'Rhetoric and change in innovation policy: The case of South Africa'. *Science, Technology and Society*, 18(2), 189–211.

Kaplinsky, R. and Manning, C. 1998. 'Concentration, competition policy and the role of small and medium-sized enterprises in South Africa's industrial development'. *The Journal of Development Studies*, 35(1), 139–161.

Kaplinsky, R., Memedovic, O., Morris, M. and Readman, J. 2003. 'The global wood furniture value chain: What prospects for upgrading by developing countries, the case of South Africa', United Nations Industrial Development Organization (UNIDO, Vienna.

Kaplinsky, R. and Morris, M. 2014. 'Developing industrial clusters and supply chains to support diversification and sustainable development of exports in Africa', Report for the African Export-Import Bank, Cairo.

Khuzwayo, S.S. 2015. 'Evaluating the role of business incubators in South Africa'. Thesis submitted for a Master of Arts degree at the University of KwaZulu-Natal. http://hdl.handle.net/10413/14263.

Kraak, A. 2023. 'Initiating an economic and skills turnaround in the local furniture innovation system of the Southern Cape: an "intermediation" and "innovation" perspective'. PhD thesis, School of Economics, University of the Johannesburg.

Lundvall, B.Å. (ed). 1985. *Product Innovation and User-Producer Interaction*. Aalborg: Aalborg University Press.

Lundvall, B. and Borras, S. 1999. *Targeted Socio-Economic Research. The Globalising Learning Economy: Implications for Innovation Policy*. Luxembourg: Office for Official Publications of the European Communities.

Maskell, P. and Lorenzen, M. 2004. 'The cluster as market organisation'. *Urban Studies*, 41(5/6), 991–1009.

Masutha, M. 2012. 'Small business incubators in South Africa: Emergence, geography and local impacts'. MA thesis, University of Johannesburg.

Morris, M. and Jackson, C.A. 2002. 'Final report on factors impacting on the competitiveness of key export value chains in the furniture sector'. Report commissioned by the Policy Support Programme of the Department of Trade and Industry. Industrial Restructuring Project, School of Development Studies, University of Natal.

Moss, T., Medd, W., Guy, S. and Marvin, S. 2009. 'Organising water: The hidden role of intermediary work'. *Water Alternatives*, 2(1), 16–33.

Nadvi, K. 2016. 'What role for small enterprises? Industrial clusters, industrial policy and poverty reduction', in Weiss, J. and Tribe, M. (eds). *Routledge Handbook of Industry and Development*. Parbhoo: Routledge.

Nelson, R., Dosi, G., Helfat, C., Pyka, A., Saviotti, P.P., Lee, K., Dopfer, K., Malerba, F. and Winter, S. 2018. *Modern Evolutionary Economics: An Overview*. Cambridge: Cambridge University Press.

Papia, S.P. 2006. 'Factors determining success/failure in business incubators: A literature review of seventeen countries'. Worcester Polytechnic Institute, pp 2–81.

Ponte, S. and Sturgeon, T. 2014. 'Explaining governance in global value chains: A modular theory-building effort'. *Review of International Political Economy*, (21), 195–223.

Schmitz, H. 1999. 'Collective efficiency and increasing returns'. *Cambridge Journal of Economics*, 23(4), 465–483.

Szogs, A., Cummings, C. and Chaminade, C. 2011. 'Building systems of innovation in less developed countries: The role of intermediate organizations supporting interactions in Tanzania and El Salvador'. *Innovation and Development*, 1, 283–302. doi:10.1080/2157930X.2011.615601.

Ward, M., McLean, D., Kraak, A., Jenkin N. and Mushangai, D. 2018. *The School Desks and Conservation Initiative: An Evaluative Review*. Johannesburg: Jobs Fund.

Watkins, A., Papaioannou, T., Mugwagwa, J. and Kale, D. 2015. 'National innovation systems and the intermediary role of industry associations in building institutional capacities for innovation in developing countries: A critical review of the literature'. Research Policy, 44(8), 1407–1418.

Weaver, A. and Osterman, P. 2014. 'The new skill production system: Policy challenges and solutions in manufacturing labour markets' in Locke, R. and Wellhausen, R.L. (eds). *Production in the Innovation Economy*. Cambridge, MA: MIT Press.

Yusuf, S. 2008. 'Intermediating knowledge exchange between universities and businesses'. *Research Policy*, 37, 1167–1174.

INTERVIEWS

Interview with Jeanne le Roux, owner of Creative Design, maker of bespoke design furniture, Friday, 6 May 2016.

Interview with Paul Cloete, lecturer in wood technology at Saasveld campus, Nelson Mandela University, George, Friday 6 May 2016.

Interview with Michael de Beer, senior manager, School Desks and Conservation Initiative (SDCI), George factory, Wednesday 7 June 2017.

FIVE

Frugal and reverse innovation in the medical devices industry in South Africa

ZAMANZIMA MAZIBUKO-MAKENA

INTRODUCTION

The medical devices industry plays a critical role in the healthcare system of a country, particularly in the prevention, diagnosis and treatment of various diseases as well as in patient monitoring (Chandan et al., 2021). There are more than 10,000 different types of medical devices globally at varying degrees of complexity and cost, including surgical instruments, medical imaging devices, in-vitro diagnostics, and prostheses (WHO, 2011; Kale and Wield, 2019). However, most medical devices in low- and middle-income countries (LMICs) have been designed for use in high-income countries (Marks et al., 2019). The World Health Organization has reported that LMICs have lagged in the development and manufacturing of medical devices, particularly ones appropriate to and affordable in local contexts (WHO, 2012; 2016). Instead, these countries depend on imported medical devices, most of which are costly and/or incompatible with local settings and socioeconomic dynamics (Marks et al., 2019).

South Africa has an emerging medical devices manufacturing sector, which is mostly limited to assembly and lower-end products, with a few exceptions (Fitch Solutions, 2021). South Africa's medical devices industry is largely dependent on imports. Moreover, the number of start-up medical device manufacturers in the country has been declining (Maharaj and Sunjka, 2019). There has, however, been a rising interest in the medical device industry in South Africa in the past few years, which was deepened by the unfortunate realities exposed by the Covid-19 pandemic. The pandemic laid bare the importance of robust innovation and production capability in the key area of medical devices to ensure greater resilience and sustainability in health systems, and to enable a more agile response to public health crises. The need to localise the manufacturing of medical devices became even more urgent. Aside from the benefits of having context-specific medical devices, many see the medical devices industry in South Africa as an opportunity for economic growth, job creation, localisation, a reduction of trade imbalances and a reduced reliance on imports (SAMRC, 2022).

However, the research and development of medical devices is capital intensive; there is inadequate funding and government support across the full value chain; and there is unclear market guidance for and pathways to commercialisation (SAMRC, 2022). These are some of the challenges faced by medical device firms and the reasons some of their technologies fail to reach commercialisation.

This chapter examines the kinds of medical devices that have been successfully commercialised in South Africa and the conditions under which this occurred. It also explores the contribution of medical innovation to the country's development goals, particularly Chapter 10 of the National Development Plan (NDP, 2013). Additionally, the chapter discusses how some so-called 'frugal innovations' in healthcare extend their journeys to more developed countries, thus becoming 'reverse innovations'. Low- and middle-income countries have increasingly been providing new sources of global innovation, and thus offering firms worldwide fresh opportunities for innovation. The location and focus of innovation have become broader and there is a need to adjust innovation management theories, models and frameworks. The theoretical foundation for the analysis is drawn from innovation literature, particularly frugal and reverse innovation as well as national health innovation systems literature.

Through exploring the journey of three South African medical device innovations, this chapter expands the discussion on the role of innovative medical device manufacturing firms as sources of frugal product innovation. The chapter also identifies the determinants and consequences of, and agents involved in, reverse innovation for medical technologies. Importantly, the chapter draws attention to the critical role of government and strong health systems in advancing innovations for public health. In this respect, the chapter argues for a broader analytical lens with closer attention paid to access and societal impact.

FRUGAL AND REVERSE INNOVATION

This chapter explores the notions of frugal and reverse innovations, which have similar characteristics but also clear differences. These concepts are adopted as useful analytic lenses through which to view the case studies that will follow in later sections. 'Frugal innovation' is the term used for innovations intended for markets in emerging economies, typically designed with consideration for the contexts in these markets. This means that consideration is given to factors such as the need to keep costs low, and to concentrate on core functionalities and optimal performance (Weyrauch and Herstatt, 2017; Zeschky et al., 2014). Frugal innovation may take place outside of emerging economies but it is certainly directed at consumers in developing countries or indeed poorer consumers in developed countries. Previously, the term frugal innovation was used to describe a context in which there is a lack of resources for development and affordable prices for intended customers. In its current formulation, however, it is applied to a population's unsatisfied demands and to needs left unaddressed by established institutions (Bhatti and Ventresca, 2013). Frugal innovations thus also contribute to addressing social needs, such as the provision of healthcare, at more affordable prices (Rosca et al., 2017). Harris et al. (2020) found that the term 'frugal' took on added meanings in the course of the Covid-19 pandemic: they report that it was applied to the repurposing, reusing and rapid deployment of new technologies.

The concept of reverse innovation was theorised by Immelt et al. (2009). It offers different insights into product flows and associated innovations in a globalised world. Reverse innovation is 'any type of global innovation that, at some stage during the innovation process, is characterised by a reverse flow of innovation from a developing country to an advanced country, and that is eventually introduced to an advanced country's market' (Von Zedtwitz et al., 2015). While the term challenges the notion of high-income countries as best at innovating and the initiators of healthcare transformation, it is also thus a term that can seem paradoxical; on the one hand, it challenges the notion of high-income countries as being the only sources of innovation and healthcare transformation, but the term 'reverse' also perpetuates exactly this notion.

HEALTHCARE SYSTEMS AND HEALTH INNOVATION

A healthcare system may be seen as an innovation system in which performance depends on the quality of the relationships between the people and institutions within the system. A national health innovation system is a sectoral innovation system which comprises varied actors and associated expertise (Consoli and Mina, 2009). For that reason, the definition of a health innovation system is wide-ranging, and its outcomes include new drugs and devices as well as clinical services (Djellal and Gallouj, 2005; Pammolli et al., 2005).

The fields of innovation systems and global health policy merged in the mid-2000s following considerable emphasis on the role of science in advancing new drugs, vaccines and diagnostics in solving the world's health problems (Cassiolato and Soares, 2015). The ability to improve the health of individuals depends on much more than new discoveries or having the tools or the medications to diagnose or treat diseases. Noticeably, it also requires the healthcare system to have the ability to absorb and roll out new technologies through existing services with minimal disruption and maximum effect. Consoli and Mina (2008) highlight that in seeking to make a system effective for the provision of healthcare, it is necessary to incorporate a number of activities, skills and different types of technical and practical knowledge. All of these require effective mechanisms of coordination to achieve the overall goal of patient care (Consoli and Mina, 2008).

The concept of a health innovation system therefore includes broader aspects of institutions, standards and procedures within a national innovation system, particularly those that are connected to the provision of healthcare, including financing and research (Cassiolato and Soares, 2015). Specifically, the health innovation system involves actors that co-create value through their interconnections to achieve sustainable healthcare improvements through innovation and technology development. The degree of innovation in healthcare is highly dependent on a national health innovation system (Proksch et al., 2019).

All this means that in order to strengthen its healthcare system, South Africa must also strengthen its national health innovation system. There are some shared challenges between the two. The burden of diseases such as HIV/AIDS, TB and non-communicable diseases (such as cardiovascular diseases, diabetes, cancer and chronic respiratory diseases) is detrimental to society and perpetuates the socioeconomic marginalisation of mostly black people. As a result of its colonial and apartheid history, South Africa is reportedly the most unequal country in the world (World Bank, 2022) representing what is often referred to as a dual economy, where one economy has features of a relatively advanced capitalist economy and the other is under-developed and underfunded (Vollrath, 2009). This dichotomy is prominent in the country's healthcare system. Its private healthcare is known for its world-class facilities and care provision that is equal to that of many high-income countries. This coexists with a public healthcare system that supports 84 per cent of the population, which is acutely under-resourced, overloaded and fails to meet its undertaking for accessible quality healthcare (Mayosi et al., 2012; MISTRA, 2019). In South Africa, as globally, there is increasing emphasis on strengthening the healthcare system by supporting the 'building blocks' of health infrastructure, which includes technologies (MISTRA, 2019). There are however the same challenges of inequality: most of South Africa's population has very limited access to technology, as well as to quality healthcare.

THE MEDICAL DEVICE INDUSTRY IN SOUTH AFRICA

South Africa, with its emerging local medical devices manufacturing sector, provides an appropriate setting for research into medical device manufacturing firms as sources of frugal (and sometimes reverse) product innovation. Despite being an upper-middle-income country, South Africa shares similar institutional and structural challenges and pressures to balance economic growth and social development. Countries on the continent all face difficulties in taking innovations to market. This challenge is particularly marked in South Africa as it has world-class biomedical research. Nonetheless, the country has few companies that have successfully commercialised their products (Chakma et al., 2010; SAMRC, 2022). The sector is dominated by multinational corporations, represented by the South African Medical Device Industry Association, selling mainly imported products. Local medical device manufacturing is represented by Medical Device Manufacturers of South Africa.

The South African medical device manufacturing industry is active across a range of fields and device classes. A survey led by the South African Medical Research Council (SAMRC) revealed that South Africa has at least 136 medical device manufacturing companies with substantial diversity in sizes, turnovers, products and levels of R&D expenditure (SAMRC, 2022). Over half (53 per cent) of the survey respondents operate in the consumables field, followed by 27 per cent in the orthopaedics sector, and 14 per cent in hospital furniture; the remaining 21 per cent operate in assorted other fields. The industry produces and sells a variety of consumable medical device products ranging from medical devices for wound care to diagnostic test kits. The sector is concentrated in three provinces, with most medical device manufacturers being located in Gauteng (60), followed by the Western Cape (47) and KwaZulu-Natal (26). There has been a declining trend in company formation since 2004: more than half of the companies are older than 20 years and only seven new companies were founded in the period 2015 to 2019.

South Africa's medical devices manufacturing sector is one of the largest medical device sectors in the Middle East and Africa region. It was estimated at R21 billion in 2021 and is projected to grow to R29.6 billion by 2025 (Fitch Solutions, 2021). However, this makes up only 0.3 per cent of the global market for medical devices. Government is the major purchaser of healthcare equipment and supplies in South Africa for the public healthcare sector which comprises 7,901 facilities with 85,362 registered beds (Who Owns Whom, 2019).

CASE STUDIES: SOUTH AFRICAN MEDICAL DEVICES

Although frugal innovations in healthcare have been studied (Arshad et al., 2018), more research needs to be conducted on the commercialisation and successful diffusion of frugal innovations through public healthcare, locally and abroad. Furthermore, it is crucial to expand the discussion on the contribution of medical innovation to South Africa's development goals in the area of health. This section discusses three case studies of firms in South Africa that have successfully designed and introduced medical device innovations into the market. Specifically, the section focuses on medical devices from these three firms to provide insight into the conditions that lead to the development of medical innovations in South Africa; the kinds of medical devices that are successfully commercialised; and the support required for the medical devices to thrive, and, in some cases be adopted, abroad.

Case Study 1: The Sinapi chest drain
Background and context: The problem of gun violence in South Africa is among the most acute in the world, with gun-related deaths estimated at

20 per day (Masters et al., 2021). Penetrating chest trauma (injuries such as gunshot and stab wounds) is one of the leading causes of admission to South African emergency departments (Keegan, 2005; Masters et al., 2021). This results in excessive pressure on trauma facilities with associated cost implications. It is thus valuable to have these traumas effectively and efficiently managed to ensure short hospital stays and minimal complications. For years, cases of pneumo-/haemothorax[1] (the condition of having air (pneumothorax) or blood (haemothorax) in the chest cavity) have been treated using standard underwater bottle drainage. An underwater seal chest drainage system is used to re-establish correct air pressure to the lungs, re-inflate a collapsed lung as well and remove blood and other fluids (Zisis et al., 2015). The Sinapi chest drain was launched by Sinapi Biomedical to provide a more cost-effective treatment than with existing chest drainage systems (Cooper and Hardcastle, 2006).

The firm: Sinapi Biomedical is a Stellenbosch-based medical device firm that focuses on providing the most affordable possible products (Devex, 2023). It is owned and managed by a mechanical engineer with diverse industrial experience and has been fully operational since 2006 (Sinapi, 2020). The firm has advanced engineering and manufacturing capabilities, with over 150 people in its employ and it frequently collaborates with academic institutions, either the relevant Engineering Department or the Medical School at Stellenbosch University (Sinapi, 2020; Devex, 2023). Since its establishment, Sinapi has successfully commercialised several affordable products, such as its chest drain, aimed at improving access to healthcare in South Africa and other developing countries (Sinapi, 2020; Devex, 2023).

Medical device: The Sinapi chest drain is an external medical device made of plastic that incorporates a fluid reservoir, a one-way valve and an air-leak detection system (Cooper and Hardcastle, 2006). It is connected to a thoracic intrapleural catheter to allow fluid and air to drain from the thoracic cavity. The Sinapi chest drain incorporates a mechanical (Scheffler) valve, which allows for faster evacuation

---

1 A haemothorax, pneumothorax, or the combination of both (haemopneumothorax) can occur as a result of a wound to the chest, such as from a bullet, stabbing, or broken rib.

of liquids and air from the chest, makes patient management easier and supports early patient mobility (Cooper and Hardcastle, 2006). The advantages of a Sinapi drain over a standard underwater bottle drainage include: a) a smaller, lighter device, which facilitates greater patient mobility and comfort; b) a 'closed system' fluid drainage that protects nursing staff from exposure to body fluids; and c) fast, easy attachment to any size chest catheter without the need to add water (Cooper and Hardcastle, 2006).

Frugality: The Sinapi chest drain was developed to provide a more affordable way to manage trauma injuries. The technology costs less than R300 (approximately US$15 at time of writing) (Hardcastle, 2021); only one Sinapi chest drain is required for a patient's entire hospital stay because it can be emptied rather than be replaced (Sinapi, 2022); removing the need for bottle changes also reduces sterilisation costs, In addition, a clinical trial showed that the Sinapi chest drain has an average drainage time of 61.04 hours compared to 81.47 hours with a standard underwater seal (Hardcastle, 2006). This means a patient's hospital stay is reduced, resulting in further cost savings. The Sinapi chest drain can thus be considered a frugal innovation.

Reverse innovation: The Sinapi chest drain carries the CE marking, which indicates that a product has been deemed to meet European Union (EU) safety, health and environmental protection requirements. It is required for products marketed in the EU manufactured anywhere in the world, and it thus facilitates access to the European market and free movement throughout the European Single Market (BSI, 2023). The Sinapi chest drain is currently exported to Europe.

Case Study 2: The Medical Diagnostech Covid-19 Rapid Screen Test

Background and context: The Covid-19 pandemic exposed the deficiencies in medical device manufacturing supply chains and distribution models, which resulted in shortages of testing reagents, diagnostic test kits, personal protective equipment and respiratory devices. The supply of Covid-19 diagnostics became a concern, particularly for low- and middle-income countries. In order to address this shortage in South Africa, the SAMRC partnered with the South

African government, academia and business to provide support for the development and scaling up of local reagents and point-of-care tests for SARS-CoV-2. This was to ensure rapid and robust options for South Africa with locally produced diagnostics and reduced dependence on international provisions. Medical Diagnostech was one of the enterprises to receive funding to develop and supply antigen-based test kits for the management of Covid-19 in South Africa.

The firm: Medical Diagnostech (Pty) Ltd was established in 2010 as a developer and manufacturer of lateral flow rapid diagnostic test kits. The firm manufactures rapid diagnostic test kits using its trade-secret methodology for increased sensitivity and early detection. Lateral flow tests are manufactured under ISO 13485[2] accreditation and include tests for alcohol consumption, drugs of abuse, HIV, malaria, pregnancy, fertility/ovulation and Covid-19. Medical Diagnostech also offers manufacturing and development services for innovative lateral flow components and test kits, as well as other medical-related products including sanitisers and surgical scrubs. The firm has an in-house laboratory with a three-member R&D team and makes use of student interns from the University of the Western Cape (Chakravarty, 2022).

Medical device: Medical Diagnostech's rapid antigen test, the SARS-CoV-2 Antigen Device, is a rapid visual immunoassay for the qualitative detection of the Covid-19 nucleocapsid protein (N-protein) antigen from nasopharyngeal swabs (HealthPulse, 2022). It is intended for professional use to diagnose acute infection and reveal the patient's current infection status. The Medical Diagnostech rapid antigen test was approved by South African Health Products Regulatory Authority (SAHPRA) in December 2021 (SAMRC, 2022). Since then, Medical Diagnostech has partnered with Audere, a digital health non-profit organisation, which produces tech-based solutions to delivering health equity in underserved communities worldwide (Audere, 2022). This partnership has resulted in the launch of a self-test version, in combination with the mobile phone application, HealthPulse TestNow: South Africa's first Covid-19 antigen self-test (SAMRC, 2023). The

---

2 ISO 13485 is the medical industry's optimal medical device standard, which ensures that all medical devices meet the proper regulatory compliance laws and customer needs.

application provides detailed instructions on how to perform the self-test and assists in interpreting the results through image capture of the rapid test device (SAMRC, 2023).

Frugality: Medical Diagnostech develops test kits that are cheaper than alternative ones. The firm focuses on the market for low-income groups, particularly in the African market, thus promoting Africa's self-sufficiency (HealthPulse, 2022). The manufacturing facility is ISO 13485 certified, complete with some equipment designed and fabricated locally to reduce costs (Chakravarty, 2022).

Reverse innovation: Medical Diagnostech targeted the South African market for its rapid antigen test. The company seemingly has no intention of marketing it outside the country; thus there is no reverse innovation achieved.

Case Study 3: The Lodox Scanner

Background and context: The diamond company De Beers faced a substantial loss of profits with some of its miners smuggling diamonds in the mid-1980s and '90s. The company's relatively advanced engineering team was asked to develop a whole-body scanner that would be able to detect even the smallest diamonds in or attached to human bodies. An X-ray body scanner was developed and used henceforth in this industry. Some of the engineers however saw potential for this innovation in the medical field too and formed a separate company to further develop this scanner.

The firm: Lodox Systems (Pty) Ltd was formed in 2002 as a result. The state-owned Industrial Development Corporation (IDC) of South Africa is the major shareholder of Lodox Systems and funds ongoing research, development and product improvements.

Medical device: Lodox developed the initial X-ray body scan further to enable a whole-body scan to be carried out at high speed (13 seconds), using only low radiation. The effectiveness and high speed of Lodox imaging significantly reduces the treatment time of patients with major injuries, allowing for imaging of a large number of patients in a very short time. The machine is used in trauma units and forensic pathology laboratories.

Frugality: The Lodox scanner was not regarded by its developers as a frugal innovation. Rather it was recognised as an advanced technology with universal benefits. However, the Lodox scanner has some frugal aspects as described below, including that it offers a better solution than a conventional, imported X-ray scanner but at a notably lower cost (Chakravarty, 2022). Research by Rao (2013) shows that, as with the Lodox scanner, in some cases frugal innovations can be created with high technology. In an analysis by Chakravarty (2022), it was found that the costs of buying and owning the Lodox scanner are significantly lower than for conventional X-ray scanners. The reduced purchasing price is a result of lower R&D costs in comparison to high-income countries. Chen et al. (2010) found that the cost of a single-image Lodox/Statscan study is lower than the sum of multiple X-ray studies. Furthermore, the scanner can be operated by health workers with minimal training, thus there is no need for a radiologist. Lastly, the Lodox scanner requires less infrastructure (radiation proofing) and is locally manufactured, repaired and maintained, further adding to its frugal characteristics.

Reverse innovation: Lodox Systems (Pty) Ltd has various partner firms around the globe selling its scanner and a full subsidiary in Ohio, USA. Lodox installations for use in trauma units and forensic pathology laboratories can be found around the globe (North America, South America, Europe, Asia and the Middle East). In addition, the firm has obtained regulatory approval for the scanner in other countries. The Lodox scanner is thus a successful reverse innovation.

THE DETERMINANTS OF SUCCESS AND SOCIETAL RELEVANCE FOR MEDICAL DEVICES

Appropriate innovation

The three case studies show that more often than not, an important driver of successful innovation is being developed within context, meaning that there was a specific need for it in that particular market. This ensures that successful innovations are often both usable and desirable in the context for which they are designed. For example, as previously mentioned, trauma injuries are common in South Africa and thus medical innovations that assist in managing trauma injuries are critical and in demand. The value of the Sinapi chest drain and the Lodox scanner in addressing the burden on hospitals caused by gunshot and knife wounds made their success probable. Similarly, Medical Diagnostech's rapid antigen tests were produced at a time of very high demand during the pandemic.

Relevance to context does not only make for commercial success: it can also mean that an innovation has social benefits. For example, widespread trauma injuries are often directly linked to the socioeconomic conditions of a population group. Innovations developed to alleviate such adverse socioeconomic conditions have been referred to as public interest technologies. Emulating the framework of public interest law, public interest technology aims to ensure technology is 'designed, deployed, and regulated in a way that protects and improves the lives of people, centring values of equity, inclusion, and accountability where the public interest is at stake' (Ford Foundation, 2023).

All three case studies can be considered public interest technologies. The Sinapi chest drain addresses a major problem in the South African healthcare system. So too does the Lodox scanner, even though it was initially designed to detect stolen diamonds in mines. The Medical Diagnostech rapid antigen test provided an affordable solution for South Africa at a time when there was a desperate need for urgent health responses to the pandemic.

Adoption into a healthcare system

As described previously, a country's health system is part of its broader national innovation system. However, an NIS that is functioning optimally is not enough to guarantee the adoption of a new medical technology. Rather, a country's health system has to be receptive to the technology, and have the resources for it. Crucial to this process is evidence of a technology's effectiveness, lower cost and superiority in a clinical setting in comparison to available products. Government provision of access to patients and/or clinical facilities to develop and test the prototypes offers opportunities to develop such evidence, and thus supports the technologies' introduction into the healthcare system. In the three case studies, the South African government supported the uptake of the medical devices into the healthcare system by providing access to public research facilities and allowing for testing in public research facilities and government hospitals. For example, Groote Schuur Hospital, a public academic hospital, participated in the prototype testing and clinical trials of the Lodox scanner. Following an animal trial undertaken at Stellenbosch University in 2002, which found the Sinapi chest drain to be 100 per cent effective, samples of the chest drain were used at Tygerberg Hospital, a government hospital. Adoption of Medical Diagnostech's rapid antigen tests was ensured from the start: government recognised the extent of the need for such a test even before development was complete.

Partnerships and funding

Partnerships were key to the success of all three medical devices discussed. The University of Cape Town had a significant role in the successful development of the Lodox scanner as it collaborated with De Beers in the early phases of development when the diamond company was seeking to detect stolen diamonds. Once the value of the Lodox scanner had been proven, the Industrial Development Corporation (IDC) came on board in 2010 as a key shareholder and funder. The IDC is fully owned by the South African government and aligned with the national policy direction as set out in the NDP. The institution provided the required financial means to develop the scanners for both local and overseas markets. Moreover, government hospitals provided the local market for the scanner, with Groote Schuur Hospital testing the first prototype early on (Lodox, 2023).

For the Medical Diagnostech rapid antigen test, the South African Medical Research Council (SAMRC) – a government entity mandated to improve the health of people in South Africa through research, innovation, development and technology transfer – provided grants to assist the firm with completing the development of its testing kit (SAMRC, 2022). The grant built on existing development and the firm utilised its already-operating infrastructure, capacity and expertise to develop the Covid-19 testing kit. A collaboration that included Business 4 South Africa, the IDC and the Department of Trade, Industry and Competition (DTIC) was established to plan for downstream scale-up and manufacturing of the testing kit (SAMRC, 2022). The firm also has an arrangement with the University of the Western Cape that allows it to recruit student interns from the university.

Sinapi receives support from the Technology Innovation Agency (TIA), a national public entity, and DTIC (Sinapi, 2023). The firm has also received some grants from international donors. However, its main sources of funds are commercial banks (Chakravarty, 2022). Sinapi has various global health partnerships and associations including one with the global health non-profit PATH (Programme for Appropriate Technologies in Health) and Grand Challenges Canada, a Canadian non-profit organisation that funds solutions to critical health and development challenges in low- and middle-income countries. Sinapi has also partnered with Stellenbosch University and Northwestern University in Illinois, USA.

In all three case studies, the relevant firms had strong partners with financial backing, as well as collaborations with local universities and hospitals. The linkages formed by these firms constitute part of a health innovation system that worked to ensure the success of their innovations. In the Lodox case, the IDC provided substantial financial backing albeit not in the early R&D phases. The rapid antigen testing kit also received financial support from government entities when Medical Diagnostech required the funds to complete development.

Firms that produce successful technology-intensive innovations often have sizable government support and strong academic connections. They are able to tap into these connections and well-established partnerships to find support for their innovations. It has thus been argued that government's role should include resource mobilisation and establishment of the conditions for widespread market commercialisation (Cozzens, 2012; Mazzucato, 2011). A lack of funding and connections has been the major downfall of many innovations.

However, in a study on medical technology firms in South Africa (Chakravarty, 2022), it was found that funds from government were not a substantial component of R&D support. Rather, support came in the form of product testing in clinical trials in academic hospitals or incubation facilities. Public research facilities and hospitals have been a source of support and an avenue for market creation. However, many firms are unable to make it to the point at which they can receive such support: their innovations do not make it past the R&D stages due to a lack of funding. Minimal or no support in the initial stages therefore needs to be addressed, although government's involvement in taking the technologies to the commercialisation stage can be lauded.

Firm-level strategy

As much as the environment in which firms innovate is important, firms' strategies also play an important role in the success of their innovations. This is evident from the successful reverse innovations and the medical technologies discussed in this chapter. The case studies reveal that reverse innovation was intrinsic to the firms' strategies from early on. These firms have a clear strategy for the journey they desire for their medical technology innovations, from the types of partnerships they establish to the types of accreditation they pursue. Sinapi acquires the CE marking for all its technologies, which allows the firm to export to Europe. Furthermore, the company has long-term associations with international organisations such as PATH. This lays the groundwork for the firm's innovations to gain access to the international market. Similarly, Lodox has acquired FDA approval and other international accreditations. In addition, Lodox has established international partnerships and has various partner firms selling its scanner around the globe, including a full subsidiary in the USA.

In contrast, Medical Diagnostech targets the South African market, particularly the low-income groups not catered for by large companies. Seemingly, there is no immediate desire to export its testing kits and the technology will thus be an unlikely candidate for reverse innovation.

CONCLUSION

It is evident from the case studies in this chapter that medical technologies developed within the country for which they are initially intended – in this case, South Africa – solve local challenges. In-depth knowledge of a local ecosystem assists in the development of innovations within the right context. Furthermore, as has been seen with the innovations reviewed, frugal innovations have a crucial role to play in healthcare. This is particularly the case in low- and middle-income countries but high-income countries also find value in such innovations and often adopt them in their countries.

An encouraging lesson to be drawn from the case studies in this chapter is that there is a solid foundation for a medical devices industry in South Africa, built by private firms working in collaboration with universities and other STI institutions to produce successful local innovations. These firms have both simple and complex technology capabilities and produce devices appropriate for local and sometimes export markets. The South African healthcare system, as fragmented as it is, plays an important role in the development and uptake of these medical devices.

This means that a clear avenue to boosting local innovation would be strengthening South Africa's healthcare system, to allow it to have more capacity for facilitation and adoption. As evident in the case studies, the firms responsible for successful medical innovation had access to government research facilities for prototyping and testing medical devices in a clinical environment. A strong recommendation therefore is that government takes note of the crucial role that such access plays, and takes steps to further provide it. Furthermore, testing medical devices in a clinical setting has another benefit for local innovation. Staff and patients are provided the opportunity to contribute to an ongoing culture of innovation in the healthcare system.

Another recommendation to emerge from these case studies is that government needs to come on board early in the R&D stages of the innovation process to ensure success. As discussed, it did not do so in the case of the Lodox scanner and it was evident that the company was only able to go on to successful commercialisation as it had the means to develop a prototype without government support. Existing funding instruments need to play a bigger role in the R&D stages of innovation and in continuing investment in the commercialisation of new technologies.

The importance of academia in this entire system of innovation has also been evident. A further recommendation then is that firms take the steps necessary to leverage the knowledge contained in these institutions, including establishing academic partnerships. These connections can be an important step in converting ideas into medical products and solutions that meet customers' needs.

In general, a case can be made for government's role to include the mobilisation of resources, in academia and elsewhere, and the facilitation of the conditions for market commercialisation. Government cannot play such a role without cohesive legislative and policy frameworks to support local innovation, manufacturing and skills development. The right policies can facilitate greater cooperation and collaboration between stakeholders, and the innovation culture necessary for South Africa to build on its successes in this sector.

REFERENCES

Arshad, H., Radic, M. and Radić, D. 2018. 'Patterns of frugal innovation in healthcare'. *Technology Innovation Management Review*, 8, 28–37.

Audere. 2022. https://www.auderenow.org/, accessed 28 June 2023.

Bhatti, Y. and Ventresca, M. 2013. 'How Can 'Frugal Innovation' Be Conceptualized?'. Said Business School Working Paper Series, University of Oxford.

BSI Group. 2023. 'CE Marking: Gain Market Access in Europe'. BSI, https://www.bsigroup.com/en-ZA/Our-services/Product-certification/ce-mark/, accessed 29 May 2023.

Cassiolato, J.E. and Soares, M.C.C. 2015. 'Innovation systems, development and health: An introduction', in *Health Innovation Systems, Equity and Development*. Rio de Janeiro: E-papers Serviços Editoriais.

Chakma, J., Masum, H. and Singer, P.A. 2010. 'Can incubators work in Africa? Acorn Technologies and the entrepreneur-centric model'. *BMC International Health and Human Rights*, 10, S7, https://bmcinthealthhumrights.biomedcentral.com/articles/10.1186/1472-698X-10-S1-S7#citeas, accessed 15 November 2022.

Chakravarty, S. 2022. 'Resource-constrained innovation in a technology-intensive sector: Frugal medical devices from manufacturing firms in South Africa'. *Technovation*, 112, 102397.

Chandan, B.V., Balamuralidhara, V., Gowrav, M.P. and Motupalli, V. 2021. 'Applications of medical devices in healthcare industry'. *Journal of Evolution of Medical and Dental Sciences*, 10 (38), 3419.

Chen, R.J., Fu, C.Y., Wu, S.C., Wang, Y.C., Chung, P.K., et al. 2010. 'Diagnostic accuracy, biohazard safety, and cost effectiveness-the Lodox/Statscan provides a beneficial alternative for the primary evaluation of patients with multiple injuries'. *The Journal of Trauma*, 69(4): 826–30.

Consoli, D. and, Mina, A. 2009. 'An evolutionary perspective on health innovation systems'. *Journal of Evolutionary Economics*, 19(2), 297–319.

Cooper, C. and Hardcastle, T. 2006. 'Xpand chest drain: Assessing equivalence to current standard therapy – a randomised controlled trial'. *South African Journal of Science*, 44, 4.

Cozzens, S. 2012. 'The distinctive dynamics of nanotechnology in developing nations', in Aydogan-Duda, N. (ed). *Making It to the Forefront: Innovation, Technology, and Knowledge Management.* New York: Springer, pp. 125–138.

Devex, 2023. 'Sinapi Biomedical'. Devex, https://www.devex.com/organizations/sinapi-biomedical-111868, accessed 29 May 2023.

Djellal, F. and Gallouj, F. 2005. 'Mapping innovation dynamics in hospitals'. *Research Policy*, 34, 817–835.

Fitch Solutions. 2021. 'South Africa Medical Devices Report Q3 2021'. Fitch Solutions Group Limited, London.

Ford Foundation, 2023. 'Public interest technology and its origins'. Ford Foundation, https://www.fordfoundation.org/work/challenging-inequality/technology-and-society/public-interest-technology-and-its-origins/#:~:text=Public%20interest%20technology%20(PIT)%20is,should%20be%20created%20at%20all, accessed 29 May 2023..

Gadelha, C. 2010. 'The health economic complex in Brazil: Modes of coordination and implications for NIS in the health area', 8th Globelics International Conference, Kuala Lampur, Malaysia.

Govindarajan and Ramamurti, 2011. *Reverse Innovation in Health Care: How to Make Value-Based Delivery Work*. Harvard Business Publishing: Massachusetts, United States.

Harris, M., Bhatti, Y., Buckley, J. and Sharma, D., 2020. 'Fast and frugal innovations in response to the COVID-19 pandemic'. *Nature Medicine* 26(6), 814–817.

HealthPulse, 2022. 'Audere and South Africa-based Medical Diagnostech partner to bring Africa's first home-grown COVID-19 antigen test to market with digital companion App'. *HealthPulse*, https://www.healthpulsenow.org/news-medical-diagnostech-partner, accessed 28 June 2023.

Hossain, M. 2021. 'Frugal innovation and sustainable business models'. *Technology in Society*, 64, 101508.

Immelt, J.R., Govindarajan, V. and Trimble, C. 2009. 'How GE is disrupting itself'. *Harvard Business Review*, 87(10), 56–65.

Kale, D. and Wield, D. 2019. 'In search of the missing hand of "collaborative action": Evidence from the Indian medical device industry'. *Innovation and Development*, 9(1), 1–23.

Keegan, M. 2005. *The Proliferation of Firearms in South Africa, 1994–2004.*

Johannesburg: Gun Free South Africa.

Lodox, 2023. Lodox, https://lodox.com/about/, accessed 3 July 2022.

Maharaj, I and Sunjka, B.P. 2019. 'A strategic framework for start-up medical device manufacturers in South Africa'. *South African Journal of Industrial Engineering*, 30(3), 63–76.

Malodia, S., Gupta, S. and Jaiswal, A. K. 2020. 'Reverse innovation: A conceptual framework'. *Journal of the Academy of Marketing Science*, 48, 1009–1029.

Mapungubwe Institute for Strategic Reflection (MISTRA). 2019. *Epidemics and the Health of African Nations*, Mazibuko, Z. (ed.). Johannesburg: MISTRA.

Marks, I.H, Thomas, H., Bakhet, M. and Fitzgerald, E. 2019. 'Medical equipment donation in low-resource settings: A review of the literature and guidelines for surgery and anaesthesia in low-income and middle-income countries'. *BMJ Global Health*, 4(5): e001785.

Masters, J., Laubscher, M., Graham, S., Marais, L., Ferreira, N., Held, M. et al. 2021. 'The gunshot-related injuries in trauma (GRIT) study: A profile of patients affected by gunshot-related orthopaedic injuries across South Africa'. *South African Medical Journal*, 111(7), 655–660.

Mayosi, B.M., Lawn, J.E., Van Niekerk, A., Bradshaw, D., Abdool Karim, S.S., Coovadia, H.M. et al. 2012. 'Health in South Africa: Changes and challenges since 2009'. *Lancet*, 8, 380(9858), 2029–2043.

Mazzucato, M. 2011. 'The entrepreneurial state'. *Soundings*, 49(49), 131–142.

Medical Diagnostech: https://medi-tech.co.za/.

National Planning Commission (NPC). 2013. 'National Development Plan Vision 2030', https://www.gov.za/issues/national-development-plan-2030, accessed 9 March 2023.

Pammolli, F., Riccaboni, M., Oglialoro, C., Magazzini, L., Salerno, N. and Baio, G. 2005. *Medical Devices Competitiveness and Impact on Public Health Expenditure*. Entreprise Directorate-General, European Commission, Bruxelles.

Proksch, D., Busch-Casler, J., Haberstroh, M.M. and Pinkwart, A. 2019. 'National health innovation systems: Clustering the OECD countries by innovative output in healthcare using a multi-indicator approach'. *Research Policy*, 48, 169–179.

Rao, B.C., 2013. 'How disruptive is frugal?'. *Technology in Society*, 35(1), 65–73.

Rosca, E., Arnold, M. and Bendul, J.C. 2017. 'Business models for sustainable innovation: An empirical analysis of frugal products and services'. *Journal of Cleaner Production,* 162, 133–145.

Simula, H., Hossain, M. and Halme, M. 2015. 'Frugal and reverse innovations – Quo Vadis?'. *Current Science,* 109(9), 1567–1572.

Sinapi, 2020. Sinapi, https://sinapibiomedical.com/#about, accessed 13 September 2022.

South African Medical Research Council (SAMRC). 2022. 'The

Medical Devices Landscape in South Africa'. SAMRC, https://www.samrc.ac.za/sites/default/files/attachments/2023-03/SAMRCMedicalDeviceLandscapeReport-2022.pdf, accessed 17 March 2023.

South African Medical Research Council (SAMRC). 2023. 'South Africa's first Covid-19 antigen self-test launched'. SAMRC, https://www.samrc.ac.za/press-releases/south-africas-first-covid-19-antigen-self-test-launched, accessed 28 June 2023.

Vollrath, D. 2009. 'The dual economy in long-run development.' *Journal of Population Economics*, 14(4), 287–312.

Von Zedtwitz, M., Corsi, S., Søberg, P.V. and Frega, R. 2015. 'A typology of reverse innovation'. *Journal of Product Innovation Management*, 32(1), 12–28.

Weyrauch, T. and Herstatt, C. 2016. 'What is frugal innovation? Three defining criteria'. *Journal of Frugal Innovation*, 2(1), 1–17.

Who Owns Whom. 2019. *The Supply and Manufacture of Medical and Surgical Equipment and Orthopaedic Appliances*. Gqeberha, South Africa: Who Owns Whom.

World Bank, 2022. 'New World Bank Report Assesses Sources of Inequality in Five Countries in Southern Africa', World Bank, https://www.worldbank.org/en/news/press-release/2022/03/09/new-world-bank-report-assesses-sources-of-inequality-in-five-countries-in-southern-africa#:~:text=South%20Africa%2C%20the%20largest%20country,World%20Bank's%20global%20poverty%20database, accessed 24 February 2023.

World Health Organization (WHO). 2011. 'Core medical equipment'. WHO, https://www.who.int/publications/i/item/WHO-HSS-EHT-DIM-11.03, accessed 23 May 2023.

World Health Organization (WHO). 2012. *Local Production and Technology Transfer to Increase Access to Medical Devices. Addressing the Barriers and Challenges in Low- and Middle-Income Countries*. Geneva: World Health Organization.

World Health Organization (WHO). 2016. 'Towards improving access to medical devices through local production: Phase II Report of a case study in four sub-Saharan countries'. WHO, https://iris.who.int/bitstream/handle/10665/206545/9789241510141_eng.pdf?sequence=1, accessed 8 May 2023.

Zeschky, M.B., Winterhalter, S. and Gassmann, O. 2014. 'From cost to frugal and reverse innovation: Mapping the field and implications for global competitiveness'. *Research Technology Management*, 57(4), 20–27.

Zisis, C., Tsirgogianni, K., Lazaridis, G., Lampaki, S., Baka, S., Mpoukovinas, I. et al. 2015. 'Chest drainage systems in use'. *Annals of Translational Medicine*, 3, 43.

SIX

Life and death in the national system of innovation (NSI): The role of public sector innovation

GECI KARURI-SEBINA, MJUMO MZYECE, PIERRE
SCHOONRAAD AND NSIZWA DLAMINI

INTRODUCTION

The importance of the public sector in and for innovation has received increasing focus and attention in recent years (OECD, 2015, 2017). This includes the role of governments in shaping innovation systems, creating conditions for innovation and being innovative themselves (Arundel et al., 2019; Mazzucato et al., 2021). However, there have also been massive challenges and criticisms levelled at the role of the state in public sector innovation (PSI). The critiques levelled range from overly bureaucratic operations to centralisation, lack of transparency, corruption, inadequate skills and professionalism and unconducive institutional arrangements (CPSI, 2021).

In this chapter, the authors explore a series of questions in relation to public sector innovations (PSI) in South Africa. Firstly, the chapter contends with the stereotypical view that innovation is being stifled by, or has been dying at, the hands of the state. This question requires taking a look at innovation as enabled and/or inhibited by the state, and at the public sector as an innovator itself, i.e., innovating within the service. Secondly and linked to the first question is, is the prevailing national system of innovation (NSI) conception and configuration put in place by the state supportive of public sector innovation? Lastly, if indeed the state has not been innovative or conducive to innovation, what has driven PSI then, and why?

The authors consider prevailing paradigms and the innovation policies and strategies that have been influencing innovation practices and performance. Local case studies are then used to help elucidate lessons from practical experiences. The chapter also looks to international literature to determine whether there are similarities or lessons to be found elsewhere. This pursuit raises epistemological and methodological challenges, which require consideration of what an appropriate analytical framework for PSI might be. It also raises questions about whether and how case studies of public sector innovation failures (and not only 'best practices') could be used to develop useful insights for learning and innovation in the public sector.

Ultimately, the paper seeks to determine what changes or factors for success in innovation policy (Schot and Kanger, 2018) might shift the public sector towards better enabling effective innovation in South Africa.

METHODOLOGY

The research was approached as part of a qualitative study. The intention was to enable the researchers to draw on their own valuable knowledge and experiences, as they are embedded in public institutions and/or affiliated to academia. Two of the authors are currently public sector officials, and two are former civil servants currently working in academia. The qualitative approach also allowed the researchers to construct and re-construct the scope and findings of the research study to illustrate the various determinants and concepts under analysis without distorting or reducing their meaning (Rahman, 2017).

First, existing theories and perspectives in the literature about public sector innovation were reviewed: this literature includes academic and so-called 'grey literature'.[1] The literature relating to South Africa's NSI pursuit is also considered. The concepts derived are then used to construct an analytical framework that can be used heuristically to interrogate the efficacy of public sector innovation. Next, a set of purposively selected PSI case studies are presented and analysed. These were selected to represent a top-down perspective (large-scale government or corporate-driven innovations, which tend to be most frequently referenced in popular discourse about PSI failures), plus bottom-up innovations (community-driven solutions, an area in which there is great emerging potential). Although the case studies selected are not entirely representative or generalisable, they were chosen to give some dimension to the exploratory analysis. Finally, findings are discussed in relation to the research questions.

INNOVATION, INNOVATION SYSTEMS AND THE PUBLIC SECTOR

Historically, a national system of innovation is one of three major framings for science, technology and innovation (STI) policy, alongside innovation for growth, and – more recently – transformative change (Schot and Steinmueller, 2018). The innovation for growth framing was articulated and implemented in industrialised countries in the aftermath of the Second World War with significant investments in research and development (R&D) to drive long-term economic recovery and growth. The national systems of innovation framing arose from the 1980s onwards as scholars began to question the linear innovation model underpinning the innovation for growth framing. Although the role of government is cardinal to the national systems of innovation framing – for instance in the quadruple helix model, which focuses on the interaction of government, industry, university and civic innovation activities and outcomes – innovation in the public

---

1   Grey literature is a term used for information produced outside of commercial publishing and distribution channels. It can include papers and publications from government, business, industry and academia.

sector per se is not explicitly addressed.

Most recently, emerging in the 2010s, the 'transformative change' framing has called for transformation through applying innovation to contemporary environmental and societal challenges such as climate change, inequality, poverty and pollution, and directing innovation towards systemic solutions such as the United Nations' Sustainable Development Goals (SDGs) initiative (Ghazinoory et al., 2020; Lundvall, 2022:12). Schot and Steinmueller (2018: 1565) argue that the transformative change framing is complementary to the two earlier framings, but that it should be prioritised because it addresses several key shortcomings in the earlier framings and integrates multiple actors in holistic ways. For example, civil society and citizens are seen as playing crucial innovation roles in the transformative change framing, not just one of providing demand for firm-level innovation. Furthermore, under this framing public policy can be translated into transformative public missions. As such, the frame can be linked to the mission-oriented innovation policy paradigm (Mazzucato, 2018) in terms of government planning and implementation.

Lundvall et al. (2009: 6) define a national system of innovation (NSI) – although they use the alternative, equivalent term 'national innovation system (NIS)' – as:

> ... an open, evolving and complex system that encompasses relationships within and between organisations, institutions and socio-economic structures which determine the rate and direction of innovation and competence-building emanating from processes of science-based and experience-based learning.

This definition includes both the narrow STI and the broad DUI (doing, using and interacting) conceptualisations of innovation systems (Lundvall et al., 2009: 2–7). In the South African context, the NSI is firmly aligned with the narrow definition of innovation systems and focuses largely on science, engineering and technology (SET). This is despite the fact that the Department of Science and Technology (DST) White Paper on Science, Technology and Innovation, the key policy document on South Africa's NSI, explicitly states that it aims to 'adopt a broader conceptualisation of innovation beyond R&D' (DST, 2019: 33). Among its other policy intents, the White Paper on STI also aims to 'strengthen government's role as an enabler for innovation' by several means: it aims 'to address market failures, taking the lead in making high-risk investments' and says that 'to help entrench a culture of innovation in government, the DST will work with the Centre for Public Service Innovation (CPSI) and other relevant national, provincial and local agencies' (DST, 2019: 41–42). Importantly, although the White Paper on STI sets the medium- to long-term policy direction for South Africa's NSI, it is not an implementation plan. 'Rather, the implementation of the White Paper will be directed through successive decadal plans. To ensure policy coherence and maximum responsiveness to the needs of society, these decadal plans will be developed in partnership with the relevant NSI actors' (DST, 2019: 12).

ROLES OF THE PUBLIC SECTOR IN THE INNOVATION SYSTEM

Differences between the public and private sectors
To understand the role of the public sector in innovation, it is useful to step back and discern the key differences between the public sector and the private sector. Because the boundary between the public and private sectors is permeable and changes with time and circumstances (Flynn and Asquer, 2017: 1–2), it is extremely difficult, if not impossible, to distinguish clearly and unambiguously between the two sectors. Nevertheless, four general distinctions can be made between the public and private sectors even though none of them are absolute (Flynn and Asquer, 2017: 4–5):
1. public goods and services vs. private goods and services (for example, public goods and services generally produce positive externalities and are non-excludable);
2. the public sector is mainly financed by taxation rather than direct payments by individual customers;
3. who employs the service providers and who owns the facilities (typically public services are provided by public employees using publicly owned assets); and

4. most importantly, whether the underlying motivation for serving and satisfying customers is the value of public service rather than profit.

Generally speaking, there are two types of innovations (Gault, 2020), both of which the public sector is engaged in: *product innovations* involving new or improved goods and services, and *process innovations* involving new or improved organisational processes. Public sector innovation is the implementation of new ideas, methods or practices to create new or improved public goods, services and processes (CPSI, 2021). For public goods and services, government (national, provincial and municipal) and government departments and agencies are the key providers and citizens are the key beneficiaries. On the other hand, public sector process innovation involves internally facing innovations such as e-administration, e-recruitment and green buildings. Furthermore, a distinction is drawn between such public sector innovation and innovation in which other kinds of non-private organisations are the main actors, science councils, higher education institutions, non-governmental organisations and so forth.

The Copenhagen Manual (Innovation Barometer, 2021: 51) highlights how public-sector innovation differs from private-sector innovation in terms of its predominant logic (political vs. market); purpose (public good vs. competitive advantage); general attitude towards copying (free copying vs. intellectual property rights); predominant collaboration mode (horizontal vs. vertical); and relative risk propensity and appetite (low vs. high).

THE ROLE OF THE PUBLIC SECTOR AS AN INNOVATION ENABLER

Governments have long played roles in fostering private sector innovation through (Boghani and Jonash, 1993):

1. procurement;
2. reducing the technical, commercial and financial risks of innovation;
3. facilitating innovation by collaborating on advanced research and development (R&D) and product development; and

4. using standards and regulations to stimulate innovation.

In South Africa, the public sector's involvement in these four roles has been largely uncoordinated, and the use of procurement to foster innovation has been under-utilised. There are however occasional cases where this has not been the case: a contemporary example of the South African government successfully enabling innovation is the launch of the Africa Medical Supplies Platform (AMSP). This is a digital marketplace to enable the supply of Covid-19-related critical medical equipment to African Union (AU) member states (Presidency, 2020).

THE ROLE OF THE PUBLIC SECTOR AS AN INNOVATOR

Beyond the traditional role of fostering innovation in the economy, the public sector also innovates within. According to Mulgan (2014: 5), '... public sector innovation involves creating, developing and implementing practical ideas that achieve a public benefit'. As such, public sector innovation is distinct from, but complementary to, creativity and entrepreneurship.

Chen et al. (2020) propose a typology for classifying innovation within the public sector. This typology is comprised of two: 'innovation focus' and 'innovation locus'. The first, innovation focus, includes three public value creation processes: strategy, capacity and operations. The second, innovation locus, encompasses both internal and external orientation. Together, these result in six types of public sector innovation:

1. **Mission innovation:** introduction of a new worldview, mission or purpose for the organisation as a whole (strategy value creation process + internal orientation).
2. **Policy innovation:** introduction of new benefits and obligations for the organisation as a whole to solve societal problems (strategy value creation process + external orientation).
3. **Management innovation:** introduction of a new management practice, process, structure or technique to improve the organisation's ability to further organisational goals (capacity value

creation process + internal orientation).

4. **Partner innovation:** establishment of new partnerships to improve the organisation's ability to further organisational goals (capacity value creation process + external orientation).

5. **Service innovation:** introduction and delivery of new services to achieve organisational goals (operations value creation process + internal orientation).

6. **Citizen innovation:** establishment of new platforms to facilitate citizen collaboration to achieve organisational goals (operations value creation process + external orientation).

THE CASE FOR AND AGAINST THE PUBLIC SECTOR AS AN INNOVATION ACTOR

There are views that run counter to the idea that the state *can* play an active role both as an innovator and as an innovation enabler. These broadly revolve around three issues:

1. **Appropriateness critique:** Liberal views about the appropriate role of governments, with the automatic assumption that it should be minimal at best, and innovation left to markets (Muraille, 2019);

2. **Capability critique:** Debilitating culture, structure and capacities – the view that the debilitating culture, structure and capacities of most public bureaucracies result in inevitable inefficiency. This hampers their capacity to succeed in either innovation role (Cinar et al., 2019); and

3. **Performance critique:** What is anecdotally assumed to be generally negative experiences and poor track records of public bodies being anything other than just funders, or else obstacles to innovation (King, 2022).

Despite these critiques and cynicisms, there have been cogent arguments made that states *should* play key roles in the innovation ecosystem – 'as shareholder, policymaker, regulator and operator' (Mazzucato et al., 2021: 9). This has been argued in terms of governments' specific legitimacies and innovation capabilities considered to be 'based on underlying values, [and] which can be better recognised and supported to achieve sustainable innovation outcomes and more inclusive service delivery' (Plantinga, 2021). It has been further argued that there are certain clearly defined, mission-critical societal objectives 'whose realisation requires a strong, not weak, state that is able to co-create markets, and work with a variety of stakeholders in realising missions' (Mazzucato et al., 2021: 7). This therefore locates the state centrally in national innovation systems, and 'requires strengthening the institutional capabilities of the state across different spheres of government, especially at the coalface of public service delivery at the local level' (Mazzucato et al., 2021: 19).

BARRIERS AND RISKS TO PUBLIC SERVICE INNOVATION

Since public sector innovation does not exist in a vacuum, but in an environment of structured organisation, certain organisational factors may impede or trigger it. To further complicate matters, a specific factor can be either a barrier or a driver depending on the broader context (Bekkers et al., 2013). A recent study puts barriers to public sector innovation into four categories (Cinar et al., 2019) (see Table 6.1).

In the South African context, there are opportunities and challenges associated with the implementation of the White Paper on STI since its adoption in 1996 (NACI, 2020). These illustrate policy innovation and interaction-specific 'barriers' as types of impediments to public sector innovation, respectively.

Barriers can either constitute specific constraints (Bekkers et al., 2013) or could be viewed as the absence of key success factors (EU, 2013: 15–16), thus referred to as the 'lack of...' Drivers on the other hand can help to create enabling conditions for innovation, e.g., resource availability. These two concepts are discussed together, in most of the literature, as inadequate or absent drivers weakening enabling conditions (EU, 2013: 15–16). In addition, a barrier such as lack of funding at one stage of the innovation journey may be an enabler rather than a constraint as it could force frugal innovation (Hindocha et al., 2021: 3), whilst at another stage could lead to failure.

An important factor closely associated with barriers and drivers

Table 6.1: Barriers to public sector innovation

Organisational barriers	Interaction-specific barriers	Innovation-characteristics barriers	Contextual barriers
Barriers linked to the internal context in which innovation takes place. • Ineffective administration of innovation-process activities • Resistance or lack of support from specific actors • Lack of available resources • Inappropriate organisational structure and culture • Lack of skills, knowledge and expertise	Barriers linked to interactions and collaborations can arise out of linkages with other actors such as: • Public service organisations • Citizens and NGOs • Businesses as suppliers or contractors • Politicians and political entities • Businesses as users or co-creators • International organisations • Other	Barriers linked to the characteristics of innovations, as perceived by adopters. • Incompatibility • Complexity • Switching costs • Lack of interoperability • Platform/ software problems • Inflexibility • Other	Barriers linked to context can arise from: • Laws, regulations and policies • Lack of standardisation • Geography • Other

Source: Cinar et al. (2019)

which warrants separate discussion is 'risk', including uncertainty and shocks (Flemig et al., 2016: 429). Innovation is after all strongly associated with risk-taking with high odds for failure. In a public sector context where many wicked[2] problems exist, failure can further come

---

2   A wicked problem is a social or cultural problem that's very difficult or even impossible to solve because of its complexity.

from too many shocks at a time when the innovation has not matured. Failure can also result from barriers to innovation as identified in the third transformative innovation policy framing of Schot et al. (2019: 25). Yet, very little empirical work has been conducted on the nexus between risk-taking and innovation performance (García-Granero et al., 2015; Flemig et al., 2016: 425). Whilst the NSI is structured as an enabler for higher-risk investment (DST, 2019: 41), the White Paper is silent on navigating the risks associated with innovations. Brown and Osborne (2013: 195) distinguish between risks as 'known knowns' and uncertainty as 'unknown knowns'. Shocks can be viewed as unknown unknowns. Brown and Osborne (2013) proceed to categorise risk as *consequential* (risks to the individual citizen, e.g., when a digitised service excludes a legitimate recipient); *organisational* (e.g., job losses); and *behavioural* (negative consequences at community or environmental levels). Unintended consequences can indeed be the death of innovation and, as emphasised by Flemig et al. (2015), technocratic risk management narrowly linked to financial management within the public sector is inadequate to support public and social innovation.

Most of the barriers, drivers and risks discussed in the literature are external to the innovation journey itself. Separating these from the innovator or innovation team can lead to a superficial judgement of the efficacy of the innovation or to ineffective innovation policy (Flanagen and Uyarra, 2016).

Flanagen and Uyarra (2016: 177) rightfully decry the idealistic, tool-boxing, coordination-reliant and atemporal nature of innovation policies. They point out that these policies take little account of the complexity of the actual innovation journey from the perspective of the innovator(s). Specifically, agency and the need to sustain momentum are overlooked. Innovation is the product of human creativity and action, not of an industrial or policy process. Forsman (2021), when reflecting on the innovation failure of small, medium and micro enterprises (SMMEs), noted that the 'common factor for innovation failure is the occurrence of several incidents during the innovation process that slowly contribute to complete failure'. Dhliwayo (2017), identifies agency, facilitation and participation as key elements, although he frames these as forms of public sector entrepreneurship.

The ability (or inability) of individuals and teams to navigate the social networks underpinning systems and processes (Pedraza-Fariña, 2017), foster collaboration, explore inter-dependencies, navigate risks and leverage opportunities become key factors in success or failure (Courvisanos, 2007). As such, 'agency', as a relational, deeply human construct, could provide an additional framing for understanding the success and failure of innovations.

A WORKING ANALYTICAL FRAMEWORK

Based on the above discussion, the two cases below are used to explore how the determinants of success or failure of innovation in the public sector – barriers and drivers, risk and agency – impacted on the outcomes of an initiative. These determinants are present at individual, team, organisational and systems levels and many cut across. For example, the barriers related to innovation characteristics and those related to context, mentioned above, present at both organisational and systems levels.

INNOVATION CASE STUDIES

Two case studies with rich longitudinal insights related to the framework above are discussed below. The first was initiated as a top-down, leadership-enabled innovation, and the second as a bottom-up, social needs-driven innovation.

Case 1. Top-down State Innovation Projects: The Maponya Mall Urban Thusong Centre

The Minister of Public Service and Administration, Mr M.R. Baloyi, launched the Maponya Mall Urban Thusong Service Centre (MMUTSC) in February 2011 as 'part of integrating public services and bringing them closer to the people' and 'as a *pilot model* of an integrated service delivery point for a range of government services which include, amongst others, applications for identity documents, social grants and employment opportunities' (emphasis added) (DPSA,

Table 6.2: Examples of Analytical Determinants

| FACTOR | EXAMPLES OF WHAT THESE FACTORS CAN IMPACT AT DIFFERENT LEVELS: | | |
	Individual/team	Organisational	System(s)
Barriers and drivers	Lack of skills and capacity Funding Personal traits	Lack of incentives Bureaucracy, management, leadership Sharing of knowledge	Lack of flexibility in laws and policy Structural constraints Political factors Social and technological factors Theoretical and policy failure
Risk, un–certainty and shocks	Consequences of failure (negative performance appraisal) Unintended consequences such as the exclusion of certain individuals	Culture of risk avoidance (negative consequence management practices) Job losses	Negative consequences such as dependency or unemployment Wicked problems
Agency	Ability and support to navigate the structure of social relations underlying processes	Ability and support to navigate inter-institutional dynamics	Ability and support to navigate policy and legislative dynamics

Source: Compiled by the authors

2011: 11). The model was inspired by Citizen Assistance Service Centres in Bahia State in Brazil, which won the 2004 UN Public Service Award and was subsequently visited by the Minister for the Public Service and Administration and officials from the Department and Centre for Public Service Innovation in October 2004.

Although it became one of the most successful Thusong Service Centres (TSCs) (DPSA and GCIS, 2019), it remains a pilot model that has not been successfully scaled. According to the 2010/11 Annual Report of the DPSA, within two months of opening its doors, the Maponya Mall Urban Thusong Centre had provided 10,693 citizens with services from the Departments of Home Affairs and Labour, Gauteng Department of Roads, Transport Gauteng Enterprise Propeller, Gauteng Provincial Government, Professional Job Centre and the NYDA.

From the inception of the Thusong model, it was clearly articulated that the key factor for the success of the TSC would be intergovernmental collaboration, enabled by Memoranda of Agreement. In addition to offering citizens access to multiple government services, the TSC extends the additional convenience of being open on Saturdays.

Despite the clear benefits to citizens, the TSC initiative and the intended scaling were hampered by two challenges, according to subsequent annual reporting by the DPSA. These were operational challenges, such as procurement and cost recovery, from participating departments and broader challenges related to funding and ownership of the Thusong Service Centre programme. Some departments simply did not contribute to the operational costs and in 2021 the outstanding lease contribution of one of the entities amounted to R2,107 million (DPSA, 2021).

Institutional management and oversight in the DPSA further shaped the priorities related to the centre, and emphasis gradually shifted away from experimentation towards the development of a broader framework. Whereas the pilot project was launched by the DPSA's Governance Branch as an Integrated Public Administration Reform project, it was moved to the Policy, Research and Analysis Branch in 2015/16, with the restructuring of the DPSA. The focus was now internally on the operational management of the centre and no longer on the piloting of an innovation in public sector reform. The policy objective also shifted to developing an appropriate model for the governance and co-ordination of service centres with the DPSA's only role being to guide the provision of ICT and broadband connectivity.

There is uncertainty as to what will happen when the current lease commitment comes to an end in June 2024. A number of observations, based on the DPSA's reporting, relating to the failure to mainstream this innovation are discussed below.

Initial barriers were easily managed through the provision of funding from the DPSA (ring-fenced by National Treasury) and operational management capabilities. The availability of funding further enabled the DPSA to mitigate risks such as non-payment by participating entities. However, the inability to navigate inter-institutional dynamics and to finalise a multilaterally agreed management framework for a broader Thusong Centre Programme has meant that the initiative, after 11 years, has not succeeded in progressing beyond that of a pilot. Whereas high levels of agency were present at the start of the pilot (such as obtaining funding from Treasury and getting the buy-in of several departments and entities), this agency eroded over time as the vision for the programme was blurred by operational challenges and non-adoption by service delivery departments.

The provision of enabling funding was thus not sufficient to overcome the interaction-specific barriers described by Cinar et al. (2019). In addition, regular leadership changes at political and executive management levels further created contextual barriers, whilst eroding agency and ownership of the pilot. The transition at organisational level from an experimentation mindset (to demonstrate efficacy and scaling potential) to an operation management and maintenance approach (by making the pilot an extension of the activities of the department), effectively stopped any future commitment to scaling.

Case 2. Community-level Innovations: The MeMeZA Community Alarm System

South African urban areas face challenges that are associated with fast-growing populations. These are a result of the influx of people from rural areas in search of opportunities. This unplanned migration into cities 'without adequate spatial planning, urban design or financial allocation to accommodate the transfer and relocation of people' (Singh, 2019: 6) leads to a sharp growth in informal settlements. Policing under these circumstances becomes a big challenge. The MeMeZa Community

Alarm System sought to solve this challenge.

In 2012, the South African Police Services in the Honeydew Cluster, located in and around Johannesburg, Gauteng, approached the Centre for Public Service Innovation (CPSI) to request assistance. They were seeking help with a solution that would improve police response to incidences of crime in Diepsloot, a settlement within the cluster – particularly those committed within Diepsloot's informal settlements. The police were only responding more than 24 hours after crimes had been committed. This was mainly because when the crimes were committed victims' cell phones were stolen, which made it difficult for them to alert the police. Furthermore, when crimes were reported, the police found it difficult to locate the exact sites where the crimes were committed due to the lack of proper street addresses in informal settlements.

Efforts to deal with this challenge saw the CPSI collaborate with The Innovation Hub (TIH) who, through its open innovation platform (OpenIX), were able to identify a number of potential solutions in conceptual or pre-commercial stages of development (CPSI, undated: 8).

The start-up company that was the closest match was MeMeZa Shout, which was headed by Ms Thuli Mthethwa, who developed the solution as a survivor of crime herself. The system consists of an electronic device that is installed in households. If triggered, the alarm sends a text message to the police sector vehicle, the police station and members of the Community Policing Forum (CPF). It also makes a loud noise, which attracts the attention of neighbours. The alarm can also be triggered silently. The innovation lies not in the device itself but in the use of appropriate technology to activate community networks, encourage proactive policing, improve response times and strengthen community participation in creating safer neighbourhoods (Isafiade et al., 2020).

This solution was piloted in Diepsloot through a collaborative effort between the CPSI, TIH and the SAB Foundation. It involved the deployment of alarms in selected households. The statistics from the pilot programme were promising: serious crimes were reduced by 60 per cent with a 9 per cent decrease in the murder rate and a 26 per cent reduction in sexual offences (OECD: 2014), suggesting the potential to improve police response times and reduce crime (Suleiman et al., 2020: 260). The solution was further replicated in 23 Gauteng schools to protect the institutions' ICT infrastructure. Here again, the solution was impactful as it reduced theft of ICT equipment by 50 per cent (CPSI, undated: 31).

Despite these successes, the solution has yet to be sustainably scaled and formally integrated into policing. Several high-level meetings were held at which Diepsloot and Honeydew Cluster police and community members presented on how the solution had proved helpful. This points to clear barriers within state bureaucracy that prevent solutions from being scaled. The first is a lack of flexibility in procurement legislation that would allow government departments to test and scale community-based innovations. Flexibility in the legislation is further needed for the government departments to then procure innovations that prove successful without having to go through a tender process which puts start-up companies at a significant disadvantage (UNDP, 2018). A second constraint is risk aversion in management decisions, planning and budgeting. The potential of new and alternative solutions is not weighed against the consequences of continuing the status quo.

It can further be argued that the state is still not receptive to social innovations that come from communities. This is despite the fact that there is a legislative instrument for this in the form of the National Treasury Practice Note No 11 of 2008/2009 which facilitates the submission of unsolicited proposals (National Treasury: 2008/9); the burden of evidence required however assumes the solution is at commercialisation stage. Many potential social innovations may require significant further development and thus further experimentation before they can be offered as a bid. The result is that those solutions that do get piloted, like MeMeZa, are because of the individual agency of the officials guiding the process. Several individuals within the state (notably from TIH, CPSI, SAPS Honeydew Cluster and the Civilian Secretariat for the Police) helped MeMeZa to navigate constraints, overcome policy and institutional stumbling blocks, and access funding to ensure that at least the solution was tested and piloted in a government environment to satisfy the requirements for unsolicited proposal (CPSI, undated: 17).

However, individuals within the government departments that are potential beneficiaries are less likely to assist in the scaling of such solutions. This is mainly because scaling requires buy-in from top leadership, dedicated 'champions' and budgeting and incorporation into operational and annual plans. There is thus a need for policy mechanisms that will allow leadership to adopt, fund and scale innovations in a more agile manner (UNDP, 2018). Currently many officials, despite understanding the potential service delivery benefits, are not willing to provide dedicated support. This is because they perceive themselves as facing consequential risk in terms of both the procurement process itself and the potential for a new solution to fail, which would result in them confronting 'consequence management'.

MAKING THE CASE FOR A HUMAN-CENTRED SYSTEM FOR PUBLIC SECTOR INNOVATION

Considering the barriers, drivers, risk-related behaviour and agency discussed above, as well as the lessons arising from the case studies examined, it is not possible to make a simple case for the public sector as either a destroyer or an enabler of innovation in South Africa. From the number of entries for awards initiatives, such as the national Public Sector Innovation Awards and the Gauteng Accelerator Programme (GAP) Innovation Competition, it is clear that there is not a dearth of innovation associated directly with the public sector. A more nuanced narrative is needed; a view that recognises that officials innovate at institutional level despite barriers, and that social and entrepreneurial innovators only succeed with great effort, patience and support from within the state bureaucracy. In contrast, the role of the state as an enabler of innovation beyond the mandated institutions of the NSI is severely constrained.

As observed by Cavalcante and Camões (2017) from their analysis of Brazilian public sector innovations, successful 'bottom-up' innovations mostly relate to institutional and process reforms whilst, as Kotter (1996) observed in his seminal work, 'top-down' innovations are led and are more disruptive in nature. This suggests that the type of innovation is a function of the respective levels of agency that innovators have. As is illustrated by the two case studies, the failure or success of an innovation is dependent on sustained human agency. One way of countering the negative consequences of loss of agency, not only for innovation but also for the realisation of most policy intentions, is to institutionalise mechanisms and processes that are human-centred.

Creating pathways for experimentation in a risk-controlled environment, institutionalising agile and design-thinking methodologies and ring-fencing bridging funding are some of the policy interventions to explore. These measures should create safe spaces for experimentation through mechanisms such as living labs or regulatory 'sandboxes' (Attrey et al., 2020). Sandboxes 'promote flexibility and innovation in the digital age' (OECD, 2023) for both officials and innovators. Schot and Kanger (2018) identify the notion of 'shielding' – the creation of national policy which allows for shielding from regulations which prevent further developments. The Transformative Innovation Policy Consortium (TIPC) framing of this concept of shielding offers another potential mechanism to explore to afford innovators protection, especially social and civic tech innovators[3] from outside government. This protection and support would allow innovators the space to demonstrate the efficacy of their solutions. Importantly, governance mechanisms should recognise not only the product/service aspect of what defines innovation but also enable the process aspect.

CONCLUSIONS AND RECOMMENDATIONS

This paper's title attempts to confront the common but blunt narrative that South Africa's public sector should not or cannot innovate, and that it hampers innovation in the country. Rather than just defend against that stereotypical narrative, the authors offer a more nuanced and constructive story about what has been happening in the South African system, and what could be learned from it. The authors

---

3   The term 'civic tech' refers to the use of technology to enhance civic participation.

take the opportunity to also think through an appropriate analytical framework for guiding policy considerations that relate to public sector innovation.

In concluding and seeking lessons for moving forward, it is useful to consider the final research question, which was whether the prevailing NSI conception and configuration in South Africa is supportive of public sector innovation. This study concludes that more deliberate and practical consideration of public sector innovation within the broader NSI is required, beyond what the current White Paper alludes to. Currently, the role of the public sector in the NSI is poorly framed and focused on at both national and sub-national levels. These shortfalls result in poor performance by actors within the innovation system despite the aspiration to 'strengthen government's role as an enabler for innovation' (DST, 2019). Imagining a government that can enable experimentation and dynamic innovation would require attention to the limiting conditions (barriers and risks) encountered within the state.

In addition, public sector innovation requires policy that is human-centred and developmental in nature. This is important for the challenges around both the innovations themselves and around how innovators are enabled to address such challenges: i.e., how the innovators can be assisted to use their ingenuity and agency to address obstacles to innovation. Here, the authors propose the formation of a public sector innovation living lab that will foster collaborative arrangements for both state and non-state actors. The proposed lab must focus on macro-societal challenges, leveraging cross-sectorial networks that include public-sector leaders, academics and innovators. It can provide space for experimentation and for policy to be developed.

The proposed living lab can be located within a cross-cutting national entity or agency – for example, to ensure that resources and political support are available – but ownership should be shared and horizontal integration ensured in order to provide access to various service sectors, and so enable agile experimentation. It is through this safe space for experimentation that, for example, new innovations from the community can be assessed for impact rather than individual bureaucrats within the state being left to make decisions about which innovations should thrive and which should die. A safe space such as this would ensure that new innovations can be tested and, if need be, supported for scaling. The anticipated outcome of this experiment would be the emergence of policies that would enable innovators from within both communities and the state to address challenges to innovation in the public sector. These policies include the procurement ones which are cited as one of the barriers to public sector innovation.

The conditions in innovation ecosystems also need to be considered. The cases presented demonstrate the need to allow for process flexibility to accommodate the nature of an innovation (e.g., top-down, bottom-up), and not force everything into a single, system-determined mould (the 'cookie cutter' approach). The environment should allow space for failure, active de-risking and alternative risk-management practices at various levels – policy, planning, resourcing, performance management and auditing.

Demand-side mechanisms also need strengthening to foster greater efficiency in the South African innovation system. The ever-so-often disconnect between what is produced through the NSI, decision-makers and public officials at the coalface of service delivery is resulting in many failures or unscaled innovations. In times of austerity and resource constraints, it is even more imperative to find ways of using public systems and programmes to stimulate and support both public and private demand for innovation, including among SMMEs (OECD, 2011). This would help to boost innovation without relying on new programme spending, and focus innovation towards meeting social demands in critical areas such as health, energy, food security and the environment (Adesida et al., 2021).

Finally, although the paper's title speaks to the goal of successful, sustained innovation because (or in spite of) the public sector's effective role within an NSI, it is also useful to recognise the complex and dynamic nature of socio-technical needs and conditions. For this reason, we need mechanisms to manage dynamic innovation 'life and death' cycles, including how to prevent failure, capacity chasms, a lack of bridge funding, and – in the TIPC framing – protect new niches whilst retiring innovations that have played their course.

REFERENCES

Adesida, O., Karuri-Sebina, G. and Kraemer-Mbula, E. 2021. 'Can innovation address Africa's challenges?'. *African Journal of Science, Technology, Innovation and Development*, 13(7), 779–784.

Arundel, A., Bloch, C., Ferguson, B. 2019. 'Advancing innovation in the public sector: Aligning innovation measurement with policy goals'. *Research Policy*, 48(3), 789–798.

Attrey, A., Lesher, M. and Lomax, C. 2020. 'The role of sandboxes in promoting flexibility and innovation in the digital age'. OECD Going Digital Toolkit Notes, No. 2, Paris: OECD Publishing.

Bekkers, V.J., Tummers, L.G. and Voorberg, W.H. 2013. 'From public innovation to social innovation in the public sector: A literature review of relevant drivers and barriers'. Paper presented at Erasmus University, Rotterdam.

Boghani, A.B. and Jonash, R.S. 1993. 'The role of government in fostering innovation'. *PRISM*, Q3, 23–27.

Brown, L. and Osborne, S.P. 2013. 'Risk and innovation'. *Public Management Reviews*, 15, 186–208.

Cavalcante, P. and Camões, M. 2017. 'Public innovation in Brazil: An overview of its types, results and drivers'. Discussion Paper, No. 222, Institute for Applied Economic Research (IPEA), Brazil.

Centre for Public Service Innovation (CPSI). 2021. 'Feasibility Study: CPSI'. Centre for Public Service Innovation, Pretoria, unpublished.

Centre for Public Service Innovation (CPSI). Undated. 'CPSI entrenching innovation in the public sector: Selected sase studies'. Centre for Public Service Innovation, Pretoria, pp. 7–34.

Chen, J., Walker, R. M. and Sawhney, M. 2020. 'Public service innovation: A typology'. *Public Management Review*, 22(11), 1674–1695.

Cinar, E., Trott, P. and Simms, C. 2019. 'A systematic review of barriers to public sector innovation process'. *Public Management Review*, 21(2), 264–290.

Courvisanos, J. 2007. 'The ontology of innovation: Human agency in the pursuit of novelty'. *History of Economics Review*, 45(1), 41–59.

Department of Science and Technology (DST). 2019. 'White Paper on Science, Technology and Innovation'. The Department of Science and Technology, Republic of South Africa, Pretoria. https://www.gov.za/sites/default/files/gcis_document/201912/white-paper-science-technology-and-innovation.pdf, accessed 10 June 2022.

Department of Public Service and Administration (DPSA). 2011. 'Annual Report'. The Department of Public Service and Administration, Republic of South Africa, Pretoria.

Department of Public Service and Administration (DPSA). 2021. 'Annual

Report'. The Department of Public Service and Administration, Republic of South Africa, Pretoria.

Department of Public Service and Administration (DPSA). 2018. 'Review of the Thusong Service Centre: Service Delivery Model'. The Department of Public Service and Administration, Republic of South Africa, Pretoria.

Dhliwayo, S. 2017. 'Defining public sector entrepreneurship: A conceptual operational construct'. *The International Journal of Entrepreneurship and Innovation*, 18(3), 153–163.

European Commission. 2013. 'Powering European Public Sector Innovation: Towards A New Architecture – Report of the Expert Group on Public Sector Innovation'. European Commission, Brussels. https://ec.europa. eu/futurium/en/system/files/ged/42-public_sector_innovation_-_ towards_a_new_architecture.pdf, accessed 2 July 2022.

Flanagen, K. and Uyarra, E. 2016. 'Four dangers in innovation policy studies – and how to avoid them'. *Industry and Innovation*, 23(2), 177–188.

Flemig, S., Osborne, S. and Kinder, T. 2015. 'Risk definition and risk governance in social innovation processes: A conceptual framework'. LIPSE Project Working Paper 4, European Union, Brussels.

Flemig, S., Osborne, S. and Kinder, T. 2016. 'Risky business: Reconceptualizing risk and innovation in public services'. *Public Money and Management*, 36(6), 425–432.

Flynn, N. and Asquer, A. 2017. *Public Sector Management* (7th ed). London: SAGE Publications.

Forsman, H. 2021. 'Innovation failure in SMMEs: A narrative approach to understand failed innovations and failed innovators'. *International Journal of Innovation Management,* 25(9).

Garcia-Granero, A., Llopis, O., Fernandez-Mesa, A. and Alegre, J. 2015. 'Unravelling the link between managerial risk-taking and innovation: the mediating role of a risk-taking climate'. *Journal of Business Research*, 68(5), 1094–1104.

Gault, F. 2020. *Measuring Innovation Everywhere: The Challenge of Better Policy, Learning, Evaluation and Monitoring*. Cheltenham: Edward Elgar Publishing Limited.

Ghazinoory, S., Nasri, S., Ameri, F., Montazer, G.A. and Shayan, A. 2020. 'Why do we need "problem-oriented innovation system (PIS)" for solving macro-level societal problems?'. *Technological Forecasting and Social Change*, 150, 11–18.

Hindocha, C.N., Antonacci, G., Barlow, J. and Harris, M. 2021. 'Defining frugal innovation: a critical review'. *BMJ Innovations*, 7(4), 1–10.

Innovation Barometer. 2021. 'Copenhagen Manual: A guide on how and why your country can benefit from measuring public sector innovation'. https://www.innovationbarometer.org/copenhagen-manual, accessed 16 June 2022.

Isafiade, O., Ndingindwayo, B. and Bangula, A. 2020. 'Predictive policing using deep learning: A community policing practical case study', 12th EAI International Conference, AFRICOMM 2020, Ebene City, Mauritius, 2–4 December, 269–286.

King, R. 31 March 2022. 'Should government leave innovation to the private sector?'. World Economic Forum, https://www.weforum.org/agenda/2022/03/should-government-leave-innovation-to-the-private-sector/, accessed 10 July 2022.

Kotter, J.P. 1996. 'Leading change: Why transformation efforts fail'. *Harvard Business Review*, https://hbr.org/1995/05/leading-change-why-transformation-efforts-fail-2, accessed 8 September 2022.

Lundvall, B-Å., Vang, J., Joseph, K. J. and Chaminade, C. 2009. 'Innovation system research and developing countries', in Lundvall, B-Å., Joseph, K.J., Chaminade, C. and Vang, J. (eds). *Handbook of Innovation Systems and Developing Countries*. Cheltenham: Edward Elgar Publishing, 1–30.

Lundvall, B-Å. 2022. 'Transformative policies for sustainable innovation systems'. *Lund Papers in Economic History*, 239.

Mazzucato, M. 2018. 'Mission-oriented innovation policies: Challenges and opportunities'. *Industrial and Corporate Change*, 27(5), 803–815.

Mazzucato, M., Qobo, M. and Kattel, R. 2021. 'Building state capacities and dynamic capabilities to drive social and economic development: The case of South Africa'. UCL Institute for Innovation and Public Purpose, Working Paper Series (IIPP WP 2021/09), https://www.ucl.ac.uk/bartlett/public-purpose/wp2021-09, accessed 12 May 2022.

Mulgan, G. 2014. 'Innovation in the public sector: How can public organisations better create, improve, and adapt?'. NESTA, https://media.nesta.org.uk/documents/innovation_in_the_public_sector-_how_can_public_organisations_better_create_improve_and_adapt.pdf, accessed 16 June 2022.

Muraille, E., 2019. 'Ethical control of innovation in a globalized and liberal world: Is good science still science?'. *Endeavour*, 43(4), 1–14.

National Advisory Council on Innovation (NACI). 2020. 'A Review of the National Research and Development Strategy (NRDS) and Ten-Year Innovation Plan (TYIP)'. https://www.naci.org.za/index.php/new-data-sets-to-support-innovation-policy, accessed 16 July 2022.

Organisation for Economic Co-operation and Development (OECD). 2023. 'OECD Going Digital Toolkit Notes', No. 2, Paris: OECD Publishing.

Organisation for Economic Co-operation and Development (OECD). 2017. 'Fostering innovation in the public sector'. OECD Publishing, Paris. http://dx.doi.org/10.1787/9789264270879-en, accessed 10 November 2022.

Organisation for Economic Co-operation and Development (OECD). 2015. 'The innovation imperative in the public sector: Setting an agenda for action'. OECD Publishing, Paris. http://dx.doi.org/10.1787/9789264236561-en, accessed 11 November 2022.

Organisation for Economic Co-operation and Development (OECD). 2014. 'Memeza shout community safety alarms'. OECD Publishing, Paris. https://oecd-opsi.org/innovations/memeza-shout-community-safety-alarms/, accessed 20 August 2022.

Organisation for Economic Co-operation and Development (OECD). 2011. 'Demand-side Innovation Policies'. OECD Publishing, Paris. https://www.oecd.org/innovation/inno/demand-sideinnovationpolicies. htm#TOC, accessed 2 July 2022.

Pedraza-Fariña, L.G., 2017. 'The social origins of innovation failures'. *SMU Law Review*, 70(2). https://scholar.smu.edu/smulr/vol70/iss2/6, accessed 22 October 2022.

Plantinga, P. 2021. 'Innovation and the public service: Achieving inclusive service delivery'. Centre for Open Science, https://ideas.repec.org/p/osf/socarx/e2xaz.html, accessed 18 October 2022.

Presidency of South Africa. 18 June 2020. 'COVID-19: African Union Chair, President Ramaphosa launches the Africa Medical Supplies Platform, Africa's unified continental response to fight the pandemic'. https://www.thepresidency.gov.za/press-statements/covid-19%3A-african-union-chair%2C-president-ramaphosa-launches-africa-medical-supplies-platform%2C-africa%E2%80%99s-unified-continental-response-fight-pandemic, accessed 16 June 2022.

Rahman, S. 2017. 'The advantages and disadvantages of using qualitative and quantitative approaches and methods in language "testing and assessment" research: A literature review'. *Journal of Education and Learning*, 6(1), 102–112.

Schot, J. and Kanger, L. 2018. 'Deep transitions: Emergence, acceleration, stabilisation and directionality'. *Research Policy*, 47(6), 1045–1059.

Schot J., Kivimaa P. and Torrens J. 2019. 'Transforming experimentation: Experimental policy engagements and their transformative outcomes', Transformative Innovation Policy Consortium, https://www.tipconsortium.net/resource/transforming-experimentation-experimental-policy-engagements-and-their-transformative-outcomes, accessed 18 October 2022.

Schot, J. and Steinmueller, W.E. 2018. 'Three frames for innovation policy: R&D, systems of innovation and transformative change'. *Research Policy*, 47(9), 1554–1567.

Singh, D. 2019. 'Policing for safe cities and citizen security in urban South Africa: A fundamental human right'. *Just Africa*, 1, 6–14.

Suleiman, M.M., Kuliya, M., Surajo, A.Z. and Musa, J. 2020. 'ICT is an integral strategy for crime prevention and detection'. *Academic Leadership*, 21, 249–267.

United Nations Development Programme (UNPD). 2018. 'Round table of public sector innovation funding mechanism', https://www.undp.org/south-africa/speeches/roundtable-public-sector-innovation-funding-mechanism, accessed 10 June 2022.

Uyarra, E., Edler, J., Garcia-Estevez, J., Georghiou, L. and Yeow, J. 2014. 'Barriers to innovation through public procurement: a supplier perspective'. *Technovation*, 34, 631–645.

SEVEN

Government-led technological missions: An assessment of the PBMR, SKA and HySA projects

NQOBILE XABA AND XOLILE FUKU

INTRODUCTION

This chapter aims to investigate the successes and failures of three high-technology projects that represent government-led technology missions: the Pebble Bed Modular Reactor (PMBR), the Square Kilometre Array (SKA) and Hydrogen South Africa (HySA). This will be undertaken through an assessment of a failed project, the PBMR;[1] a successful one, the SKA; and HySA, a project whose outcome has yet to be classified as it is only entering the commercialisation phase.

The term 'success' in this chapter is limited to delivering a pilot plant or project; positive impact on broader communities is not considered. The research methodology entailed an analysis of relevant literature,

---

1 'PBMR' will be used in this chapter to denote both the PBMR company and the technology itself.

including reports and articles published by reliable sources. The three projects were assessed against factors that included technology transfer; prototyping and commercialisation; economic viability and markets; and human capital development.

The final section of the chapter considers lessons for current and upcoming technology projects. Questions are raised and recommendations are made regarding South Africa's capacity to succeed in these projects.

Although the projects discussed in this chapter do not themselves constitute innovations, they do seek to promote technological advancements within their respective value chains and fields. The PBMR was designed to address South Africa's energy shortage and build the country's capabilities in nuclear energy. The HySA project is also concerned with energy solutions: it is aimed at building South Africa's capability in hydrogen and fuel cell technologies by beneficiating PGMs. The SKA project, however, aims to build capabilities within a different field: astronomy. The three projects then will be assessed in terms of different factors. The PBMR and HySA, which are both aimed at creating products for the market, will be assessed for technological, economic and market viability. The SKA project, however, will be assessed for sustainability, effective governance and potential wider socioeconomic benefits.

CASE STUDY 1: SOUTH AFRICA'S ADOPTION OF THE PEBBLE BED MODULAR REACTOR (PBMR)

The PBMR is a small, high-temperature reactor that uses helium gas as a coolant medium to remove heat. It was intended to have the capacity to be built relatively quickly as it has a small modular design that is easily replicable (McKune, 2010). Enriched uranium is kept in ceramic, ball-sized 'pebbles', using graphite as a moderator; these pebbles are cooled by gas rather than water.

The PBMR technology was suitable to South Africa as it is more thermally effective than the conventional pressurised water reactors that the country currently uses at its Koeberg nuclear power plant. The PBMR is clean, cost competitive and produces small quantities of manageable nuclear waste.

The PBMR prototype was first in operation in Germany from 1966 to 1988, when it was decommissioned due to political considerations and because it had fulfilled all planned research experiments (Adam, 2020; PBMR, 2005). The idea of a 5MWe pebble bed reactor for South Africa was first proposed to Eskom by the company Integrated Systems Technology Holdings (Pty) Ltd (IST), which provided electronic systems for Armscor – the state's arms manufacturing and procurement agency (Fig, 2010). IST was formed by nuclear scientists and engineers who had been active in South Africa's bomb programme, and was an early partner with Eskom.

One of the engineers from IST, Dr Johan Slabber, had taken a personal interest in high-temperature reactors. Dr Slabber visited the father of the German HTR, Prof. Rudolf Schulten, at the University of Aachen in 1988 where they discussed the viability of applying the technology in South Africa. Dr Slabber persuaded the company to propose the idea of a 5MWe pebble bed reactor to Eskom to serve remote inland sites. Slabber was able to convince Armscor to commission IST to come up with a design and feasibility study for a pebble bed-type reactor to power nuclear submarines. By 1993, when Armscor money fell away, the proposal had reached a point at which IST could offer development of the pebble bed reactor to Eskom. From 1993 onwards, Eskom took increasing control of the project. In July 1995, Eskom appointed IST to undertake a series of feasibility studies, which were completed by April 1997. The South African government backed the project's initial feasibility study in 1995 and approved a detailed feasibility phase in the year 2000 (Fig, 2010).

After reconsidering a joint venture agreement with IST (in which Eskom held 51 per cent), Eskom entered into a contractual relationship with IST and granted its nuclear division a R260 million contract to develop the PBMR design. Eskom's Council had formally accepted that the PBMR was a priority project by 1998. Eskom formed the Pebble Bed Modular Reactor (Pty) Ltd (PBMR Co.) in 1999, which Eskom initially owned fully (Fig, 2010).

South Africa officially announced the programme in 1998, with the expectation that a demonstration plant would be completed in 2004 and would cost R2 billion. Eskom issued a letter of intent to buy 24 units of the new technology for South Africa in the hope that global sales would follow (McKune, 2010).

Knowing the risks of being the sole owner and also to enable access to technology, Eskom offered other companies, parastatals and government shares on a subscription basis; the shares were relative to respective contributions to the PBMR company. Those offered PBMR shares included the Industrial Development Corporation (IDC) of South Africa; Exelon, a US-based nuclear reactor operator company; and the British Nuclear Fuels Ltd (BNFL).[2] In 2003, BNFL ceased further payment to Eskom due to the company being close to bankruptcy. Similarly, Exelon pulled out in 2002 saying it was switching from being a technology developer to being an electricity supplier as discussed in the following sections. The loss of these investors had serious implications for the success and commercialisation of PBMR technology. Nominal foreign ownership would have been valuable later in the process too, in the form of assistance with dealing with regulators in other jurisdictions, and with commercialising and exporting the product (Fig, 2010).

Assessment of the programme

The PBMR was initially promoted as an export-oriented technology which, by 2004, would deliver the means for commercially available PBMRs to be made for order. However, the target date for commercialisation was deferred: first to 2009 and then to 2014. By 2009, a full decade after the adoption of the programme, there was still no sign of a demonstration plant and the date set for this changed again to 2030 (McKune, 2010).

The PBMR was conceived as a high-risk project and for it to succeed it had to be able to operate reliably, be technologically and economically viable and be commercially available to buyers. The project was also intended to increase local manufacturing; provide a solution for energy shortages; establish South Africa as a player within

---

2   BNFL was a major owner of nuclear reactors in the United Kingdom (Fig, 2010).

the nuclear power systems value chain; and transform the geopolitical landscape establishing Africa as a powerful leader in PBMR technology.

i. Technological viability

The reliability and viability of the PBMR technology were questionable from the start as South Africa only bought the PBMR patent from Germany after other, more technologically advanced countries had already tried and rejected the technology. Most of the world's major nuclear power design nations (USA and Germany) had extensively studied HTR technology, which is like the PBMR. Despite these nations' technological capacities, the HTR technology had reached a commercial-scale prototype and then failed.

There were also risks related to the design of the technology that were overlooked or underestimated. The first was the gas turbine. The PBMR used a helium-driven gas turbine, which was an unproven technology; it proved to be one of the biggest failures of the PBMR and a critical factor in the project's demise. In 2002, PBMR changed contractors in an effort to overcome this failure, but by 2009 the decision was taken to abandon the gas turbine in favour of the conventional steam cycle. Changing the contractor and procuring the gas turbine were steps taken to try to hasten the construction of the demonstration plant. However, the switch to a gas turbine entailed design changes which further delayed the project.

China, in contrast, persisted with decades of research and successfully connected its first high-temperature gas-cooled modular pebble bed (HTR-PM) reactor into a grid that uses a helium-driven gas turbine (Patel, 2022; World Nuclear News, 2021; Zhang et al., 2016). China succeeded – where South Africa had failed – in averting the main risk of using the helium-driven gas turbine. Beijing's Chinergy Company Ltd and South Africa's PBMR Company signed a memorandum of understanding in order to explore possible benefits in cooperating over the projects that both countries were developing. There were some similarities in design between companies and there were also some significant variations. However, South Africa could have exploited this agreement to learn from the Chinese design and avert the risks of using the gas turbine in their own design.

A second risk concerned the size of the plant, which was originally scaled to 267 MW, and then later scaled to 400 MW. However, the power output was scaled up without an increase in the physical size of the plant. Such a significant deviation from the capacities of the original design would have created new problems, but the design incongruities were never identified or addressed.

ii. Economic viability

The PBMR was chosen because it was deemed to be less expensive to build than the existing pressurised water reactor (PWR) at Koeberg. However, it can be challenging to calculate construction and operating costs with accuracy. In the initial stages of the PBMR, it was estimated that commercial units could be constructed for less than US$1,000/kW overnight[3] (excluding finance charges meaning that a unit that was then anticipated to produce 110 MW would cost US$110 million (then roughly R600 million)).

When the project was first launched in 1998 it was estimated that the demonstration plant would cost just over R1 billion. This estimate increased to R31 billion in 2009, shortly after the project was abandoned. This escalation of costs suggests poor management and oversight by Eskom, the PBMR company board and the South African government. A total of R9.2 billion was spent on the PBMR project, of which R7.4 billion was provided by government prior to the construction of the demonstration plant and an associated fuel plant. A further estimated R31 billion was needed to get the project to the demonstration phase, with the expectation that a demonstration plant would be commissioned in 2018.

iii. Market viability

Eskom predicted a market for 30 units annually when the PBMR project was first made public, of which 20 would be exported and 10 would be installed in South Africa. Its first potential customer

---

3 'Overnight' is the term used for the costs of a construction project in which no interest is incurred in the course of construction.

was Exelon,[4] a US-based nuclear reactor operator company, which expressed interest but provided the PBMR with only a letter of intent to purchase. This letter expired in 2002 when Exelon withdrew its commitment, saying that it was switching from being a technology developer to an electricity supplier. Eskom had also put forward a letter of intent to purchase but it never committed to buying any units. However, when Exelon abandoned its commitment then Eskom followed suit, withdrawing its own intent to buy. Around the same time, Eskom also made the decision to no longer invest in the project on the grounds that it was not developing new technologies any more. Subsequently, the South African government withdraw all funding. However, Eskom still remained a shareholder. This constituted poor marketing strategy by the South African government: the fact that its own state-owned company did not commit to buying the reactors badly undermined global market confidence. This lack of market confidence was compounded by the fact that South Africa had no prior experience in PBMR technology (Thomas, 1999; 2011).

CASE STUDY 2: THE SQUARE KILOMETRE ARRAY (SKA)

The SKA is an intergovernmental project that aims to build a radio telescope in Australia (low-frequency) and South Africa (mid-frequency). The core of the high- and mid-frequency dishes will be in South Africa's Karoo desert. Australia will serve as the host nation for the low-frequency antennas (Adam, 2020). The SKA, which has 10 full members (South Africa, Australia, China, Germany, Canada, Italy, Sweden, The Netherlands, New Zealand and the United Kingdom) and one associate member (India) is the only international initiative in the European Strategy Forum of Research Infrastructures (ESFRI). More than 67 organisations from 20 different countries are participating, along with information, computing and telecommunication (ICT) industry leaders from around the world. The SKA will be constructed

---

4   Eskom had previously owned 100 per cent of the company, but decided to diversify. Exelon was offered 12.5 per cent in exchange for investment. Exelon withdrew from the project in April 2002 (Fig, 2010).

in the Southern Hemisphere in phases: Phase 1 (SKA 1) began in South Africa and Australia in 2022 (Britz, 2022). There are plans for Phase 2 (SKA 2) to be built in the SKA African Partner nations of Botswana, Namibia, Ghana, Zambia, Mauritius, Madagascar, Mozambique and Kenya. The advantages offered by the SKA project are that its telescopes will operate at a wide range of frequencies, be 50 times more receptive than a typical radio telescope and produce the highest-resolution visuals in all of astronomy (Carilli and Rawlings, 2004; Gastrow et al., 2016; Van Ardenne et al., 2012).

The SKA is divided into different components that will combine to create the final SKA Observatory, which will be run by an international collaboration made up of top experts in their respective specialities. It is critical to remember that the SKA will comprise two telescopes, SKA1-LOW and SKA1-MID in Australia and South Africa respectively, each of which will provide its own elements subsystem. Each telescope will have its own unique element product tree created during the pre-construction phase. All these products will, to the greatest extent possible, be based on a single design, except for the low-frequency array products that will be deployed in Australia and the dish products that will be deployed in South Africa (Carilli and Rawlings, 2004; Gastrow et al., 2016; Van Ardenne et al., 2012).

Project assessment of SKA

The science objectives of the SKA are broad and ambitious, with a focus on resolving some of the unanswered questions in astrophysics that date back to the so-called 'cosmic dawn'. The SKA will have considerable influence in its own right, but also on next-generation facilities. Between 50 and 70 per cent of the SKA's time will be spent on key science projects, which are deep investigations that require a lot of telescope time and are intended to produce ground-breaking discoveries. The remaining resources will be used for conventional, smaller-scale studies, depending on their levels of technical and scientific viability. Scientists from the observatory's member nations will have most of the available telescope time allocated to them.

The SKA's design has changed over time to take account of advancing technology and budgetary restrictions, much like any scientific endeavour. Before formal design work started on the SKA 1 project, the SKA Organisation Board set a cap of €650 million on costs (Cartlidge, 2019). The deployment baseline for the infrastructure, which has been regularly adjusted to reflect inflation, was fixed at €691 million at the latest update in December 2017. In June 2019, the first stage of the SKA project, SKA 1, was anticipated to cost €914 million (Cartlidge, 2019). This increased cost estimate will be subject to a critical review of the design of the entire SKA 1 system, and to ongoing overall cost audits (Berry, 2021; Carilli and Rawlings, 2004; Gastrow, et al., 2016; Schilizzi et al., 2007; Van Ardenne et al., 2012).

i. Sustainability

SKA has invested a lot of effort in aligning with the recommendations made by the European Strategy Forum on Research Infrastructures (ESFRI) task force on research infrastructure sustainability. Such sustainability requires a governance structure that will last for the duration of the project; financial stability; and policies that guarantee that the SKA is positioned sustainably in its host nations and will provide a compelling case for the socioeconomic benefits of membership in the project. The ability to inspire a consistent, sizeable commitment to support operations is an indication of sustainability for a research infrastructure. This calls for a multidisciplinary strategy that combines a legislative foundation for governing, a policy climate that facilitates financial stability, and scientific and socioeconomic arguments in support of these. There is progress in all domains of the SKA project, with the creation of the Square Kilometre Array Observatory (SKAO), the establishment of the intergovernmental organisation (IGO) tasked with delivering and operating the SKAO, and approval for the telescope's development in 2020 (Berry, 2021; Carilli and Rawlings, 2004; Gastrow et al., 2016; SKAO, 2023; Van Ardenne et al., 2012).

To prove its readiness and capabilities to host the SKA project, South Africa had to first construct the Karoo Array Telescope (KAT)-7. The KAT-7 is a seven-dish radio telescope array created as an engineering prototype for the 64-dish MeerKAT array. The South African government had to enact legislation to protect areas to guarantee the security of the SKA project. The Astronomy Geographic Advantage (AGA) Act of 2007 limited radio and electrical interference, and so helped facilitate funding for astronomy research. The AGA Act identifies so-called Astronomy Advantage Areas (AAAs). Under the Act, living in an AAA has implications for residents and municipalities. To date, the only areas identified as AAAs are Northern Cape Province, excluding Sol Plaatje Municipality, the Karoo Core AAA and the Karoo Central AAA within it. The Karoo Core AAA contains the main host site of the MeerKAT. Government regulations created an environment that was favourable for SKA sustainability, and KAT-7's construction and completion demonstrated South Africa's capacity to host the larger MeerKAT.

ii. Governance

The SKA adopted a strategy, used to good effect by the European Research Infrastructure Consortium, to advance from an unofficial partnership to the creation of a UK corporation to oversee the design process prior to construction. Then, following a decision made by SKA member nations in 2015, work started on creating an international organisation (the SKA Observatory) that would oversee the facility's advancement and management. A convention on astronomy resulted in the signing of a treaty by 15 countries to oversee the delivery of the world's largest radio telescope. This crucial choice was made to ensure a sustainable governance system in the long term. The best practices from all pertinent global and European examples were considered when building the IGO. It functions similarly to other long-standing intergovernmental infrastructure organisations like CERN (European Council for Nuclear Research), ESA (European Space Agency) and ESO (European Southern Observatory). The IGO is an independent organisation but some aspects of its rules were borrowed from the UN system (DSI, 2019). It is responsible for the operation of the SKA project which is promoted in accordance with the principles stated in the convention and is governed by a committee that has been elected by the members (Carilli and Rawlings, 2004; Gastrow et al., 2016; Van Ardenne et al., 2012). The IGO operates, and has appropriate legal standing and benefits in member countries in accordance with international law.

iii. Socioeconomic Benefits

The SKA is intended to encourage creativity and innovation across international industries and aid technological advancement. These will produce social benefits that will be realised prior to the telescope's ultimate astronomical breakthroughs. Additionally, market trends created by these technological advancements will be beneficial in other disciplines. For countries that take part in the SKA, being at the cutting edge of these advancements may have significant socioeconomic advantages. In addition, SKA's activities in computing will have benefits for the industries entailed in collaboration: systems reliant on analysing enormous amounts of information from globally disparate sources might benefit from spin-off improvements. Areas such as data management, data mining and analytics, imaging algorithms, remote visualisation and pattern matching may benefit from innovations sparked by the SKA's requirements.

The SKA is making a significant contribution towards a global knowledge-based economy. It has done this in part by opening the way for developing countries to contribute to this economy on an unparalleled scale. The facility's presence will also create job opportunities on the ground, in sites such as science museums and visitor centres for astro-tourists, and in the development of learning resources connected to the SKA.

However, potential benefits are not confined to developing nations. To design, develop, operate and manage all related services for the SKA, thousands of workers from numerous nations and professions will be required. In addition, as many of the workers involved in the project will be conducting remote research with telescopes, SKA will have a genuinely worldwide presence, thus facilitating opportunities in institutions around the globe. Therefore, the SKA has a potentially enormous impact on skills development globally (Carilli and Rawlings, 2004; Gastrow et al., 2016; Van Ardenne et al., 2012). The project has the potential to become the first interdisciplinary research infrastructure with education and outreach integrated into its progress from the start, encouraging youth to use the telescopes and develop related skills (Gastrow et al., 2016; Hall, 2005; Rawlings et al., 2004).

CASE STUDY 3: HYDROGEN SOUTH AFRICA (HYSA)

In September 2008, South Africa's DSI officially launched Hydrogen South Africa or HySA, a long-term (15-year) programme within its Research, Development, and Innovation (RDI) strategy for hydrogen and fuel cell technologies. The HySA programme aims to beneficiate the extensive Platinum Group Metal (PGM) reserves in the country. HySA consists of three Competency Centres (CCs): HySA Infrastructure, HySA Catalyst and HySA Systems (HySA, 2015; Lorentzen and Petersen, 2009). The first is housed at North-West University and aims to improve the mining and processing of platinum-group metals through novel approaches to and uses for small- and medium-scale hydrogen generation.

The second, HySA Systems was established at the University of the Western Cape by the South African Institute for Advanced Materials Chemistry (SAIAMC). It is a centre for systems integration and for the assessment of technological competency, focused on hydrogen and fuel cell technologies. Metal hydrides, HT-PEM fuel cells and HT-MEAs are being developed, prototyped, tested and put into service by HySA Systems for hydrogen storage and compression systems (HySA, 2015; Lorentzen and Petersen, 2009).

The third, HySA Catalysis Centre of Competence is jointly hosted by Mintek and the University of Cape Town (HySA, 2015; MISTRA, 2013). The Centre's main goals are to establish a fuel cell supply chain, in both the private and the public sectors, with the assistance of regional manufacturing partners and to transform South Africa into a significant global exporter of catalysts and fuel cell components. The scope of HySA Catalysis includes the catalysts and catalytic equipment that are used in the first phase of fuel cell and hydrogen value chains. It also entails the development of human capital, including a pool of South African engineers and scientists with expertise in the fuel cell sector (Bessarabov et al., 2012; HySA, 2015; Lorentzen and Petersen, 2009).

Assessment of the programme

It is useful to take stock of HySA's goals before assessing the programme, and throughout this section HySA's achievements are assessed against its stated aims. South Africa embarked on this technology project in energy and PGM beneficiation (fuel cell and hydrogen) as part of its science, technology and innovation strategy. It planned to supply 25 per cent of the global market in fuel cell catalysts by 2020 to maximise the value of its estimated 80 per cent share of the world's platinum group metal (PGM) reserves (HySA, 2015; Du Preez, 2022; MISTRA, 2020;). HySA seeks to develop membrane electrode assembly (MEA) and the ability to manufacture internationally competitive catalysts at commercially viable scales to gain any market share in the fuel cell catalyst market. Initially, Mintek and UCT created the Pt/C catalyst 'ySA-V40 as the first product. Future fuel cell sales will largely be made up of today's catalyst technology. It is possible that companies that have shown they can reliably produce catalysts at commercial scale and can innovate using current state-of-the-art technology will dominate the catalyst market (HySA, 2015; Lorentzen and Petersen, 2009; Turner, 1999).

i. Technological viability

One of HySA's main goals is to demonstrate its ability to achieve both technological and financial viability. Some of its achievements thus far include the creation of pilot plant manufacturing facilities/capabilities for HFC components and systems in South Africa; collaboration with important national and international HFC industries; development of a local supply chain of SMMEs; creation of commercial/industrial agreements with national and international HFC players; and publication of research in journals with high impact factors.

A small-scale hydrogen production facility was built by the HySA Infrastructure team. The system is made up of two 15 kWh lead-acid battery banks with charge controllers, a Proton S-10 PEM electrolyser, a hydrogen storage unit, and a 6 kW photovoltaic array. It is used to generate hydrogen from the energy from the PV panels; any excess energy is stored in battery banks for use in power outages (HySA, 2015; Lorentzen and Petersen, 2009; MISTRA, 2015). The system is used to investigate various power management techniques, configure system elements and perform research on various control strategies. The goal of the project is to create a locally produced hydrogen manufacturing process that is reliable and suitable for off-grid and dispersed small-scale applications, such as cluster residences in remote regions, healthcare facilities or localised fuelling stations. Despite the development of all these small-scale systems, the fuel cell market has not undergone a significant shift that has benefitted the South African economy, as the technology is stagnating and the nation continues to experience unabated load reductions, which the fuel cell technology was expected to help offset (Bessarabov et al., 2012; DSI, 2007; Hu et al., 2020; Singla et al., 2021).

With this in mind, scientists are researching different catalysts to boost the cost-effectiveness and efficiency of hydrogen fuel cells. Approximately 50 per cent of the total cost of large-scale manufacturing in a typical proton exchange membrane (PEM) fuel cell is borne by platinum group metal (PGM)-based catalysts. Two materials-based strategies that have been pursued to reduce costs are through utilising fewer PGM catalysts and developing substitute PGM-free catalysts. These are some of the strategies that HySA is exploring. Significant loss of stability occurs in the PEM fuel cell power generation unit, when PGM catalyst loading is reduced in a membrane electrode assembly (MEA), or when PGM-free catalysts are used (Bessarabov et al., 2012; DSI, 2007; Hu et al., 2020; Singla et al., 2021).

Additionally, there is a sizable knowledge gap between device integration and material innovation. For instance, high-performance electrocatalysts frequently show unwanted rapid deterioration in MEAs. The development of PEM fuel cells is severely constrained by this. Research is currently being conducted to better understand the degradation of low-PGM and PGM-free catalysts in fuel cell MEAs and to develop material-based solutions. Researchers at the Argonne National Laboratory of the US Department of Energy (DoE) recently produced and studied non-platinum fuel cell catalysts, which are compounds that speed up crucial fuel cell operations (James, 2021). The study provides a greater knowledge of the mechanisms that make these catalysts successful, and the new findings could aid in the development of even more efficient and cost-effective catalysts. This demonstrates that HySA is on the right track with the research strategies employed for fuel cell catalysts.

ii. Economic viability

The goals and outcome of the HySA programme will be of benefit to South Africa in the following ways: increased economic growth; a stronger South African skill base; better positioning the country to make a significant contribution to curbing the impact of climate change; and averting potential future export penalties due to a high carbon footprint. One of the most effective ways to meet South Africa's energy needs and reduce greenhouse gas emissions in other sectors is to employ fuel cell and hydrogen technologies. In addition, fuel cell technology can be used to address energy inequality and poverty, since this technology can be deployed to areas where there is limited grid capacity. Globally, hydrogen (green) is one of the key elements that is needed to achieve net zero emission targets. Therefore, there is a growing demand for these technologies locally and globally to combat climate change (Bessarabov et al., 2012; James, 2021; Kongkanand and Mathias, 2016). The HySA programme is well positioned to address South Africa's need to diversify its energy mix, and the imperatives of widening energy access and addressing energy poverty using hydrogen technologies.

iii. Markets

Fuel cells and the related hydrogen infrastructure constitute new technologies that promise to boost South Africa's platinum industry and open up new markets for it. For instance, Vehicle Projects Inc. Colorado, as the prime contractor, collaborated with Trident South Africa and Battery Electrics, Inc. to develop a hybrid locomotive as a demonstration for Anglo American Platinum Limited (Bessarabov et al., 2012; James, 2021; Kongkanand and Mathias, 2016; Sasaki et al., 2010). The locomotive is propelled by lithium-ion batteries and Ballard PEM stacks. In South Africa's mining sector, there are at least four thousand of these locomotives in use. In addition to other opportunities that have been mentioned, these locomotives show the potential market for fuel cell use in the mining industry in South Africa. Further, there is a potential to use hydrogen-powered fuel cell trucks for mining activities, and fuel cell-powered heavy vehicles for road transport of goods. Additionally, South Africa has developed the Hydrogen Society Roadmap (HSRM) and it's implementation is underway. The roadmap explores how South Africa can best use and deploy hydrogen and hydrogen related technologies as part of its transition to a low carbon and climate resilient society (HSRM, 2022). These are potential markets within South Africa that the country has planned to invest in.

LESSONS FROM THE CASE STUDIES

The three projects covered are important technological projects that the South African government has undertaken and invested national resources into. They are therefore critical in the discourse on South Africa's science, technology and innovation policy and strategy. This section discusses some of the lessons derived from these three technological projects. Project successes and failures will be discussed in this context.

Lesson One: Set and monitor realistic timelines for projects.
The trajectory of the PBMR project is a powerful testament to the crucial importance of setting realistic timelines for innovation projects. The PBMR was initiated in South Africa in 1998 and the demonstration or pilot was expected by 2004 at the latest. That goal was not realised. But there was not sufficient assessment of why such an important milestone had been missed: was it a case of unrealistic timelines, with a project that simply required more time to reach fruition, or was the project floundering for other, less-remediable reasons? Those questions were not identified and addressed. Instead, the project was abandoned completely some 12 years later in 2010, when government entirely cancelled all plans for a demo and pulled all funding. Rigorous and insistent attention to timelines, and ongoing assessment of whether these are realistic or not, are crucial to the success of innovation projects.

Lesson Two: Draw on the experiences of countries that have developed similar technology.
The PBMR technology was new in a country with no history of developing and licensing nuclear technology. South Africa failed

to learn from other countries, including Germany, the USA, Japan, France and the UK who all had experience with this technology (Thomas, 2011). This failure to heed lessons from other countries was due to South Africa's blinkered focus at the time on developing nuclear energy and its determination to be a global player in the nuclear sector.

South Africa also missed the opportunity to learn from China's research path. China signed a licensing deal with Germany for high-temperature gas coolant reactors around the same time as South Africa did, in 1989. However, China used the conventional steam cycle for its pebble bed technology. If South Africa had taken cognisance of this development, the country might have abandoned the gas turbine earlier and so avoided delays in the completion of its project. Instead, South Africa followed a flawed approach for a long time, missing relevant research and opportunities to assess the implications of this research for South Africa's own project.

China managed to build the HTR-10 plant, a 10 MW high-temperature gas-cooled experimental reactor for demonstration at Tsinghua University's Institute of Nuclear and New Energy Technology (Thomas, 2011; World Nuclear News, 2021). This reactor operated from the year 2000 and reached full power in 2003. China has recently launched a precursor to this plant, the HTR-PM: a plant that features two small reactors that drive a single 210 MWe turbine (Moormann et al., 2018; World Nuclear News, 2021). China has reached more milestones and achieved greater success than South Africa's PBMR company ever did. This success can be attributed to prioritising a demonstration plant. In addition, China involved multiple stakeholders in investment into and ownership of its project, unlike South Africa. Such diversity fosters greater accountability, which facilitates effective budget and project planning, execution and management. The lack of these factors was critical in the PBMR's many setbacks.

It is worth noting that the SKA project has some of this diversity as it is funded by multiple partner countries and thus has varied stakeholders. This results in the sharing of risks and financial responsibilities, which mitigates the possibility of a central funder pulling out of the project or failing to meet commitments, as has happened with South Africa's PBMR.

Lesson Three: Manage budget constraints and have a marketing strategy in place.

The trajectory of the PBMR project suggests a lack of effective budgeting and marketing. Firstly, the PBMR plant's assumed lifespan was excessively long and ignored the need to retire old plants when new, more economical ones become available. In addition, the PBMR company had no established customer base and no committed buyer. Focused feasibility studies and a tighter marketing strategy would have encouraged interest in the reactors from investors other than South Africa. This might have opened up additional sources of funding, and so helped with managing budget constraints.

The SKA differs from the two energy projects discussed in that it does not necessarily produce a marketable product. However, some marketable innovations that are driven by the needs of the SKA have emerged in other areas within the sector. For example, the EMSS Antenna company developed a world-first, low-noise, stable receiver for the MeerKAT radio telescope. The company was formed by PhD students from Stellenbosch University, and it was able to innovate and respond directly to gaps in the technology needed for the SKA project. Similarly, other South African companies – namely Power Adenco Joint Venture (Pty) Ltd, Vivo Technical, Zutari and EMCOM (DSI, 2022) – have been recently awarded contracts for SKA infrastructure to the combined value of R1.2 billion (DSI, 2022).

Additionally, South Africa's SKA has developed an innovative industry called astro-tourism. The Northern Cape offers visitors 'dark sky' experiences through innovative astro-tourism activities in South Africa. Once fully established and widely advertised, the distinctive experiences will have the potential to tap into a very specific market in South Africa (Gastrow et al., 2016; Rawlings et al., 2004; Van Ardenne et al., 2012).

HySA, unlike the SKA project, has a direct relationship with the market: it is well placed to ensure the beneficiation of PGMs through the hydrogen economy. In this sense, it occupies a specific niche in South Africa, with unique potential for facilitating the marketing of South Africa's PGM by-products such as catalysts for electrolysers and fuel cells. For example, through the creation of a green hydrogen sector,

HySA could potentially increase South Africa's export markets in the automotive sector, steel industry, chemicals and agricultural sectors.

Lesson Four: The value of building capabilities in the sectors in which technology projects are located.

The SKA project has proven to be an excellent example of how an innovation project can prompt the growth of skills and experience with a wider sector, and of the value that accrues from building up that skilled pool. Prior to the SKA project, South Africa's astronomy sector had very limited skills and experience on which to draw. The SKA project changed that: the Human Capital Development (HCD) Programme was established in 2005 in response to this need. The programme offers assistance at all academic levels to build expertise in pertinent radio astronomy, engineering and science fields. It aims to keep a consistent flow of young people engaged in relevant research and study programmes, and to ensure that adequate supervision and teaching resources are available for the students. The programme is also open to students from the SKA African Partner nations. More than a few hundred awards have now been given out to universities and students, and by 2014, 600 bursaries, grants, fellowships, and five research chairs had been created (Gastrow et al., 2016).

SKA has also used the MeerKAT facility as an opportunity to expand the skills required for the operation and maintenance of the facility. Artisan and technician training programmes have been established, with defined timelines for producing the required numbers of highly skilled workers. These programmes are on track to meet this demand within the deadlines set. In the towns close to the SKA site in the Karoo, the SKA HCD programme has helped with the hiring and secondment of maths and science teachers, offering scholarships for students to go to Carnarvon High School, establishing cyberlabs and e-learning centres, and training locals to manage cyber-centres.

Overall, South Africa's competitiveness on the international market has significantly increased as a result of its participation in the SKA project, and the country's skills in this arena are now internationally recognised. This was achieved through research aimed at anticipating the skills that would be required for the sector, and significant financial support from state actors for relevant courses, facilities and opportunities within the higher education system. These state interventions have resulted in a rapid increase in the competencies available to employers over the past 10 years. It is however important to note a major concern in one area of skills development: local TVET colleges lack the apabilityes to develop the skills required at an intermediate level – for example, those needed by technicians and artisans (Gastrow, 2015).

HySA has also had a transformative effect within the wider hydrogen and fuel cell technology sector, achieved by building a knowledge economy in that sector. HySA achieved this through the establishment of the competency centres – discussed in Case Study Three above – housed at three South African universities. The most notable effect of these initiatives has been the extent to which a technology that was not talked about in South Africa has moved into popular discourse and been incorporated into policy formulation. Over the years, policymakers have incorporated fuel cell and hydrogen technology into strategies to address energy requirements and transition to a low carbon economy. HySA has also fed into other policies, including the DSI's recently launched hydrogen society roadmap (DSI, 2022). The technologies have also been taken up in the private sector with mining companies dedicating resources to research into ways of using this technology.

In the case of the PBMR, there was capacity built in the sector but it was not enough to sustain this project. The PBMR initiative generated more than 100 patents between 1999 and 2004, demonstrating the strength of internal research. The project enlisted a considerable number of domestic and international subcontractors, resulting in a large supporting infrastructure. It has partnerships with institutions including the North-West University while also using facilities at the Nuclear Energy Corporation of South Africa (NECSA). Relevant skills and capabilities were being built in the country and still exist. Unfortunately, some of the nuclear engineers who worked at PBMR have now moved to the United States to work for companies contracted to develop a similar concept to the PBMR.

Lesson Five: Partnerships and collaborations with intermediary organisations, government and the private sector are crucial for effective governance, accountability and skills development.

Intermediaries have crucial functions, which are often overlooked. They are responsible for funding, strategy, planning, managerial oversight, network building and knowledge transfer (Gastrow et al., 2016). Two examples are the DSI and the NRF, both public sector organisations in South Africa. The SKA is managed by these intermediaries and they are responsible for supporting interactions between the SKA and the US-based Space Science Institute (SSI). This management by intermediaries allows for proper governance, monitoring and evaluation of the project to ensure that it stays on track. In addition, the intermediaries connect the SKA network in South Africa with networks in other countries for knowledge exchanges, funding, etc.

SKA also benefits from collaborations with international intermediaries. The African European Radio Astronomy Partnership and the National Radio Astronomy Observatory (located in the USA) are two examples of international assistance organisations. In addition, the International Astronomical Union provides assistance to the private sector. These organisations form part of the astronomy innovation system, together with the SKA's innovation network. The latter encompasses Africa, Europe, India, China and the Pacific region. African partner countries participate by offering infrastructure sites and skills development. Students, scientists and engineers from these nations work on SKA operations. Collaboration has also been important in demand-led skill development, as mandated by SKA. This has involved successful partnerships and coordination between businesses, government and education and training institutions.

The SKA project office in South Africa, which also serves as an intermediary, is the main coordination hub for the whole project. As this project office is part of a network of international innovation networks, it resembles an industry-wide association. This office is uniquely different from the other two main intermediaries, the DSI and the NRF, in that it prioritises sector demands over national development objectives. The SKA office is categorised as a public–

private intermediary, a categorisation that reflects this intermediary's special characteristics. The success of the SKA can thus be attributed to intermediaries, partnerships and collaborations.

Similar to the SKA project, HySA is led by an intermediary organisation, the DSI, in collaboration with research institutions and industry. The DSI and NRF are the public sector intermediary organisations responsible for ensuring funding for HySA. Furthermore, HySA serves as the chair of the International Partnership for Hydrogen and Fuel Cells and the Economy (IPHE), a 22-member, intergovernmental organisation whose mission is to facilitate the transition to energy systems that use hydrogen and fuel cell technologies (IPHE, 2023). The organisation serves as a platform for partners to share resources, foster collaborations, provide accurate information to policymakers and monitor developments in hydrogen and fuel cell technologies to inform necessary activities.

Such international collaboration at institutional level has enhanced HySA's capacity to build a strong knowledge base in fuel cell and hydrogen technologies in South Africa. It has done this by employing international experts, as well as by establishing competency centres, training postgraduate students and establishing research chairs. To further build South Africa's skills pool, HySA has tapped into bilateral agreements between the DSI and other countries. Collaboration with intermediaries has been central then to HySA's capacity to build a knowledge base and develop local skills, which have in turn been crucial in South Africa having the expertise to take the HySA project to the next phase of commercialisation.

HySA's collaborative efforts also point to another valuable lesson, namely the importance of engaging government policymakers in the development of new technologies. As is evident from HySA's trajectory, such engagement greatly increases the possibility of policymakers taking cognisance of a new technology and therefore facilitating further recognition from the private sector.

Management of the PBMR was very different from that of either the SKA or HySA. The PBMR was managed by the Board, and by Eskom, a state-run enterprise. These structures resulted in a lack of proper governance, which in turn led to the demise of the PBMR project.

CONCLUSION AND RECOMMENDATIONS

South Africa has embarked on huge technology projects in energy, astronomy and PGM beneficiation (with a focus on the use of fuel cell and hydrogen technologies) as part of its science, technology and innovation strategy. This chapter has discussed three of these projects and reflected on the factors that contributed to their successes and failures.

South Africa's ambitions of being competitive, even a leader, in nuclear energy led the PBMR team to believe that South Africa would succeed with high-temperature nuclear reactors where other countries had failed. This was despite clear evidence that the high-temperature reactor was not viable. Since the announcement of China's high-temperature gas-cooled modular pebble bed (HTR-PM) reactor, Moormann and colleagues (2018) have continued to issue warnings about the safety of operating and waste management in new PBMRs. These authors say that there is still insufficient knowledge of core behaviour, dust physics and fuel materials to render the technology safe.

Despites is potential promise, the PBMR project should have been abandoned long before it was finally halted due to the early emergence of unresolved problems. These included shifting timelines, escalating costs, changes in plant design and, most importantly, an inability to deliver a demonstration plant. The South African government continued to support this project despite strong indications that it would be best to do otherwise, possibly because of the government's relentless pursuit of nuclear energy.

South Africa winning the SKA bid was a huge accomplishment; the SKA is a national flagship project and a symbol of world-class scientific and technology achievement. The SKA has therefore received major political support, which has ensured that priority has been given to the policy and funding required for the project's success. Some of the key positive outcomes identified in the SKA case study were international acknowledgement of South Africa's scientific and technical prowess in the fields of astronomy and physics, and significant developments in ICT capacity and data-processing techniques. Other gains for South Africa are SKA spin-off programmes aimed at building human capacity in relevant fields, including development of South Africa's human capacity programmes and its engineering capabilities.

However, the SKA does face challenges to its continued success, and it is important that these are acknowledged and addressed. For example, the SKA's collaborations with government, business and education have presented substantial challenges because these partnerships have been at institution level, each one of these is an individual entity with its own goals and processes. It is important therefore to adopt systems thinking that takes account of the entire innovation 'ecosystem', and to recognise the differing roles that public and private intermediaries can play in the functioning of this ecosystem. Public-private intermediaries are important in coordination, and private intermediaries can have significant influence on policy. The necessity for a cooperative effort, which includes government, industry, academic institutions and other organisations is becoming increasingly clear.

In addition, large science initiatives, like the SKA, face challenges in keeping up with the shifting skills needed to accommodate rapid technological progress within a global network. As a result, it is extremely difficult to coordinate the skills of supply-side and demand-side actors. The SKA differs from other high-technology industries in that major roles are played by governments and local and international science facilities rather than transnational corporations.

The HySA project has done excellent work in capacity building to ensure that South Africa has a knowledge economy in this sector. Although the HySA programme is well established, it is critical that public-private partnerships are established to develop markets for fuel cells and hydrogen technologies: this may be a deciding factor in whether the project succeeds or not. The success of the HySA must go beyond creating a knowledge base in this field to commercialisation of the technology in South Africa.

To this end, the industrial component of HySA's collaborations needs to be strengthened (MISTRA, 2020). Increased investment by the private sector and industry is going to be the key to unlocking fuel cell and hydrogen markets for the commercialisation stage of these technologies. This should be accompanied by policies to create an enabling environment for the business sector, including small businesses, to be a receptive market for hydrogen technology. For instance, the update of the Integrated Resource Plan (IRP)[5] should explicitly include fuel cell and hydrogen technologies as part of the national energy mix and solutions for it. This will in turn create confidence in the private sector about the future viability of the technology, which will encourage further investment in the technological sector. The DSI has already taken a step in this direction with the establishment of the Hydrogen Society Roadmap, which is a progressive initiative that will encourage the development of markets for fuel cell and hydrogen technologies in the country.

The success of the HySA programme therefore rests on the creation and strengthening of partnerships with the private sector, research institutions and government. These partnership or lack thereof will ultimately determine the success or failure of the next commercialisation phase. To hasten the widespread adoption and commercialisation of fuel cell technology, South Africa must consider adopting a different approach for the HySA programme from the one used to expand capabilities in astronomy. For instance, in the USA, ElectroCat[6] coordinates R&D activities at national laboratories and facilitates academic and industrial partners' access to world-class tools and expertise. South Africa could consider embracing the ElectroCat approach to propel the HySA programme to success, in comparison with the current model in which the DSI serves as an intermediary.

Resources allocated to the PBMR did not yield good returns as poor decisions were made regarding the management of the project and relevant technology. This resulted in over a decade of funding without any demonstration plant being built and so investors pulled

---

5 Integrated Resource Plan is South Africa's electricity planning document, which details South Africa's electricity demand and how this demand will be met (DMRE, 2019).
6 ElectroCat consortium aims to increase US competitiveness in manufacturing fuel cells and hydrogen production water electrolysers by addressing the primary challenges to the widespread implementation of this technology. Industry and academia engages with ElectroCat by participating through competitively selected U.S. Department of Energy-funded projects or via standard national laboratory partnerships. See https://www.electrocat.org/.

out, leaving the state as the sole funder of the project. South Africa could have learned from other countries that have pursued this type of technology with limited success, or sought assistance from experts in the field to resolve some of the technical issues with the technology. Many varied factors account for the difficulties faced by the PBMR, but the major issue was the failure to establish a global innovation network that South Africa could benefit from. This was vital as South Africa lacked experience in developing high-temperature nuclear reactors.

South Africa has shown with the SKA that it has what it takes to succeed with large technology projects. The SKA has a strong innovation network to tap into and political backing. These assets are underpinned by capable intermediary organisations, which have provided support; strong interactive capability within the SKA organisation itself; a high level of responsiveness from the research institutes in South Africa to meet SKA's requirements for niche expertise; and a dense network structure within the astronomy sector. Policymakers should note the value of this alignment within the astronomy sector to derive interventions that can be applied in similar technology projects to facilitate success.

South Africa's achievements in HySA and the SKA have been due to the DSI and NRF's capacity to design, manage and execute such projects. While this should be noted and replicated, it is important to recognise that government departments and institutions face severe resource challenges in the current economic climate. It should be noted then that lessons from these two projects can be drawn on in science and technology innovation projects that are not under the auspices of the DSI. Whatever the avenue, South Africa must continue to pursue prospects for large technology projects as these have the potential to accelerate economic development and help the country reach its sustainable development goals.

REFERENCES

Adam, R.M. 2020. 'Technology, policy and politics: Critical success factors in high-technology infrastructure projects'. *Social Dynamics*, 46(3), 378–390.
Berry, S.T. 2021. 'The SKA approach to sustainable research', in Beck, H.P. and Charitos, P. (eds). *The Economics of Big Science: Essays by Leading*

Scientists and Policymakers. Switzerland: Springer, 2021, 25–31.

Britz, E. 2022. 'Blue-SKA thinking – construction begins on Square Kilometre Array'. *Daily Maverick*, https://www.dailymaverick.co.za/article/2022-12-05-blue-ska-thinking-construction-begins-on-square-kilometre-array/, accessed 10 November 2023.

Bessarabov, D., Van Niekerk, F., Van der Merwe, F., Vosloo, M., North, B. and Mathe, M. 2012. 'Hydrogen infrastructure within HySA National Program in South Africa: Road map and specific needs'. *Energy Procedia*, 29, 42–52.

Carilli, C. and Rawlings, S.R. 2004. 'Science with the Square Kilometre Array'. *New Astronomy Reviews,* 48, 1–6.

Cartlidge, E. 2019. 'Square Kilometre Array hit with further cost hike and delay'. *Physicsworld,* https://physicsworld.com/a/square-kilometre-array-hit-with-further-cost-hike-and-delay/, accessed 2 October 2023.

Department of Mineral Resources and Energy (DMRE). 2019. 'South Africa's Integrated Resource Plan'. https://www.energy.gov.za/irp/2019/IRP-2019.pdf , accessed 25 June 2023.

Department of Science and Innovation (DSI). 2007. 'National Hydrogen and Fuel Cell Technologies Research, Development and Innovation Strategy'. Department of Science and Innovation, https://www.hysa-padep.co.za/wp-content/uploads/2022/02/Document-2_National-Hydrogen-and-Fuel-Cell-Technologies-Research-Development-and-Innovation-Strategy.pdf, accessed 20 June 2023.

Department of Science and Innovation (DSI). 2018. 'Draft White Paper on Science, Technology and Innovation'. *Government Gazette*, 14 September 2018, No. 41909. https://www.gov.za/sites/default/files/gcis_document/201809/41909gon954.pdf, accessed 13 June 2023.

Department of Science and Innovation (DSI). 2019. 'Square Kilometre Array Telescope & MeerKAT projects: Briefing'. https://pmg.org.za/committee-meeting/28862/, accessed 2 October 2023.

Department of Science and Innovation (DSI). 2022. 'South African company awarded contract as construction of the world's largest radio astronomy infrastructure and telescope commences'. Media statement, 14 December 2022.

Du Preez S.P., Kozhukhova A.E. and Bessarabov D.G. 2022. 'Catalytic hydrogen combustion using platinum supported on anodized aluminium oxide adhered to metallic aluminium'. *South African Journal of Chemistry*, 76, 31–37.

Eskom. 2020. 'Request for an Expression of Interest (EOI) in PBMR'. Eskom Leadership Development Centre, Midrand, Gauteng, https://tenderbulletin.eskom.co.za/Tenders/Docs?TENDERID=43443, accessed 20 July 2022.

Fig, D. 2010. 'Nuclear energy rethink? The rise and demise of South Africa's Pebble Bed Modular Reactor'. Institute for Security Studies, Pretoria.

http://www.issafrica.org/uploads/210.pdf, accessed 22 June 2023

Gastrow, M. 2015. 'Understanding interactive capabilities for skills development in sectoral systems of innovation: A case study of astronomy and the Square Kilometre Array telescope'. https://psetresearchrepository.dhet.gov.za/show-pdf/609, accessed 30 April 2015.

Gastrow, M., Kruss, G. and Petersen, I.H. 2016. 'Connecting capabilities in highly unequal developing countries: The case of the Square Kilometre Array telescope in South Africa'. *Development Southern Africa*, 33 (3), 361–375.

Hall, P. (ed). 2005. *The SKA: An Engineering Perspective*. Dordrecht: Springer.

Hu, G., Chen, C., Lu, H.T., Wu, Y., Liu, C., Tao, L., Men, Y., He, G. and Li, K.G. 2020. 'A review of technical advances, barriers, and solutions in the power to hydrogen (P2H) roadmap'. *Engineering*, 6(12), 1364–1380.

Hydrogen South Africa (HySA). 2015. 'Hydrogen South Africa Public Awareness'. https://www.hysa-padep.co.za/about/, accessed 26 March 2022.

International Partnership for Hydrogen and Fuel Cells in the Economy (IPHE). 2023. 'Terms of reference for the International Partnership for Hydrogen and Fuel Cells in the Economy'. https://www.iphe.net/_files/ugd/45185a_b5b324e98af64196a60cc00fcd0f4293.pdf, accessed 17 April 2023.

James B., 2021. 'Fuel cell systems analysis'. *U.S. Department of Energy 2021 Hydrogen and Fuel Cells Annual Merit Review*, https://www.hydrogen.energy.gov/pdfs/review21/fc163_james_2021_o.pdf, accessed 12 June 2022.

Kongkanand, A. and Mathias, M.F. 2016 'The priority and challenge on high-power performance of low-platinum proton-exchange membrane fuel cells'. *Journal of Physical Chemistry Letters*, 7, 1127–1137.

Lorentzen, J. and Petersen, I.H. 2009. *Three New Technology Platforms. Sectors and Skills, The Need for Policy Alignment*. Cape Town: HSRC Press.

Mapungubwe Institute for Strategic Reflection (MISTRA). 2013. *South Africa and the Global Hydrogen Economy, the Strategic Role of Platinum Group Metals*. Johannesburg: Mapungubwe Institute for Strategic Reflection.

Mapungubwe Institute for Strategic Reflection (MISTRA). 2020. 'Partnerships for PGM Beneficiation Through the Hydrogen Economy: A report on MISTRA's annual roundtables 2016-2019'. Mapungubwe Institute for Strategic Reflection, Johannesburg.

McKune, C. 2010. 'Pebble Bed Modular Reactor demonstration plant is funded but not constructed'. *South African Journal of Science*, 106(5), 1–3.

Moormann, R., Kemp, R.S. and Li, J. 2018. 'Caution is needed in operating and managing the waste of new pebble-bed nuclear reactors'. *Joule*, 2(10), 1911–1914.

Minerals Council South Africa, 2022. 'Platinum key facts and figures', https://www.mineralscouncil.org.za/sa-mining/platinum, accessed 15 March 2023.

National Planning Commission (NPC). 2012. 'National Development Plan Vision 2030'. https://www.gov.za/issues/national-development-plan-2030, accessed 12 May 2023.

Organisation for Economic Co-operation and Development (OECD). 2009. 'Innovation in firms: A microeconomic perspective'. https://www.oecd.org/berlin/44120491.pdf, accessed 12 March 2023.

Patel, S. 2022. 'China starts up first fourth-generation nuclear reactor'. *Power*, 1 February. https://www.powermag.com/china-starts-up-first-fourth-generation-nuclear-reactor/#:~:text=The%20first%20of%20two%20units,20, accessed 10 October 2022.

PBMR, 2005. 'The Pebble Bed Evolution', Internet Archive Way Back Machine, https://web.archive.org/web/20070223061715/http://www.pbmr.co.za/download/Evolution%20June%2005.pdf, accessed 10 October 2023.

Rawlings, S., Abdalla, F.B., Bridle, S.L., Blake, C.A. et al. 2004. 'Galaxy evolution, cosmology and dark energy with the Square Kilometre Array'. *New Astronomy Reviews*, 48(11/12), 1013–1027.

Singla, M.K., Nijhawan, P. and Oberoi, A.S. 2021. 'Hydrogen fuel and fuel cell technology for cleaner future: A review'. *Environmental Science and Pollution Research*, 28, 15607–15626.

South African Government (SA-GOV). 2022. 'Official guide to South Africa 2021/2022: Science and Innovation'. https://www.gov.za/about-sa/science-technology, accessed 12 April 2022.

Sasaki, K., Naohara, H., Cai, Y., Choi, Y.M., Liu, P. et al. 2010. 'Core-protected platinum monolayer shell high-stability electrocatalysts for fuel-cell cathodes'. *Angewandte Chemie International Edition*, 49, 8602–8607.

Schilizzi, R.T, Alexander, P., Cordes, J.M. et al. 2007. 'SKA Memo 100: Preliminary specifications for the Square Kilometre Array'. https://citeseerx.ist.psu.edu/document?repid=rep1&type=pdf&doi=cdfe868c40f-c785af70db56b12dd6451c74edef7, accessed 20 March 2023.

Square Kilometre Array Observatory (SKAO). 22 September 2023. 'SKAO Annual Report 2022'. https://issuu.com/ska_telescope/docs/skao_annual_report_2022, accessed 10 November 2023.

Thomas, S. 1999. 'Arguments on the construction of PBMR reactors in South Africa'. Briefing Paper, SPRU, University of Sussex, http://www.nirs.org/intl/SThomasPMBRpaper.htm, accessed 23 June 2023.

Thomas, S. 2011. 'The Pebble Bed Modular Reactor: An obituary'. *Energy Policy*, 39, 2431–2440.

Turner, J.A. 1999. 'A realizable renewable energy future'. *Science*, 285(5428), 687–689. https://doi.org/10.1126/science.285.5428.687. https://citeseerx.ist.psu.edu/document?repid=rep1&type=pdf&doi=f094f0dd77748363c8aa4f26bb87e501f1369b05, accessed 20 June 2022.

United Nations (UN). 2019. 'A Framework for Science, Technology and Innovation Policy Reviews'. United Nations, https://unctad.org/system/files/official-document/dtlstict2019d4_en.pdf, accessed 13 June 2023.

United States Department of Energy (US DoE). 2023. 'Benefits of Small Modular Reactors (SMRs)'. https://www.energy.gov/ne/benefits-small-modular-reactors-smrs, accessed 24 February 2023.

Van Ardenne, A., Faulkner, A.J., Bij de Vaate, J.G. 2012. 'The SKA new instrumentation: Aperture arrays in the Square Kilometre Array', in Barbosa, D., Anton, S. Gurvits, L., and Maia, D (eds). *Paving the Way For The New 21st Century Radio Astronomy Paradigm*. Berlin: Springer.

World Nuclear News. 17 December 2021. 'Demonstration HTR-PM connected to grid'. https://www.world-nuclear-news.org/Articles/Demonstration-HTR-PM-connected-to-grid, accessed 20 July 2022.

Zhang, Z., Dong, Y., Li, F., Zhang, Z., Wang, H. et al. 2016. 'The Shandong Shidao Bay 200 MWe high-temperature gas-cooled reactor pebble-bed module (HTR-PM) demonstration power plant: An engineering and technological innovation'. *Engineering*, 2, 112–118.

EIGHT

Structural change and innovation in the mineral resource finance network

THOMAS POGUE

'The deeply wounding assault on human dignity visited daily on black South Africans by all manner of classification and control laws has been stopped in its tracks by the victory of the liberation movement. This is a magnificent achievement to be celebrated forever. At the same time it is important not to allow the brilliance of this very process to blind oneself to a fundamental problem that remains.'
– Francis Wilson (2003: 298–299)

INTRODUCTION

This chapter describes technologies from South Africa's mineral resource finance network (MRFN) and their journeys towards commercialisation. It explores two cases in which the breadth and depth of successful commercialisation vary significantly: the creation of South

Africa's modern export coal market and the development of water-based hydraulic mining technology. Building on previous analyses, this chapter describes how relationships between a technology and the economy in which it is produced co-create subsequent economic and technological opportunities. Employing the multi-dimensional analytical framework proposed by Weber and Rohracher (2012) to the conceptualisation of innovation detailed in Arthur (2009),[1] these case studies highlight changing relations between the MRFN and the broader political economy as well as the technologies' values and generation of costs. The final section reflects on these insights and explores implications for future innovation and development policies associated with the MRFN.

Each case study begins with a description of the challenge or opportunity that drove the initial development of the technology. That is followed by a review of the key components through which the technologies were developed, that is the technological domain. With that context established, the analysis details the process of the technologies' development across their respective markets, development structures and capabilities systems. The final part of the case studies reflects on key lessons from the commercialisation of these technologies, including their impacts on the broader development environment.

Comparing the legacies of these two technologies, the export coal market had a deeper impact on South Africa's production system because of the scope of this market, both domestically and internationally.

However, water-based hydraulic mining technology played a critical, although not dramatic, role in supporting South Africa's extensive deep-level mining interests through a cumulative process of system improvement. Policymakers do not seem to have considered adequately the implications of these experiences for contemporary mining and economic development policies. The penultimate section therefore considers the potential for incorporating these lessons into future policy development.

---

1   For further details on the theories and methods applied in this descriptive analysis, see Chapter 1 of this volume.

DEVELOPMENT OF A LARGE-SCALE SOUTH AFRICAN COAL EXPORT INDUSTRY[2]

Technological challenges in and opportunities for the export of coal
There were several precedents in the export of coal from KwaZulu-Natal. Coal from what was then Natal was experimented with as a bunker fuel for ships out of Durban in the early 1850s (Edgecombe and Guest, 1985). This potential led to discussion in the 1860s about developing railways to transport coal from Natal to meet the demand for bunker coal at the port of Durban. Following the development of the Witwatersrand goldfields, a rail line linking Durban with the Natal coal mines was initiated in the mid-1880s. By the time the Union of South Africa was established in 1910, Natal collieries were exporting coal through Durban, which was a major market for them, and some coal production from the Transvaal was being exported out of Maputo (Delagoa) Bay. The First World War further increased South African coal exports as the country supported the war effort.

However, after the First World War concerns emerged over the scale of South African coal exports and their potential impact on domestic demand. A 1920 Commission recommended a system of grading coal for export into 'classes' and led to the Coal Act of 1922, which gave the government authority to curtail coal exports to meet domestic needs. Further development of South Africa's industrial economy during and after the First World War led to the Fuel Research Coal Act of 1930, which granted government the authority to suspend exports in order to protect supply for the domestic market.

The Second World War once again expanded the export market for South African coal as the war increased demand. Post-war reconstruction in Europe and elsewhere meant that the international demand for South African coal was sustained. However, further South African industrialisation again raised concerns about the adequacy (and cost) of domestic coal supplies. As a result, in 1951 the South African government banned most coal exports. This reduced exports

---

2 This case builds on the analysis by Fatima Ferraz in Ferraz and Pogue (2016).

from between 15 per cent and 33 per cent of domestic production during the 1940s to around 2 per cent from 1950 to 1970 (Eberhard, 2011). However, local producers suffered from the erosion of prices and a stagnating market on the domestic front. As a result, when government restrictions were lifted, producers found it a challenge to scale up to the level required for an export coal industry.

The nature of South Africa's coal seams posed a second challenge to the development of a large-scale export coal industry. Southern African coal deposits tend to have relatively high levels of mineral matter, which creates high ash content (Falcon and Ham, 1988). When high ash coal is used in reactors it leaves more combustion residuals, changes thermal behaviour, and tends to adhere and build up in the equipment (Jayanti et al., 2007). Therefore, for most export markets it is necessary to process the coal to reduce its ash content. Processing of South African coal dates back to the early 1900s when jig concentrators were used to reduce ash and produce higher-quality coal for domestic users. However, processing significantly improved during the 1950s and 1960s as the Fuel Research Institute of South Africa adapted dense medium processing technology that had been developed in the Netherlands (Napier-Munn et al., 2014).[3] While further work was needed to create a processing technology for the export of coal at scale, the foundations for a solution to this challenge had been established.

The development of a coal export market also necessitated improvements to and development of South Africa's transportation infrastructure. The first part of this challenge involved identifying a location where a deep-water bulk cargo port could be developed. By the early 20th century several South African bays had been identified as potential sites for the development of another port, but it was only with the industrial growth catalysed by the Second World War that development of additional cargo capacity began to be seen as an economic proposition. By the late 1960s Richards Bay had been identified as the most suitable site after several locations north of Durban had been evaluated (Zwamborn and Cawood, 1974). The site

---

3   De Korte (2010) provides a brief history of coal processing technology and the institutions that developed it in South Africa.

was chosen with the recognition that an important function of the port would be to serve the highveld region of modern-day Gauteng and Mpumalanga province, as well as the coal-producing areas of northern KwaZulu-Natal. In parallel with the decision about where to develop the deep-water port, planning for a 500km railway from the highveld to the coast north of Durban also began in the mid-1960s. Both the railway line and the deep-water port required further planning and design, but opportunities and concepts had been established.

One of South Africa's largest coal mining-finance groups, Anglo American Corporation, had initiated conceptualisation of both parts of this transportation system, as well as a broader focus on export market development. However, the scale of the initiative was beyond the purview of a single producer, even one of the largest companies in South Africa.[4] The financing of the necessary transportation infrastructure was a major challenge. Building the export coal market therefore required the development of a broad coalition that eventually encompassed the South African government and the coal mining industry, and secured a large-scale export contract.

Solutions to these challenges held tremendous opportunities. Reopening domestic coal production for export offered the prospects of foreign exchange and the diversification of revenue streams. The development of export markets also held the promise of improved mining efficiency since a greater proportion of the deposit became economic to extract. Furthermore, revenue gained through coal export duties or similar instruments could potentially be used to subsidise domestic coal consumption. In addition, development of the infrastructure necessary to export South African coal at scale offered the potential for a new regional growth centre to be built, and a bulk cargo capacity created. The lack of this capacity had hindered export opportunities in other sectors.

---

4   Berning (1971) discusses these efforts by Anglo American Corporation.

Technological domain for creating solutions in the 1960s and 1970s

This conception of technology used in this volume draws on three distinct features.[5] First, technology is the means to fulfil a human purpose. Second, technology is an assemblage of practices and components. Finally, technology exists as a collection of devices and engineering practices available to society (Arthur, 2009: 28). In the context of the two case studies in this chapter, the notion of a collection of technologies is relevant for our conceptualisation of the process of technology development. Specifically, the idea of a technological domain based around capabilities, practices and knowledge associated with mineral resources and financial development is central to this chapter.

A domain forms a constellation of technologies that emerge from parts to give potential to the whole economy (Arthur, 2009: 69–85). In both the case studies cited in this chapter, the mineral resource and finance domain played a key role in providing solutions to the challenges of commercialisation. Institutional embodiment of this domain existed in many parts of the South African political economy in this period, but the MRFN was central to its application and direction.

Hilsenrath and Pogue (2017) describe the South African MRFN as a unique, collectively coordinated governance structure with dynamic capabilities.[6] Accordingly, the MRFN formed a network of high-level organisational coherence. Through its distributed dynamic capabilities, the MRFN defined a critical component in the technology domain in which these technologies were able to be developed. A few components of the MRFN are particularly relevant to this case. These include research organisations such as the Fuel Research Institute of South Africa, the Coal Mining Research Controlling Council and the Chamber of Mines Research Organisation (COMRO) collieries

---

5   See Chapter 1 in this volume for further details.
6   The MRFN concept is related to the idea of a mineral-energy complex described by Fine and Rustomjee (1996) and historically contextualised by Freund (2010), but in addition to being a system of accumulation the MRFN possesses distributed dynamic capabilities accumulated through socially embedded and contingent historical processes.

research laboratory. Several industry bodies were also important including the Chamber of Mines of South Africa (COMSA), the Transvaal Coal Owners' Association (TCOA), and the Natal Coal Owners' Association (NCOA). These organisations played important roles in the development of the necessary technologies to establish large-scale coal exports, including facilitating the financial packages and realising the scale required of the market contracts that made initiation of the project viable.

Recent historiographic analyses by Scerri (2016) and Beinart and Dubow (2021) provide important context for understanding the features of South Africa's evolving technological domains. Beinart and Dubow (2021) identify several functions of the Council for Scientific and Industrial Research (CSIR) and the Industrial Development Corporation (IDC) that were important. In this regard, the complex and dynamic structure of relations across the MRFN is worth noting. In the 1950s the IDC played a leading role in creating Foskor to mine phosphate deposits in Phalaborwa, in contrast with the limited assistance it would later provide to facilitate the establishment of the export coal industry. The development of Foskor prevented Anglo American Corporation from mining those deposits and seems to have been part of an effort to promote the mining interests of white, predominantly Afrikaans-speaking sectors of the community, and limit the growth and influence of Anglo American Corporation and associated white, predominately English-speaking, mining finance groups (Beinart and Dubow, 2021: 279). During this period in the 1950s, interventions by the IDC focused on strategic and capital-intensive industries, which were important parts of the evolving MRFN structure.[7] This augured well for the financial needs of the coal export project, and so facilitated a supply push for the project.

---

7 A major investment led by the IDC was in the commercialisation of the Fischer-Tropsch oil-from-coal technology that eventually led to the establishment of the South African Coal, Oil and Gas Corporation (Sasol); for a description, see Hilsenrath and Pogue (2016: 62–65).

Technological journeys and establishment of an export coal industry

The successful development of a large-scale export coal industry depended on solutions to several interdependent challenges. One of the key challenges was establishing overseas demand for South African coal. Domestic priorities in the 1950s led to a focus on coal-based energy and industrial development to ensure energy security. This was particularly the case as international pressure on the National Party (NP)-led government posed rising challenges to its apartheid development model (Fine and Rustomjee, 1996). By the 1960s coal mining was playing a critical but supportive role in the MRFN, providing inexpensive energy. Coal mining was thus a low-profit venture, with correspondingly limited opportunity for profitable investment, dependent on inefficient mining techniques (Marquard, 2007). In this environment, the development of export markets created an opportunity to generate higher value from South Africa's coal production thereby increasing its appeal as an investment and also facilitating the adoption of more efficient mining practices (Eberhard, 2011). Of equal importance to the South African economy was that the export market's development created the capacity to cross-subsidise less expensive, low-grade coal for domestic consumers. Lastly, the apartheid government was facing an increased flight of foreign capital and international calls for sanctions in protest at its racist policies, particularly after the Sharpeville Massacre in 1961. Therefore, export coal also represented a strategically important source of foreign currency earnings. Consequently, government opposition to coal exports in the 1950s had transformed in the 1960s to tacit support. This was particularly the case within the broader MRFN where the IDC had begun working with mining finance houses to develop necessary transportation infrastructure.

To secure the investment needed for this transportation infrastructure, the IDC needed to be able to assure investors of long-term export market demand. In order to do that, they needed to ensure that an adequate supply of low-ash, export-grade South African coal could be provided at scale. As a result, in the early to mid-1960s, planning and design of the necessary railway and port infrastructure began along with the pursuit of an overseas client. By the late 1960s the search for a large-scale client led to the TCOA assuming the lead in both securing the necessary client and ensuring approval by the South African state for exports. This was the case despite the Anglo American Corporation continuing to play a central role in efforts to build an export coal industry,

In 1965 the South African government decided on Richards Bay as the best site for development, after carrying out an analysis of potential deep-water ports. In 1967, the CSIR undertook aerial surveys and soundings of the Richards Bay lagoon along with hydraulic modelling and morphology studies of the bay (Zwamborn and Cawood, 1974). Campbell (1976) details the process of designing and planning what would become the Richards Bay deep-water harbour. Another consequence of the decision about a harbour location was that in 1965 planning commenced for a rail line from the Vryheid coal mining district in what is now northern KwaZulu-Natal to the Richards Bay harbour, with additional plans for a line onward to Ermelo beginning in 1967 (Hill, 1976).

Construction on the first section of the line to Richards Bay started in mid-1968 despite the absence of any customers with a long-term commitment to buying South Africa's coal. In the meantime, building on the dense, medium processing work of the Fuel Research Institute of South Africa and further overseas development, Anglo American Corporation began designing the technology required to provide low-ash coal at scale for the export market (SAIMM, 1997: 212–213). As a result, by the early 1970s, several of the conditions necessary for the long-term export of South African coal were in place. Recognising this, in 1971 Japan committed to a long-term purchasing agreement for South African coal. Tokyo wanted an alternative to the coal supplies from established producers in the United States and Australia. The Japanese contract provided the assurance of demand needed to move forward with the deep-water harbour and in May 1972, following authorisation through an act of parliament, construction began (Zwamborn and Cawood, 1974).

Legacy of coal export technologies

The rail line to Vryheid was completed in 1972 and the Richards Bay Coal Terminal opened in 1976. Even before the completion of either project, several related industries had already been established in anticipation. For instance, construction of the Alusaf Aluminium Smelter at Richards Bay started in 1969 and began production in 1971 (Civil Engineer, 1976). By 1976 Richards Bay had expanded into fertiliser manufacturing with a phosphoric acid and two sulphuric acid plants commissioned as well as plant-to-mill maize and flour (Grové, 1976). Throughout the 1970s, the capacity of the coal terminal was continually expanded from an initial 12 million tonnes per annum to 24 million tonnes per annum by the end of the decade (Dunn, 1980). Subsequent expansions have taken the design capacity of the coal terminal to 91 million tonnes per year. Dry-bulk, liquid bulk and break-bulk terminals, bulk metal facilities and wood-chipping export facilities have supported the further development of an import and export market. In the 1980s, Richards Bay supported and grew further from the relocation and subsequent growth of Bell Equipment, a material-handling equipment manufacturer and supplier. The town of Richards Bay has a population in excess of 50,000 residents; it forms part of the uMhlathuze local municipality, which has a population of over 330,000.

The Richards Bay population forms a sizable part of the wider uMhlathuze municipality. Despite this, a notable aspect of its development has been the relatively limited connection between the businesses of Richards Bay and the surrounding communities. In many ways this was by design: the Richards Bay development was intended to support industrial decentralisation and to draw on the pool of available black, African labour in what was then the surrounding impoverished 'homeland' of KwaZulu (Grové, 1976). The current limited linkages between Richards Bay and its surrounds can thus be understood as a testament to the entrenched and enduring nature of South Africa's racially based spatial development.

Hall (2000) raises this legacy in his review of the policy underlying the South African Spatial Development Initiative programme. Identifying the important relationship between institutional structures his analysis questions the ability of spatial development policies to realise transformation without increasing local decision-making agency (Hall, 2000: 99–100). In this context while 'successfully' bridging the innovation chasm, the question remains whether the chasm was bridged for social benefit or at the very least whose definition of social benefit.

The development of the large-scale export coal industry produced various legacies. With hindsight the 'success' of the technologies entailed in creating that legacy can be questioned. The development of the export market supported domestic coal-based energy production as well as the expansion of Sasol's capacity in the 1970s and 1980s (Eberhard, 2011). However, as concerns grow about the need to reduce human-generated greenhouse gases, the dependence that subsidy created can be seen as more of a liability, particularly as path dependency challenges – like those of spatial development – create barriers to changing South Africa's energy base. The evolving demand for export coal has created another unintended legacy of the technology associated with this expansion technology. Burton et al. (2018) have described how an increased demand for lower calorific value coal in the Pacific market has changed the potential for exports to subsidise the domestic coal used in power generation. Eskom-tied mines have suffered from underinvestment by the SOE, and this has exacerbated the potential impacts of this market shift, and increased the costs entailed in solving South Africa's current energy crisis (Burton et al., 2018: 9).

DEVELOPMENT OF HYDRAULIC TECHNOLOGIES WITHIN THE SOUTH AFRICAN MRFN

Hydraulic mining technologies: opportunities and technological challenges

The development of hydraulic technologies in South Africa is a story of incremental innovations. These innovations facilitated improved operating efficiency and economic viability in several of the country's deep-level gold mines and in some of its platinum mines. The desire for the technological change emerged from apparent equipment efficiencies, a perceived need to reorganise stoping practices, improvements in market demand for gold, increasing challenges of extracting gold economically at depth, and a potential to leverage complementarities from other equipment.[8]

Several of the properties of hydraulic equipment seemed to give it an advantage over pneumatic equipment. First, hydraulics had about three times the rate of efficiency on the stopes as established pneumatic technologies (Marshall, 1975). Hydraulic technologies also accommodated a greater range of pressures than pneumatics, which equated to potentially more power at the stope face (Clement, 1975; Marshall, 1975; Whillier, 1975). Hydraulic rock drills also had uniform stress wave amplitude, which means that with the same energy as a pneumatic rock drill there is less peak stress in a hydraulic drill, or at equal peak stress levels significantly more energy content is delivered in a hydraulic drill. As a result, hydraulic drills promised to be more economic than pneumatic drills in the wear of drill steel. Lastly, mechanical and exhaust noise in hydraulic drills tended to be substantially lower than that in pneumatic drills.

Despite these advantages, hydraulic equipment also posed challenges in comparison with pneumatic equipment. Perhaps the most important of these challenges was that pneumatic equipment was an established technology in South Africa's deep-level gold mines, with associated organisational routines and tacit knowledge. These created a technological lock-in, which forms a barrier to change (David, 1985). In addition, hydraulic equipment tended to be more complicated and less robust than its pneumatic counterparts. Further development held the promise of resolving these challenges, but at least initially they meant that pneumatic equipment had distinct advantages over hydraulic equipment which was therefore less likely to be introduced.

Other challenges arose in deep-level mining, including higher temperatures and the longer transportation time required to get workers to the gold-bearing deposits. This had already become more significant in established mines along the central Witwatersrand. In the 1970s, however, gold mines were coming online in the areas of

---

8   See Pogue (2006) for further details on the technology's efficiencies and complementarities with other equipment.

what was then Orange Free State (OFS, later renamed Free State) and Far West Rand (FWR). Mining of the gold-bearing reef there started at greater depths. In this environment cooling became increasingly important, but cooling had previously been done on the surface and transported, under pressure, underground. As mining took place at deeper levels the problem of losing the cooled air, or of it becoming hotter, during transportation became more significant. Refrigeration units were moved underground as a result and by the 1970s COMRO began researching and developing the use of chilled mine service water to directly cool the surface underground. As it became clear that chilled mine service water was a superior way of creating a tolerable work environment at depth, one advantage of hydraulic technology emerged, namely that a hydro-hydraulic power system could directly supply energy and cooling without the need for separate compressed air and cooling systems (Wagner and Joughin, 1989: 337–338). This was further supported by the recognition that, at depth, the latent energy of mine service water, which had to be removed anyway, was sufficient to power the hydraulic equipment.

Realisation of the integrated hydro-hydraulic power and cooling system's advantages necessitated that the drills and other equipment also be hydro-hydraulic (all water) based. That created another significant challenge since at that point the hydraulic equipment deepened on an emulsion (oil) to lubricate and protect the metals from the corrosive effects of the mine service water. If the advantages of integrated hydro-hydraulic power were to become a reality, it would require developing new hydro-hydraulic equipment technology that eliminated the need for an oil emulsion and potential release of oil into the environment.

Perhaps the biggest boost for hydraulic mining technologies was the ending of the Bretton Woods international monetary system. This happened in 1971 when the United States ended the convertibility of US dollar to gold at a fixed price. Under the Bretton Woods system South Africa and 43 other nations had agreed to fix their currencies to the US dollar, and the US dollar in turn was fixed to gold at a set price. From 1958, the US dollar was fixed to gold at US$35 an ounce. However, inflation created a growing gap between the nominal and real price of gold. When the United States abandoned the fixed exchange rate system in 1971, the average price of gold began to rise substantially.[9] This increased price meant that South Africa's gold reserves at depth became more economically viable to mine. Effective hydraulic mining technology further expanded that advantage by increasing the portion of gold deposits that were above the minimum cost to mine.

The realisation of the improved gold price also required that the mines address the colour bar as its racial occupational mobility restriction on black African miners limited the mines' ability to develop lower-cost skilled labour.[10] A further challenge related to the migrant labour system that had supported mine viability by enabling the mines to use deprivation in rural South Africa and neighbouring Southern African nations to supply mine labour. However, the deprivation that accompanied the system began to meet resistance from the newly independent nations in the early 1970s (Crush et al., 1991). Therefore, the South African MRFN simultaneously sought to develop skilled labour by repealing the colour bar and replacing unskilled labour with new technologies like hydraulic mining technology. Thus while the potentially significant benefits of hydraulic mining technologies were recognised, realisation of those benefits was far from certain as efforts to develop hydraulic technologies were initiated.

Technological domain for creating solutions in the 1970s and 1980s

The development of hydraulic mining technologies in the 1970s and 1980s presents considerable overlap with the features of the technological domain noted in the previous case. However, the tension between collaboration and confrontation in the MRFN was more overt in this case than in that of developing coal exporting technology.

Constrained by a static gold price, the MRFN had systematically used the migrant labour system to suppress the real earnings of black African miners to the point that Wilson (1972) was able to convincingly argue that their real wages in the early 1970s were likely lower than

---

9 By August 1981 the spot price of gold had risen to over 10 times its August 1971 value (World Gold Council, 2022).
10 See Johnstone (1976) for a history of the colour bar in South African mining.

they were in 1911. With mounting resistance to cheap labour, there was growing pressure to change the organisation of work in the mines and the broader system of production. This growing need for transformation of the established technological domain meant that there was greater receptivity to new mining methods such as hydraulic mining technologies.

The distributed nature of the dynamic capabilities of the MRFN was also a critical component of the technology domain in which its technologies were developed. The central role of COMRO in this process has been described previously, along with the important contributions made by COMSA and its Technical Advisory Committee and later its Research Advisory Committee and its Gold Producers Committee (Pogue, 2006). Professional societies like the Association of Mine Managers and the South African Institution of Mining and Metallurgy supported the open collaborative innovation model employed by COMRO during this period by offering channels for the diffusion of knowledge about these new technologies.

Technological journeys and establishment of hydraulic mining technologies[11]

Preparatory research on technologies to improve the efficiency of deep-level gold mining began with COMRO's Mining Research Division in the mid-1960s. However, the most important development in the research process occurred in 1974 when COMRO committed to a 10-year research initiative to develop underground mechanisation technologies. COMRO initiated a mechanisation research programme divided between conventional and revolutionary technologies, using a collaborative sourcing model in partnership with mining equipment manufacturers. A drag-bit miner, which operated like a chainsaw to remove the gold-bearing host rock, was a promising revolutionary technology early on. It worked best though with high-pressure water jets, which created early potential for the use of a pure water (hydro) system (Hood, 1976). Emulsion-hydraulic technologies

---

11 See Pogue (2006) for further details of hydraulic mining technologies' development.

were initially investigated as an alternative to pneumatics within the conventional technology programme as emulsion-hydraulic power held particular promise over established electrical power systems (Joughin, 1982). Significantly, South Africa engaged an international learning network in its initial development of emulsion-hydraulic drills. Substantial challenges to low emulsion drills were overcome in this initial era of development, with solutions that included the development of additional seals (Walczak, 1984), micro-oil emulsions (Wymer, 1976) and a mechanism to rotate drill steel (Veldsman and Pretorius, 1983). By the early 1980s these efforts in emulsion-hydraulic technologies had created optimism about the potential for a suite of hydraulic technologies for deep-level gold mining based on a hydro-hydraulic system.

Even as operational trials were being carried out with emulsion-hydraulic technologies, COMRO initiated the development of a hydro-hydraulic power system. Through a series of prototypes, COMRO advanced the technology to a point where by 1985 a hydro-hydraulic power system was being tested along with ancillary equipment on the Kloof gold mine in Gauteng near Carletonville (Brown et al., 1986). While the hydro-hydraulic power system advanced through relatively straightforward incremental technological enhancements, the challenges associated with the emulsion-hydraulic drills created further difficulties as COMRO moved to the development of a hydro-hydraulic drill. The organisation worked with a series of domestic and international drill manufacturers to address these challenges. One such challenge was boundary lubrication, needed where contact between two surfaces occurs. After experimenting with a range of materials rubber products were used for static seals and polymers for dynamic seals and bearings (Harper, 1990). Hybrid steels were also developed in collaboration with US and UK steel manufacturers to withstand corrosive service water. However, after several experiments an existing steel was found to provide sufficient corrosion resistance (Howarth, 1990). Development of the hydro-hydraulic mining technology continued and by the early 1990s a commercially viable hydro-hydraulic system was being utilised.

Legacy of hydraulic mining technologies

Through a multi-decade programme, the MRFN managed to develop robust hydraulic technologies suitable for South Africa's narrow tabular gold and platinum deposits. Domestic manufacturing and consulting services continue to provide most of the technology. In that regard, this case is a story of successful technological development. During the technology's development, South Africa was able to leverage its scientific and engineering capabilities as the country progressed from being a technological learner to international leadership. In this case, the technological domain during initial development and application was one of the international engagements during an era of apartheid isolation. These world-class science and engineering capabilities form another illustration of science under apartheid, where the MRFN worked within the system for transformation and to ensure its own survival (Beinart and Dubow, 2021: 300).

The transformation of the South African MRFN innovation ecosystem was an important context for these technologies' developments. Especially important was the dissolution of COMRO and its merger into South Africa's Council for Scientific and Industrial Research (CSIR).[12] That change preserved some of the capabilities and institutional knowledge of this important applied science and technological institution. However, the shift also introduced new challenges as the CSIR confronted its own organisational relevance (Maharajh, 2016: 188). This limited opportunities for broader, coordinated introduction and application of the technologies. That change in the institutional environment also supported the lock-in and path dependency associated with established technologies rather than broader adoption of these novel hydraulic technologies.

Another important factor limiting the broader adoption and diffusion of these technologies within mining environments was the relatively unique nature of the gold and platinum deposits for which they were developed. While mining environments necessitated solutions to increasingly challenging operating conditions on the mines,

---

12 For details of the dissolution of COMRO and its transfer to the CSIR, see Pogue (2006).

that urgency was not as significant in other mining environments. This meant that maintenance practices differed across the mines and those differences imposed additional costs to wider adoption.

PROSPECTS FOR LEVERAGING MRFN CAPABILITIES FOR TRANSFORMATION AND COMMERCIALISATION

This chapter described two sets of mining technologies that were successfully developed into commercial viability. Despite this success, further application and utilisation of these technologies are relatively limited, although these opportunities seemed and still seem possible. There are a multitude of challenges to the successful commercial application of a technology. One of these is the combinatorial nature of technology (Arthur, 2009: 167–189): a technology's use may only become apparent as other technologies are developed or their associated relevance is recognised. Another constraint on the development of a technology's application may be changes within or among operational or technological networks. These networks may call forth or impede the application of a technology by connecting or disconnecting agents and resources that might facilitate development. Capacity and capabilities are further factors influencing the application of a technology. They determine the combination of resources and know-how available to apply the technologies. In this section we consider how these influences contributed to commercialisation, or lack thereof, in our two technologies. We also consider the role of innovation and development policy since democracy in advancing opportunities for commercialisation.

In both case studies, changes in production and innovation networks transformed the challenges and opportunities impacting on the technologies' commercialisation. Those challenges and opportunities were defined by historically specific development paths, which simultaneously reflected and embodied the broader socio-political structure. Scerri (2016: 372–376) has, in past years, identified the need to consider this historical specificity when considering the evolution of national systems of innovation. In the context of his analysis evolution of these systems relates directly to the question of commercialisation for whom. To what extent then did the commercial success of the technologies in the case studies perpetuate inequity in a pre-democratic South Africa? What role did these technologies have in advancing inclusive transformation in a democratic South Africa?

The development of export coal technologies was shown to reinforce and support the policies of the apartheid regime in several ways, but this development also created critical infrastructure, expanded international trade, and built market opportunities in other sectors. However, that infrastructure and associated opportunities were not leveraged to advance transformation and inclusive development (Hall, 2000). Similarly, coal exports and associated greenhouse gas emissions have supported an alarming energy production trajectory in a world increasingly impacted by climate change. A more transformational perspective might consider how the export coal infrastructure (including the knowledge infrastructure) could be used to advance technologies and resource development, such as biomass energy, which address the challenges of climate change.

As part of the entrenched production system of the time, the initial development of hydraulic technologies supported the systems that upheld the poverty and deprivation of the period such as migrant labour and the profit and associated political-economic power of a racially excluding MRFN. Some of the issues around racial exclusion in the MRFN have been addressed since democracy through black economic empowerment, the promotion of majority black-owned mining companies, and the demise of the migrant labour system. However, the transformational impact of the hydraulic technology[13] could be increased by the application of the technology in other industrial and sustainable energy sectors.

In no way should the application of the technologies to a more transformational agenda suggest that their realisation is not inherently challenging. Such a reorientation of technologies involves a challenging process of mutually co-adapting and co-creating new opportunities across the technological domain and economy (Arthur, 2009: 191–202).

---

13 See Pogue (2006: 200–202) for a description of non-resource-based markets for hydraulic technologies.

It requires the identification and development of the necessary markets, as well as the re-design of production and technology structures to utilise the new domain. Such a process might seem possible, but these are typically processes of structural change that play out over relatively long periods of time rather than three-to-five-year development plans (Arthur, 2009: 156–159). The ability to adapt in this way is highly dependent on more than just knowledge, but also on capabilities and in the case of the MRFN, its distributed dynamic capabilities.[14]

Another major influence on the impact of the technologies was the change that occurred in the MRFN's distributed dynamic capabilities during the 1990s, as South Africa transitioned to democratic rule. These changes also redefined the potential to further leverage the opportunities the technologies created and to minimise associated challenges. One of the forces for change was the globalisation and regionalisation of many mining groups, which accelerated the degradation of the MRFN's alignment and coordination.[15] Another important influence on the MRFN was the policies promoting black economic empowerment and transformation. Black economic empowerment and other transformation policies have tended to focus on advancing access to ownership and leadership in the minerals and mining industry for historically disadvantaged South Africans (Moraka and Van Rensburg, 2015). This has propagated a focus on ownership targets and control rather than on systemic human capital development, the transformation of inequitable production systems, and the general development of technologies to promote more inclusive operations. These policies follow other policies of the state in perpetuating inherited dysfunction because of a narrow focus on limited issues rather than consideration of broader social welfare and institutional rigidities (Scerri and Maharajh, 2016: 371).

These two dynamics – globalisation and regionalisation – along with a narrow focus on ownership and control combined to change not just the nature of the MRFN, but also its functions. As a result, the

---

14 See Hilsenrath and Pogue (2017) for a description of distributed dynamic capabilities in the South African MRFN and their evolution.
15 See Carmody (2002) for a description of this post-apartheid globalisation of major South African business groups.

potential to redefine and modernise resource-based development in a more progressive and inclusive manner has largely been neglected.[16] A further challenge associated with the change in dynamic capabilities was the reduction in resources for the innovation ecosystem. The scale of this reduction was massive: annual funding in the early 2010s was a fraction of its levels in the 1970s and 1980s when South Africa was near the global forefront of mining research and development (Macfarlane and Singh, 2017). The dissolution and transition of COMRO to the CSIR was a clear manifestation of change in knowledge system investment by the MRFN.

The loss of technological capabilities impacted on the management of the overall technological domain, and on the coordination of knowledge within it as well as its application to other areas. This process relates to how deep knowledge in one technology can be leveraged into deep knowing in another technology. It is a developed capability that requires an ability to pursue science without expectation of particular commercialisation value (Arthur, 2009: 159–163). One can fairly question whether the MRFN innovation system was ever at a point where it was generating science for science's sake but, with hindsight, the dissolution of the MRFN's capabilities during the transition to democracy seems to have reduced opportunities to leverage its technologies.

The South African government recognised the need to rebuild technological capabilities and so, in 2015, it convened the Mining Phakisa, a government initiative that brought together all stakeholders in the industry. The Mining Phakisa adopted the South African Mining Extraction Research, Development & Innovation (SAMERDI) strategy, which aimed to revitalise the development of mining technology through a series of research programmes and the establishment of the Mandela Mining Precinct at the former COMRO facility in Johannesburg. This was intended to be a hub for the coordination and facilitation of mining research and development (Singh, 2017). The SAMERDI strategy defined a broad pathway to

---

16 See for example Ville and Wicken (2013) for a description of a resource-based diversification development model used in Australia and Norway.

modernise South African mining by 2030. However, its programme to develop the necessary workforce skills, called Successful Application of Technology Centred Around People (SATCAP), has a relatively narrow focus on formal qualifications. The SAMERDI strategy thus represents an important, but relatively limited, effort to revitalise South African mining technology and associated capabilities, rather than a more fundamental reflection on the country's technological legacies and a systemic attempt to address associated path dependencies in the development of human capabilities.

Mphahlele and Scerri (2016) identify the need to address broader capabilities in the labour force and the school system as critical deficiencies in South Africa's transformation since democracy. In addition to advocating for policy that addresses the massive shortcomings of the basic education system, they highlight the importance of reconciling the philosophical discontinuities between apartheid-era technological domains and inclusive African conceptualisations (Mphahlele and Scerri, 2016: 236). This recognition of the complicated and multidimensional nature of transformation in mining technology is framed within a broad conceptualisation of a national system of innovation. However, the policy needed to facilitate this change remains largely unfulfilled.

Finally, there is one more factor that should be added to the considerations above. Hausmann et al. (2007) argue that measures of mining's 'product space' indicate that the opportunities provided by the mining sector may be more limited than previously. The implications of this are that the decline in new South African mining technologies may merely reflect more limited opportunity, and therefore not warrant policy interventions to boost the development and commercialisation of new technologies.

CONCLUSION

These cases demonstrate how the MRFN was able to successfully commercialise technologies before and during South Africa's transition to democracy. This chapter reviewed the route to commercialisation for these technologies, drawing attention to the extent to which opportunities were mediated by apartheid institutions. These institutions created a legacy for technological development as well as path dependencies and challenges to transformation for inclusive and equitable growth. Change in this context involves a process of what Arthur refers to as 'revolutions and redomaining' (Arthur, 2009: 145–165). These require the creation of new rules as well as the evolution of unspoken practices, cultures and expectations that facilitate institutional and social change and redefine the trajectories of technological purposes. In this chapter, it is contended that a process of interrogation that considers and addresses these legacies is a necessary condition for policy that supports the transformation of existing technological domains. It is necessary to recognise and explicitly address these legacies in order to realise the benefits of South Africa's mineral wealth.

REFERENCES

Arthur, W.B. 2009. *The Nature of Technology: What It Is and How it Evolves*. New York: Free Press.

Beinart, W. and Dubow, S. 2021. *The Scientific Imagination in South Africa: 1700 to the Present*. Cambridge: Cambridge University Press.

Berning, F.S. 1971. 'Filling the energy gap'. *Optima*, 21(21), 81.

Burton, J. Caetano, T. and McCall, B. 2018. 'Coal transitions in South Africa: Understanding the implications of a 2°C-compatible coal phase-out plan for South Africa'. IDDRI & Climate Strategies, https://www.iddri.org/sites/default/files/PDF/Publications/Catalogue%20Iddri/Rapport/20180609_ReportCoal_SouthAfrica.pdf, accessed 1 October 2022.

Brown, C.J., Tupholme, E.R. and Wymer, D.G. 1986. 'The application of hydro-power to deep-level mining'. *South African Institute of Mining and Metallurgy*, 113–133.

Campbell, N.P. 1976. 'Planning and construction of the new deep water harbour at Richards Bay'. *The Civil Engineer in South Africa/Die Siviele Ingenieur in Suid-Afrika*, 257–265.

Carmody, P. 2002. 'Between globalisation and (post) apartheid: The political economy of restructuring in South Africa'. *Journal of Southern African Studies*, 28(2), 255–275.

Civil Engineer. 1976. 'Alusaf: Richards Bay Pioneer'. *The Civil Engineer in South Africa/Die Siviele Ingenieur in Suid-Afrika*, November-Supplement, 7.

Clement, D. 1975. 'A comparison between hydraulic and pneumatic rockdrills'. *The Journal of The Southern African Institute of Mining and Metallurgy*, 75(8), 218–220.

Crush, J., Jeeves, A. and Yudelman, D. 1991. *South Africa's Labour Empire: A History of Black Migrancy to the Gold Mines*. Oxford: Westview Press.

David, P.A. 1985. 'Clio and the economics of QWERTY'. *American Economic Review*, 75(2), 332–337.

Dunn, M.B. 1980. 'Richards Bay coal terminal'. *The Civil Engineer in South Africa/Die Siviele Ingenieur in Suid-Afrika*, 57–61.

Eberhard, A. 2011. 'The future of South African coal: Market, investment and policy challenges', Program on Energy and Sustainable Development (PESD) Working Paper, No. 100, Stanford University, https://fsi-live. s3.us-west-1.amazonaws.com/s3fs-public/WP_100_Eberhard_Future_ of_South_African_Coal.pdf, accessed 1 October 2022.

Edgecombe, R. and Guest, B. 1985. 'An introduction to the pre-Union Natal Coal industry', in Guest, B. and Sellers, J.M. (eds). *Enterprise and Exploitation in a Victorian Colony: Aspects of the Economic and Social History of Colonial Natal*. Pietermaritzburg: University of Natal Press, pp. 308–351.

Falcon, R. and Ham, A.J. 1988. 'The characteristics of Southern African coals'. *The Journal of The Southern African Institute of Mining and Metallurgy*, 88(5), 145–161.

Ferraz, F. and Pogue, T. 2016. 'Mining and the South African national system of innovation', in Scerri, M. (ed). *The Emergence of Systems of Innovation in South(ern) Africa: Long Histories and Current Debates*. Johannesburg: Mapungubwe Institute for Strategic Reflection (MISTRA), pp. 279–326.

Fine, B. and Rustomjee, Z. 1996 *The Political Economy of South Africa: From Minerals-Energy Complex to Industrialisation*. London: Hurst & Co.

Freund, B. 2010. 'The significance of the minerals-energy complex in the light of South African economic historiography'. *Transformation: Critical Perspectives on Southern Africa*, 71, 3–25.

Grové, E.L. 1976. 'Richards Bay railway and harbour complex – Present and future economic benefit to the country'. *The Civil Engineer in South Africa/Die Siviele Ingenieur in Suid-Afrika*, 11, 266–268.

Hall, P.V. 2000. 'Regional development and institutional lock-in: A case study of Richards Bay, South Africa'. *South Africa Critical Planning*, 7, 87–102. https://luskin.ucla.edu/sites/default/files/007%20Hall.pdf, accessed 1 October 2022.

Harper, G.S. 1990. 'Application of engineering polymers in the mining industry'. *Journal of the South African Institute of Mining and Metallurgy*, 12, 365–375.

Hausmann, R., Hwang, J. and Rodrik, D. 2007. 'What you export matters'. *Journal of Economic Growth*, 12(1), 1–25.

Hilsenrath, P. and Pogue, T. 2017. 'Distributed dynamic capabilities in

South Africa's mineral resource finance network'. *Technology in* Society, 49, 57–67.

Hood, M. 1976. 'Cutting strong rock with a drag bit assisted by high-pressure water Jets'. *Journal of the South African Institute of Mining and Metallurgy*, 77(4), 79–90.

Howarth, D. 1990. 'The field evaluation of alternative materials and protective systems for mine water piping'. *Journal of the South African Institute of Mining and Metallurgy*, 90(9), 225–239.

Jayanti, S., Maheswaran, K. and Saravanan, V. 2007. 'Assessment of the effect of high ash content in pulverized coal combustion'. *Applied Mathematical Modelling*, 31(5), 934–953.

Johnstone, F.A. 1976. *Class, Race and Gold: A Study of Class Relations and Discrimination in South Africa*. London: Routledge & Kegan Paul.

Joughin, N.C. 1982. 'The development of equipment for stoping in South African gold mines'. Proceedings of the 15th Common Wealth Mining and Metallurgical Institute Congress, 395–401.

De Korte, G.J. 2010. 'Coal preparation research in South Africa'. *The Journal of the Southern African Institute of Mining and Metallurgy*, 110(7), 361–364.

Maharajh, R. 2016. 'Racial capitalism, apartheid, and the negotiated post-apartheid constitutional democracy', in Scerri, M. (ed). *The Emergence of Systems of Innovation in South(ern) Africa: Long Histories and Current Debates*, Johannesburg: Mapungubwe Institute for Strategic Reflection (MISTRA), pp. 179–223.

Marquard, A. 2007. 'The development of energy policy in South Africa'. PhD thesis, University of Cape Town.

Marshall, T.C. 1975. 'A comparison between hydraulic and pneumatic rockdrills'. *Journal of the South African Institute of Mining and Metallurgy*, 75(7), 181–184.

Macfarlane, A. and Singh, N. 2017. 'Mining research and development reborn – the Mining Precinct', *Journal of the South African Institute of Mining and Metallurgy*, 117(12), 9–10.

Moraka, N.V. and Van Rensburg, M.J. 2015. 'Transformation in the South African mining industry: looking beyond the employment equity scorecard'. *Journal of the South African Institute of Mining and Metallurgy*, 115(8), 669–678.

Napier-Munn, T.J., Bosman, J. and Holtham, P. 2014. 'Innovations in dense medium technology', in Anderson, C.G., Dunne, R.C., and Uhrie, J.L . (eds). *Mineral Processing and Extractive Metallurgy – 100 Years of Innovation*. Denver: Society for Mining, Metallurgy & Exploration, pp. 265–275.

Pogue, T.E. 2006. 'Lessons for the future: The origins and legacy of COMRO's hydraulic technology programme'. *Journal of the South African Institute of Mining and Metallurgy*, 106(8), 515–525.

Southern African Institute of Mining and Metallurgy (SAIMM). 1997. 'Proceedings, 100th Annual General Meeting, 1997'. *The Journal of The Southern African Institute of Mining and Metallurgy*, 97(5), 211–216.

Scerri, M. (ed). 2016. *The Emergence of Systems of Innovation in South(ern) Africa: Long Histories and Current Debates.* Johannesburg: Mapungubwe Institute for Strategic Reflection (MISTRA).

Scerri, M. and Maharajh, R. 2016. 'The policy environment and policy options for the South African system of innovation', in Scerri, M. (ed). *The Emergence of Systems of Innovation in South(ern) Africa: Long Histories and Current Debates.* Johannesburg: Mapungubwe Institute for Strategic Reflection.

Scerri, M. and Mphahlele, L. 2016. 'The human factor in the evolution of systems of innovation', in Scerri, M. (ed). *The Emergence of Systems of Innovation in South(ern) Africa: Long Histories and Current Debates.* Johannesburg: Mapungubwe Institute for Strategic Reflection.

Singh, N. 2017. 'Weathering the "perfect storm" facing the mining sector'. *Journal of the South African Institute of Mining and Metallurgy*, 117(3), 223–229.

Veldsman, T.H. and Pretorius, K. 1983. 'An analysis of current organizational arrangements for the pneumatic drilling system on a gold mine with reference to the introduction of the hydraulic drilling system'. Chamber of Mines Research Organization Report, No. 33(83).

Ville, S. and Wicken, O. 2013. 'The dynamics of resource-based economic development: Evidence from Australia and Norway'. *Industrial and Corporate Change*, 22(5), 1341–1371. https://doi.org/10.1093/icc/dts040, accessed October 2022.

Wagner, H. and Joughin, N.C. 1989. 'The use of research in management'. *Journal of the South African Institute of Mining and Metallurgy*, 89(11), 333–340.

Walczak, Z.J. 1984. 'The application of hydraulic rock drills in gold mining', Minemech 84 Symposium, 19 September, South African Institution of Mechanical Engineers.

Weber, K.M. and Rohracher, H. 2012. 'Legitimizing research, technology and innovation policies for transformative change: Combining insights from innovation systems and multi-level perspective in a comprehensive "failures" framework'. *Research Policy*, 41(6), 1037–1047.

Whillier, A. 1975. 'Note: Hydraulic rockdrills and their effect on the underground environment'. *Journal of the South African Institute of Mining and Metallurgy*, 75(9), 245–246.

Wilson, F. 1972. *Labour in the South African Gold Mines 1911–1969.* Cambridge: Cambridge University Press.

Wilson, F. 2003. 'Understanding the past to reshape the future: Problems of South Africa's transition', in David, P.A. and Thomas, M. (eds). *The*

Economic Future in Historical Perspective. Oxford: Oxford University Press, pp. 297–313.

World Gold Council, 2022. 'Gold spot prices', https://www.gold.org/goldhub/data/gold-prices, accessed 1 October 2022.

Wymer, D.G. 1976. 'Dilute oil-in-water emulsion as a hydraulic fluid for gold mine stoping machinery'. Chamber of Mines Research Report, 12–20.

Zwamborn, J.A. and Cawood, C.H. 1974. 'Major port developments at Richards Bay with due regard to preserving the natural environment'. *The Civil Engineer in South Africa/Die Siviele Ingenieur in Suid-Afrika*, 2, 79–86.

Part Three

*Public policy and innovation
system navigation*

NINE

Death by centralisation: Exploring disjunctures and opportunities for city-driven innovation systems in South Africa

STACEY-LEIGH JOSEPH AND GECI KARURI-SEBINA

INTRODUCTION

Cities can bring innovation to life by using levers and competencies that they already hold. Africa's emerging megacities can unleash their potential as drivers of economic transformation if they can be viewed and managed less as static administrative regions and more as dynamic innovation ecosystems (Nawrot et al., 2017: 1). This is despite the challenges African cities face.

Yet, innovation systems studies have tended to focus on the level of national systems of innovation (NSI), where the discourse on government-led innovation has inadequately interrogated the weaknesses of local systems of innovation (LSI). This discourse has also not addressed adequately the lack of functional linkage between local governments and national system frameworks in countries like South Africa (Joseph and Karuri-Sebina, 2022). This gap coincides with a growing focus on the role of cities in driving national development, including in Africa (SACN and Wits, 2017; Nawrot et al., 2017: 223) due to their inherent proximity to local initiatives and activities.

Joseph and Karuri-Sebina (2022) have argued however that the local state, exemplified by case studies of three major African cities (Tshwane, Nairobi and Accra), plays an inadequate role in local innovation and production systems, and therefore contributes very little as a lever for the achievement of inclusive economic development and general mitigation of inequality. The study identified a number of challenges that must be addressed to promote innovation-driven development at city level. These include decentralising power and authority; fostering alignment between national development planning and local strategies; recognising the importance of informal economies in cities; and building trust between actors at the local level.

This paper makes the case that cities, despite these challenges, can use their already mandated functions to better harness innovation and that they don't have to wait for national impetus. City governments (municipalities) already have constitutional authority and legal mandates for local development planning, for example. And if a city is able to effectively play its role of driving innovation it will not only succeed in strengthening its LSI but also make a crucial contribution to vertical alignment that would make for a more functional NSI.

Based on the fact that city governments (municipalities) already have constitutional authority and legal mandates around certain key local development roles,[1] the research questions for the study are:

- What can be done within the existing competencies and frameworks of cities to better support local innovation?

---

1 As envisaged in the 1998 White Paper on Local Government, key functions are meant to be decentralised to municipalities (mostly metros) with the capacity to carry these out. Thus, functions such as housing delivery, spatial planning and land management, and certain transport functions, have progressively been decentralised to the local level. These are governed by policies such as the Comprehensive Plan for the Development of Human Settlements (also known as Breaking New Ground) and the Spatial Planning and Land Use Management Act.

- How could this support be levered towards strengthening both local systems of innovation and a more functional national system of innovation?

THE ELEPHANTS IN THE ROOM

There are two main critiques that might immediately be levelled against our framing, which are useful to recognise and contextualise.

1. South Africa does not have a functional NSI (or LSI).

NSIs should ideally include a range of key actors, both public and private, their innovation activities, and the various relationships that facilitate knowledge and resource-flows between them to create an effective system (Wilson et al., 2020). This synergistic formation is important in order for countries to develop the kinds of innovation and ideas that can drive their economies. These innovation systems and activities are even more crucial in developing countries with critical development needs. However, NSIs have to be grounded within local contexts and realities and thus cannot take a cookie-cutter approach. A functional and effective NSI is one that is also appreciative of and devolved to the local level, getting close to the people's socioeconomic realities and dynamics (Muchie and Baskaran, 2009: 147). This means that local-level plans and ideas can be further tailored, across different locations, to address the needs of a particular context and area through the formation of a local system of innovation (LSI). The LSI derives its strength and value from its proximity to local actors within a particular space.

However, the above is the ideal, and it has been argued that South Africa does not even have a functional NSI (see Chapter 11 in this volume). Furthermore, the link between the country's weak national framework and what there might be of local innovation systems is at best tenuous; it might therefore be considered to be quite a leap to claim that there is an NSI–LSI nexus to be leveraged to drive innovative and inclusive development. It can also be argued that it is necessary to consider a different conception of how local innovation could work and in turn strengthen national frameworks through a bottom-up approach – one that recognises local contexts and realities, rather than a mechanical and formulaic implementation of a theoretical national framework. This study broadly accepts these arguments. Despite this, it aims to look at an NSI/LSI (or more accurately, 'nsi' and 'lsi' denoting less the theoretical form than the functional notion of the systems) relationship, which considers the qualities and interventions necessary for an effective innovation approach driven by contextualised experiences and activities. We therefore use the NSI/LSI terminology flexibly, more in the nsi/lsi sense; less the form than the idea of the functions even if structured less formally.

2. Municipalities are incompetent.

The performance of South African municipalities has been mixed since 1998 when they were established in their present form. However, while successive audit reports have pointed to issues of corruption, maladministration and poor performance, there have also been improvements especially where cities were able to attract officials with the necessary skills and experience. The 2020/21 report from the Auditor-General showed some improvements in audits of the metros and intermediate cities but noted that the audit findings in a number of these have also worsened (AGSA, 2021). These issues, worsened by the impact of the Covid-19 pandemic and lockdowns, have caused disillusionment with the capacity of local government to adequately deliver services and efficiently manage towns and cities. Evidence of this waning faith in local government ranges from private citizens increasingly operating off-grid, impacting on the potential revenue streams of municipalities, to private sector actors carrying out the jobs of municipalities (e.g., fixing potholes or managing traffic). This is exacerbated by the ongoing instability of coalition governments and poor political leadership at the local level, which have impacted further on service delivery implementation and the ability of local governments to achieve and drive long-term spatial transformation.

However, the 1998 White Paper on Local Government clearly envisioned the local sphere as the key driver for the transformation of South Africa's towns and cities. Ultimately, the municipalities that had the capacity and capabilities were to take on devolved functions (e.g., transport, planning and the development of human settlements) that are crucial in reshaping and redesigning the apartheid spatial legacy (SACN, 2016a). It was at this level that local government was to play a coordinating role. But local government was not intended to act on its own; it would have needed to be supported by other core actors (i.e., the private sector, civil society and knowledge industries), forming a quadruple helix. By creating an enabling environment for these various actors, local government would have the potential to drive and support urban systems of innovation (SACN, 2016a). Ultimately, it remains true that this is the sphere of government which is the closest to the people and thus arguably best placed to respond to critical local issues in an inclusive and transformative manner.

Figure 9.1: The quadruple helix

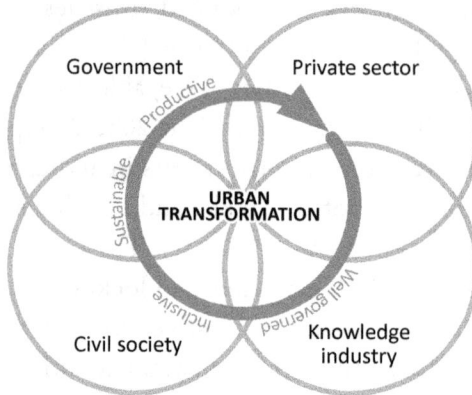

Source: SACN (2016a: 288)

Therefore, despite the institutional challenges bedevilling local government, its relevance remains. This is not to suggest that these challenges should be ignored, but rather that consideration be given to how local government might fulfil its constitutional mandate, rather than dismissing its part in a system that is actually structured around its role. (It is beyond the scope of this chapter to prove the efficacy of such a structure.) The goal of developmental local government remains official policy and intent, and thus cannot simply be ignored on the basis that there is doubt about its present capabilities.

METHODOLOGY

This qualitative study is based on a single case study of the City of Tshwane. The city was chosen because of its particularities, which include being the administrative capital of South Africa and its additional role as the concentration of innovation institutions in the country. Both these features imply a practical proximity to the NSI in the form of national government, innovation agencies, science councils, universities, inter- and multi-national NGOs and corporates, diplomatic core, think tanks and other education and training institutions. If any local government in South Africa were to expressly work with or benefit from the NSI as a set of national programmes and infrastructures, it would be the City of Tshwane. Whilst this makes for somewhat unique and privileged circumstances, which are not necessarily generalisable, these optimal conditions were appropriate for this exploratory, qualitative research, which aims to explore the status of linkages between the NSI and the LSI, and the possibilities for a strengthened municipal role. It is worth noting that although the authors recognise the role of all the actors in the quadruple helix, the emphasis of this chapter is on the role of government in driving and supporting innovation. As noted previously, transformative development cannot occur without communities themselves, industry and knowledge actors playing specific roles. However, as local government is intended to be the enabler and the interface amongst these role players, this paper focuses on its role and how local government functions to drive local innovation.

The data for the study included a Tshwane focus group, supplementary key informant interviews and secondary data drawn from a literature review and city-level document analysis. The choice of methods was based on interpretivist approaches, which consider reality to be socially constructed (Bogdan and Biklen, 1998: 3). The method was deemed suitable for the exploratory nature of this study, which seeks to understand how the institutions and the actors within them are engaging.

The informant interviews were carried out with one relevant national and local government informant each, all senior managers responsible for NSI/LSI programmes or interactions. Semi-structured interviews of 60–90 minutes each were conducted; these served as the basis for framing key questions and responses about the study propositions.

An additional hour-long engagement was held with a municipal-level manager responsible for overseeing innovation in Tshwane City to co-design the focus group. This group consisted of 8–12 people (8 consistently: officials from different parts of the municipal administration of Tshwane, from the innovation and support units to line staff in delivery departments like water and policing). Once eligible interviewees had given their official consent to participate, they were invited by the City to take part in a focus group facilitated by the two authors. Participants were assured of anonymity, and it was agreed that all raw data was to be anonymised and made available back to the City.

The focus group process was used to explore participants' common understanding of their LSI context, as well as to invite structured input into the study questions. A facilitated process, which included the use of collaborative tools (Jamboard)[2] and foresight methods (the 'Three Horizons' framework),[3] was used to explore the future of the LSI within the NSI and to consider how transitioning to a more effective ecosystem might be enabled.

Finally, the documentary evidence collected included Tshwane's innovation strategy and plans, the Municipal Innovation Maturity Index conducted in 2021 by the Department of Science and Innovation, and innovation capability assessments shared with us by the City.

INNOVATION SYSTEMS

An innovation system can be defined as 'the set of economic, political and institutional relationships occurring in a given geographical area,

---

2 Jamboard is a digital whiteboard that allows collaboration in real time using either the Jamboard device, a web browser or a mobile app.
3 The 'Three Horizons' framework describes three patterns of action and how the relative prevalence of these change over time. It describes a phased process of change from the established patterns of the first horizon to the emergence of new patterns in the third one, via the transitional activity of the second horizon (https://medium.com/activate-the-future/the-three-horizons-of-innovation-and-culture-change-d9681b0e0b0f).

which generates a collective learning process leading to rapid diffusion of knowledge and best practice' (Rantisi, 2002: 590). However, innovation cannot occur in a vacuum; it requires a systemic approach that facilitates learning and engagement amongst multiple and diverse actors (Lundvall, 1992: 91). Innovation systems can be national, regional, sectoral or technological (Carlsson et al., 2002: 233). They play an important role in long-term economic development and include all economic, political and social factors affecting innovation such as financial systems, organisation of private firms, elementary, secondary and university education systems, labour markets, culture, regulatory policies and innovation institutions (Atkinson, 2014: 1; Hlophe and Dlamini, 2018: 13).

An NSI is a framework in which innovation activities are realised within an economy (Rodriquez and Bielous, 2016). Legislation, interactions and relations between various actors, innovation policy measures and other factors directly or indirectly affect the circumstances in which innovation is realised (Beraha and Duricin, 2022: 84). Studies that map out the NSI use the triple helix model, highlighting government, industry and academia as the important actors in the system and the interactions and subsystems, which influence the innovation process (Hlophe and Dlamini, 2018: 13). Despite the existence of an NSI in South Africa, critics highlight that it lacks vertical and horizontal policy integration, arguing that the country's national innovation policy is rooted in a linear, narrow path of supply-driven technology and has a top-down perspective approach (Raphasha, 2015: ii).

If the NSI is about a top-down network of economic agents, institutions and policies, then the LSI refers to the bottom-up, locality-based arrangements and relationships. LSIs are characterised by geographical agglomeration and clustering, which supports product specialisation (Oyelaran-Oyeyinka and McCormick, 2007: 4–5). Local innovation refers to the creation of ways of doing things that are new and improved in the local context within which they have been developed. It can also be defined as innovation processes that take place in a specific location, leverages the people and resources from that particular locale, works to address problems or take advantage of opportunities that are locally relevant (Hoffecker, 2018: 3). Local resources include the knowledge base of local institutions and firms; dense networks of the formal and informal institutions that support production and innovation; collaborations and interactions between key agents and institutions (suppliers, producers and so on); and technical knowledge structures (Oyelaran-Oyeyinka and McCormick, 2007: 5).

The recognition of both the NSI and the LSI suggests roles both for nation states as well as for local governance actors.

The role of the state in innovation systems

When functional NSIs are being developed, the government needs to play a role in the provision of policies, institutions, conducive environments and resource allocation. It also needs to be involved with funding the rate of innovation and envisioning the direction of innovation (Hlophe and Dlamini, 2018: 13; Mazzucato, 2015: 627). The state should play a meaningful and supportive role to enable industrial research and development (R&D). It should also spark innovation elsewhere (Mazzucato, 2015: 635).

The OECD (2017) recommends that governments have a range of risk management and governance policies in place to mitigate unintended consequences. It is important to note that even if the state can think big and formulate bold policies, it will not always succeed because the innovation process is uncertain (Mazzucato, 2015: 632). However, failure does not have to be seen as the negative outcome of investment in innovation. The lessons and experiences from failed interventions are critical for providing insight to improve future initiatives. An acceptance that failure is part of the innovation process will result in greater willingness to engage in innovation. This is because there will be some recognition of the exploration undertaken, whether a particular innovation has succeeded or failed.

The role of cities in innovation systems

Cities are hubs and sources of productivity, innovation, economic growth and development (Nawrot et al., 2017: 4). They are also constantly evolving and adapting their systems to respond to changing contexts. They do this by developing policies, programmes and services so that they can address changes in demographic, cultural, social, economic and environmental needs (OECD, 2017). Local public sector innovations allow them to address changes and come up with solutions. According to Concilio et al. (2019: 43) cities are considered key environments for the emergence of innovative interactions and relationships because creatives and innovative industries tend to localise in or proximity to urban environments.

In Africa, cities are characterised by overcrowding, poor infrastructure and limited connectivity to the international economic system. African cities are underperforming as potential centres of creativity and innovation (Nawrot et al., 2017: 1). Cities need sufficient investment in capacity building so that local governments can create innovative solutions to global changes which in turn can push local governments/cities to be more innovative (OECD, 2017).

South Africa has a rich political, cultural, economic and geographic spread of district innovation systems. These are characterised by actors such as the local and regional offices of both national and provincial departments, NGOs, science councils, finance institutions, local municipalities, business chambers, traditional authorities, local development agencies and private consulting firms (Ndabeni and Rogerson, 2016: 3). Based on the White Paper on Local Government (CoGTA-RSA, 1998), local municipalities have a developmental mandate to address the historical legacy of apartheid as well as to provide services and infrastructure to their residents. However, many municipalities in South Africa are not in a position to meet their developmental mandate because of high levels of poverty and unemployment (Jacobs et al., 2018). Some municipalities fail to attract sorely needed private and public investments and the effects of this lack of funding are exacerbated by wasteful expenditure and weak accountability (Jacobs et al., 2018).

Municipalities are thus under pressure to find innovative solutions to local development problems. According to Jacobs et al., (2018), when innovation is mentioned in the strategies of municipalities it tends to be restricted to periodic transfers of new or substantially improved technology into local areas. They need to rather foster innovation-driven, local, socio-economic development tailored to local circumstances so that all involved gaining lasting benefits from the innovations (Jacobs et al., 2018). However, municipalities are facing several challenges to being innovative. These challenges include organisational and cultural barriers, fragmented politics and policy silos (OECD, 2017).

Innovation surveys in South Africa have focused on formal enterprises, usually in big cities or towns (Jacobs et al., 2018). Of course, formal industries have an important role to play in driving, supporting and contributing towards innovation, for their own benefit and that of the broader society in which they exist. Countries like Germany, Japan and the United States have transformed their economies with the adoption of an NSI, the creation of innovation zones and investment in the knowledge and research development necessary to drive innovation (Lal and Shipp, 2013: 18).

However, given the levels of informality in African cities, not recognising the role of the informal sector is a crucial omission. There is significant potential in the informal sector and the kinds of creativity needed to address the developmental challenges faced by African cities. Focusing on the informal sector provides an opportunity for 'Africa's youthful urban population to take on the challenge (if supported and adequately enabled) to drive economic transformation and innovation' (Joseph and Karuri-Sebina, 2022; Karuri-Sebina, 2017). In most African countries the informal sector accounts for the largest share of their economies (Muller, 2013) and the informal sector in Tshwane similarly accounts for a significant share, though not as big as in some countries. So, focusing on smaller, mostly informal entrepreneurs could potentially both address the issue of youth unemployment and day-to-day socio-economic challenges, and boost broader contributions to the economy. This untapped reserve of new ideas and creative energy has been demonstrated internationally (Rantisi, 2002: 600) and so must be a key focus of innovation interventions.

The case for centring cities

Our current notions of national innovation systems grew out of the seminal scholarship of the late 20th century which defined an NSI as 'a network of institutions in the public and private sectors whose activities and interactions initiate, import, modify and diffuse new technologies' (Freeman, 1987), and articulated its characteristics and conditions (Lundvall, 1992; Nelson, 1993; Edquist, 1997), including in the developing world (Muchie et al., 2003; Cassiolato and Vitorino, 2009; Lundvall et al., 2011). It was argued early on that regional and local innovation systems, given their specificities, cohesion and situated capacities could be the more fruitful levels for innovation systems functioning and analysis (Cooke et al., 1997; Tödtling and Kaufmann, 1999: i; Rantisi, 2002: 591). This is true for developing regions like Africa where local innovation systems have often been found to be context-specific (Ferretti and Parmentola, 2015: 12) and governments play significant roles in the innovation systems (Yusuf and Stiglitz, 2001: 244).

Nevertheless, strong arguments have more recently been made that African countries (Adesida et al., 2021: 782), and their emerging major urban conurbations in particular (Nawrot et al., 2017: 224; Joseph and Karuri-Sebina, 2022), could potentially be crucial drivers of economic transformation if they could function as dynamic innovation ecosystems. Nawrot et al. (2017: 231) propose the reciprocal potential for African cities to stimulate innovation growth while at the same time having any innovations enhance sustainable urban development. In relation to this, they propose defining the 'megacity innovation ecosystem' as (Nawrot et al., 2017: 231):

a network of interconnected institutions, actors, and participants connected to a defined platform of an urban agglomeration of a megacity with ability to interact, adopt, and evolve within its diverse environment by creating new structures, forms, and value that enable the system to evolve to new levels.

In this system, the crucial key actors, who relate to each other, include city authorities, the private sector, academia and NGOs as well as other institutions and individuals.

However, African innovation systems have typically been characterised by the fragmentation of actors and their linkages

(Intarakumnerd and Virasa, 2002: 3). In addition to cross-actor challenges (Adesida et al., 2016: 3), functional inter-governmental dislocations (Mitullah, 2012: 1) within the critical government sector mean that the innovation ecosystems are not typically coherent, healthy or enabling. Consider, for instance, the dimensions of the framework for analysing innovation systems within a city proposed by Nawrot et al. (2017) – see Table 9.1.

Local government is increasingly constrained, with fewer resources, more challenges and greater demands on it to resolve the developmental challenges that continue to haunt South Africa. If it is to come to grips with these issues, it will have to figure out the most creative and effective ways to do so. Investing in local urban infrastructure is one critical way that cities can drive this necessary transformation. Investments in land, transport and infrastructure in built environments do not only change the physical nature of the city; they also have the potential to enable the creativity and innovation possible in an urban agglomeration. Thus, the proximity of various industries, their scale and diversity, could all contribute towards enabling new ideas and interests in innovations that would address local needs (Quigley et al., 2005; Concilio et al., 2019). Local economic development initiatives are important also because they provide strategic opportunities for enabling local activity that can potentially be scaled up to fit with the broader national economic strategy of the country. Besides the functions mentioned here, Table 9.2 outlines the legislated responsibilities of local government which could be seen as potential areas for innovative interventions.

SOUTH AFRICA'S NATIONAL SYSTEM OF INNOVATION (NSI)

The OECD review of South Africa's NSI observed that government is the sole actor for financial allocation, R&D performance, innovation and evaluation with public R&D funds channelled through its four-tiered institutional framework (Patra and Muchie, 2017: 12). The Department of Science and Innovation (DSI) is responsible for coordinating and managing science, technology and innovation (STI) activities and policies relating to finance, procurement, regulations,

Table 9.1: Distribution of innovation system mandates

Dimensions of City Innovation Systems	Mix of Government Powers and Functions		
	National	**Provincial**	**Local**
People	• Enterprises	• Enterprises	• Individuals • Households • Enterprises
Infrastructure	• Transportation • Housing • Management of energy • Renewable resources	• Transportation, housing • Renewable resources	• Transportation, housing • Distribution of energy • Renewable resources
Environment	• Pollution, climate, haze	•	• Pollution, climate
Communication	• ICT • Early warning systems	• Early warning systems	• Cities management
Urban planning	• Spatial planning	• Spatial planning	• Spatial planning • Land use management
Legal frameworks	• Legislation • Procedures • Policies	• Policies	• Policies • Bylaws
Education	• Tertiary education • Triple helix collaboration between government, private sector, and academia	• Secondary education • Triple helix collaboration	• Triple helix collaboration
Culture	• Public funding and assistance	• Public funding and assistance	• Public funding and assistance
Connectivity	• Internally and globally	•	• Internally

Source: Nawrot et al. (2017)

Table 9.2: Functions of the three spheres as per Schedules 4 and 5 of the South African Constitution, 1996

CONCURRENT FUNCTIONS – SCHEDULE 4	EXCLUSIVE PROVINCIAL FUNCTIONS – SCHEDULE 5 (A)	LOCAL GOVERNMENT MATTERS – SCHEDULES 4(B) AND 5(B)	
shared competencies of the national and provincial government, i.e., both spheres can enact laws in these functional areas.	exclusive legislative competence over the functions, including providing regulatory frameworks to supervise municipalities around local government matters listed in Schedule 5 (B).	a municipality 'has the right to govern, on its own initiative, the local affairs of its community' and has 'the executive authority and the right to administer the local government matters' assigned to it. This authority includes the power to make and execute by-laws (as per Sections 151(3), 156(1), and (2) of the Constitution).	
• Agriculture • Local airports • Consumer protection • Education • Health • Housing • Public transport • Welfare services • Police • Environment • Nature conservation • Pollution • Road traffic • Property transfer fees • Tourism trade • Vehicle licensing	• Abattoirs • Ambulance services • Archives other than national archives • Liquor licences • Museums other than national museums • Provincial planning • Provincial cultural matters • Provincial recreation and amenities • Provincial sport • Provincial roads and traffic • Veterinary services excluding regulation of the profession	• Schedule 4 (Part B) • Air pollution • Building regulations • Child-care facilities • Electricity and gas reticulation • Fire-fighting services • Local tourism • Municipal airports • Municipal planning • Municipal health services • Municipal public transport • Municipal public works (limited) • Pontoons, ferries, jetties, piers and harbours, excluding the regulation of international and national shipping and matters related thereto • Storm-water management systems in built-up areas • Water and sanitation services limited to potable water supply systems and domestic waste water and sewage disposal systems	• Schedule 5 (Part B) • Beaches and amusement facilities • Billboards and advertisements in public places • Cemeteries, funeral parlours and crematoria • Cleansing • Control of public nuisances • Control of undertakings that sell liquor to the public • Facilities for housing, care and burial of animals • Fencing and fences • Licensing of dogs • Licensing and control of undertakings that sell food to the public • Local amenities • Local sports facilities • Markets • Municipal abattoirs • Municipal parks and recreation • Municipal roads • Noise pollution • Pounds • Public places • Refuse removal, refuse dumps and solid waste disposal • Street trading • Street lighting • Traffic and parking

Source: SACN (2016b: 7)

governance and other areas that influence the innovation process (Hlophe and Dlamini, 2018: 18). Other important institutions in South Africa's NSI are the state-funded research councils: the Council for Scientific and Industrial Research (CSIR); Council for Mineral Technology (MINTEK), which specialises in mineral research; Medical Research Council (MRC); Human Sciences Research Council (HSRC); and the Agricultural Research Council (ARC) (Hlophe and Dlamini, 2018: 18). The Technology Innovation Agency (TIA) and the National Intellectual Property Management Office (NIMPO) are also important in the NSI as they assist industries in absorbing and assimilating technologies and R&D output (Hlophe and Dlamini, 2018: 18). The NSI in South Africa is supported by the country's dynamic university system, which plays a huge role in the development of human resources and in conducting research (Hlophe and Dlamini, 2018: 18). South Africa's White Paper on Science and Technology highlighted the development of a technological economy (Hlophe and Dlamini, 2018: 18). This was the impetus for the establishment of a Council on Higher Education (CHE) in 1998, technology transfer offices, incubators and a number of funding instruments for the commercialisation of R&D outputs, which has fostered university-industry collaboration (Hlophe and Dlamini, 2018: 18).

However, while the NSI in South Africa seems active and complicated, Booyens et al. (2018: 749) suggest that there is little empirical evidence of local level innovation systems. They note that the character of local innovation networking does not fit into the NSI framework, which emphasises territorially bound knowledge and formal institutions. However, the recent MIMI assessment (ASSAf and DSI, 2021: 26) shows that there is in fact evidence of networking within various municipalities, though in an ad hoc manner. Tshwane's local innovation strategy not only attempts to align with the national development agenda but deliberately, and crucially, locates its approach within the Gauteng region to align with a region-wide approach. The City's vision emphasises the importance of collaboration with local-level stakeholders 'to co-create and build city-wide innovation capability' (CoT, 2019: 8).

Public sector innovation (PSI) is concerned with addressing the

Figure 9.2: South Africa's national system of innovation

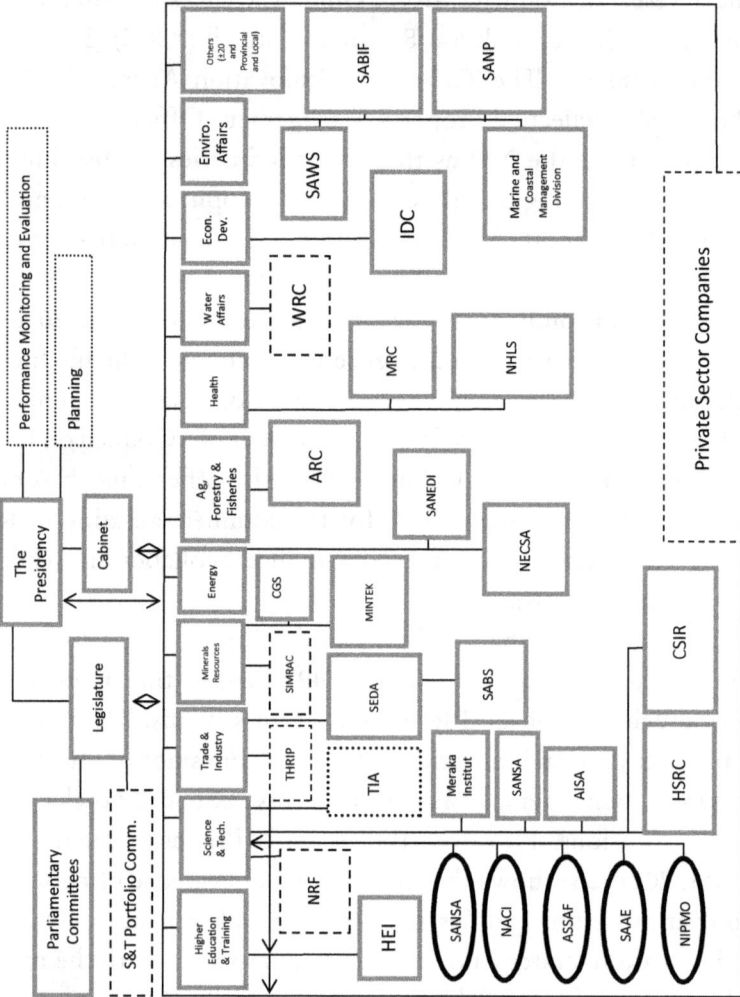

Source: Pogue and Kraemer-Mbula (2013: 13)

challenges faced by the public sector and advancing public services (Hart et al., 2020). The public sector can use innovation to improve performance and reduce costs (Plantinga and Adams, 2021). Inclusive PSI demands strong networks and investment in financial and human resources. It also requires officials with innovation capabilities to enable the introduction of innovations along with balancing the requirements necessary for enhancing economic growth, governance and social wellbeing (Hart et al., 2020). South Africa is at a key point of reflection in how it approaches both innovation and public administration as linked objectives (Plantinga and Adams, 2021). For South Africa, the public sector's relationship to innovation entails a role in economic development leading to a strong interconnection between internal and external innovation outcomes (Plantinga and Adams, 2021).

The importance of decentralisation

'While economies of scale in innovation and transfer argue in favour of standardised, centralised approaches, the decentralised approach allows tapping into local knowledge about constraints, possibilities and priorities, which may enhance local demand for innovations on offer' (Pamuk et al., 2014: 227–228). Some argue that over-centralisation kills initiatives and innovations (Makara, 2018: 23). However, it has also been argued that focusing on decentralised approaches can ignore possible economies of scale in R&D and systemic binding constraints, which may require sectoral responses; therefore a balance is required (Makara, 2018: 235). Decentralisation needs to be implemented with purpose and commitment in order for it to work well (Makara, 2018: 31). It allows for a closer connection to communities and numerous other actors who operate within the local context. In illustrating why the IT and tech revolution was so successful, Mazzucato (2015: 631) references the American government's investment in a network of decentralised public and private actors.

In addition to the constitutional mandate of local government outlined in the White Paper on Local Government, the White Paper on Science, Technology and Innovation also specifies important roles for local government (DST, 2019: 37). As noted, municipalities already have constitutional authority and legal mandates related to developmental local government. They are assigned certain powers and functions to which resources ought to be allocated in planning and budgeting cycles. They are well placed to understand and be responsive to local needs, to engage optimally with local innovators and actors, to customise responses to local peculiarities, to ensure buy-in and efficacy of service delivery, and to enable local participation, investment and diffusion. However, instead there are often accusations of demands imposed on municipalities without the commensurate allocations of funding required to deliver – the so-called 'unfunded mandates' (Chaumba et al., 2008).

Yet, South Africa is still centralised fiscally (also politically and economically), which means that local government cannot drive economic development very much, and doesn't have strong leverage with other key parts of society (corporations, academic and research institutions).[4] Arguments for centralisation are not always explicit: they sometimes rely on assumptions of municipal incompetence or incapacity, presumed coherence in verticality, challenges with silo mentalities, or considerations about the efficiencies of scaling and replication. Indeed, all of these concerns might appear to benefit from a more centrally coordinated approach. However, overly centralised approaches may cause the death of innovation – up there with other killers of innovation activity. These include macroeconomic uncertainty, political instability, unfavourable institutions, poor/lack of infrastructure, lack of information on innovation, technologies and markets, risk-averse enterprises, barriers to business start-up, poor or lack of policies, lack of funds, high cost of innovation, domination of the market by established enterprises, low investment in quality education, limited skills (worsened by brain-drain) and lack of a culture that encourages entrepreneurship and innovation (Mudombi and Muchie, 2014: 315). An appropriate role for central governments would be the provision of guidance and support to address these challenges without stifling

---

4   Issues of corruption, maladministration and instability in local government politics has resulted in a general lack of trust in the ability of local government to effectively manage services and longer-term sustainable development in the local space. This is evidenced from surveys such as the one done by Afrobarometer and the Institute of Justice and Reconciliation.

the initiatives that are taking place. In addition, supporting successful initiatives could provide the impetus and recognition that would allow them to be scaled or replicated. This oversight and support role would be much more useful and relevant than trying to dictate or centralise which and how local interventions should take place.

Tshwane's current innovation context

The 2021 Municipal Innovation Maturity Index (MIMI) (ASSAf and DSI, 2021) measured the state of municipal innovation maturity in South Africa against the scoring matrix as shown in Table 9.3:

Table 9.3: Criteria for assessing the maturity of innovation practices in municipalities

Level 1	Level 2	Level 3	Level 4	Level 5	Level 6
Limited, if any	Defined	Applied	Managed	Entrenched	Share Learnings
Limited, if any, awareness or evidence of innovation on the part of individual officials or the organisation.	Innovation is defined. Officials understand innovation principles and innovation strategies are in place, but there is little, if any, evidence of innovation.	Innovation is applied, there is evidence of implementation in certain departments of the municipality. Innovation is repeatable, but irregular.	Innovation in managed, Innovation occurs on an on-going basis and processes in relation to this are managed well in the municipality.	Innovation principles and practice are entrenched throughout the municipality. Innovation officials seek to optimise and evaluate solutions and improve on these continuously for internal benefit.	Innovation is open and outward looking. New knowledge is applied creatively, based on evidence, in diffent context and shared with others outside of the organisation.

Source: ASSAf and DSI (2021: 8)

The 2021 Municipal Innovation Maturity Index scored Tshwane at three, which means that innovation is applied and that there is evidence of implementation in certain departments of the municipality. And while the innovation is repeatable, it is irregular. The highest maturity rating is level six, which means that innovation is open and outward-looking, and new knowledge is applied creatively, based on evidence, in different contexts and shared with others outside of the organisation (ASSAf and DSI, 2021: 26). The assessment confirmed that a lack of political support, from either stakeholders or local political leadership, was one of the biggest stumbling blocks to the city moving ahead and being able to entrench innovation.

Yet, despite this, there is a lot happening in the city that should be highlighted and built upon.[5] Tshwane has a wealth of knowledge and information within close proximity. However, these are not being shared strategically nor targeted in a manner that would encourage creativity and learning (Joseph and Karuri-Sebina, 2022). In addition, the lessons (including failures) from pilots and other small-scale interventions by the different actors are not readily shared. Tshwane is missing a crucial opportunity to facilitate a flow of information and knowledge between businesses, local economic actors and other institutions. It is also missing a chance to further link up informal and formal networks in the city, mobilise community engagement and encourage participation from the private sector. By building stronger partnerships, the beginnings of which exist, the City could tap into a growing interest in innovation among the youth and could also begin to focus on specific groups, e.g., increasing the participation of women in innovation.

Interviews and the roundtable discussion with Tshwane officials suggest that there is interest, space and capacity within the City to upscale its current interventions. This might also result in more trust and willingness to financially support creative solutions. Officials admit that they have good strategies and that there is some support from senior management (though they say that more can be done). These positives can be harnessed and collaboration needs to be a key feature of a successful strategy.

FINDINGS AND ANALYSIS: TSHWANE CASE STUDY

A case has been made for the role of local governments in Africa to drive innovation in order to address the ongoing need for

---

5 Examples of innovative initiatives include the proposed Barter Bank (referred to later in this chapter) as well as the Tshwane Inter-University Innovation Challenge (a partnership driven project to support emerging young entrepreneurs) for which Tshwane won a Public Sector Innovation Award, https://www.iol.co.za/pretoria-news/news/tshwane-in-running-for-prestigious-innovation-award-a8788201-aedd-4816-b6f0-ac775e9cc591.

transformative and inclusive development. City and local governments still remain best placed to drive and support innovative solutions to local-level problems. Yet, local officials consistently pointed out over-centralisation as an ongoing issue that hampers the ability of local authorities, impacting on the resources and support received for innovative activities.

In South Africa, the importance of innovation to address the country's most pressing needs has been recognised and invested in for more than two decades (DST, 2019). The NSI provides guidance on how to implement and support innovation within the South African context. As outlined earlier, this has been accompanied by investments in a range of national bodies and initiatives aimed at driving and supporting innovative solutions and interventions. While encouraging, one of the major challenges with implementing the NSI has been its devolution to the sub-national sphere, despite the recognition of the importance of LSI in the 2019 policy. According to a national-level informant in the study, the implementation of regional and national innovation support programmes has fallen short. Instead, local support has tended to entail interventions with communities or universities where national government has supported baseline and feasibility studies for any proposed interventions. Even though the strength of the national system is its 'helicopter view' and its potential to play a strong coordinating function, it has not been able to realise these roles. Instead, the NSI is centralised at the national level without the clarity and devolution that is required to implement the system at the regional and local levels. Rather than the coordinating function that the national state is best placed to play, it is part of an existing top-down approach. This approach in effect means that local authorities have to interpret the NSI to create their own LSIs but with insufficient consultation and support to ensure that what is articulated at the national level speaks to the challenges at the local, and at the same time supports local-level initiatives to address these.

The outcomes of the focus group with Tshwane officials and a series of interviews with informants drawn from both local and national government are summarised in this section below. The findings are grouped under four themes: coherence, planning, funding and opportunities.

A coherent innovation system

National government functions better as a coordinator of the support and platforms for the country's shared innovation system at various levels. A better understanding of the role of municipalities in the NSI from all stakeholders, and better alignment between national- and local-level plans and timelines, would allow for greater synergy. A national-level respondent noted that municipalities should focus not only on the big solutions but should also think about how to use innovation to deliver basic services or improve basic implementation. This could be supported by national government by acknowledging and foregrounding any local innovation initiatives that have been successful or shown potential to address local, day-to-day challenges.

Instead, rather than a broader, macro vision for innovation in South Africa (which the NSI is presumed to represent and ensure), 'innovation' seems to have been left to the interpretation of various actors, resulting in differing understandings of innovation, which have hampered long-ranging and effective initiatives. A functional system would be one where all actors would bring their different skills and ideas into an innovation space. Or as one of the local respondents put it '[an innovation system is one where] thousands of active citizens are solving current, relevant problems in South Africa with appropriate, supported solutions'. The respondent suggested that this could even be formalised – in the form of an open innovation platform for private companies, community actors and members of the public sector to share their challenges and collectively innovate and work towards solving commonly identified problems.

Such a vision is not incommensurate with that of the National Development Plan's broader vision for South Africa's development. It also aligns with the City of Tshwane 2055 Strategy. While the coherence could be achieved top-down through the NSI, perhaps this is also where local government has a role to play. It could begin to provide the articulation of what these visions look like if facilitated and supported locally, and what would be needed for this to happen. Cities could leverage and determine their role in the NSI by providing clarity at the level of the LSI and demonstrating the potential for innovation through their existing channels and responsibilities. This would be another way of providing a clearer sense of how the NSI could be coordinated, localised and supported through locality-specific plans and initiatives.

Planning alignment

Unfortunately, the NSI and LSI do not speak to each other due to a lack of planning alignment, most importantly the inability to adequately recognise local-level plans and initiatives. Thus, although the LSIs are meant to respond to the broader national framework, there has been little consultation to drive this. Though there are instances where local municipalities have been consulted, these are not regular or systematic enough to ensure that sufficient alignment takes place. It emerged from engagement with local Tshwane officials that, in their experience, broader economic decision-making is done in a way that does not consider the role that local municipalities and actors play despite their importance in driving local economic development.

It was suggested that language may be one of many reasons why these kinds of ideas do not find resonance in the broader political economy landscape and amongst those who make economic decisions and policies. Respondents from both local and national levels acknowledge the lack of alignment, particularly between the NSI and LSI. Factors that contribute towards this non-alignment include insufficient communication and engagement; a persistent silo mentality across various departments, and changes in the political system which affect buy-in and support for innovation programmes. However, there seems to be agreement about the fact that the local sphere is best placed to support sustainable and appropriate interventions. To give effect to this, better alignment with national strategic planning cycles, particularly with the IDP, needs to be realised.

Tshwane officials are better equipped than most to understand their role in driving innovation as they serve in one of the municipalities in South Africa that are best supported and resourced to drive innovation at the local level (ASSAf and DSI, 2021). This is due to the initial support they received from national political leadership when the innovation unit was established. This political buy-in and understanding from national government is what drove the work of the unit in its early years and helped to establish it as one of the innovation leaders in the municipal space. The location of Tshwane and its proximity to a large number of universities and educational institutions, government departments and private sector actors have meant that it is well placed to coordinate and enable the connections needed to drive innovation. This has allowed Tshwane to introduce a range of innovative solutions and to support community-driven interventions. Examples of this are the establishment of the innovation hub as well as township incubators, which provide support to emerging entrepreneurs and innovators. Tshwane has won many accolades for driving innovation, including international recognition for the work it does. The change in administration has meant that more work needs to be done to convince the new political leadership to continue supporting the LSI. Unfortunately, this has also led to low morale amongst staff. But when pushed about what the municipality could still do and what works, informants expressed a number of ideas and a commitment to continue pushing for Tshwane leadership to buy into the innovation agenda.

Funding for innovation

While both national and local government have dedicated funding available for innovation, financing is often considered to be insufficient. One of the major challenges, however, seems to stem from the fact that there is very little co-funding of initiatives. Besides the availability of funding for public sector initiatives, it is also not clear where other actors (private and community) are able to apply for and access funding for their initiatives. Respondents noted that the challenge is not a lack of funding in the system but rather that the funding is not coordinated or administered effectively. Another issue expressed is that although funding seems to be available for innovation projects, much of the focus is on 'creating the next Wakanda'[6] and not enough thought is given to how existing funding at municipal level is used in innovative ways to support basic service delivery.

The lack of shared vision for what an innovation-driven system

---

6   Wakanda, or the Kingdom of Wakanda, is a fictional country in North East Africa featured in comic books by Marvel Comics. Wakanda was supposedly isolated for centuries only to become one of the most technologically advanced nations in the world.

looks like and how it should operate is perhaps best illustrated by the issue of funding. According to local officials, the national Department of Science and Innovation should make available a lot more funding for local initiatives. National department officials, however, suggest that the issue is one of co-funding and that local municipalities should use the resources that they have to close the gaps between government departments and innovation units. This would help to ensure that innovation would be less of a once-off or project-specific intervention and is instead mainstreamed into the daily work of the municipality. Innovation, for the most part, remains the domain of the innovation unit rather than co-owned across the municipality with available funding focused on projects that are rarely scaled up. An example given was an idea for launching a barter bank in Tshwane. This is an internationally recognised innovation where services are paid for through exchanges rather than money, most successfully pioneered in France. Despite this, when the idea was mooted by the Tshwane innovation unit as an innovative option for South Africa, it was met with a lot of hesitancy across the municipality and wider government institutions. For a country with high levels of unemployment and a large informal sector,[7] this presented an opportunity to grow businesses that have great potential but little cash flow. City officials argued that innovation systems should result in thriving businesses, communities being supported to contribute towards innovation-driven solutions, and a safe, equitable and cohesive city where major developmental challenges are addressed and services are delivered efficiently and effectively. But how this should be steered and funded – and by whom – is not clear.

Cities like Tshwane have been forerunners in creating local systems of innovation that speak to local development challenges and strive to support innovative responses that will be appropriate and sustainable. However, these local processes and initiatives are not joined up within

---

7   The Quarterly Labour Force Survey (QLFS) for the third quarter of 2022 shows the unemployment rate for those aged 15–24 as 59.6% and 40.5% for those aged 25–34 years. Overall, the official national rate stands at 32.9%. The informal sector accounts for 3 million jobs, compared to the 10.8 million in the formal sector (StatsSA, 2022).

the broader system. Local officials lament that the NSI is not a coherent and clear system from which it is possible to derive information, access resources and relevant actors, etc. Poor access to available resources has been a challenge resulting in many promising ideas not receiving support or seeing the light, despite the White Paper on Science, Technology and Innovation outlining a vision for joining up various actors and stakeholders. This is not encouraging for the wider NSI, given that innovation is by nature a process of trying, failing and learning over a long period of time.

What opportunities exist despite centralisation?

The thesis of this chapter is that, despite these challenges, there are nevertheless opportunities that cities could be leveraging to build their LSI. Some examples of these are:

1. The IDP as a co-development space

Both the City of Tshwane and the national DSI affirm that the municipality certainly has an important proximity advantage, making it better able to directly engage with community-based needs and resources. An important and legislated instrument for municipal planning and engagement with communities is the Integrated Development Plan (IDP) specified in the Municipal Structures Act (No. 117 of 1998). As a co-produced framework for local development, IDPs are meant to help coordinate the work of different spheres of government into a coherent plan to deliver development and improve the quality of life for the people in a community. The question or opportunity is whether the IDP process could be used not only as a list of service demands but also as a framework or basis for building an innovation ecosystem, which would bring a range of system actors and actions into the scope of development strategies and planning.

2. Transforming places through Spatial Development Frameworks

Innovation systems have a strong spatial character; they are enabled by proximity, scale, access and relational arrangements. South Africa's Municipal Systems Act No. 32 of 2000, Section 26 requires Spatial Development Frameworks (SDFs) to form part of municipalities'

IDPs. As a spatialised interpretation of a place's vision and investment propositions, the SDF is core to municipalities' economic, sectoral, spatial, social, institutional and environmental strategies. It also intended to ensure a high level of buy-in from all stakeholders. Other spatial planning legislation that cities could leverage is the Spatial Planning and Land Use Management Act No. 16 2013 (SPLUMA). SPLUMA places local municipalities at the centre of spatial planning and decision-making related to land use management, enabling them to tackle their local socio-economic challenges directly through spatial transformation interventions. Cities could use the SDF and SPLUMA as instruments for economic clustering and innovation system coordination.

3. Building resilience through disaster management

LSIs have opportunities to show their key innovation capacities for building local resilience in times of disaster. This was evident during the Covid-19 pandemic. South Africa has a Disaster Management Act 57 of 2002, which specifies explicit, multi-level protocols focused on optimising prevention, response and mitigation capabilities. These draw on local systems that have explicit roles and are nested within regional and national systems. Local municipalities are expected to regularly update their disaster management plans, and so Tshwane could be explicit about supporting multi-level innovation and learning in and beyond times of disaster.

4. Strengthening localised public investments

Tshwane could build on its existing initiatives, e.g., the incubators that have been created in townships like Mabopane to think about the fourth industrial revolution in the African context. There could be more living labs to test solutions, document failures and scale up innovations that work. The cost of these investments should not be borne by Tshwane alone. Rather, the idea of co-funding should be further explored with the national government, the private sector and academia. An external innovation fund, managed through partnerships between key actors, could contribute towards scaling up research and innovation within the city. Tshwane needs to take on the role of coordinating these initiatives and building the trust and support needed for mainstreaming innovation across the city. If this buy-in and support is achieved, the innovation agenda may be buffered from changes in leadership. Also, an active citizenry with a stake in the outcomes of these interventions will lend more sustainability and long-term support to the innovation mandate. This could also push politicians to be more accountable especially post local government elections where programmes may be affected by new incoming administrations and a change in political focus.

5. Coordinated innovation ecosystem building

Because of their local proximity and relationships, cities can play a direct role in building and strengthening innovation ecosystems. Their networking would provide them with the access and intelligence required to understand how best to coordinate and enable actors and innovations. This may include direct opportunities to provide a platform themselves where ecosystems are weak, or less indirect opportunities to support existing and emerging ecosystems as a partner, sponsor or consumer of innovation.

6. Support to other innovation actors

Tshwane has a wealth of untapped resources and potential. As noted, it is replete with universities and research institutions with which it could build stronger local partnerships to implement the LSI. Through these partnerships local communities, entrepreneurs and informal sector businesses could access mentors and support to become active innovators and participants in driving local innovations. If investment in these actors begins to happen at an earlier stage, e.g., exposing young people to the idea of innovation at schools or through public programmes and providing the resources for them to begin to develop and innovate around new ideas, the long-term benefits to the city and its residents will be exponential. Partnering with academia, businesses and the public will allow Tshwane to play a more coordinating and enabling role to drive and facilitate innovation in its midst.

7. *Being a learning platform*

Innovation systems rely on learning and competence building. Cities are both problem- and learning-rich contexts. Tshwane's concentration of knowledge institutions, coupled with the City's internal innovation and knowledge management capabilities mean that the stage is set for the City to offer local learning at a depth that national structures would struggle to offer.

8. *Growing internal support for innovation*

But more could be done internally, within the municipality and across its departments. Tshwane has an emerging community of practice with some managers and leaders who encourage free thinking and initiative. The innovation unit should capitalise on this space by creating and reinforcing a culture of learning, experimentation and documentation of these lessons and experiences. Structured research management programmes and internal ideation sessions are some of the ways that this could be done. These might allow employees to more organically consider ideas and opportunities (despite internal constraints and a still-ongoing silo approach in government) for innovating together within the City to solve collective problems and issues. This internal culture could then spill over into how the City and its officials respond to development and service delivery issues within the communities they serve. Such openness to innovation and trying new ideas for dealing with persistent problems might strengthen alignment and compliance with existing innovation programmes and standards. It might also encourage the mainstreaming of an innovation agenda across the City's internal departments and programmes, potentially leading to better availability of funding for innovative responses.

CONDITIONS TO WORK TOWARDS

There are possibilities, but actualising and beneficiating them require intervention as the current course is ineffectual. It is clear from this research that an LSI does exist in Tshwane, and that it is both supported and recognised though not functioning optimally. Tshwane has interventions that are outlined in its innovation strategy, and it has received funding support from the DSI for a series of initiatives that it has implemented across the city. Yet, as discussed in this paper, Tshwane has not been able to take full ownership of its innovation agenda due to both internal and external factors.

Internally, there is a need in the city for a shared understanding of innovation, as well as greater political awareness, support and championship of the LSI role. This, along with institutional commitment to adequate investment, support and ecosystem-building sets a stronger course for the City. There are expectant and active communities and stakeholders which are an asset, but inadequate tactics and operational systems to coordinate and leverage these and other strengths systematically are an obstacle. If the City could make some progress in these areas, beginning with leveraging existing opportunities and instruments in the short term, then it could be more locally effective and also strengthen its hand in steering upwards and laterally into the NSI.

Innovation and the LSI function are not well or commonly understood in municipalities, and interpretations range from interventions to address basic social needs to creating Wakanda. Even amongst innovation actors within the city, there is a relative lack of awareness of or focus on what municipalities themselves can do. Officials are often caught up in their sector-specific roles, rather than innovating in their work to find traction and buy-in for doing things in a more creative and effective way across the city system. Tshwane has thus not fully appreciated the extent to which it could and should drive and harness innovation in the day-to-day service delivery activities of the city. If the City can get this right, perhaps Wakanda would become less of a pipedream as more actors within the city might begin to see the value and potential of doing things differently.

But there are clearly roles and interventions that national government would have to undertake if the LSI–NSI system is to work. Shared understanding and political recognition are also necessary. National government has to be committed not only to playing a more effective policy and coordination role, but also to co-producing and co-resourcing programmes, and supporting innovation capability formation in municipalities. It also has to remove unnecessary obstacles (including lack of funding, dismissiveness about local ideas, and barriers to engagement between national and local government) and be responsive to local (bottom-up) advocacy towards enabling healthy innovation ecosystems. National government can furthermore play an important strategic knowledge-sharing role.

CONCLUSIONS AND RECOMMENDATIONS

South Africa's NSI has very much been a national-level conversation held, steered and beneficiated by national-level institutions and actors with very little articulation with local governance (municipal or civic) roles or spatial development. This national-local disjuncture is obvious from engagement with actors at both ends who report on the gaps. But it is also evident in the outcomes of the NSI, which are often not visible in local communities, i.e., the coexistence of NSI capabilities (represented by the concentrated presence of education and R&D institutions and infrastructures) and underdevelopment in many African cities (Karuri-Sebina, 2011). Furthermore, if one were to interrogate municipal strategies and plans to identify references to the NSI, one would not find many, if any (Karuri-Sebina, 2011).

This paper has sought to argue that South Africa has an NSI, but it is weak, and it is also disconnected from even weaker LSIs. Even though national policies refer to the LSI role, there is no robust national framework for specifying local roles or interfaces. Furthermore, there remains poor championship and capabilities at both ends to steer either their own side or the other. This has translated into weak local innovation ecosystems, even though the demand is there in the form of expectant and vibrant communities and local innovators. Yet there remains poor recognition of the strategic roles that local municipalities could play to manage upwards to facilitate the strengthening of LSIs and LSI-NSI linkages, even within their existing powers and functions (for which some examples have been given).

It is imperative that Tshwane focus on its LSI role as an important way to do 'the basics' of local governance and development. It is impossible to convince others of big visionary ideas if basic things do not work. This erodes trust, and impacts on the ability to sell ideas like the barter bank. Especially the private sector but also very importantly, local communities, will find it very hard to buy into the idea of being active participants if the City is not ensuring that it meets its service delivery mandate to improve the day-to-day lives of its residents. The existing mandates, mechanisms and potentials that Tshwane holds – from planning and financing instruments to platform and support roles – are important places for the City to start being more strategic and tactical.

Finally, national government must figure out how to better enable cities to do the above. A low-hanging fruit would be to reconsider how engagement takes place and to begin to foster better alignment and support for local initiatives. A city like Tshwane or any other city provides the perfect opportunity to test and learn. While Tshwane does the hard work of fostering an innovation-driven mindset at the local level, it is up to national government to actively support these efforts through funding, alignment and scaling of innovations that work so that other local municipalities can benefit from these lessons.

REFERENCES

Academy of Science of South Africa (ASSAf) and Department of Science and Innovation (DSI). 2021. 'The Launch of the National Rollout of the Municipal Innovation Maturity Index (MIMI) (A tool to measure innovation in municipalities)'. https://doi.org/10.17159/assaf.2021/0076, accessed 27 February 2023.

Adesida, O., Karuri-Sebina, G. and Kraemer-Mbula, E. 2021. 'Can innovation address Africa's challenges?'. *African Journal of Science, Technology, Innovation and Development*, 13(7), 779–784.

Adesida, O., Karuri-Sebina, G. and Resende-Santos, J. (eds). 2016. *Innovation Africa: Emerging Hubs of Excellence*. UK: Emerald Group Publishing.

Auditor-General of South Africa (AGSA). 2021. 'Consolidated General Report on Local Government Audit Outcomes: MFMA 2020-21', https://www.agsa.co.za/Portals/0/Reports/MFMA/2020-21/MFMA%20GR%202020-21%20General%20Report%20interactive.pdf?ver=2022-06-15-090741-193, accessed 16 August 2022.

Atkinson, R.D. 2014. 'Understanding the US national innovation system'. The Information Technology & Innovation Foundation, https://www.researchgate.net/publication/321790571_Understanding_the_US_National_Innovation_System, accessed 20 August 2022.

Beraha, I.A. and Đuričin, S.O. 2022. 'The effects of innovation policy on science-to-business collaboration: The case of Serbia', in Rua, O. (ed). *Impact of Open Innovation on the World Economy*. USA: IGI Global, 83–110.

Bogdan, R. and Biklen, S.K. 1998. *Qualitative Research for Education*. Boston: Allyn & Bacon.

Booyens, I., Hart, T.G. and Ramoroka, K.H. 2018. 'Local innovation networking dynamics: Evidence from South Africa'. *The European Journal of Development Research*, 30(4), 749–767.

Carlsson, B., Jacobsson, S., Holmén, M. and Rickne, A. 2002. 'Innovation systems: Analytical and methodological issues'. *Research Policy*, 31(2), 233–245.

Cassiolato, J.E. and Vitorino, V. (eds). 2009. *BRICS and Development Alternatives: Innovation Systems and Policies* (Vol. 1). New York: Anthem Press.

Chaumba, B.C., Lahiff, E., Matsimbe, Z., Mehta, L., Mokgope, K. et al. 2008. 'The Politics of Decentralisation in Southern Africa'. Future Agricultures Consortium Policy Process Briefing for WDR, Sustainable Livelihoods in Southern Africa, Stellenbosch.

City of Tshwane (CoT). 2019. 'Innovation Strategy'. Tshwane.

Concilio, G., Li, C., Rausell, P. and Tosoni, I. 2019. 'Cities as enablers of innovation', in Concilio, G. and Tosoni, I. (eds). *Innovation Capacity and the City*. UK: Springer, 43–60.

Cooke, P., Uranga, M.G. and Etxebarria, G. 1997. 'Regional innovation systems: Institutional and organisational dimensions'. *Research Policy*, 26(4/5), 475–491.

Department of Cooperative Governance and Traditional Affairs (CoGTA). 1998. 'The White Paper on Local Government'. https://www.cogta. gov.za/cgta_2016/wp-content/uploads/2016/06/whitepaper_on_Local-Gov_1998.pdf, accessed 3 May 2023.

Department of Science and Technology (DST). 2019. 'White Paper on Science, Technology and Innovation'. https://www.dst.gov.za/images/2019/ White_paper_web_copyv1.pdf, accessed 20 August 2023.

Edquist, C. 1997. 'Systems of innovation approaches: Their emergence and characteristics', in Edquist, C. (ed). *Systems of innovation: Technologies, Institutions and Organizations*. UK: Pinter Publisher Ltd, 1–35.

Ferretti, M. and Parmentola, A. 2015. 'Local innovation systems in emerging countries', in *The Creation of Local Innovation Systems in Emerging Countries*. US: Springer, Cham, 7–36.

Hart, T.G., Booyens, I. and Sinyolo, S. 2020. 'Innovation for development in South Africa: Experiences with basic service technologies in distressed municipalities'. *Forum for Development Studies*, 47(1), 23–47.

Hlophe, T.G. and Dlamini, T.S. 2018. 'Mapping the national system of innovation in eSwatini'. *African Review of Economics and Finance*, 10(2), 10–43.

Hoffecker, E. 2018. 'Local innovation: What it is and why it matters for developing economies'. D-Lab Working Papers: NDIR Working Paper 01, MIT D-Lab, Cambridge.

Intarakumnerd, P. and Virasa, T. 2002. 'Broader roles of RTOs in developing countries: From knowledge creators to strengtheners of national innovation system'. Science, Technology and Innovation Conference, JFK School of Government, Harvard University, 23–24.

Jacobs, P., Sinyolo, S., Jonas, S. and Fakudze, B. 2018. 'Innovation for equitable local socioeconomic development: action agenda for resource-poor municipalities', HSRC Policy Brief, July. http://hdl.handle.net/20.500.11910/12467, accessed 12 March 2023.

Joseph, S. and Karuri-Sebina, G., 2022. 'Enabling inclusive economic ecosystems in Africa: Is there a role for city governments?'. Southern Centre for Inequality Studies, Working Paper. https://wiredspace.wits.ac.za/server/api/core/bitstreams/6695b949-9793-4dc3-bc33-704a4bec23f9/content, accessed 12 March 2023.

Kalan, S. 27 June 2022. Interview with author, online.

Karuri-Sebina, S. 2011. 'Towards an Inclusive NSI'. Input paper on Social Innovation and Sustainability, Science and Technology Ministerial Review Committee on the National System of Innovation. Unpublished.

Karuri-Sebina, G. 2017. 'Entrepreneurship, innovation-driven economies and emergence', Second edition of the International Conference on the Emergence of Africa (ICEA), Abidjan, 28–30 March 2017.

Lal, B. and Shipp, S. 2013. 'National innovation systems: Invention to innovation', in Stirling-Woosley, S. (ed). *Unlocking the Potential of the U.S.–Japan–Europe Relationship*. USA: German Marshall Fund of the United States.

Lundvall, B.A. 1992. 'National systems of innovation: Towards a theory of innovation and interactive learning'. *The Learning Economy and the Economics of Hope*. London: Pinter.

Lundvall, B.Å., Joseph, K.J., Chaminade, C. and Vang, J. (eds). 2011. *Handbook of Innovation Systems and Developing Countries: Building Domestic Capabilities in a Global Setting*. UK: Edward Elgar Publishing.

Makara, S. 2018. 'Decentralisation and good governance in Africa: A critical review', *African Journal of Political Science and International Relations*, 12(2), 22–32.

Mazzucato, M. 2015. 'Innovation systems: From fixing market failures to creating markets'. *Revista do Serviço Público*, 66(4), 627–640.

Mitullah, W. V. 2012. 'Decentralized service delivery in Nairobi and Mombasa: Policies, politics and inter-governmental relations (No. 2012/92)'. *WIDER Working Paper*.

Muchie, M. and Baskaran, A. 2009. 'The National Technology System

Framework: Sanjaya Lall's contribution to appreciative theory'. *Institutions and Economies*, 1(1), 134–155.

Muchie, M., Gammeltoft, P. and Lundvall, B.Å. 2003. 'Putting Africa first. The making of African innovation systems'. Denmark: Aalborg University Press.

Mudombi, S. and Muchie, M. 2014. 'An institutional perspective to challenges undermining innovation activities in Africa'. *Innovation and Development*, 4(2), 313–326.

Muller, J. 2013. 'Another path: Local systems of innovation in the South'. *Forum for Development Studies*, 40(2), 235–260.

Nawrot, K.A., Juma, C. and Donald, J. 2017. 'African megacities as emerging innovation ecosystems', in Kleer, J. and Nawrot, K.A. (eds). *The Rise of Megacities: Challenges, Opportunities and Unique Characteristics*. London: World Scientific Europe, 221–258.

Ndabeni, L.L., and Rogerson, C.M. 2016. 'The role of science technology and innovation in local economic development'. Department of Science and Technology, Pretoria.

Nelson, R.R. (ed). 1993. *National Innovation Systems: A Comparative Analysis*. Oxford University Press on Demand.

Organisation for Economic Co-operation and Development (OECD). 2017. *Fostering Innovation in the Public Sector*. Paris: OECD Publishing.

Oyelaran-Oyeyinka, B. and McCormick, D. 2007. *Industrial Clusters and Innovation Systems in Africa*. Japan: United Nations University Press.

Pamuk, H., Bulte, E. and Adekunle, A.A. 2014. 'Do decentralized innovation systems promote agricultural technology adoption? Experimental evidence from Africa'. *Food Policy*, 44, 227–236.

Patra, S.K., and Muchie, M. 2017. 'Role of innovation system in development of biotechnology in South Africa'. *Asian Biotechnology and Development Review*, 19(1), 3–30.

Plantinga, P. and Adams, R. 2021. 'Rethinking open government as innovation for inclusive development: Open access, data and ICT in South Africa'. *African Journal of Science, Technology, Innovation and Development*, 13(3), 315-323.

Pogue, T. and Kraemer-Mbula, E. 2013. 'Erawatch Country Reports 2012: South Africa' 10.13140/RG.2.2.13965.54247.

Statistics South Africa (StatsSA). 2022. 'Quarterly Labour Force Survey, Quarter 3, 2022'. Pretoria: Statistics South Africa. chrome-extension:// efaidnbmnnnibpcajpcglclefindmkaj/https://www.statssa.gov.za/ publications/P0211/Presentation%20QLFS%20Q3%202022.pdf, accessed 12 September 2023.

Quigley, J., Wilhelmsson, M. and Andersson, R. 2005. 'Agglomeration and the spatial distribution of creativity'. *Papers in Regional Science*, 84, 445–464.

Rantisi, N.M. 2002. 'The local innovation system as a source of "variety":

Openness and adaptability in New York City's garment district'. *Regional Studies*, 36(6), 587–602.

Raphasha, P.I. 2015. 'Integrating national and regional innovation policy: The case of Gauteng in South Africa'. Doctoral dissertation, Graduate School of Business Administration, University of the Witwatersrand, https://core.ac.uk/download/pdf/188775497.pdf, accessed 21 August 2022.

Rodríguez, N.B. and Bielous, G.D. 2016. 'Exploring the impact of university-industry linkages on firms' innovation: Empirical evidence from Mexico', in De Pablos, P.O. (ed.). *Handbook of Research on Driving Competitive Advantage through Sustainable, Lean and Disruptive Innovation*. Spain: IGI Global, 590–613.

South African Cities Network (SACN). 2016a. 'State of Cities Report 2016: Johannesburg', http://www.socr.co.za/wp-content/uploads/2016/06/SoCR16-Main-Report-online.pdf, accessed 12 August 2023.

South African Cities Network (SACN). 2016b. 'State of South African Cities Report 2016: The People's Guide'. https://www.sacities.net/wp-content/uploads/2020/03/SoCR16-Peoples-Guide-web.pdf, accessed 25 August 2023.

South African Cities Network (SACN) and University of the Witwatersrand. 2016. 'BRICS Cities: Facts and Analysis'. https://www.sacities.net/wp-content/uploads/2020/02/BRICS-Cities-Facts-and-Analysis-2016-min-1.pdf, accessed 5 August 2023.

Tödtling, F. and Kaufmann, A. 1999. 'Innovation systems in regions of Europe—a comparative perspective'. *European Planning Studies*, 7(6), 699–717.

Wilson, S. Maharaj, C. and Maharaj, R. 2020. 'Formalising the national innovation system in a developing country'. *The West Indian Journal of Engineering*, 42(2).

Yusuf, S. and Stiglitz, J. 2001. 'Development issues: Settled and open'. in Meier, G.M. and Stiglitz, J.E. (eds). *Frontiers of Development Economics: The Future in Perspective*, New York: Oxford University Press, 227–268.

TEN

Moving beyond national systems of innovation: Insights from antiretroviral localisation

DAVID WALWYN

INTRODUCTION

South Africa's economy is in dire straits (Tregenna et al., 2021: 1). The gross domestic product (GDP) per capita has declined since 2011 and in dollar terms is now back to the same level as 2007 (World Bank, 2021). Based on the expanded definition, unemployment has risen to 44.4 per cent of the labour force and 60 per cent of the population is below the upper-middle-income country poverty line (StatsSA, 2021; World Bank, 2021). Furthermore, on a per capita income basis, South Africa is one of the most unequal countries in the world, with a reported Gini coefficient of 0.68 (World Bank, 2021).

The country's recent economic performance is a disappointment to many South Africans, but particularly to its science, technology and innovation policy practitioners. It was one of the first countries in the world to have applied the policy framework of national systems of innovation (NSI) and has adhered to this structural approach since 1996: it adopted its first White Paper on Science and Technology (DACST, 1996) and more recently the White Paper on Science, Technology and Innovation (DST, 2019). The NSI framework seemed to provide the ideal answer to many of the legacy issues inherited by the post-1994 democratic government, including a lack of inclusiveness and coherence, a strong focus on military technology and extreme fragmentation of the science system (DACST, 1996).

However, the expected benefits of a systems approach have not fully materialised. Its theoretical framework has been unable to provide sufficient directionality, to develop new industries, to increase substantially citizen participation in the science and technology infrastructure, and to address the core issues of inequality, poverty and employment (NACI, 2020).

The result of these cumulative failures is a crisis of democracy and legitimacy. Although many state departments need to take responsibility for the socioeconomic failures, it is also opportune to reconsider the NSI framework, and how to reshape its tenets to improve the prospects of a full economic recovery in the next decade. Notwithstanding issues such as criminality, corruption, skills emigration and cadre deployment (Peter et al., 2018), South Africa's inability to reconfigure its economy is as much a failure of innovation policy as it is of other initiatives to rescue a country so deeply mired in its institutional past and context (of institutional racism and colonialism). These other initiatives have included attempts to broaden participation and inclusiveness in the economy, introduce greater competition, reduce poverty and raise employment (NPC, 2012).

In this chapter, the essence of an alternative approach to industrial development is outlined, supported by a reflection on attempts to establish an antiretroviral (ARV) active pharmaceutical ingredient (API) manufacturing industry in South Africa. The chapter is a theoretical contribution to the literature and the proposals have not been tested or validated in the broader community of policy practitioners and experts. It has been developed as a novel contribution to the industrial development of upper-middle-income countries such as South Africa and Argentina, which have experimented with the

NSI approach and failed, so far, to escape the middle-income trap (Andreoni et al., 2021).

The chapter begins by providing a brief overview of HIV and the use of ARVs. This section is necessary as background information for the chapter's case study of how an approach to innovation and industrial development, based on the NSI framework, has not succeeded in a developing country. In the next section, the context for South Africa's innovation policy, which shaped the efforts to build active pharmaceutical ingredients (API) manufacturing, is presented, followed by the case study of the local manufacture of ARV active pharmaceutical ingredients, and how the logic of the NSI failed to support this initiative. In the final section, the lessons from this analysis are summarised and then used to propose a new model for industrialisation, more closely aligned with the Sustainable Development Goals (SDGs) and with a clearer vision of how to overcome the barriers to development in Africa over the last 25 years.

BACKGROUND

Prevalence of HIV

Although somewhat overshadowed by the Covid-19 pandemic, HIV continues to be a major public health risk, with globally about 680,000 AIDS-related deaths per year and 1.5 million new infections, despite the use of antiretroviral treatment and pre-exposure prophylaxis (PrEP) (Clinton Health Access Initiative, 2021). Globally, 38.4 million people are living with HIV (PLHIV), of whom 27.5 million are on ARV treatment (known as ART) (World Health Organization, 2023). Southern Africa is an epicentre of HIV, with about 19 million PLHIV in the region (Clinton Health Access Initiative, 2021; UNAIDS, 2021b). South Africa itself has an adult prevalence level of close to 20 per cent, a total of 7.8 million PLHIV and about 5.6 million patients on antiretroviral (ARV) treatment (Van Schalkwyk et al., 2021: 5652), as shown in Figure 10.1.

Figure 10.1: Number of PLHIV and patients on ART

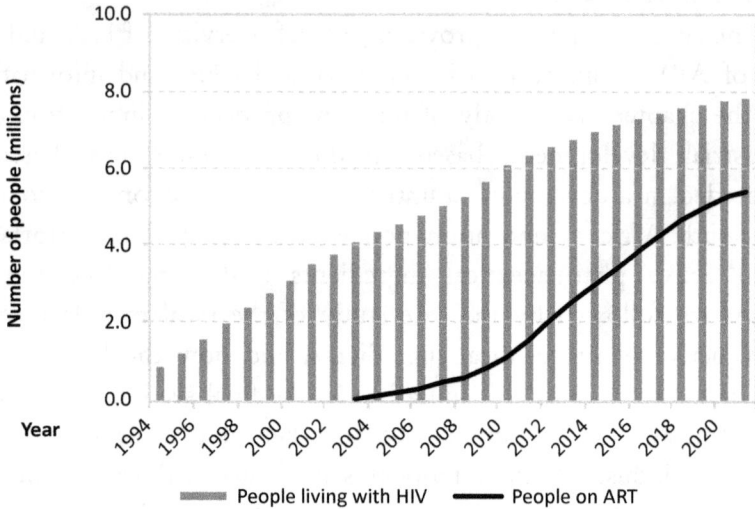

Source: Own data and Van Schalkwyk et al. (2021: 5652)

The prevalence of infection and the number of people who would eventually require ARV treatment (ART) were evident from the early days of the pandemic (Walwyn, 2004: 19–23). Although these projections were based on simplistic assumptions about changes in behaviour (or lack thereof) and the impact of public health campaigns on HIV prevention, the high levels anticipated duly materialised.

Even by 2010, the quantity of medicine required for ART in the region was daunting and there were early questions about who could make the APIs, and how these would be formulated and distributed. In the next section, the extent and cost of the demand within the region are discussed in detail. Appreciation of these quantities, and how the components of ART have changed over time, are important in understanding the extent of the market demand that arose and how this opportunity for pharmaceutical manufacturers was contested.

Development and cost of antiretroviral treatment
The development of ARVs has been profoundly effective in reducing new infections and AIDS-related deaths, and allowing PLHIV to lead normal lives. The first ARV to be approved was zidovudine (AZT)

in 1987, followed by didanosine in 1991, zalcitabine in 1992 and stavudine in 1994 (Vella et al., 2012: 1231–1241; Palmisano and Vella, 2011: 44–48). Interestingly, with the exception of zidovudine, none of the early drugs are still in widespread use, mainly due to toxicity and treatment protocols.

The introduction of two key drugs, lamivudine and tenofovir, together with the implementation of triple therapy, whereby patients are treated with three active ingredients simultaneously, revolutionised HIV treatment and led to the standard of care to which PLHIV now have access in most countries. The standard regimen, also referred to as the first-line regimen, is now a single tablet, fixed-dose, once-daily combination of three drugs. This three-drug regimen is necessary due to HIV's high mutation rate and hence the rapid development of resistance to single therapy.

The cost of ART, measured as the treatment cost per patient per year, depends on the country and the regimen. In developed countries, such as the United States, treatment costs vary from US$36,000 to US$48,000 (McCann et al., 2020: 601–603). In developing countries, at least 75 per cent of patients have access to generic drugs for which the treatment costs are US$70 (first-line regimen) and US$230 (the second-line option) (Clinton Health Access Initiative, 2021).

The total annual cost in South Africa of ART, including diagnostics and patient care, is about R28.2 billion, or 44 per cent of the total health budget (National Treasury, 2022). The actual expenditure on ARV drugs is estimated to be R7.5 billion, assuming an average treatment cost of US$79 per patient per year (similar to the 2019 tender prices for TLD).

The affordable cost of treatment, and its universal access, has been a success story for AIDS activists and international donor organisations. In the 1990s, when ARVs were launched, treatment costs were prohibitive and led to low rates of uptake in developing countries (Vella et al., 2012: 1231–1241). However, the increasing public outcry over health disparities between rich and poor countries, and support from multilateral organisations, led to the generic manufacturing of key drugs in India and China, with prices falling to fractions of the products over the next decade (UNAIDS, 2021a).

The most widely used APIs in South Africa, prescribed over the period from the start of the epidemic to 2020, are listed in Table 10.1.

Table 10.1: Main components of ART in South Africa; 2004 to 2024 (figures in tonnes per annum)

ARV API	2008	2010	2014	2020	2024 (forecast)
Stavudine (d4T)	7	2	0	0	0
Zidovudine (AZT)	70	50	36	15	15
Didanosine (ddI)	13	4	24	0	0
Nevirapine (NVP)	44	53	36	5	5
Lamivudine (3TC)	63	110	81	86	606
Tenofovir (TDF)	0	0	292	517	575
Efavirenz (EFV)	285	460	0	150	0
Dolutegravir (DTG)	0	0	0	10	96
Emtricitabine (FTC)	0	20	195	307	0
Total	481	698	663	1,090	1,297

Source: Author's data and Van Schalkwyk et al. (2021: 5652)

The initial regimens were based on stavudine/didanosine/zidovudine, but this combination of drugs was found to be highly toxic and not well tolerated by many of the initial patients. Some of the side effects were acidosis (which could be fatal), lipodystrophy, sleep disruption and nausea (Tseng et al., 2015: 182–194). The first of many combination ARVs was introduced in 2006 with the launch of Atripla (tenofovir, emtricitabine and efavirenz), although it was nearly a decade before this specific combination became available within South Africa's public health sector (Simelela et al., 2015: 256–261), as shown in Figure 10.2.

The present South African regimens for ART, somewhat simplified, are listed in Table 10.2. The recent preference for tenofovir, lamivudine and dolutegravir (TLD) over Atripla explains the resurgence in the use of lamivudine (3TC) and the decline in emtricitabine (FTC).

Figure 10.2: South African market volumes for the main ARV APIs; 2003 to 2025 (figures in tonnes per annum)

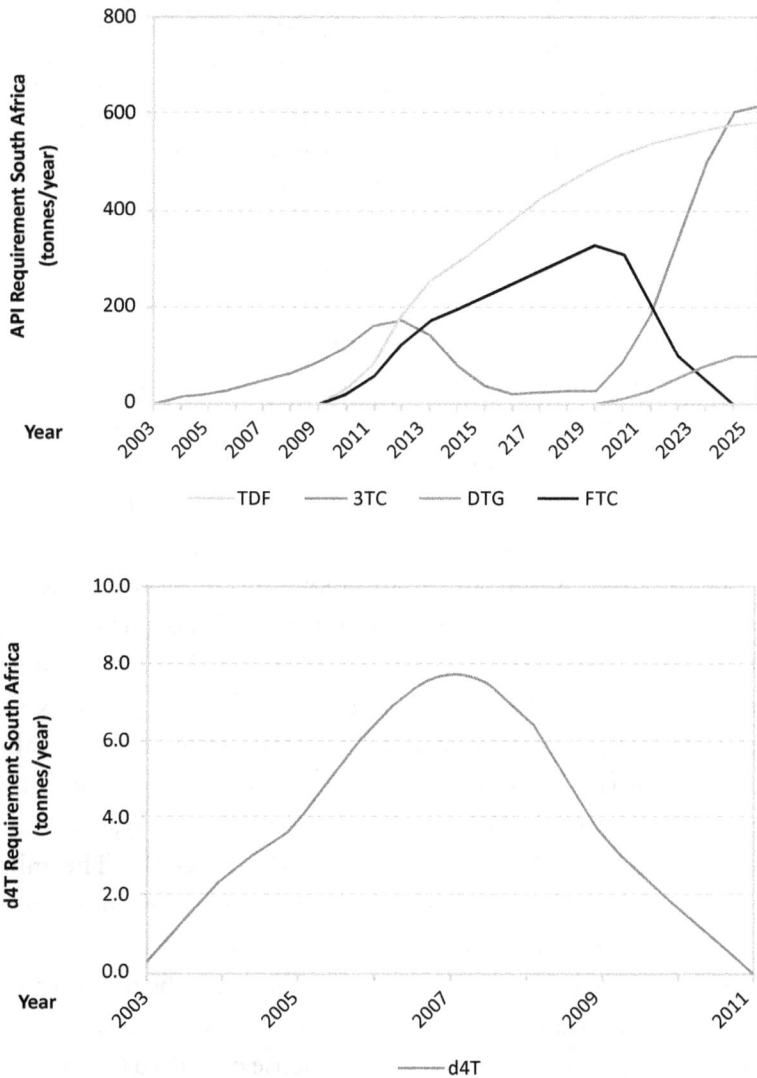

Source: Author's own data and Walwyn (2013: 19)

Table 10.2: Main components of the present guideline for ART in South Africa

First Line Adult (1L) (Fixed Dose Combination)	Second Line Adult (2IL)	Paediatric Formulations
Dolutegravir (DTG) 50 mg/day Tenofovir (TDF) 300 mg/day Lamivudine (3TC) 300 mg/d	AZT/TDF + 3TC/FTC + Lopinavir or Atazanavir or DTG	Various combinations of AZT, Nevirapine, 3TC, Abacavir and DTG depending on age and weight

Source: National Department of Health (2020: 3)

The opportunity for local manufacturing

Pharmaceutical manufacturing is perhaps one of the most contested domains within and between countries. Who gets to own the intellectual property, to what extent it is enforced, who makes the profits and how prices are determined are all critical questions which arise regularly and reach controversial conclusions.

The conflict is fundamentally about the tension between public health, or the right to health, and its access cost, or the right to profit (Walwyn, 2013: 17–23; Harrelson, 2001: 175–203). These questions emerged again recently in the international furore over the Covid-19 vaccines. Inequities in vaccine access resulted in renewed calls, and some initiatives, to build local manufacturing capacity and increase the resilience or self-sufficiency of national health systems (Loembé and Nkengasong, 2021: 1353–1362; Walwyn, 2021). The initiatives of domestic manufacture were resisted by the drug industry, which acted to protect its intellectual property and undermine localisation initiatives (Davies, 2022). For those familiar with the public campaigns for affordable access to HIV drugs in the 1990s, the initiatives and the industry response brought on a strong sense of déjà vu (Walwyn, 2022).

In South Africa, the Council for Scientific and Industrial Research (CSIR), together with other public-funded organisations, began in the early 2000s an initiative to develop the manufacturing technology for ARV APIs, with the intention of building at least a portion of the necessary regional capacity to ensure security of supply. This move was in response to the high initial costs for ART, strong resistance from the major drug companies to waiving their commercial and intellectual property rights, and the unaffordability of a widespread public health programme in South Africa.

The approach was broadly based on the science, technology and innovation policy of that period, as reflected in the White Paper on Science and Technology (DACST, 1996) and the National Research and Development Strategy (DST, 2002). The White Paper was particularly formative. It was adopted by the South African government at least eight years before work had begun on the localisation of ARV APIs and it had already been absorbed into the annual performance plans and strategies of public research organisations such as the CSIR and the Medical Research Council (Walwyn, 2006: 274–274).

Moreover, it was apparent at the time that the technological capabilities to realise such an important objective were already present in the country's research organisations. These institutions covered all areas of pharmaceutical process development including the chemistry and engineering expertise needed to reproduce patented routes, improve upon them, and develop cost-competitive processes (Al-Bader et al., 2009: 427–445; Jeenah and Pouris, 2008: 351–354).

The starting point for the localisation effort, as undertaken by the CSIR, was to decide on the target molecule(s), a choice complicated by the changing nature of the treatment regimens as more became known about issues such as tolerance, toxicity, drug resistance, cost and availability. The work began with zidovudine and stavudine (Gordon et al., 2011: 258–265), and then later included tenofovir when it became apparent that this API was well tolerated and highly effective (Riley et al., 2016: 742–750; Walwyn, 2013: 17–23).

The rationale for local research, development and innovation (RDI) had several components in addition to health access/security. For instance, in terms of the WTO's Trade-Related Aspects of Intellectual Property (TRIPS) agreements,[1] any member country that wishes to invoke the compulsory licensing provisions of TRIPS must show

---

1 The World Trade Organization (WTO) Agreement on Trade-Related Aspects of Intellectual Property Rights (TRIPS) sets standards for copyright protection and also establishes minimum standards for the enforcement of intellectual property rights.

evidence of local capacity (Abbott and Reichman, 2007: 921–987). Moreover, the spectre of large-scale ART in South Africa raised issues of foreign exchange and local industrial development. There had already been significant work on local pharmaceutical production (Kudlinski, 2014; Walwyn, 2004: 19–23), which had concluded that its growth was limited by the small regional market, insufficient to support a viable manufacturing entity. For the first time, this broad principle was not applicable, with the regional market being about 45 per cent of the global market and the quantities of API being at least several hundreds of tonnes per year, many times higher than most drugs and well above the limit of viability.

Articulation of the ARV 'opportunity' in this way emphasises the epistemic basis upon which the systems of innovation framework, or more correctly the narrow version of the NSI approach, resides. The latter's claim is that industrial development results from strong innovation policies, particularly policies that support the efforts of firms to develop knowledge and capability relating to specific product or service opportunities (Edquist and Johnson, 1997: 41–63). The fundamental elements of the NSI framework are intensive public–private research and development (R&D) as a means of developing new knowledge, training and innovation through doing, using and interacting, lowering the cost of capital and building networks between actors (Edquist, 2010: 14–45). Within this theoretical perspective, and its associated theory of change, the key priorities for the development of local ARV API manufacture would be increased investment in local R&D, human resources, capital infrastructure and international networks.

However, the theory of change implicit in the NSI framework is not the only approach. There are multiple views, based on varying emphases on the role of firms, the extent of state intervention, the power of markets, the importance of competition and the necessity of networks. In the next section, four approaches to industrial development are briefly outlined, leading to a critique of the NSI approach and finally to a proposed alternative.

INNOVATION AND PHARMACEUTICAL PRODUCTION

In the introduction to this chapter, it was noted that national systems of innovation and industrial production are deeply mired in their institutional past and context, making reconfiguration difficult to achieve. Although disintegration happens of its own accord, and the perpetuation of existing socio-technical systems requires only minimal effort, the alignment of new actors to create a cohesive force for change is both complicated and challenging. In the case of this chapter, this force led to new pharmaceutical manufacturing. Capability and sustainable development have to be constructed layer upon layer with painstaking care, sometimes taking generations, but can disappear in an instant as a key actor fails to participate or a critical input weakens.

The way in which this construction takes place depends on context and ideology. In this section, four different approaches are described briefly, emphasising different policy targets and roles for the main actors. The four approaches are techno-economic (often referred to as engineering and finance), industrial policy, systems of innovation and socio-technical reconfiguration.

Techno-economics and firm-level innovation
The first approach adopts a neo-classical perspective on economic development. This considers such development as a process driven by unfettered markets and the rational allocation of limited resources for opportunities for investment and market expansion. The latter are identified through techno-economic assessment of multiple options. Firms are central to this model, and firm-level innovation is essential in the identification and realisation of these opportunities. This construction derives from two ideological assumptions: the first is that development is the consequence of the action of individuals who can exercise their agency within an environment that is unconstrained by regulation or state control. The second is that the analytical tools and methodologies deployed to support such action are objective and divorced from powerful actors who seek to influence the analytical outcomes.

As is always the case when routines become normative, users of these tools are oblivious to their performativity and the way in which both assumptions and calculations prevent new entrants and new ideas from emerging (Walwyn and Kraemer-Mbula, 2021: 102131). More importantly, the strategy underplays the importance of the political economy, the role of the state and how the economic/industrial structure may act against the realisation of investment opportunities (Mondliwa and Roberts, 2021: 312–336).

There are various ways in which the strategy can be characterised. As shown in Figure 10.3, the perspective aligns with the centrality of agency, the notion that industrial development is the consequence of actions taken by firms and the individuals within these firms. The state plays a limited role in this process, other than the provision of public goods (infrastructure, public health, education and security) and in the maintenance of a stable policy/fiscal environment.

Figure 10.3: Firms as the 'star of the show'

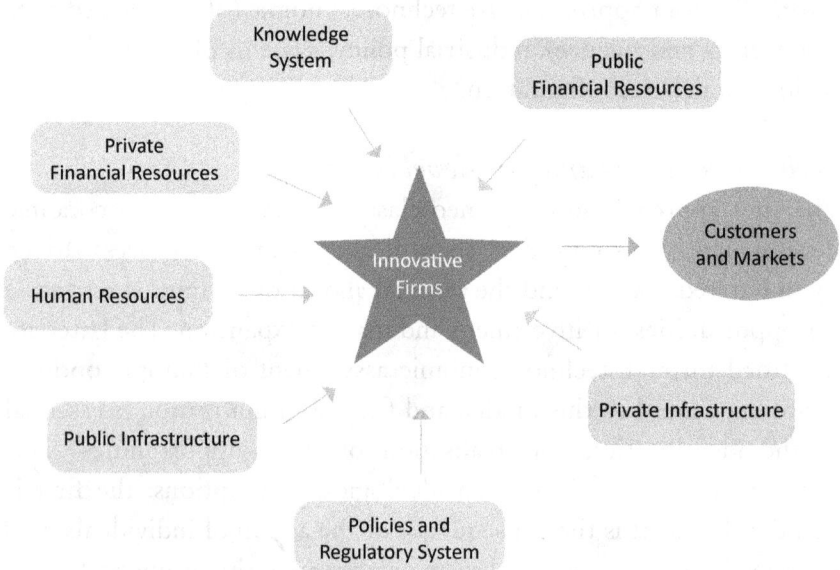

Source: Author's own complilation

Sectoral Structure and Industrial Policy

The second strategy is an approach to sectoral transformation based on industrial policy. The main assumption in this approach is that firms are constrained by structural issues that cannot be overcome by individual actors. In many cases, firms do not have the power or resources to change the enabling conditions in their environments, such as the availability of public goods, the pool of human resources or the availability of financial capital. These constraints can only be changed by powerful actors, particularly governments, or through collective action by large groups with an aligned interest.

The presumption of industrial policy in this approach is clear, i.e., that a strong interventionist state is required in order to overcome market barriers and failures. This perspective fell from favour under the strongly neo-liberal approaches of the decades since the 1980s. The result was that targeted policies focusing on specific sectors or actors were phased out, leaving a suite of horizontal, supply-side policy portfolios, which reduced the role of direct state subsidies in supporting new markets or internal industries (Criscuolo et al., 2022b).

More recently, however, this view has been challenged and industrial policy is resurging as governments realise that horizontal approaches provide insufficient directionality and support for emergent firms, whose success is critical to the imperatives of inclusive development and climate action (Criscuolo et al., 2022a). Notwithstanding this interest, studies of policy effectiveness indicate few successes, with many interventions, although well intentioned, failing to deliver the desired results on account of poor coordination with other policies, crowding out of private investment and capture of the benefits by powerful actors with vested interests (Criscuolo et al., 2022b; Morris et al., 2020: 1–23).

Innovation policy and sense-making

A third strategy is centred on innovation policy and the NSI framework. In South Africa, innovation policy has followed the NSI approach since 1996 and accepted, mostly without in-depth critical analysis, the link between innovation and economic growth. To quote from the opening chapter of the White Paper on Science and Technology (DACST, 1996: 12):

> Innovation will improve the lives of all the country's people in two ways: through progressively increasing economic growth and enhanced participation in the economy, but, just as importantly, by innovative and pervasive personal and social development of the nation's people.

The NSI concept is an acknowledgement that the interaction between technology, economy and society is better described as a seamless web of actors, organisations and institutions, rather than as an orderly sequence of logical events. Indeed, it could be called a chaotic abundance of relationships, some aligned and some conflicting. It is a socio-technical framing that considers innovation as a complex co-creation of discovery and learning, a process involving a system of actors, organisations and institutions, which contribute simultaneously to the attainment of specific goals and outcomes. The important factor is not static capabilities but knowledge flows and openness, sitting alongside specific initiatives to protect infant industries.

The framing has failed to ignite national consciousness about the importance of STI and its link to development due to the low level of technical education and the inability to prioritise technological innovation across South Africa. Technology has an oppressive past in this country, strongly linked to conflict, terror and exploitation, and this legacy slows down the creation of a new socio-technical imaginary through a process of sense-making and localisation (Kahn, 2019: 116–125).

Even when a new faith in science has been developed, efforts to localise pharmaceutical knowledge-making have stalled and failed (Pollock, 2014: 848–873). In this chapter, I argue that the reason for this lack of success is that the NSI framework, as implemented within South Africa, and specifically in its narrow form, is overly focused on supply-side interventions that rely on firm-level agency and the incentivisation of firm-level behaviours. Examples of such incentives include tax credits for research and development, training grants and financial support for equipment upgrading. This supply-side focus aligns closely with other neo-liberal economic policies, which have dominated international trade agreements since the end of the Second World War. These are captured by the various rounds of World Trade

Organization agreements and are divorced from the challenges faced by middle-income countries with weak innovation systems (Davies, 2019).

It is important, at this point, to consider whether the weaknesses outlined in the previous paragraph and elsewhere in the chapter are the consequence of South Africa's adoption of the narrow, rather than the broad, approach to the NSI framework. There are clear and fundamental differences between the two systems (Lundvall et al., 2002: 213–231). The narrow version focuses almost exclusively on firm-level innovation, emphasising the need for technological capability, R&D and innovation processes as drivers of innovation. The approach also considers how firms within a specific industry or sector interact with each other, as well as with other stakeholders such as research institutions, universities and government bodies to create and diffuse new technologies and knowledge (Malerba, 2002: 247–264). It prioritises the role of formal practices, such as intellectual property rights, patents and government policies in shaping innovation outcomes.

The broad version of the NSI approach takes a more comprehensive view and looks beyond just the activities of firms within a specific industry or sector (McKelvey, 1997: 200–222). It considers the broader social, economic and institutional context, thereby acknowledging that innovation is influenced by factors such as culture, institutions, networks and historical path dependencies (Lundvall, 2022: 1–18). This version of the NSI approach emphasises the importance of interactive learning, knowledge networks and systemic interactions between different actors in fostering innovation (Lundvall, 2016: 406).

Although the broad version does address the importance of the political economy, it fails to address the need for directionality in innovation policy (Schot and Kanger, 2018: 1045–1059); the politics of underdevelopment (Banerjee and Duflo, 2019); and erosion of learning through migration. In the next section, a fourth strategy, which introduces stronger measures for breaking path dependencies and supporting new niche entrants, is outlined.

Socio-technical systems and transition theory

Weaknesses in the approaches of techno-economics, industrial policy and the (narrow) NSI approach lead to a fourth strategy based on a multi-level perspective (MLP). The MLP is a 'middle-range' theory, which depicts processes of change, particularly the reconfiguration of socio-technical systems, to make them more sustainable (Geels and Turnheim, 2022). This perspective draws on several theoretical understandings of change including neo-Schumpeterian economics, historical institutionalism and the social construction of technology.

Transition is considered to happen as a consequence of multi-level and multi-actor struggles between the dominant socio-technical system (regime), the threat of new entrants (niche level) and unpredictable changes to the exogenous landscape (see Figure 10.4). Moments of opportunity (for change) arise when there is congruence or simultaneity between new landscape pressure, stronger and more aligned contestation from niche players, and a growing weakness in the dominant regime. These windows may or may not lead to transition; the events are random, open-ended and have uncertain outcomes.

The construct of a socio-technical system is an important element of MLP. The system is considered to be a diverse configuration of components, including scientific knowledge, industry structures, products, markets, consumption patterns, infrastructure, policy, and cultural meaning which have 'material, relational and institutional dimensions' (Geels and Turnheim, 2022). These dimensions become firmly embedded over time, making them highly resistant to change.

Figure 10.4: The multi-level perspective

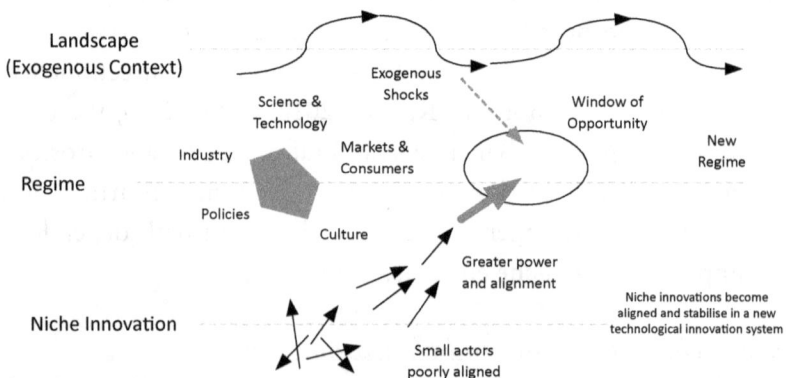

Landscape (Exogenous Context)

Exogenous Shocks

Science & Technology

Window of Opportunity

Industry

Markets & Consumers

New Regime

Regime

Policies

Culture

Greater power and alignment

Niche innovations become aligned and stabilise in a new technological innovation system

Niche Innovation

Small actors poorly aligned

Source: Adapted from Geels (2019: 188)

The MLP defines four distinct phases in transition. These are: first, radical innovations take place at the niche level, initially in a discordant and incoherent fashion; second, the niche players become aligned over time (murmurate) and reach a critical mass; in the third phase, these innovators are sufficiently powerful to be able to challenge the regime; finally, if this challenge happens synchronously with the weakening of the regime following exogenous shocks and hence landscape pressure, then a new technological configuration is able to emerge. MLP maintains that changes in socio-technical systems cannot take place without niche management and regime destabilisation and emphasises a proactive strategy of countering regime resistance, pathway dependence, incumbency and lock-in. Mechanisms for this strategy are a combination of relational aspects (alliances and dependencies), institutions (cultural norms and practices) and techno-economics (capital investments and fixed assets).

A typology of the various models for industrial development mentioned in this chapter is shown in Figure 10.5. The typology, adapted from a prior publication (Geels, 2020: 119894), uses the two orthogonal axes of positivist/constructivist and collectivist/individualist, with examples of relevant theories and the innovation approaches in this chapter inserted into the relevant quadrant. For instance, the techno-economics approach, in which individuals and firms have agency and autonomy to pursue new opportunities unconstrained by the structures or contexts within which they operate, is inserted into the bottom left quadrant. Similarly, MLP, which is strongly influenced by neo-institutionalism, is placed in the top right quadrant, where structure is important and institutions are performative (Roberts and Geels, 2019: 221–240).

Four different policy approaches to sectoral development have now been reviewed. It has been argued that the first three models have limited applicability as theories of change for developing countries. These operate within a context of the political economy in which agency-based theories of change, which emphasise the importance of learning, human resource development and rational choice, take no cognisance of the structural constraints and struggles of developing countries, such as the migration of scarce skills and capital flight. In the

Figure 10.5: Representation of the four approaches to industrial development based on their paradigmatic assumptions

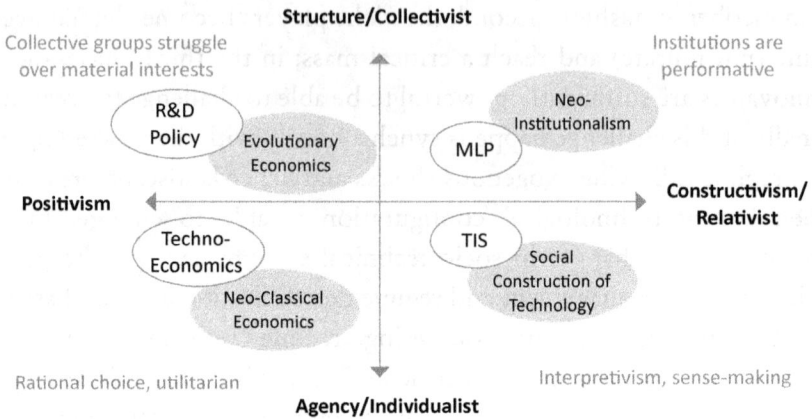

Source: Adapted from Geels (2020)

next section, this argument is illustrated by the various attempts made to establish ARV manufacture in South Africa. The analysis concludes with how these approaches were undermined by the country's context and how an alternative approach to economic transition may have been more successful.

ATTEMPTS TO ESTABLISH ANTIRETROVIRAL MANUFACTURE IN SOUTH AFRICA

Arvir and iThemba: Entry through innovation

The combination of a significant local market for ARV APIs and advances in the CSIR's research programme for manufacturing technology resulted in the establishment in 2007 of a private company, Arvir, with a mandate to commercialise ARV API technology. The company was funded by the Technology Innovation Agency, which is a Schumpeterian-type development agency based in Pretoria, funded by the national government (Kaplan, 2021: 259–277).

The company's initial focus was the novel technology for the production of β-thymidine, a key intermediate in the production of zidovudine and stavudine. At this time, the South African treatment regimen included both APIs, with a total annual market of about

8 tonnes of stavudine and 70 tonnes of zidovudine. However, shortly thereafter stavudine was found to be highly toxic and the product was withdrawn from treatment regimens. As a result, the company's research focus switched to tenofovir and lamivudine, and it began the process of obtaining the technology and partners to support local manufacture.

The development of tenofovir is a fascinating story of multiple partners in various countries, including the Czech Republic, Belgium and the United States (Walwyn, 2013: 17–23). Interestingly, the initial clinical work was undertaken by Bristol Myers Squibb, which was sceptical of the molecule's prospects and granted all the intellectual property to an ex-employee who then established Gilead Sciences, which is now a multi-billion dollar company built almost entirely on tenofovir. Initially expensive to manufacture (> US$3,000 per kg in 1997, when the drug was first approved by the Federal Drug Administration), the cost fell considerably following the licensing of several generic Indian manufacturers, reaching US$550 per kg in 2010 and US$182 per kg in 2021 (Clinton Health Access Initiative, 2021; Walwyn, 2013: 17–23).

Even in 2010, it was apparent that in Gilead's access countries, the margin on tenofovir and lamivudine API manufacture would be small as a consequence of bulk procurement by aid organisations and the intense competition between Indian and Chinese pharmaceutical companies. For Arvir to compete, it would need a competitive manufacturing technology and a level of demand-side support, such as an offtake agreement, from the National Department of Health and the National Treasury.

Unfortunately, it was not the moment to be seeking support through the public procurement system for ARVs. The prevailing Minister of Health was Manto Tshabala-Msimang, well known for her anti-ARV views and openly hostile to any initiative which may lead to the establishment of an ARV manufacturing business. Although she was replaced in 2008, her department continued her anti-localisation stance, arguing that it would lead to higher prices and reduced access for PLHIV. This argument overrode both the government's industrial policy, which explicitly mentioned strengthening pharmaceutical manufacturing (Department of Trade and Industry, 2015), and even the policy of the ruling party, the African National Congress (ANC), which in 2007 had adopted the following resolution at its Polokwane Conference: 'The ANC should explore the possibility of a state-owned pharmaceutical company that will respond to and intervene in the curbing of medicine prices.'

Developing tenofovir manufacturing technology transpired to be an easier task than offtake agreements. The details of the process route had already been published, following efforts by the Clinton Health AIDS Initiative (CHAI) to ensure that the drug was globally available at an affordable price (Fortunak et al., 2014: 15–29; Ripin et al., 2010: 1194–1201). CHAI was also keen to see more producers in the market and happy to support technology transfer from its international partners. It is noted that throughout the conceptualisation phase, the importance of innovation and the use of a globally competitive process were recognised and prioritised, hence the funding from the Technology Innovation Agency.

However, attempts to raise capital to support the construction of the manufacturing facility were made contingent on the offtake agreement, and the latter was never forthcoming. By 2010, Arvir had depleted its funding and was forced to close, but the work on tenofovir continued in another pharmaceutical start-up, iThemba Pharmaceuticals. The latter was also funded by the Technology Innovation Agency, but was focused on the discovery of new drugs for the treatment of tuberculosis (Pollock, 2014: 848–873). The tenofovir work at iThemba resulted in an improved synthetic route, the details of which were patented (Edlin et al., 2014) and later published (Riley et al., 2016: 742–750).

Unfortunately, the process has never been commercialised in South Africa for reasons which illustrate the core thesis of this chapter, i.e., weaknesses in the narrow NSI approach as a framework for industrial development. Further in this chapter, there is discussion of the technology's fate, the reasons for this thesis and how the example of ARV APIs suggests the adoption of a new approach. Arvir and iThemba were not alone in the ARV API space, and we now consider the experience of Ketlaphela, which employed a different strategy but ended with the same outcome.

Ketlaphela: Entry through licensing and foreign investment

Ketlaphela was established in 2011 in order to develop ARV API manufacturing in South Africa (Abbott, 2021). It is a subsidiary of a state-owned company, Pelchem, which has direct links to the nuclear energy infrastructure at Pelindaba and was mandated to explore new opportunities for chemical manufacture. Ketlaphela was one such project (it is ironic that the name aptly translates as 'I will survive no matter what'), with the initial objective of producing efavirenz (EFV), at that time a central component of ART.

Around 2010, Lonza and Pelchem entered into formal discussions about the establishment of a fully integrated pharmaceutical manufacturing company at the Pelindaba site. Lonza had already been making EFV under contract for Merck but had also developed an improved process, which it was now offering to Pelchem. Lonza is a contract manufacturer based in Switzerland and outward technology transfer is not part of its standard business practice. However, at the time, the company was in financial distress and the proposed deal with Ketlaphela allowed it to earn additional revenue and stay in the ARV market.

Ketlaphela seemed an ideal solution to four crucial issues of the time, namely the predicament of Pelchem and its need to diversify; the industrial policy objective of building local pharmaceutical manufacturing capability; Lonza's own economic woes; and finally, access to essential medicines (Abbott et al., 2021). Notwithstanding these powerful drivers to its possible success, the initiative failed, the reasons for which are now discussed.

In the first place, the National Treasury was unwilling to grant a controlling stake in Ketlaphela to Lonza. In its view, Ketlaphela was established as a state-owned entity and access to the ARV tender in the proportion that was being demanded (40 per cent of the tender to be set aside for the venture) could not be granted to a company that was not controlled by the state (Abbott et al., 2021). Secondly, Lonza was unhappy about the slow decision-making processes of the South African government.

Finally, and most importantly, the facility was expensive, requiring a capital expenditure of R1.5 billion. National Treasury was required to contribute R568 million of this as an initial cash grant, and further grant funding of R1.5 billion, bringing the total operational subsidy to R2.04 billion or about R4,295 per kg of API (the weighted average selling price of API at the time was R3,240 per kg). A feasibility study undertaken for National Treasury in 2013 calculated that the return on shareholder funds for Lonza, if all the funding streams were to be granted, would be at least 45 per cent, as compared to the 20 per cent as stated in the proposal. This indicated that the Swiss company was insistent on an extremely high rate of return, certainly out of all proportion relative to returns in other sectors or even areas of its own domestic business. This single point brings into stark reality the perceived level of risk for such an investment by an international chemical company, and questions whether a strategy aimed at international technology transfer could be successful.

In response to Lonza's withdrawal, National Treasury instructed Pelchem to issue a public tender for a new partner, which was closed in 2015. Only one company submitted a bid, and this submission did not meet the tender's minimum criteria, with the result that the initiative was left without a technology partner and private sector investor. Ketlaphela's strategy was then changed to a phased approach to the production of ARV APIs. This entailed the initial establishment of a small pilot plant for API manufacture, combined with the importing of finished products from an international supplier in order to gain an initial market share in the ARV tender. It was envisaged that over time the company would extend its footprint through backwards or upstream integration by undertaking local formulation using a contract facility and imported APIs and then establishing larger-scale API manufacturing for its key products.

However, Pelchem was not able to raise support for its new business plan from National Treasury and the project came to a complete standstill, although there are still the occasional resurrections in the media (Tomlinson, 2020). Several reasons have been cited for the National Treasury decision, including the general failure of state-owned entities such as Eskom and South African Airways, which posed a large risk to the fiscus and led to a general reluctance by National Treasury to countenance new entities. Other factors in the

Treasury's decision were the erosion of political support for public–private partnerships, which were not fully supported by government after 2009; the absence of a black empowerment partner acceptable to government; the reluctance by the National Department of Health to grant 40 per cent of the ARV tender to a single supplier; strong opposition from the existing formulators (Aspen and others) to the entrance of a new pharmaceutical company; and weak support at Cabinet level for the industrial policy of the Department of Trade, Industry and Competition (DTIC).

As of end 2020, Ketlaphela is reported to be marketing hand sanitiser only, and there is no evidence that it has gained any traction in the ARV market. Repeated attempts to do so have been undermined by a combination of factors, as noted in the earlier paragraph, with the most important being the failure of the state to grant adequate protection to the development of a new industry. Such protection would require the simultaneous implementation of a supportive innovation policy (to allow the development of the necessary technological capability and counteract regime resistance); an industrial policy (to support investment in local manufacturing infrastructure); and, most importantly, a health policy (to prioritise local manufacture as a niche or emergent sector and grant it preferred provider status).

All of these elements of the diagnosis indicate a failure of the state across a range of departments and not only those responsible for technological innovation. Ascribing the failure of the ARV API initiatives to only innovation policy, rather than the overall mix of policies (Walwyn and Naidoo, 2020: 33–46), is not the intent of this chapter or the illustrative example. Instead, it is suggested that some of the important issues are overlooked by the present policies based on the NSI approach. In the next section, a new approach to economic transitions, which could address these policy weaknesses, is outlined.

A NEW APPROACH TO ECONOMIC TRANSITION

The focus of this chapter is 'optimal strategies for industrial development', which links closely to the overall theme within the book of the general failure of innovation policy. With specific reference to South Africa, it is argued that the NSI approach, as a guiding framework for innovation policy, has been sub-optimal, largely as a consequence of inadequate attention to issues of political economy. Instead, capability, agency and firm-level innovation have been placed at the centre of the policy (Walwyn, 2019). Structural inequalities are not considered, other than through the assertion that the provision of knowledge and education as public goods will allow these inequalities to dissipate over time. Such assumptions are misleading; the opposite trajectory has characterised innovation systems within middle-income countries since the theory was introduced.

Prior studies have already highlighted the shortcomings of the NSI as a theoretical model for policy construction in developing countries (Foster and Heeks, 2013: 333–355; Kraemer-Mbula and Wamae, 2010: 65–90; Lundvall, 2007: 95–119). Several concerns have been noted, including a lack of attention to infrastructure and the informal sector; inadequate directionality and attention to issues of sustainability (Kaplinsky and Kraemer-Mbula, 2022: 104394); an overemphasis on firm-level innovation; and a poor understanding of the destructive pattern of multinationals involved in the extractive industries. In general, these authors have explained the failure of innovation policy in South Africa since 1994 as the lack of supportive and aligned policies within all areas of government, with the result that the utility of the NSI was not able to be realised (Kraemer-Mbula and Maharajh, 2021: 467–488). The validity of the NSI has been left untouched in these analyses.

It is, perhaps, time to reconsider the devotion to the NSI. The NSI subscribes South Africa's economy to a game which it cannot win because this game is based on a set of rules that prevent it from doing so. It emphasises firm-level agency, Ricardian economics and competitiveness, an agenda which is counter-development and it ignores the structural constraints faced by middle-income countries (Banerjee and Duflo, 2019). It has been argued that South Africa remains underdeveloped because developed countries need it to be so. They need to access raw materials at prices below the true cost of their extraction and production; the country remains in a middle-income trap because the state and the environment have to carry the burden of reproduction. In this sense, South Africa subsidises wealth creation in developed countries. It produces human resources that leave the country, it creates surplus value that leaves the country, and it generates intellectual property that leaves the country (Global Financial Integrity and African Development Bank, 2013).

The persistence of failure and South Africa's limited success with the NSI approach as a means of achieving medium- and high-tech industrialisation suggests that a new approach is required. Clearly, technological innovation as an isolated policy objective is no silver bullet. If government has been slow to establish congruence within it on innovation policy, the policy itself needs to be revised and updated to its context.

The question is 'What is a suitable alternative?' A number have already been documented, including transformative innovation policy (Schot and Steinmueller, 2018: 1554–1567) and inclusive innovation, although the latter also adopts systems of innovation approach (Foster and Heeks, 2013: 333–355). These new frameworks deal with the questions of inclusion and directionality, but, at least from the perspective of this author, fail to adequately address constraints to development, referred to as the 'forces of underdevelopment', as a consequence of the political economy. Such a gap has already been acknowledged in recent innovation literature, stating that 'the failure to centrally problematise the importance of power relations in society at large' haunts the school of innovation studies (Kaplinsky and Kraemer-Mbula, 2022: 104394).

This weakness leads to an alternative approach based on the MLP (Geels, 2020: 119894; 2010: 495–510), supplemented by the framework of technological innovation systems (TIS) (Hekkert et al., 2007: 413–432). MLP was developed to understand and accelerate sustainability transitions. As already mentioned, it is a middle-range theory, drawing from multiple theoretical strands including evolutionary economics, neo-institutionalism, the social construction of technology and strategic niche management (Keller et al., 2022: 14–28). Similarly, TIS is a mixture of innovative systems thinking with theoretical insights from studies on the social construction of technology.

The most significant difference between the narrow approach to NSI and MLP approaches is that the latter directly acknowledges that most socio-technical systems will be characterised by a strong regime, developed over a long period and entrenched through networks and sociotechnical institutions. The regime will generally resist any attempt to change the status quo. Instead, it will act to preserve the relationships of power, the attributes of privilege and the ongoing material gain that these networks and institutions supply. In this sense, agency has little importance; change must begin with the identification of the power relations within the system, how they recruit agents and then use these agents to reproduce themselves.

Industrial development in South Africa is a good example of a 'wicked problem' for which there is no simple solution. Instead, the problem must be approached in a transdisciplinary way using experimental policies that have already been applied to manage transition in other areas such as sustainability and income disparity (Termeer et al., 2019: 167–179; Peters, 2017: 385–396). Middle-income countries already have attained a level of development with well-established sectors and markets, and, of importance to this chapter, mechanisms of lock-in, cohorts of incumbents and pathway dependencies. Together, these factors comprise socio-technical regimes, such as the dominant patterns of production within the mobility and energy sectors, which resist change and evolve complex mechanisms to protect their privilege (Davies, 2019).

Any theoretical framework, which seeks to develop optimal strategies for industrial development must be able to recognise and respond to the present incumbents. Such features are precisely the strength of MLP developed, as already noted, to deal with sustainability transitions. Applying MLP to the industrial development of middle-income countries allows us to benefit from more than a decade of experience with the framework across a range of sectors, including mobility, energy and agriculture.

Apart from the issue of regimes and meso-level resistance, the MLP is a process-centred framework, highlighting which processes are necessary for transition. It treats change as a non-linear process which is both unpredictable and random. Moments of transition are characterised by unexpected windows of opportunity, often opened through major events at the landscape level such as pandemics and warfare. The final strength of the framework, which I wish to spotlight in this chapter, is the importance of strategic niche management, combined with the necessity of building alignment through actor collaboration and murmuration (Schot and Geels, 2008: 537–554).

CONCLUSION

This analysis of attempts to establish ARV API manufacture in South Africa has highlighted the weaknesses of the (narrow) NSI approach to industrialisation. Although the projects were able to overcome their technological hurdles, strategic niche management of the initiatives by the state was necessary to facilitate entry into local markets and competition against Indian and Chinese producers. This support was not forthcoming, with the result that the initiatives failed, despite the existence of many factors in their favour, including issues relating to health security and longer-term sustainability.

The author's vision of a country escaping its middle-income trap, its dire poverty and its high levels of unemployment through the localisation of value-adding manufacturing is, surprisingly, not a widely shared vision. Although the international community and multinational agencies have become attached to systems of innovation as a methodology and framework for the development of policies and programmes, the approach can be readily undermined by more powerful actors within the private firms of developed countries. The outcome, in South Africa at least, indicates that the narrow NSI framework is inadequate for counteracting geopolitical imbalances for developing countries and suggests that a more astute approach, which is cognisant of the political economy, should be adopted.

For this reason, I have argued for an entirely different approach to innovation and development, one that is based on a broad framing of the NSI approach, the more recent work of sustainability transitions and the concept of the X-curve in transitions management (Loorbach et al., 2017: 599–626) and the MLP (Geels, 2020: 119894). This last approach, together with TIS, should be used by the Department of Science and Innovation and its agencies in the implementation of policies for economic development. This recommendation will require the training of a new cohort of political economists who are aware of geopolitical imbalances and are able to participate in a meaningful way in projects involving the commercialisation of local R&D.

The final word, perhaps, belongs to the profound insights of Lundvall (2022: 6), who noted:

> the idea of transformational innovation policy is not alien to innovation system research ... it has taken inspiration from the historical and analytical understanding of evolution as a pulsation of path-breaking radical change and path-dependent incremental learning.

It is greater attention to radical change through path-breaking that is now required for developing countries such as South Africa to succeed with economic change.

REFERENCES

Abbott, F.M., Abbott, R., Fortunak, J., Gehl Sampath, P. and Walwyn, D. 2021. 'Opportunities, constraints and critical supports for achieving sustainable local pharmaceutical manufacturing in Africa, with a focus on the role of finance: Final Report'. Nova Worldwide, FSU College of Law, Law, Business & Economics Paper 21-03, https://doi.org/10.33009/osf-php_report, accessed 17 September 2021.

Abbott, F.M. and Reichman, J.H. 2007. 'The Doha Round's public health legacy: Strategies for the production and diffusion of patented medicines under the amended TRIPS provisions'. *Journal of International Economic Law*, 10(4), 921–987. doi: 10.1093/jiel/jgm040.

African National Congress (ANC). 2007. 'ANC 52nd National Conference 2007 Resolutions'. https://web.archive.org/web/20090411003225fw_/http://www.anc.org.za/ancdocs/history/conf/conference52/resolutions.pdf, accessed 23 December 2020.

Al-Bader, S., Frew, S.E., Essajee, I., Liu, V.Y., Daar, A.S. and Singer, P.A. 2009. 'Small but tenacious: South Africa's health biotech sector'. *Nature Biotechnology*, 27(5), 427–445.

Andreoni, A., Mondliwa, P., Roberts, S. and Tregenna, F. 2021. *Structural Transformation in South Africa: The Challenges of Inclusive Industrial Development in a Middle-Income Country*. Oxford: Oxford University Press.

Banerjee, A.V. and Duflo, E. 2019. *Good Economics for Hard Times: Better*

Answers to our Biggest Problems. London: Penguin UK.

Clinton Health Access Initiative. 2021. 'HIV Market Report: The State of the HIV Market in Low- and Middle-Income Countries'. CHAI, Boston, https:// chai19.wpenginepowered.com/wp-content/uploads/2021/10/2021-CHAI-HIV-Market-Report.pdf, accessed 13 June 2023.

Criscuolo, C., Gonne, N., Kitazawa, K. and Lalanne, G. 2022a. 'Are industrial policy instruments effective? A review of the evidence in OECD countries'. OECD Science, Technology and Industry Policy Papers, No. 128, OECD Publishing, https://doi.org/10.1787/23074957, accessed 13 June 2023.

Criscuolo, C., Gonne, N., Kitazawa, K. and Lalanne, G. 2022b. 'An industrial policy framework for OECD countries: Old debates, new perspectives', OECD Science, Technology and Industry Policy Papers, No. 127, OECD Publishing, https://doi.org/10.1787/0002217c-en, accessed 13 June 2023.

Department of Arts, Culture, Science and Technology (DACST). 1996. 'White Paper on Science and Technology'. Department of Arts, Culture, Science and Technology, Pretoria, https://www.gov.za/sites/default/files/gcis_document/201409/sciencetechnologywhitepaper.pdf, accessed 20 February 2023.

Davies, M. 2022. 'Covid-19: WHO efforts to bring vaccine manufacturing to Africa are undermined by the drug industry, documents show'. *British Medical Journal*, 376, 304. doi: https://doi.org/10.1136/bmj.o304.

Davies, R. 2019. *The Politics of Trade in the Era of Hyperglobalisation: A Southern African Perspective*. Geneva: South Centre.

Department of Science and Technology (DST). 2002. 'South Africa's National Research and Development Strategy'. Department of Science and Technology, Pretoria, https://www.gov.za/sites/default/files/gcis_document/201409/rdstrat0.pdf, accessed 13 June 2023.

Department of Science and Technology. 2019. 'White Paper on Science, Technology and Innovation'. Department of Science and Technology, Pretoria. https://www.dst.gov.za/images/2019/White_paper_web_copyv1.pdf, accessed 13 June 2023.

Department of Trade and Industry (DTI). 2015. 'Launch of the Industrial Policy Action Plan IPAP 2015/16–2017/18', https://www.gov.za/speeches/launch-industrial-policy-action-plan-ipap-201516-%E2%80%93-201718-7-may-2015-0000, accessed 1 August 2016.

Edlin, C.D., Riley, D. and Walwyn, D. 2014. 'A process for the preparation of (r)-9-[2-(phosphonometh-oxy)propyl]adenine (pmpa). PCT, UK, (Patent Application WO2014033688 A1). https://patentimages.storage.googleapis.com/24/31/84/93db21f9b4cabd/WO2014033688A1.pdf

Edquist, C. 2010. 'Systems of innovation perspectives and challenges'. *African Journal of Science, Technology, Innovation and Development*, 2(3), 14–45.

Edquist, C. and Johnson, B. 1997. 'Institutions and organizations in systems of innovation', in Edquist, C. (ed). *Systems of Innovation'*. Abingdon:

Routledge, pp. 41–63.

Fortunak, J. M., de Souza, R. O., Kulkarni, A. A., King, C. L., Ellison, T. and Miranda, L. S. 2014. 'Active pharmaceutical ingredients for antiretroviral treatment in low-and middle-income countries: a survey'. *Antiviral Therapy*, 19(3), 15–29.

Foster, C. and Heeks, R. 2013. 'Conceptualising inclusive innovation: Modifying systems of innovation frameworks to understand diffusion of new technology to low-income consumers'. *The European Journal of Development Research*, 25(3), 333–355.

Geels, F.W. 2010. 'Ontologies, socio-technical transitions (to sustainability), and the multi-level perspective'. *Research Policy*, 39(4), 495–510. doi: 10.1016/j.respol.2010.01.022.

Geels, F.W. 2019. 'Socio-technical transitions to sustainability: A review of criticisms and elaborations of the multi-level perspective'. *Current Opinion in Environmental Sustainability*, 39, 187–201.

Geels, F.W. 2020. 'Micro-foundations of the multi-level perspective on socio-technical transitions: Developing a multi-dimensional model of agency through crossovers between social constructivism, evolutionary economics and neo-institutional theory'. *Technological Forecasting and Social Change*, 152, 119894. doi: https://doi.org/10.1016/j.techfore.2019.119894.

Geels, F.W. and Turnheim, B. 2022. *The Great Reconfiguration*. Cambridge: Cambridge University Press.

Global Financial Integrity and African Development Bank. 2013. 'Illicit financial flows and the problem of net resource transfers from Africa: 1980–2009'. Global Financial Integrity; International Monetary Fund. SSRN 2334910, http://iffoadatabase.trustafrica.org/iff/illicit_financial_flows_and_the_problem_of_net_resource_transfers_from_africa_1980-2009.pdf, accessed 6 June 2022.

Gordon, G.E., Bode, M.L., Visser, D.F., Lepuru, M.J., Zeevaart, J.G. et al. 2011. 'An integrated chemo-enzymatic route for preparation of beta-thymidine, a key intermediate in the preparation of antiretrovirals'. *Organic Process Research & Development*, 15(1), 258–265. doi: 10.1021/Op100208x.

Harrelson, J.A. 2001. 'TRIPS, pharmaceutical patents, and the HIV/AIDS crisis: Finding the proper balance between Intellectual Property Rights and compassion'. *Widener L. Symp. J. HeinOnline*, 7, 175–203.

Hekkert, M.P., Suurs, R.A., Negro, S.O., Kuhlmann, S. and Smits, R.E. 2007. 'Functions of innovation systems: A new approach for analysing technological change'. *Technological Forecasting and Social Change*, 74(4), 413–432. doi: 10.1016/j.techfore.2006.03.002.

Jeenah, M. and Pouris, A. 2008. 'South African research in the context of Africa and globally: Science policy'. *South African Journal of Science*, 104(9), 351–354.

Kahn, M. 2019. 'The contract between science and society: A South African case study'. *Science and Public Policy*, 46(1), 116–125. doi: 10.1093/scipol/scy042.

Kaplan, D. 2021. 'Challenges and constraints for government agencies supporting firm-level innovation: Some reflections from South Africa', in Daniels, C., Dosso, M. and Amadi-Echendu, J. (eds). *Entrepreneurship, Technology Commercialisation, and Innovation Policy in Africa*. Cham: Springer, pp. 259–277.

Kaplinsky, R. and Kraemer-Mbula, E. 2022. 'Innovation and uneven development: The challenge for low-and middle-income economies'. *Research Policy*, 51(2), 104394.

Keller, M., Sahakian, M. and Hirt, L.F. 2022. 'Connecting the multi-level-perspective and social practice approach for sustainable transitions'. *Environmental Innovation and Societal Transitions*, 44, 14–28.

Kraemer-Mbula, E. and Maharajh, R. 2021. 'Innovation and technological change in South Africa', in Oqubay, A., Tregenna, F. and Valodia, I. (eds). *The Oxford Handbook of the South African Economy*. Oxford: Oxford University Press, pp. 467–488.

Kraemer-Mbula, E. and Wamae, W. 2010. 'Adapting the innovation systems framework to Sub-Saharan Africa', in Kraemer-Mbula, E. and Wamae, W. (eds). *Innovation and the Development Agenda*. Paris: OECD, 65–90.

Kudlinski, A. 2014. 'The South African pharmaceutical sector case study.' (Unpublished), prepared for WHO Local Production and Public Health Advocacy Think-tank Group.

Loembé, M.M. and Nkengasong, J.N. 2021. 'COVID-19 vaccine access in Africa: Global distribution, vaccine platforms, and challenges ahead'. *Immunity*, 54(7), 1353–1362.

Loorbach, D., Frantzeskaki, N. and Avelino, F. 2017. 'Sustainability transitions research: Transforming science and practice for societal change'. *Annual Review of Environment and Resources*, 42(1), 599–626. doi: 10.1146/annurev-environ-102014-021340.

Lundvall, B. Å. 2007. 'National innovation systems – analytical concept and development tool'. *Industry and innovation*, 14(1), 95–119.

Lundvall, B. 2016. *The Learning Economy and the Economics of Hope*. London: Anthem Press.

Lundvall, B.-Å. 2022. 'Transformative innovation policy–lessons from the innovation system literature'. *Innovation and Development*, 1–18.

Lundvall, B.-Å., Johnson, B., Andersen, E.S. and Dalum, B. 2002. 'National systems of production, innovation and competence building', *Research Policy*, 31(2), 213–231.

Malerba, F. 2002. 'Sectoral systems of innovation and production'. *Research Policy*, 31(2), 247–264.

McCann, N.C., Horn, T.H., Hyle, E.P. and Walensky, R.P. 2020. 'HIV antiretroviral therapy costs in the United States, 2012–2018'. *JAMA Internal Medicine*, 180(4), 601–603.

McKelvey, M. 1997. 'Using evolutionary theory to define systems of innovation', in Edquist, C. (ed). *Systems of Innovation: Technologies, Institutions and Organizations*. Routledge: Abingdon, pp. 200–222.

Mondliwa, P. and Roberts, S. 2021. 'The political economy of structural transformation', in Andreoni, A., Mondliwa, P., Roberts, S. and Tregenna, F. (eds). *Structural Transformation in South Africa: The Challenges of Inclusive Industrial Development in a Middle-Income Country*. Oxford: Oxford University Press, pp. 312–336.

Morris, M., Robbins, G., Hansen, U. E. and Nygaard, I. 2020. 'Energy and industrial policy failure in the South African wind renewable energy global value chain: The political economy dynamics driving a stuttering localisation process'. University of Cape Town, South Africa, 1–23.

National Advisory Council on Innovation (NACI). 2020. 'A Review of the National Research and Development Strategy (NRDS) and Ten-Year Innovation Plan (TYIP)'. National Council on Innovation, http://www.naci.org.za/index.php/new-data-sets-to-support-innovation-policy/, accessed 13 June 2023.

National Department of Health. 2020. '2019 ART Clinical Guidelines for the Management of HIV in Adults, Pregnancy, Adolescents, Children, Infants and Neonates'. South African Government, Pretoria, https://sahivsoc.org/Files/DoH%20Adult%202019_Final_version2.pdf, accessed 6 June 2022.

National Treasury. 2022. 'Vote 18: Health'. http://www.treasury.gov.za/documents/national%20budget/2022/ene/Vote%2018%20Health.pdf, accessed 5 June 2022.

National Planning Commission (NPC). 2012. 'Our Future - Make It Work: National Development Plan 2030'. National Planning Commission, Pretoria.

Palmisano, L. and Vella, S. 2011. 'A brief history of antiretroviral therapy of HIV infection: success and challenges'. *Annali dell'Istituto superiore di sanitÃ*, 47, 44–48.

Peter, C., Friedenstein, H., Bhorat, H., Chipkin, I., Mondi, L. et al. 2018. *Shadow State: The Politics of State Capture*. New York: NYU Press.

Peters, B.G. 2017. 'What is so wicked about wicked problems? A conceptual analysis and a research program'. *Policy and Society*, 36(3), 385–396.

Pollock, A. 2014. 'Places of pharmaceutical knowledge-making: Global health, postcolonial science, and hope in South African drug discovery'. *Social Studies of Science*, 44(6), 848–873.

Riley, D.L., Walwyn, D.R. and Edlin, C.D. 2016. 'An improved process for the preparation of tenofovir disoproxil fumarate'. *Organic Process Research and Development*, 20(4), 742–750.

Ripin, D.H., Teager, D.S., Fortunak, J., Basha, S.M., Bivins, N., et al. 2010.

'Process improvements for the manufacture of tenofovir disoproxil fumarate at commercial scale'. *Organic Process Research & Development*, 14(5), 1194–1201. doi: https://doi.org/10.1021/op1001337.

Roberts, C. and Geels, F.W. 2019. 'Conditions for politically accelerated transitions: Historical institutionalism, the multi-level perspective, and two historical case studies in transport and agriculture'. *Technological Forecasting and Social Change*, 140(3), 221–240.

Schot, J. and Geels, F.W. 2008. 'Strategic niche management and sustainable innovation journeys: Theory, findings, research agenda, and policy'. *Technology Analysis & Strategic Management*, 20(5), 537–554.

Schot, J. and Kanger, L. 2018. 'Deep transitions: Emergence, acceleration, stabilization and directionality'. *Research Policy*, 47(6), 1045–1059.

Schot, J. and Steinmueller, W.E. 2018. 'Three frames for innovation policy: R&D, systems of innovation and transformative change'. *Research Policy*, 47(9), 1554–1567.

Simelela, N., Venter, W.F., Pillay, Y. and Barron, P. 2015. 'A political and social history of HIV in South Africa'. *Current HIV/AIDS Reports*, 12(2), 256–261.

Statistics South Africa (Stat SA). 2021. 'Quarterly Labour Force Survey; Quarter 2, 2021'. Statistics South Africa, Pretoria, http://www.statssa.gov.za/publications/P0211/P02112ndQuarter2021.pdf, accessed 25 October 2021.

Termeer, C. J., Dewulf, A. and Biesbroek, R. 2019. 'A critical assessment of the wicked problem concept: Relevance and usefulness for policy science and practice', *Policy and Society*, 38(2), 167–179.

Tomlinson, C. 5 June 2020. 'What ever happened to Ketlaphela?'. *Spotlight*, https://www.spotlightnsp.co.za/2020/06/05/in-depth-what-ever-happened-to-ketlaphela/#:~:text=In%20March%202013%20it%20was,dam%20in%20Pelindaba%2C%20Northern%20Cape, accessed 12 November 2020.

Tregenna, F., Ewinyu, A.K., Oqubay, A. and Valodia, I. 2021. 'Challenges and complexities of the South African Economy', in Oqubay, A., Tregenna, F. and Valodia, I. (eds). *The Oxford Handbook of the South African Economy*. Oxford: Oxford University Press, pp. 3–25.

Tseng, A., Seet, J. and Phillips, E. J. 2015. 'The evolution of three decades of antiretroviral therapy: Challenges, triumphs and the promise of the future'. *British Journal of Clinical Pharmacology*, 79(2), 182–194. doi: 10.1111/bcp.12403.

UNAIDS. 2021a. 'Big drops in the cost of antiretroviral medicines, but COVID-19 threatens further reductions', UNAIDS, Geneva, https://www.unaids.org/en/resources/presscentre/featurestories/2021/may/20210503_cost-of-antiretroviral-medicines, accessed 3 June 2022.

UNAIDS. 2021b. 'Country Data: South Africa'. UNAIDS, Geneva, https://

www.unaids.org/en/regionscountries/countries/southafrica, accessed 13 June 2023.

Van Schalkwyk, C., Dorrington, R.E., Seatlhodi, T., Velasquez, C., Feizzadeh, A. and Johnson, L.F. 2021. 'Modelling of HIV prevention and treatment progress in five South African metropolitan districts'. *Scientific Reports*, 11(1), 5652. doi: 10.1038/s41598-021-85154-0.

Vella, S., Schwartländer, B., Sow, S.P., Eholie, S.P. and Murphy, R.L. 2012. 'The history of antiretroviral therapy and of its implementation in resource-limited areas of the world'. *Aids*, 26(10), 1231–1241.

Walwyn, D. 2004. 'The economic benefits of the local production of ARV active pharmaceutical ingredients'. *AIDS Management Report*, 2(5), 19–23, https://www.researchgate.net/publication/371510004_The_Economic_Benefits_of_Local_Production_of_ARV_APIs, accessed 13 June 2023.

Walwyn, D. 2006. 'The CSIR at 60'. *South African Journal of Science*, 102(7/8), 274–274.

Walwyn, D. 2013. 'Patents and profits: A disparity of manufacturing margins in the tenofovir value chain'. *African Journal of AIDS Research*, 12(1), 17–23.

Walwyn, D. 2019. 'Why South Africa should revert to greater protection for some of its industries'. *Conversation Africa*, https://theconversation.com/why-south-africa-should-revert-to-greater-protection-for-some-of-its-industries-120103, accessed 29 June 2020.

Walwyn, D. 27 October 2021. 'Rwanda and Senegal will host Africa's first COVID-19 vaccine plants: What's known so far'. *The Conversation*, https://www.wipo.int/wipo_magazine/en/2021/04/article_0002.html, accessed 5 June 2022.

Walwyn, D. 13 March 2022. 'How drug companies are sidestepping the WHO's technology transfer hub in Africa'. *The Conversation*, https://theconversation.com/how-drug-companies-are-sidestepping-the-whos-technology-transfer-hub-in-africa-179029, accessed 5 June 2022.

Walwyn, D.R. and Kraemer-Mbula, E. 2021. 'Captives of capital? Exploring economic models as recursive and performative agents'. *Energy Research & Social Science*, 78, 102131.

Walwyn, D.R. and Naidoo, S. 2020. 'Policy mixes and overcoming challenges to innovation in developing countries: Insights from a mixed methods study of South Africa's manufacturing sector'. *African Journal of Science, Technology, Innovation and Development*, 12(1), 33–46. doi https://www.tandfonline.com/doi/full/10.1080/20421338.2019.1610250.

World Bank. 2021. 'Country Data; South Africa'. World Bank, https://data.worldbank.org/country/south-africa, accessed 25 October 2021.

World Health Organisation. 2023. 'The Global Health Observatory: HIV'. WHO, https://www.who.int/data/gho/data/themes/hiv-aids, accessed 17 April 2023.

ELEVEN

Chasms of understanding: Testing the innovation chasm construct

MICHAEL KAHN

This chapter examines two enduring South African myths: the 'innovation chasm' and 'lost technologies and/or opportunities'. Using four case studies of innovations to inform the argument, it critiques these notions and their adoption in South African research and innovation policy. Deconstructing the paradigmatic factors that create the 'innovation chasm', system behaviour is then analysed through the lens of a social contract for science, and policy recommendations are put forward.

Democratic South Africa inherited a modest-sized, racially skewed innovation system that had served the agricultural, energy, financial, industrial and security interests of the previous order. The institutions of that innovation system – universities, public research organisations and industry laboratories – had contributed to industrial diversification, import substitution and minority rule. Heart transplants, atomic bombs, hominids and weapons systems captured imagination and territory (Dubow, 2006). A helicopter view of the then South Africa might have described her as 'CalAfrica', a state comprising a wealthy core and an impoverished periphery in which the state owned the commanding heights of the economy alongside a private sector based on the minerals–energy–financial complex. The CalAfrica is a play on the 1970s name 'Belgindia' that Brazilian economist Edmar Bacha introduced to describe the inequalities of his native land: in this instance, it refers to California and Africa. The name continues to enjoy widespread usage, given the massive inequalities in South Africa, an outlier among emerging economies on many scores such as Gini, Palma Ratio, HIV+, TB, stunting and unemployment, and an average wage in US$ purchasing power parity on par with the United Kingdom. Hence the moniker CalAfrica that avoids the pejorative labelling of India, or for that matter Nigeria, Egypt or the Democratic Republic of Congo as poorer cousins.

Come 1990 the Cold War was over, the globalisation wave lapped South Africa's shores, and the information and communication technology (ICT) revolution unfolded. The market economy was suddenly available to all, as the new Russian Federation experienced, rather than to those of the previous *nomenklatura*. Much was expected of the innovation system inherited. Kenyan academic Prof. Thomas Odhiambo, a member of the 1993 International Research Development Centre (IDRC) science system review advised president-to-be Mandela on the importance of investing in science and technology, and how many African countries are only now realising the value of it. In the final IDC report, Mandela noted that the initial fear of retribution towards the public research organisations (PROs) was rapidly dispelled, to the extent that scientists appreciated the new government's protection, investment and support' (IDRC, 1995: viii).

The new government set out to modernise and deracialise the polity. The private sector grasped the opportunities for deregulation and open markets, with South Africa gaining the moniker 'Gateway to Africa'. A flood of policies offered good practice solutions to labour, environment, financing and taxation. The science community co-generated the White Paper on Science and Technology (DACST, 1996) that introduced innovation systems thinking for new institutions to achieve transformation and coordination towards a 'better life for all'. The White Paper advocated '... a basic competence in "flagship" sciences such as physics and astronomy for cultural reasons. Not to offer them would be to take a negative view of our future – the view that we are a second-class nation, chained forever to the treadmill of feeding and clothing ourselves' (DASCT, 1996: 16).

Today's helicopter view shows the persistence of CalAfrica, with massive peri-urban informal settlements, high-end strip development along rural highways, collapsed municipalities and truck trains on the inter-city trunk roads. Market access has worked for the employed, while inequality and underemployment have increased, and the centre–periphery divide continues. The expectation that a 'new' innovation system would bridge the so-called 'innovation chasm' has not been met, even as government expenditure on R&D rose from R2.6 billion (at current value) in 2001/02 to R19.4 billion (current) in 2019/20, at an inflation-adjusted rate of 5.8 per cent (DST, 2013; DSI, 2021). It will be shown that the quarter century of democracy has been accompanied by the stasis, if not failure, of the innovation system. By definition a system is multidimensional, involving purpose, inputs, processes and interests that combine to produce intended and unintended outputs and outcomes. Add the ecosystem within which any system functions and one is faced with complexity. Teasing results out of such complexity is an art form.

This perhaps explains why the South African conception of the 'innovation chasm' as an explanatory mechanism for innovation system failure was introduced. The innovation chasm has acquired paradigmatic status, gaining political expression in a techno-nationalism that claims that South African-originated technologies have been 'lost' to foreign interests. The persistent notion of the 'innovation chasm', a uniquely South African idea, will be critiqued, limited space notwithstanding. It will be argued that the 'innovation chasm', aligned with a linear model of innovation and an implicit endorsement of equilibrium economics, underpins the theory of change that characterises high-level science, technology and innovation (STI) policy.

CROSSING THE CHASM

Internationally the idea of a chasm in the diffusion and adoption of technologies was introduced by Rogers (1962) in his sociological studies of the adoption of agricultural innovations. That thinking was extended by Moore (1991) who studied the dissemination gap between 'early adopter visionaries' and 'early majority pragmatists'. Moore was not tracking the valorisation of R&D *per se* but was interested in how market-ready products and processes are disseminated. Moore's conceptualisation, 'crossing the chasm', which is the title of his best-selling book, required understanding how customer needs change, how to generate interest in new products, and how to identify a market niche. Moore's advice is based on the sociology of organisations and markets, and focuses on customer adoption and bypassing competitors, rather than the valorisation of blue-sky research. Moore resonates with the 5th century BCE philosopher, Lao Tse, who advised generals to seek the weak point in their adversaries' defences.

A construct that appears to have informed the South African notion of the 'innovation chasm' is the schematic of the 'technology colony' (Figure 11.1). CSIR executive De Wet's (1999) schematic shows how basic research, followed by applied research, design and development fails to yield dividends. Reading left to right the logic supports the linear model of innovation (Godin, 2006), across a Moore-like gap, with top-down interactions from 'overseas' sources.

Figure 11.1: The technology colony

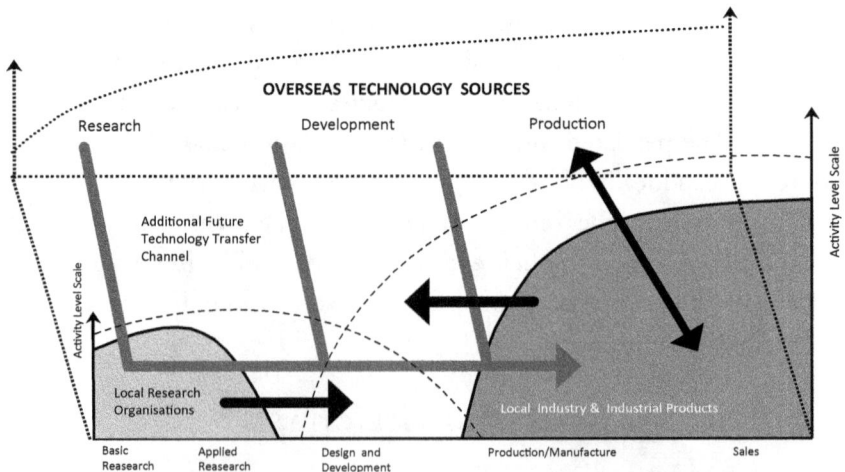

Source: De Wet (1999: 418)

In De Wet's view the national system is a technology colony dependent on advanced metropoles for research and technology, with the research agenda dependent on the metropole. Landes (1998) explains that this was to be expected of South Africa, Argentina and Brazil: these countries exported primary commodities; the foreign currency earnings from this were then used to import technologies and finished goods. Albuquerque (2003), comparing South Africa, Brazil, Argentina and India with the North, labelled their innovation systems as 'immature.' Prebisch (1950), writing on Latin America, might have said, 'told you so'. The new Department of Science and Technology then proceeded to recast De Wet's schematic, labelling the design and development/technology transfer gap as the 'innovation chasm' (DST, 2002).

Figure 11.2: The innovation chasm

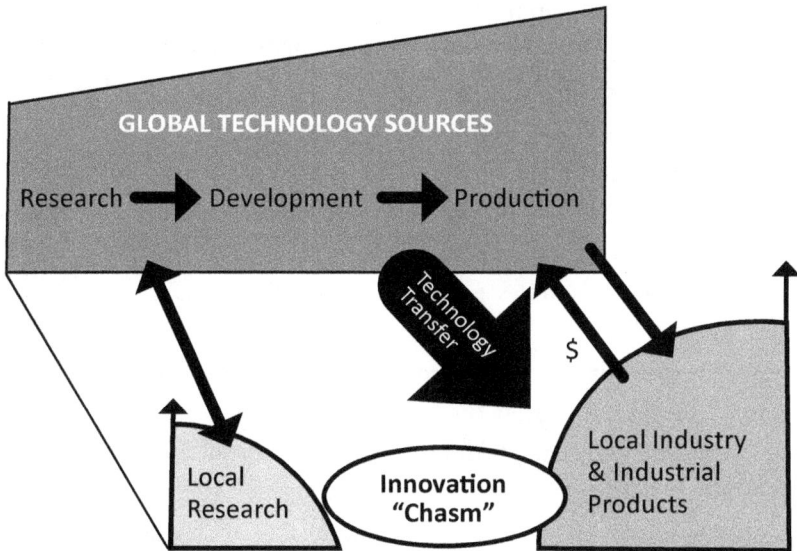

Source: DST (2002: 25)

The similarity between Figures 11.1 and 11.2 is obvious. The linear model is endorsed; foreign dominates local. The Department of Science and Technology (DST) (and Council for Scientific and Industrial Research (CSIR)) theory of change rests on the linear model of innovation, not the innovation systems approach. As Godin (2006) avers, the linear model is durable. It might be noted that the R&D strategy was a joint product of the DST and CSIR, a relationship further cemented through the proposal to move the reporting line of the CSIR from the Department of Trade and Industry to the DST, given concrete form in the location of the new headquarters of the DST within the CSIR campus.

The R&D Strategy suggested that the 'innovation chasm' between R&D results and commercialisation arose from a failure of research translation, or innovation *per se*, and this despite '… evidence of good technologies' that 'are lost or not commercialised because of a lack of innovation resources' (Godin, 2006: 41). No evidence was provided for the assertion. What is notably absent in the adaptation of the De Wet schematic is industry demand. The R&D Strategy was also silent on the importance of user-oriented basic and applied research, arguing that the valorisation problem was due to a lack of state funding, and weak protection of intellectual property. The next policy instrument was the 'Ten-Year Innovation Plan' (DST, 2008), which in all but name repeated the message of the innovation chasm. Argument redux was that 'South Africa possesses known technologies, but the challenge lies in commercialisation and coherent policy interventions for easy adoption' (Godin, 2006: 28). Lastly, the 'major obstacle to commercialisation of technological innovations is financing, due to the high risk and complexity of R&D investments' (Godin, 2006: 32). A new statutory body (the Technology Innovation Agency (TIA)) was then proposed to address the failures of coordination, integration and financing. This amounts to the claim that the science system is performing well, but that the absence of new products is due to financial market failure, not R&D market failure.

This notion of the innovation chasm subsequently gained prominence in the DST's circle of practice. Pefile (2006) writing for the CSIR lamented that many local technologies had fallen into the innovation chasm, consequential on the funding gap between 'tested R&D' and the market. The author claimed that the innovation chasm also prevailed in many developing countries that 'failed to bridge the gap between knowledge generation and knowledge application' (Pefile, 2006). An example is the call from Namibia's National Commission on Research, Science and Technology (NCRST) (2014: 49) for 'a comprehensive system of innovation that would bring together all key players … (to) overcome the innovation chasm'. South African science policy has had considerable influence across Africa via the SADC, NEPAD and the African Union; full treatment of this assertion is beyond the scope of this chapter.

The infant Technology Innovation Agency then claimed that it was 'a national public entity that serves as the key institutional intervention to bridge the innovation chasm between research and development from higher education institutions, science councils, public entities, and private sector, and commercialisation' (DSI, 2008; TIA, 2022). In their annual reports, key agencies, the National Advisory Council on Innovation (NACI, 2009), the National Research Foundation (NRF, 2012) and the Department of Science and Technology (DST, 2016) continued with uncritical advocacy of the innovation chasm. Maharajh (2011), while critical of the framing of science policy without reference to the problem of 'racial capitalism', mentions the innovation chasm in passing, as does the later work of Scerri (2016). They deal with the concept *en passant* as an element of the R&D Strategy and the Ten-Year Innovation Plan, paraphrasing the original advocacy without substantial critique for or against.

The idea of the innovation chasm was further promoted in the R&D commercialisation and technology-transfer community of practice, for example by the DSI/SARIMA/NIPMO (2021). In the academic terrain, Malele et al. (2019) accepted the innovation chasm as a '*ding an sich*' ('thing-in-itself'), conducting a survey to investigate levels of awareness of the notion at a university of technology. The study found low awareness among students and staff, and thus recommended that to 'bridge the innovation chasm, universities of technology should strengthen awareness of entrepreneurship and innovation policies and platforms through visibility and accessibility'. Finally, the notion gained additional advocacy through the Presidential Commission on the Fourth Industrial Revolution, which stated, 'Some of the work that needs to be done to take advantage of these opportunities include: closing the innovation chasm, where homegrown innovation is lost (not commercialised or lost to other markets)' (Presidency, 2020: 33).

A critical view of the ideas underlying the innovation chasm is offered by Marcus (2003) who called for universities and PROs to respond to the needs of commerce and industry: 'Working together they would form a powerful resource base for research and development.' For its part the Innovation System Review of the OECD (2007: 104) refrained from endorsing the claimed importance of the chasm and moved to identify an engineering gap '... that has much greater economic and social significance than the more frequently discussed "chasm" between R&D and implemented innovation'. Pouris (2008) debunked the claim that many technologies had been lost to South Africa. He averred that the innovation chasm notion did not serve to explain the low volume of intellectual property (IP) that emerged from the science base. In his view this phenomenon was unsurprising as the science base was not oriented to industrial needs. To the extent that respondents identified technologies that were 'lost' abroad, Pouris found these were not game-changers and refuted the claim of lost technologies. Pouris nonetheless recommended that funding and policy gaps relating to foreign companies should be addressed. Kahn (2019: 35) studied the patenting behaviour of five high-technology firms and wrote that there was evidence that the 'success of South African firms abroad suggested innovation adroitness, rather than a chasm'. A Google Scholar search for the keywords 'innovation chasm' from 1995 to 2022 generates 18 occurrences of review articles of which 13 are South Africa-authored. It would seem that the concept has attracted little academic interest. Finally, in a review of the National Research and Development Strategy and the Ten-Year Plan for Innovation (Mouton, 2021: 240), it was noted that 'the strong commitment to the linear model of innovation ... evident at a number of levels – from the explicit recurring rhetoric of the "innovation chasm" to the use of standard Frascati-type metrics that reflect the institutionalisation of the linear model at the OECD since the 1960s'.

The above comments serve as background to four case studies that examine the relationship between research and product development.

A BATTERY OF CLAIMS

In any heated discussion about lost technologies, the name of Michael Thackeray is bound to come up. From 1974 through to 1981, Thackeray worked at the CSIR on crystallography and electrochemistry, acquiring his UCT doctorate along the way. In 1981, he went to Oxford for a post-doctoral fellowship under Prof. John Goodenough. In his baggage were samples of two 'spinel' crystals, iron magnetite and manganese hausmannite. Against expectation Thackeray was able to insert layers of lithium into the hausmannite, thereby producing lithium-manganese oxide crystals that opened the way to a low-cost Li-Mn battery. Until then, expensive lithium-cobalt had done the trick; the lithium-manganese crystals were one-hundredth of the cost. Thackeray then returned to CSIR until Executive Management decided that further investment in the research would not provide 'acceptable outcomes' resulting in Thackeray moving as a lead scientist to the Argonne National Laboratory in the USA. Thackeray became the assignee of 11 provisional patents, five of which are highly cited, even though only one moved to grant status. Thackeray is internationally celebrated for his work as the highly cited author of over 200 academic papers, and 54 patent applications, nine of which date between 1981 and 1993.

The 2019 Nobel Prize for Chemistry went to Goodenough (UK-US), Whittington (US) and Yoshino (Japan), who pioneered lithium-ion battery – 'li-battery' – technology for mobiles, electric vehicles, and energy storage. Three years earlier Thackeray, in marking the 25th anniversary of the invention of the Li-battery, regretted the delay in recognising Goodenough as a Nobel Laureate. Li-batteries took seven decades of use-oriented basic research. The use was clear; the difficulties were many. The solution lay in designing crystals, standing on the shoulders of giants such as Laureates Hoffmann (USA) and Fukua (Japan), MacDiarmid (New Zealand, USA), Heeger (USA) and Shirakawa (Japan), and finally Goodenough on cobalt, and Whittingham on stability. Yoshino, at Asahi Kasei Corporation in Japan, made his discoveries in the 1980s as the consumer electronics revolution erupted.

Where was Thackeray in all this? The key research was pursued in the USA, United Kingdom and Japan. In contrast, Thackeray was working in a small group at the CSIR. MacDiarmid moved from a small innovation and research system to a large one; Thackeray did not. Yoshino worked for chemical and explosives giant Asahi Kasei, whose expenditure on lithium R&D was perhaps 50 times greater than Thackeray's at the CSIR. After moving to the USA, Thackeray's team invented the lithium-nickel-manganese-cobalt oxide cell that is used in some present-day battery technology. Thackeray made important contributions to lithium chemistry but to claim that his work at CSIR was 'lost' to South Africa is a long stretch. Social networking can play a crucial role in innovation: it can facilitate the development of knowledge nodes around areas including tradition, artisanal skills, financial capital, a spirit of change, good governance and visionary individuals (Moon, 2014). Where these accrue into knowledge nodes, technological breakthroughs emerge. Thackeray at CSIR was in a small knowledge node; Goodenough, Whittingham and Yokino played large. Once at Argonne, so could Thackeray. Was the lithium technology lost from South Africa to the United States? No. Was there an engineering gap? No, the technology was still at the discovery stage. Was the innovation chasm at work? Not in Moore's sense.

OIL'S WELL

The second case study is of African Explosives and Chemical Industries (AECI), a South African diversified chemicals company for mining, agriculture and agro-processing. With 16 US patent awards from 2011–2015, it ranks second to Sasol in holding patents in South Africa. The AECI international patent portfolio is even larger. AECI's subsidiaries include African Explosives Limited (AEL) and DetNet, the latter jointly owned with multinational Dyno Nobel. AEL maintains its own R&D facilities, producing liquid explosives for open-cast mining, and has 58 plants in more than 20 countries. DetNet was founded in 2002 following the acquisition of Altech Detonator Technologies. The decision to patent is determined by the jurisdictions in which the company is most active, namely the US, Canada and Australia. Google

Patent has detected 158 DetNet international patent applications since 2000, of which 44 moved to grant status.

AEL collaborates locally with North-West University, the University of South Africa, the University of Pretoria and the Cape Peninsula University of Technology, and internationally with the University of Melbourne, the University of Newcastle, the University of Cambridge and the University of Swansea. AECI participated in the Technological Human Resources for Industry Programme providing studentships at the Cape Peninsula University of Technology and the University of Pretoria. AEL had found that explosive gels were prone to ageing, with a reduction in blast efficiency and effectiveness. It duly provided funds and specialised equipment to research solutions to this problem to universities with complementary expertise. An improved emulsion resulted from seven years of joint research and is an example of use-oriented applied research that resulted in incremental improvements to the product (Lundvall, 1985). DetNet deepened the IP acquired through the purchase of Altech Detonator Technologies, pushing the knowledge frontier; AEL selected its knowledge partners based on their track records of knowledge production, independently of proximity. That intellectual property was protected as trade secrets. The greatest benefit of university research to AEL and to the environment is improved explosive gel shelf life and the incorporation of greater volumes of used motor oil as the hydrocarbon source. This case study illustrates pressure for innovation arising from product failure, with user innovation resulting in an in-house solution. There was no product adoption chasm as the innovator was the user. This is an example of technology gained, technology protected, technology deployed, but not technology lost. Engineering gap? Definitely not. Path dependence? Clearly so.

X-RAYS ARE A GIRL'S BEST FRIEND

The next case study is that of Lodox, selected here by virtue of its uniqueness, and its relationship with transnational corporation De Beers. This scanner has already been discussed in Chapter 5 of this volume, in the context of 'frugal' medical innovations that are globally valued. De Beers estimated that up to 20 per cent of its diamond production was being stolen, and developed a range of methods to identify miscreants. Given the dangers associated with ionizing radiation, X-rays could only be applied to a small proportion of suspects, and only occasionally. Permitted levels were substantially reduced with 1990 international health regulations and De Beers was thus under pressure to develop a low-dose X-ray technology. De Beers had expertise in high-intensity X-ray diamond sorting technologies and decided to expand its research staff from 10 to 150, recruiting many with backgrounds in military R&D (Gostner et al., 2005). Path dependence is evident.

De Beers already collaborated with UCT whose X-ray diffraction expertise goes back to the 1930s; that research laid the basis for two future Nobel laureates. There was an established tradition of intellectual exchange between natural scientists on the main campus and medical scientists at Groote Schuur Hospital. De Beers went on to fund research at the University of Cape Town, which resulted in the development of low dose Scannex X-ray detectors. In 1999 UCT and De Beers secured a three-year R5 million Innovation Fund grant to develop Scannex for medical applications. The commercial vehicle for this work was styled as African Medical Imaging (AMI), a joint venture between UCT and the National Accelerator Laboratory. From the late 1990s, the government Support Programme for Industrial Innovation (SPII) also provided funds to build the De Beers–IDC relationship, which was later expanded to include Netcare Holdings. Clinical trials were conducted at Groote Schuur Hospital from 1999–2002, leading to licensing and EU certification. Netcare Milpark Hospital was the site for the first Lodox installation.

Yet, there was a classic Moore-type marketing chasm facing Lodox. Could it become a widely adopted product? Having solved the problem of low-dose imaging, applications were sought against medical imaging giants Siemens, Philips, Fuji, Hitachi and General Electric. De Beers tried to bridge the Moore chasm but was unable to find a niche in the conventional product space. In 2002 De Beers spun out Lodox as a standalone company to focus on medical trauma applications. The spin-out included some Scannex staff with initial funding provided by De Beers and the IDC. The US Food & Drug Administration (FDA) gave regulatory approval to Lodox in 2003, and in principle the Lodox scanner could then be marketed in the USA and further afield. Lodox was granted three US patents between 2005 to 2011. In contrast, medical imaging giant Siemens Healthcare registers 33 patents a day.

In 2003 AMI developed limited angle tomography and circular scanning digital mammography that led to a US patent, and a grant from the US National Institutes of Health. Further R&D resulted in the Statscan range. As of 2009 IDC became the major investor in AMI, which rebranded itself as Cape Ray Medical and later gained ISO certification, and the CE Mark for its Pandia digital camera. In 2014 its Aceso dual modality (ultrasound and X-ray) system was subjected to phase III clinical trials and was able to begin operation the next year. Cape Ray holds four US patents and one UK patent.

Lodox technology is mature, with annual R&D expenditure at roughly 1 per cent of turnover. The high-technology components (including the X-ray generator) are imported, and account for 60 per cent of total cost, even though 75 per cent of components are locally sourced. The product is assembled, tested, qualified and certified in a small factory in Johannesburg. The 2013 TV series *Grey's Anatomy* featuring of Lodox was an advertising public gift. Lodox was shown as being of use to scan a cycling accident victim. The publicity was free yet the US market did not open up. Lodox has sold 80 machines worldwide. According to Lodox, 'the way the different components interact is unique', thereby conferring a competitive edge in a niche market. The primary market is in South Africa, where 39 units are in operation, but achieving sales volumes in the US market remains elusive. The relatively high sales in the domestic market arise from the high levels of trauma injury and death in relation to population size. The main competitor against Lodox is Adani of Russia.

The Scannex/Lodox/Statscan/Aceso story entails sequential innovations that required specific champions in De Beers, Lodox and UCT respectively. The innovations qualify as 'new to the world'. To date their markets are either niche or still evolving. One of the lessons that may be drawn from the case is the importance of networks and mobility. Staff moved from military R&D to De Beers; students moved from UCT to Lodox. Another lesson is that institutional skills matter. UCT had skills in X-ray technology that stretched back nearly a century; De Beers pioneered industrial X-ray applications. This took some 25 years of effort. Entrepreneurs and entrepreneurial states must sometimes be very patient. R&D was commercialised; knowledge was not lost; engineers did their best; markets shrugged. The inventions struggled to cross Moore's innovation chasm in an environment unsupportive of medical device registration, a matter partially resolved in the belated founding of the SA Health Products Regulatory Authority in 2017.

FROM FINITE STEPS TO THE INFINITE

The final case study is EMSS Antennas (now part of Alphawave), which exemplifies serendipity, perseverance, business and marketing. The company is based at Techno Park, which is 10 kilometres from the Stellenbosch University main campus. Company founders were recipients of military bursaries for PhD studies in electromagnetism at Stellenbosch University, a key member of the telemetry sectoral system of innovation (Kahn, 2014), with its path dependence to the earliest days of radar deployment. Following cutbacks on military R&D, the newly minted doctoral graduates of 1998 found themselves jobless and sought to capitalise on their dissertations. Through literature searches they came across the complementary work of a German researcher with whom they entered a long-term collaboration that led to a benefit-sharing agreement. They were now positioned to offer consultancy services to the SA Navy, mobile telephony companies and aviation companies. In the process they became serial innovators, so much so that by 2012 they had founded three companies: EMSS Antennas, EMSS-SA and EMSS Consulting. One of the first products was FEKO for the optimal placement of antennae on airframes. A second product was the Antenna Magus design toolkit that was marketed through a separate company, Magus Pty (Ltd). The third product was IXUS, for the determination of regulatory compliance of electromagnetic radiation sources. The EMSS group went on to derive 50 per cent of its income abroad, as a market leader for antenna placement. Development of the Karoo Array Telescope (KAT) then opened up a new market, with EMSS Antennas able to develop the antenna feed design.

EMSS Holdings has one US patent (golf ball tracing). The owners hold the view that continuous innovation renders the registration of IP of secondary importance, as is generally the case in the defence industry. EMSS won the tender to develop what is now a world-first, low-noise, stable receiver for the MeerKAT/SARAO radio telescope. The state owns the product and could go to production, but the tacit knowledge belongs to EMSS. EMSS relies on non-disclosure agreements and trade secrets and has not registered any patents in radio astronomy. IP is shared, similar to what happens among military researchers. The EMSS Group has since rebranded and restructured as Alphawave, with EMSS Antennas a partially owned subsidiary.

EMSS engaged in a process of continuous learning through the study of relevant literature, especially by maintaining its involvement in the Institute of Electrical and Electronic Engineers (IEEE) network. Foreign journals were of particular value. Staff were given leave to participate in conferences (especially IEEE), and to attend trade fairs, these two mechanisms being viewed as the most important sources for company learning. IEEE conferences have been held in South Africa since 1998, in Cape Town, Pretoria and Stellenbosch. EMSS has provided bursaries for students to study at Stellenbosch University and provides internships and employment to its graduates. The Stellenbosch University knowledge channel is valued as a source of new ideas. Consultancies from Stellenbosch University are also an important source of learning for EMSS. Over the period 1996–2018, EMSS staff published 35 papers indexed to the Web of Science, with the most highly cited receiving 20 citations.

As to the use of public funds for R&D, starting in 1998, EMSS received four Support Programme for Industrial Innovation (SPII) matching grants of R1.5 million each. The first supported the development of FEKO and the purchase of the German collaborator's algorithm and code. DTI also supported EMSS to exhibit at international trade fairs. Come 2005, the National Research Foundation assembled the Karoo Array telescope team. However, in an anonymous interview conducted by the author, it emerged that (author interviewee):

> They lacked antenna design skills, so four EMSS staff joined them … it was like skills looking for a client … the team expanded to 20 staff with R&D expenditure of around R23 million. We were responsible for the receiver design … and in determining the dish parameters. This was a risky business model since the National Research Foundation was now the sole client of a purely R&D project.

The EMSS Group was also a successful beneficiary of the early rounds of the South African government's R&D tax incentive. The formation of Alphawave and its function in supporting spinouts and start-ups closes the circle, with Alphawave supporting Stellenbosch University start-up Cargo Telematics. The EMSS-Alphawave case study is an example of a self-organising invisible college, combining serendipity, entrepreneurship, Stellenbosch University, the mobile industry, the opportunity of KAT, student and staff mobility and continuous learning. Understanding markets, penetrating them and developing niche skills were key. However, FEKO's experience of trying to capture market share in the global automotive industry was a salutary lesson regarding the Moore chasm.

Alphawave also trades in the highly competitive projectile tracking industry, a spillover to sports radar, which has been called the 'champagne' of electronics. The success of KAT, coupled with the award of the Square Kilometre Array to South Africa, has led to the 64-dish MeerKAT, for which project EMSS became a specialist service provider through a closed tender. The latter is an instance of the entrepreneurial state in action, using procurement to foster innovation. The two-person start-up of 1995 became Alphawave, a medium-sized company of 160 staff. EMSS introduced both new-to-the-world and incremental innovations. Adroit management, risk-taking, engineering skills and pivoting where necessary – the case study embraces all of these. Two state bursaries laid the basis to create a medium-sized, high-technology company.

THE REPUBLIC OF SCIENCE AND THE STATE

Alongside the above are state-funded mega projects, such as Eskom's Kusile and Medupi extreme high temperature and pressure dry-cooled coal-fed power stations, the Pebble Bed Modular Reactor (PBMR) demonstrator (see Chapter 7), the Joule electric vehicle, SARS e-filing and the Covid vaccine registration system. The three industrial projects failed, while the ICT projects succeeded.

The two frontier technology power stations, the largest dry-cooled generators in the world, came in over budget, over time and feeding a grid that was itself now unreliable. Though partnered with Japan's Hitachi and French Alstom, there were design and engineering problems from the outset. In addition there were skills deficits, corruption-plagued procurement, poor maintenance and an unreliable coal supply, and suspected acts of sabotage and theft. Hubris was followed by grim nemesis in the 2021 explosion that destroyed one of the six Medupi turbines. The cause of the explosion is not certain, though the probability is that poor adherence to the protocols needed to purge hydrogen from the cooling system was at fault. Eskom had prior experience of dry cooling at the Matimba plant that came into operation in 1993 as the then-largest dry-cooled power station in the world. Medupi and Kusile took the technology to the next level by operating at higher temperatures and pressures, 560°C and 241 bar respectively. With the goal of improved efficiency and mindful of the limited water supply, Eskom ventured into new territory. In-house research capability was maintained through the development period and there is no *a priori* reason to assume that there were some internal shortcomings. Aside from those listed earlier, it is commonplace for mega projects to go over budget, and in this case Eskom doubled the risk. Engineering gap? Yes? Chasm? No.

The PBMR, styled as the pioneer of fourth-generation safe nuclear energy, was founded in 1994 and terminated in 2010. PBMR drew on the design of the controversial high-temperature reactor known as AVR at Jülich Research Center in West Germany and attracted some of its former researchers to relocate to South Africa. PBMR entered into a memorandum of understanding with the owners of the AVR to share knowledge. The Jülich 'AVR' reactor was groundbreaking for its high temperature, high pressure, helium-cooled, pebble bed design using one per cent U-235. It operated from 1967 to 1988 and became notorious for its poor safety record, gaining the nickname 'shipwreck', with the Jülich site the most contaminated decommissioned reactor installation in the world. This was known to insiders of the day but not to the general public until 2014 when an expert panel revealed a litany of shortcomings. The PBMR fuel is based on locally manufactured highly enriched uranium pebbles with helium gas as the heat exchange medium (Nicholls, 2002). PBMR grew into an organisation of more than 200 scientists and engineers based in Centurion, with the helium gas test rig constructed at the Pelindaba site of the Nuclear Energy Corporation of South Africa (NECSA). Unlike the Chinese PBMR, which uses steam as the heat exchange medium, the PBMR design was for an extreme, high-temperature and pressure helium turbine system. Over its lifespan PBMR was granted six nuclear-related patents in Europe, four in China, three in the US and one in Canada. However, only one, a highly cited US patent, deals with the key issue of the 'TRISO' nuclear fuel 'spheres' needed for the reactor. Other patents deal with the fuel hopper and turbine design. The PBMR generated a modest patent portfolio for what was claimed to be frontier R&D but failed to retain and attract investors, burning upwards of R10 billion (then US$1 billion), a figure commensurate with the cost of the Jülich rig. A curious outcome of the termination was that some South African researchers relocated to the United States to work with X-Energy LLC, which obtained modest research funding from the US Department of Energy in 2015 and by 2019 had been granted seven US patents related to its TRISO research.

It may be that timing was against the PBMR – the global recession had irrupted, and Eskom, the only potential client, was beset by ideological policymaking. It is a stretch to label the PBMR as an example of Moore's chasm.

The Joule electric vehicle, created by Optimal Energy (Pty) Ltd, boasted a truly world-class body, and some electric drive novelty, but no international patents save for the US design patent awarded to vehicle body expert Edsel Keith Helfet. The Joule consumed in the order of R300 million with little to show for the effort. Attempts to go to scale were unsuccessful with no investors willing to provide the estimated R10 billion needed to set up a production line. Moore chasm? Absolutely? Hubristic? Yes.

As argued, it is difficult to reduce the trajectory and fate of the mega projects to the Moore chasm, let alone the paradigm of the innovation chasm. The ICT projects had a single client waiting for the product. There was no marketing required. The power stations might be labelled hubristic in that they embraced frontier technologies, for which a skills base was lacking. The Joule may also be labelled as hubristic in that South Africa had never successfully innovated a locally designed and manufactured motor vehicle into world markets. Joule was under-capitalised and over-sold. Examination of path dependence would require a more detailed examination than that presented here.

That noted, the analysis now turns to the nature of the Republic of Science. Bibliometric analysis based on the Web of Science™ Essential Science Indicators (ESIs) provides insights into research activity and innovation potential.

Activity and Citation Ratio

Figure 11.3 plots the research Activity and the Citation Ratio for the 22 ESIs. 'Activity' measures the ratio of the in-country share of an ESI to the global share of that ESI. The Citation Ratio, a proxy measure for research excellence, is the ratio of the in-country citation rate per paper to the global citation rate per paper of that ESI.

If it is assumed that the prevalence and quality of scientific publications are lead indicators for innovation, the 'implications' of the above might be as follows.

Space science demonstrates the highest activity and the highest citation ratio while material science has the lowest activity and lowest citation ratio. Thirteen of the ESIs have citation ratios close to or above the world average of unity.

From the point of view of established industry, geosciences (mining) is at world citation level, as are plant and animal sciences. However, agriculture sciences are lagging. Engineering, with low activity, is above world citation level, but chemistry must be red flagged. As to

Figure 11.3: Activity and Citation Ratio (2012–2022)

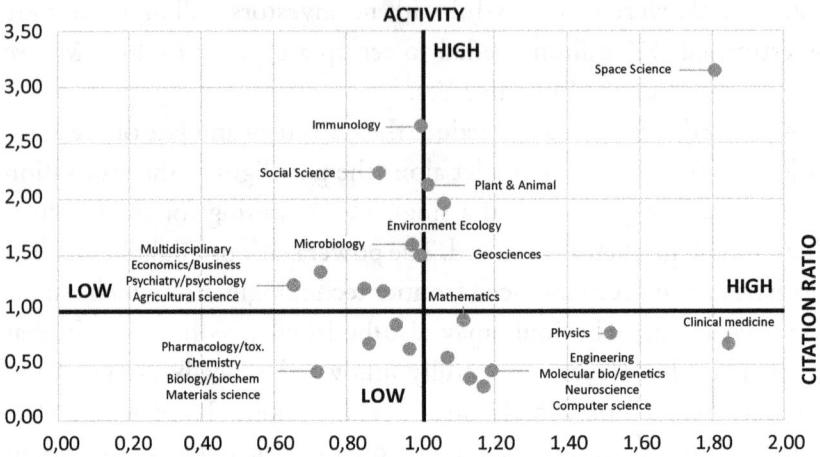

Source: Author extract from Web of Science™

future industries, computer science has very low activity yet a high citation ratio. Materials Science is red flagged. It may be a leap of faith to construct a link between the ESI research fields and the attainment of the Sustainable Development Goals, yet the performance in environment/ecology stands out as a positive.

Space science and physics show high citation ratios (and a high proportion of top papers). Researchers active in these fields are part of international big science (Kahn, 2019), which involves scores of co-authors active in the largest science systems in the world. This results in an upward pull on activity and citation ratio. The same argument holds true for clinical medicine (which includes infectious diseases). The Royal Society awards to Fanaroff, Vilakazi and Karim attest to this.

The case studies, mega projects and bibliometric analysis speak to outputs. What then of inputs? From 2001/02 to 2019/22 the number of full-time researchers per 1,000 employed in the workforce rose by 36 per cent. On the other hand, gross expenditure on R&D rose by 450 per cent. The main driver of R&D expenditure is the cost of labour plus other expenditures per employee. The message is clear. The researcher stock is static, but expenditure has boomed, implying excess remuneration. Kaplan (2008) suggested that this inflation was driven by restricted supply. However, in this chapter it is argued that the R&D workforce has enjoyed above-inflation growth driven by the power of organised labour, and has effectively participated in a form of bureaucratic capture. The upward movement of salaries is largest in the state sector, where white-collar unions are powerful. University staff has increased in number, even as numbers in the business sector have contracted. This is why the innovation system is stagnating rather than growing. The stasis of the researcher stock arises from a policy of replacement rather than expansion, coupled with the high cost of expertise and resistance to the employment of foreign expertise.

SYNTHESIS

The above begs the questions: in what research areas should scarce resources be concentrated; and from where will the corpus of researchers be found? In other words, by whom and how is selection to be made, and what resources will be needed? A stronger method of selection and project termination is required, in addition to a process in which the research agenda is set in concert with industrial policy. Such were the recommendations of the 2012 Ministerial Review (DST, 2012). These sit on the shelf and remain the key policy questions that the White Paper on Science, Technology and Innovation avoids (DST, 2019). There is a lack of focus, and a silence on attracting research skills. Indeed, were Thackeray still at CSIR, would his team have received the means to achieve the desired end? The answer might well be a flat no. On the other hand, the PBMR did gather a critical mass of researchers, a mass unparalleled since the onset of the peace dividend.

The persistence of CalAfrica and the path dependence of the economy were noted. What does this mean for the contract between science and society? Does a contract, implicit or explicit exist, and if so, does it also demonstrate path dependence? Kahn (2019) averred that the social contract might be characterised as walking on two legs. To the early 1990s, these two legs were a local variant of the Republic of Science (see Polanyi, 1962) and the Security State. The Republic of Science, the social sciences and humanities excepted, was left to pursue its own agenda of blue-sky research as part of the national project of the day (Dubow, 2006). The first 'leg' produced heart transplants and paleo-archaeological discoveries. The second leg produced howitzers and poisons even as the country became ungovernable.

Kahn (2019) averred that the two legs carried on walking even as effort was made to articulate science policy in keeping with the goal of 'a better life for all'. Under the Mandela administration, two rounds of Innovation Fund awards gave some expression to this orientation. Thereafter the humanities and social sciences component of the Republic of Science often found itself in conflict with the way the new constitutional democracy took shape. Examples of this include research on the aetiology of HIV and civil society's fight to ensure secondary constitutional rights, both of which pitted the republic against the State. As to the other leg, the technology agenda of the former Security State morphed into vanity projects such as the Rooivalk helicopter gunship, the South African Large Telescope, the Karoo Array Telescope, the Pebble Bed Modular Reactor and the Joule electric vehicle. Alongside the decline in the manufacturing base, this led to a change in the distribution of expenditure among the research fields, with the share of engineering and technology falling sharply and that of medical and health sciences, and social sciences burgeoning.

Flagship science prospered while the R&D and innovation capacity of the defence industry and state-owned enterprises weakened. The expansion of university provision was accompanied by a shift towards basic research, which now absorbs 34 per cent of gross domestic expenditure on R&D (GERD), a figure high among industrialised countries. The DST set out to support basic research and might well claim this shift as a success.

However, the share of high technology exports in total exports declined from nine per cent to six per cent from 1990 to 2020. While other emerging market economies increased the share of medium and high technology products in their export baskets, South Africa's fell. Economic growth stagnated under a perfect storm of conflicting interests and structural economic shifts.

For the above reasons it is averred that the Republic of Science is disarticulated from industrial needs. Applied research is weak in hard technologies, suggesting low prospects for addressing the challenges of new materials, engineering and computer science. While it may be argued that prowess in astrophysics and high energy physics will lead to competence in big data, application is a distant goal. Likewise, expertise in medical sciences – concentrated in the aetiology of infectious diseases, and public, environmental and occupational health – is not readily commercialised.

This chapter posed three main questions: how real is the mooted innovation chasm; is there a stock of research findings ready for commercialisation; and are proven technologies being lost? The evidence is that the innovation chasm paradigm and its extension to the claim of lost technologies has outlived any usefulness. Similarly the claim that there is a massive stock of research that is ready for commercialisation has been shown to be unhelpful.

Of the case studies discussed, one was terminated; one struggled; two prospered. That is a fair track record, hardly evident of widespread mortality. The case studies speak to innovations that had limited support from the state. The lesson from the lithium story is that size matters. The Manhattan Project is the prime example of knowledge and industrial agglomeration, where from discovery to execution a plutonium weapon was detonated but 1,600 days later (Rhodes, 1986). The same holds for Covid-19 vaccines. BioNTech developed its mRNA product through the work of 500 researchers. Oxford University/ Jenner Institute marshalled a similar-sized group of researchers to develop their adenovirus vaccine. South Africa could perhaps muster 50 vaccine researchers, with no experience in producing active pharmaceutical ingredients (APIs) or vaccine development skills.

It is just possible that an apex research and innovation agency could reduce the disarticulation. To this end the agency would require highest-level political support and would need to be led and staffed by socially aware technocrats who would act as the nose of the system, providing signals, foresight and anticipation to the innovation system actors. In the absence of such leadership, clear goals and objectives, research translation will remain an unrealised dream.

REFERENCES

Albuquerque, E. 2003. 'Immature systems of innovation: Introductory notes about a comparison between South Africa, India, Mexico and Brazil based on science and technology statistics'. Discussion Paper No. 221, CEDEPLAR/FACE/IFMG.ASGI-SA: Belo Hirozonte: CEDEPLAR.

Department of Arts, Culture, Science And Technology (DACST). 1996. 'White Paper on Science and Technology'. chrome-extension:// efaidnbmnnnibpcajpcglclefindmkaj/https://www.gov.za/sites/default/ files/gcis_document/201409/sciencetechnologywhitepaper.pdf, accessed 8 November 2023.

De Wet, G. 1999. 'Emerging from the technology colony: A view from the South'. doi:10.1109/PICMET.1999.808399, accessed 23 June 2023.

Department of Science and Innovation (DSI). 2008. 'Technology Innovation Agency (TIA) presentation to the Parliamentary Portfolio Committee 8 May 2008'. https://pmg.org.za/files/docs/080514dst.ppt, accessed 5 June 2022.

Department of Science and Innovation (DSI). 2021. 'South African National Survey of Research and Experimental Development. Statistical Report: 2019/20'. https://www.dst.gov.za/images/RD_StatisticalReport2019-20__ WEB.pdf, accessed 23 June 2023.

DSI/SARIMA/NIPMO/Kisch IP. 2021. 'South African National Survey of Intellectual Property and Technology Transfer at Publicly Funded Research Institutions Second National Survey: 2014–2018'. Department of Science and Innovation, Pretoria.

Department of Science and Technology (DST). 2002. 'South Africa's National Research & Development Strategy'. https://www.dst.gov.za/images/pdfs/ National%20research%20%20development%20strategy%202002.pdf, accessed 23 June 2023.

Department of Science and Technology (DST). 2008. 'Innovation Towards A Knowledge-Based Economy: Ten-Year Plan For South Africa (2008–2018)'. https://www.sansa.org.za/wp-content/uploads/2018/05/DST-Ten-Year-Innovation-Plan.pdf, accessed 23 June 2023.

Department of Science and Technology (DST). 2013. 'Research and Development 2010/11 Survey Statistical Report'. https://www.dst.gov.za/ images/pdfs/RD_Survey_Statistical_Report_2010-2011.pdf, accessed 23 June 2023.

Department of Science and Technology DST). 2016. 'South African Research Infrastructure Roadmap'. https://www.dst.gov.za/images/Attachments/ Department_of_Science_and_Technology_SARIR_2016.pdf, accessed 23 June 2023.

Department of Science and Technology. 2019. 'White Paper on Science, Technology and Innovation'. https://www.dst.gov.za/images/2019/White_

paper_web_copyv1.pdf, accessed 23 June 2023.

Dubow, S. 2006. *A Commonwealth of Knowledge: Science, Sensibility and White South Africa 1820–2000*. Oxford: Oxford University Press.

Godin, B. 2006. 'The linear model of innovation: The historical construction of an analytical framework'. *Science, Technology, & Human Values*, 31(6), 639–667.

Gostner, K., Roberts, S., Clark, A. and Iliev, I. 2005. 'Resource-based technology innovation in South Africa. Employment-oriented industry studies'. Human Sciences Research Council, https://repository.hsrc.ac.za/bitstream/handle/20.500.11910/9161/4263_Gostner_ResourcebasedtechnologyinnovationinSA.pdf?sequence=1&isAllowed=y, accessed 15 June 2023.

International Development Resource Centre (IDRC). 1995. 'Building a New South Africa Volume 3 Science and Technology Policy. A Report from the Mission on Science and Technology Policy for a Democratic South Africa'. Ottawa and Johannesburg: International Development Resource Centre.

Kahn, M.J. 2014. 'SMEs and the telemetry system of innovation', in Hosni, Y. (ed). *23rd International Conference for the International Association of Management of Technology*. Washington DC. Conference Proceedings, 22–26.

Kahn, M.J. 2019. 'The contract between science and society: A South African case study'. *Science & Public Policy*, 46(1), 116–125.

Kaplan, D. 2008. 'Science and Technology Policy in South Africa: A Critical Assessment of Past Performance and Proposed Future Directions'. Vienna: Research and Statistics Branch Working Paper 1/2008. United Nations Industrial Development Organization, Geneva.

Landes, D. 1998. *The Wealth and Poverty of Nations*. New York: Little, Brown.

Lundvall, B.-Å. 1985. *Product Innovation and User-Producer Interaction*. Aalborg: Aalborg University Press.

Maharajh, R. 2011. *Innovating beyond racial capitalism: A contribution towards the Analysis of the Political Economy of Post-Apartheid South Africa*. Lund: Lund University Press.

Malele, V., Mpofu, K. and Muchie, M. 2019. 'Bridging the innovation chasm: Measuring awareness of entrepreneurship and innovation policies and platforms at the universities of technology in South Africa'. *African Journal of Science, Technology, Innovation & Development*, 11(7), 783–793.

Marcus, R. 2003. 'Linking universities and business: Opinion, 16 September 2003'. *Business Day*, https://www.businesslive.co.za/bd/, accessed 5 June 2022.

Moon, F.C. 2014. *Social Networks in the History of Innovation and Invention*. Dordrecht: Springer.

Moore, G, 1991. *Crossing the Chasm*. New York: Harper Business Essential.

Mouton, J, 2021. 'A Review of the National Research and Development

Strategy (NRDS) and Ten-Year Innovation Plan'. National Advisory Council on Innovation, Pretoria.

Nicholls, D. 2002. 'The Pebble Bed Modular Reactor'. *Transactions of the Royal Society of South Africa*, 56(2), 125–130. https://doi.org/10.1080/00359190109520510, accessed 10 January 2013.

National Commission on Research, Science, and Technology (NCRST). 2014. 'The National Programme on Research, Science, Technology and Innovation 2014/15–2016/17'. National Commission on Research, Science, and Technology, Windhoek.

National Research Foundation (NRF). 2012. 'NRF Performance Report 2010–11'. National Research Foundation, Pretoria.

Organization for Economic Cooperation and Development (OECD). 2007. 'Review of Innovation Policy: South Africa'. OECD Publishing, Paris.

Pefile, S. 2006. 'Country focus. Innovation to drive development. South Africa'. *WIPO Magazine*, November, https://www.wipo.int/wipo_magazine/en/2006/06/article_0004.html, accessed 23 June 2023.

Polanyi, M. 1962. 'The republic of science: its political and economic theory'. *Minerva,* 1, 54–73.

Pouris, A. 2008. 'Science-industry relations and the SA innovation chasm: Searching for lost technologies'. Department of Trade and Industry, Pretoria.

Prebisch, R. 1950. *The Economic Development of Latin America and Its Principal Problems*. New York: United Nations.

Presidency. 2020. 'Report of the National Commission for the Fourth Industrial Revolution'. The Presidency, Pretoria.

Scerri, M. ed. 2016. *The Emergence of Systems of Innovation In South(ern) Africa: Long Histories And Contemporary Debates.* Johannesburg: Mapungubwe Institute for Critical Reflection and Analysis/Real African Publishers.

Rhodes, R. 1986. *The Making of the Atomic Bomb*. New York: Simon and Schuster.

Rogers, E. 1962. *Diffusion of Innovations*. New York: Simon and Schuster.

Technology Innovation Agency (TIA). 2022. www.tia.org.za, accessed 5 June 2022.

TWELVE

Conclusions and policy recommendations

Thomas Pogue and
Zamanzima Mazibuko-Makena

Successful commercialisation of a technology involves many factors. As technologies grow increasingly complicated the number of component technologies and the needs of these technologies themselves further influence these processes. The authors in this volume have described a range of successful and unsuccessful journeys taken in pursuit of commercialisation for technologies, as well as the co-evolution of these technologies with the economy. Various chapters also assessed the outcomes of these journeys and their relationships to issues such as development, power and agency.

In the introduction (Chapter 1), these processes were summarised and broadly framed within the national systems of innovation (NSI) approach. That context was achieved using a multi-dimensional analytical approach and a conceptualisation of technology that emphasises the recurring, applied and evolving nature of its constructs.[1] Issues

---

1 As described in Chapter 1, this conceptualisation of technology is based on Arthur (2009) and the multi-dimensional analytical framework is based on that proposed by Weber and Rohracher (2012).

associated with the development of technologies and their systemic relationships to markets, structural mechanisms and transformation were thus highlighted. Table 12.1 provides a summary of these issues and their linkages to the respective chapters.

Table 12.1: Summary of chapters and analytical framing

Chapter		2	3	4	5	6	7	8	9	10	11
Title in brief		Where innovations may come to life	Reorienting technology transfer	Intermediaries	Frugal and reverse innovation	Public sector innovation	Government-led technological missions	Structural change and innovation	City-driven innovation systems	Beyond national systems of innovation	Chasms of understanding
A) Market system failures	A-a) Information asymmetries						✓	✓			
	A-b) Knowledge spill-overs				✓			✓			
	A-c) Externalisation of costs							✓			
	A-d) Exploitation of public resources					✓		✓			
B) Structural system failures	B-a) Infrastructural failure				✓			✓	✓		
	B-b) Institutional failures	✓	✓	✓	✓	✓	✓		✓	✓	✓
	B-c) Network failures			✓				✓		✓	
	B-d) Capabilities failure		✓	✓	✓	✓	✓		✓	✓	
C) Transformational system failures	C-a) Directionality failures	✓	✓		✓	✓				✓	✓
	C-b) Demand articulation failures	✓			✓		✓	✓	✓	✓	
	C-c) Policy coordination failures	✓		✓			✓	✓	✓	✓	
	C-d) Reflexivity failures		✓		✓			✓	✓	✓	✓

In this conclusion, we revisit the chapters and our three primary research questions:

1. What impact is South Africa's commercialised research having on the achievement of the country's development goals?
2. Why are some technologies successfully commercialised and others not?
3. Which policy changes could increase the socioeconomic impact of South African technology?

Following reflections on the research questions, attention turns to their collective relationship with broader policy issues and implications. Lastly, we reflect on essential areas for further research and analysis.

THE EXTENT TO WHICH COMMERCIALISED RESEARCH SUPPORTS DEVELOPMENT GOALS

A central focus of the first section was the extent to which South Africa's development goals are being advanced by the technologies that are being commercialised. Related to this issue is the extent to which the formal structures, policies and institutions of the NSI are solving society's problems. As discussed in the Introduction (Chapter 1), these formal structures, which we refer to as the narrow NSI, stand in contrast to the broader structure of innovation networks, capabilities and know-how, which we refer to as the broad NSI.

This distinction between the formal, narrow NSI and the actual technologies being developed across the broader national system of innovation was explored in Chapter 2. In considering evidence regarding policy to foster innovation that supports development objectives, Kruss et al. explored results from the National Innovation Survey. Their examination provides evidence that most of the innovation in South Africa involves the localisation and commercialisation of existing technologies. This is shown to be especially important given that South African innovation policy is predominantly orientated towards supply-side science, research and development production. Exploring the results of the innovation survey, the authors also find both that there is a need for capabilities to adapt and adopt technologies, and that this need has been neglected by government policy. Given the importance of this gap, the authors use an innovation capabilities framework to analyse the probability of an innovation being adapted and/or modified. That provides unprecedented evidence on the alignment, or more accurately the lack of alignment, of innovation policy to the needs of innovators. As a result, the authors make three important recommendations to address this gap. First, they call for strengthening dynamic innovation capabilities, including skills development, intellectual property rights, improved access to markets and knowledge networks. Second, they suggest building capabilities to modify domestic and international technologies by facilitating collaboration to decrease technology costs and increase learning. Lastly, they recommend innovative policies, aimed at increasing market demand, to broaden capabilities to absorb and access technologies.

Chapter 3 focused on the extent to which post-democratic technology domains are either facilitating or impeding the development of socially impactful technologies. Analysing efforts to commercialise technologies at South Africa's publicly financed research institutions, Mustapha and Ralphs assess whether these institutions' efforts align with South Africa's development goals. Using the national R&D Survey, the authors consider the success that the National Intellectual Property Management Office (NIPMO) and Offices of Technology Transfer (OTTs) have had in fostering the commercialisation of their technologies. They found evidence of the impact of South Africa's institutional history on whether or not technologies addressed national transformational needs. Specifically, institutions best endowed with science and technology capacity appear to lag in development-oriented innovation. Identifying a range of institutional intellectual property capacities and their relationships to historical institutional legacies, the authors make three recommendations for facilitating public value inputs and outcomes. First, funding of public research institutions should explicitly be based on a consideration of apartheid and colonial histories, and uneven institutional development trajectories. Second, research funding should address differences between the demands of the market and those of society and its socioeconomic needs by incentivising research aimed at these needs. Lastly, such research requires distinct and additional skills and capabilities that must be integrated into existing technology transfer systems.

These chapters provide valuable insights into the need for a reorientation of policy and illustrate the benefits to be derived from further interrogation of the South African government's annual national innovation and Research and Development (R&D) surveys. The need to reframe missions to focus on technological commercialisation as an outcome, rather than on components of that process, was also apparent in these chapters' assessments of the impact of South Africa's commercialised research on its development goals. In fact, this is a recurrent theme in the descriptions of technologies' journeys to commercialisation in Section Two.

DESCRIPTIONS OF TECHNOLOGIES JOURNEYS
TOWARDS COMMERCIALISATION

Section Two includes five chapters that cover a dozen case studies. Together they identify several trajectories and systemic causes associated with successful and unsuccessful commercialisation. In Chapter 4 capabilities in intermediation are explored across two case studies of furniture clusters, in South Africa's Western Cape. Reviewing the state's efforts to build these clusters Kraak identifies a critical deficiency of capabilities contributing to the failure of these initiatives. He also identifies the need to better enhance coordination across government departments, and departmental practices that support nimble responses during the implementation of these programmes. Examining the potential use of intermediation, the chapter identifies the importance of reflection on the coevolution between technologies and their opportunity niches as well as the potential to enhance the prospects of commercialisation through systemic monitoring, evaluation and learning. Significantly, it also highlighted the multi-dimensionality of the capabilities associated with successful commercialisation.

South Africa's socioeconomic needs and development goals are central in Chapter 5. Mazibuko-Makena describes three medical devices and how the commercialisation of these assisted in realising envisioned healthcare outcomes, using the concepts of 'frugal innovation' and 'reverse innovation'. The author details how these innovations were developed with the comparatively limited resources confronting healthcare systems in low- and middle-income countries like South Africa. While these 'frugal medical devices' were bottom-up, needs-driven technologies, developed in the face of costly alternatives, they both provided important solutions to domestic challenges and found opportunity niches in high-income countries. The Lodox scanner and Sinapi chest drains are cited as illustrative cases of reverse innovation, which occurs when products from low/middle-income countries realise at least some high-income market success. The case studies thus demonstrate how South Africa's health system capabilities have been able to drive the development of technologies, which support social impact, seemingly with limited supply-side support from the state.

Two cases where the state has taken an active role in developing technologies to address South Africa's development goals are explored in Chapter 6. Karuri-Sebina et al. described significant challenges experienced by the state in shepherding these two technologies towards commercialisation. Their analysis drew on three major framings for science, technology and innovation (STI) policy, which impact on the success or failure of public sector technologies. Two factors were identified as key in both case studies: coordination failures between government departments and limited incentives within these departments for championing technologies. From the inception of the Maponya Mall Urban Thusong Centre model, it was clearly articulated that the key success factor would be interdepartmental government collaboration. As the case study shows, the lack of such collaboration ultimately undermined the wider scaling up of this initiative.

Similarly, the community-developed crime response system for informal settlements, the MeMeZA Community Alarm System, faced collaboration challenges. These arose out of an aversion to change, even when innovations provided potential solutions to recognised needs. Specifically, this case drew attention to social technologies and the challenges faced in commercialising them. This was illustrated in the author's description of the large-scale adoption required for government procurement, which requires the championing of top leadership. However, that leadership lacks incentives to support those technologies and arguably even faces many incentives to avoid supporting their adoption. Good ideas can therefore wither and be lost. This challenge is central to the failure of initiatives that are aimed at public-interest technology. Such initiatives aim to prioritise historically disadvantaged populations and create an environment conducive to desirable social outcomes for new technologies.[2] It points to a fundamental opportunity for the state to leverage the adoption of technologies to expand the impact of technological opportunities on

---

2 In addition to the references in the Introduction, see Public Interest Technology: http://newamerica.org/pit/ and Tara Dawson McGuinness and Hana Schank, *Power to the Public: The Promise of Public Interest Technology*. Ithaca: Princeton University Press, 2021.

the achievement of South Africa's development goals.

Attention in Chapter 7 turns to three case studies with high levels of scientific complexity. Such innovations lend themselves well to linear innovation processes in which research leads to development, which is then prototyped and followed by efforts to commercialise. South Africa's efforts to develop a pebble bed modular reactor (PBMR) is the focus of the first case study in Chapter 7. The authors describe the effects of overestimating the technology's immediate availability for commercialisation. They also outline the difficulties associated with high-cost technology commercialisation, given that it is not possible to ensure that winning technologies have been chosen, and that even winning technologies may take decades to deliver a return on investment.

In the second case study, Xaba and Fuku analyse the Square Kilometre Array (SKA). Their analysis follows the work of others (Kruss et al., 2015), in detailing a collaborative and relatively successful initiative to increase astrophysical knowledge, which results in incrementally larger systems – systems which develop training and knowledge pathways to complement physical technologies and their deployment. The SKA appears to be a case where local endowments are leveraged to build additional capabilities while evolving and linking partnerships across South Africa's public research institutions. However, this case study also suggests a technological enclave with relatively limited direct linkages to broader socioeconomic needs.

South Africa's efforts to develop a pebble bed modular reactor (PBMR) is the focus of the second case study in Chapter 7. The authors describe the effects of overestimating the technology's immediate availability for commercialisation. They also outline the difficulties associated with high-cost technology commercialisation, given that it is not possible to ensure that winning technologies have been chosen, and that even winning technologies may take decades to deliver a return on investment.

The final case study examines the Hydrogen South Africa (HySA) strategy to develop South African hydrogen and fuel cell technologies. The authors describe the significant promise that commercialisation of these technologies holds for South Africa. They also highlight, however, significant challenges in realising these opportunities across several institutions and government divisions. While offering a path to build technology that would facilitate South Africa's transition to a green economy, there remains uncertainty around the future commercial viability of the technologies associated with this initiative. Nonetheless, the case study also highlights how support of the technology has created emerging knowledge and capabilities that may be leveraged for related applications.

In Chapter 8, attention turns to the commercialisation of technologies within the South African Mineral Resource Finance Network (MRFN).[3] Pogue describes the development of South Africa's export coal industry and of mining equipment that enhanced the viability of the country's deep-level mineral resources. He highlights the disconnect between these technologies and South Africa's modern development goals, despite both projects being deemed a 'success'. Pogue argues instead for a broader contextual evaluation, which takes account of social costs and benefits, to be used when discussing successful commercialisation. The chapter holds that to date efforts to leverage the distributed capabilities of the MRFN have followed a relatively narrow conceptualisation of technology and innovation policy rather than a broader one, which holistically considers the needs and functions of South Africa's innovation system.

Collectively the case studies in Section Two describe a diverse array of technologies' journeys towards commercialisation. Despite the diversity of these journeys, capabilities, coordination and collaboration/networks were common themes throughout. Within our research framework these are considered structural and transformational features. While market features were alluded to, structural and transformational features were dominant in the technologies' journeys towards commercialisation. While the market did feature in the technologies' journeys towards commercialisation, structural and transformational factors played a much bigger role.

---

3 The MRFN concept is described by Hilsenrath and Pogue (2017). It is related to, but distinct from, the minerals-energy complex detailed in Fine and Rustomjee (1996) and its South African historiography reviewed by Freund (2009).

These factors also feature in the chapters in Section Three, which explore how South Africa's technology and innovation policy can better facilitate alignment to national socioeconomic needs.

POLICIES TO FACILITATE COMMERCIALISATION FOR SOCIOECONOMIC NEEDS

The chapters in Section Three identify ways to ensure that a greater number of technologies that advance South Africa's development goals and address its socioeconomic needs reach the commercialisation stage. This focus makes Section Three, in part, a response to the limitation of South Africa's commercialised research identified in Section One. Chapter 9 examined opportunities, including a re-orientation to local government for better policy coordination and coherence. Specifically, Joseph and Karuri-Sebina considered the potential to further align innovation policy and support measures with local innovation systems that build bottom-up opportunities and increase alignment with local needs. They explored the potential of local government to support both local and national systems of innovation, using a case study of the City of Tshwane. The authors argued that this does not preclude local government from fulfilling the important function of influencing the technology domain: the constellation of technologies that creates and is created by wealth and power (Arthur, 2009: 69–85). They found evidence that municipal government is uniquely positioned to create nuanced and nimble solutions that address local challenges to and opportunities for the commercialisation of technologies. They found, however, that, even when capabilities exist, local government is precluded from engaging because of difficulties in coordination between local and national levels of government. Based on this case study, the authors articulated a framework for the adoption of a more effective local system of innovation policy. If successfully implemented, such a policy would represent an important policy innovation aligned to, and advancing, local needs and the realisation of associated development goals.

Chapter 10 identified a need for alternative guidance to that currently being provided by the NSI policy framework, using failures to develop domestic HIV/AIDS medicine manufacturing as its focus. The chapter placed particular attention on the state's inability to bring the necessary finance together when a significant window of opportunity was present. In his call for an alternative, Walwyn contends that transformative needs and political-economic context should be central to building innovative capabilities and coordination. An alternative innovation strategy, based on a multi-level perspective (MLP), is advocated. Through its focus on the institutional fabric and associated political-economic challenges and opportunities, the MLP is held to offer a better framework to address key challenges and foster commercialisation for socioeconomic needs.

An extensive review of the innovation chasm is presented in Chapter 11. The analysis also calls into question the validity of associated thinking about lost technology applications. Highlighting the origins and shortcomings of the innovation chasm as a concept and policy tool, Kahn reviews four cases of commercialisation in the private sector and three cases of state-funded, large-scale projects. Reflecting on implications, a lack of control over the social contract for science was highlighted as an important source of the frustration that supports the South African lost technology/innovation chasm narrative. The chapter proposes that this has led to a misarticulation of South Africa's transformational goals by the NSI, and a disconnection from the country's industrial needs. It holds then that without a concerted effort to address this disconnect, frustration is likely to deepen and attempts to address socioeconomic needs will remain unfocused.

POLICY RECOMMENDATIONS

This volume has focused on the critical, but relatively neglected, process of technologies' commercialisation. Numerous areas with significant implications for the state's technology policy were discussed. A few of the more significant themes included:

1. Better supporting the adaption and adoption of existing technologies;
2. Increasing management of technologies' socioeconomic costs and benefits; and

3.   Improving coordination across government agencies.

Prioritise adaptation and adoption of existing technologies

It is significant that virtually every chapter in this volume identified an excessive focus in current technology policy on supplying novel technologies rather than supporting standard engineering and/ or structural deepening.[4] An important policy implication of the contributions in this book then is the recognition that the adaption and adoption of existing technologies requires distinct technology policy. As discussed in Chapter 2, it is important to profile varied firms' innovation models in order to understand national and sectoral patterns of capabilities. This information is a starting point to inform and monitor the implementation of a balance between technology demand and supply-side interventions.

This volume has identified a range of capabilities that, if developed, would support the adaptation and adoption of existing technologies. These ranged from workforce skills and a competitive environment to technology management and standards that support service. A key policy issue raised in Chapter 4 was the need for innovative thinking around the capabilities needed to increase successful technology commercialisation. Intermediation and quasi-autonomous, non-governmental organisations (quangos) seem to hold promise to build capabilities within organisations aspiring to commercialise technologies. Such organisations would also assist with efforts to overcome bureaucratic, siloed modes of operating. In addition, cross-departmental coordination, actor interaction and the sharing of knowledge resources would be facilitated.

The need to develop dynamic capabilities in the public sector was a recurrent theme in the varied descriptions of technology commercialisation in this volume. These discussions suggest the need for a systematic articulation of a range of regulatory, financial and 'soft' policy interventions aimed at tackling market and system failures. Such articulation would shape and change barriers to innovation at

---

4   In fact, only two chapters do not identify this issue: Chapter 8, which is focused on historic technology commercialisation in South Africa's mineral resource finance network, and Chapter 11 with a focus on South Africa's conceptualisation of the innovation chasm.

firm level. In this way, it would grow the innovation capabilities of all categories of firms, across the broad NSI.

This need to build capabilities is also related to the analysis of Mazzucato et al. (2021) and their call for reflection on the magnitude of the investment into human capital required for South Africa to implement state policies. This was also noted in the Higher Education, Science, Technology and Innovation Institutional Landscape (HESTIIL) Ministerial Committee's call for state intervention to establish a diverse portfolio of technologies that advance transformation and build capacity in the narrow NSI to realise South Africa's development goals (2020: 237). Central to such a reorientation towards new solutions and adaptations within given technologies are investments in the conditions necessary for commercialisation and development.

Increase focus on the socioeconomic impacts of technologies

Acemoglu and Johnson (2023) recently reflected on the distribution of the socioeconomic costs and benefits of technology throughout history. While recognising that important sceptics have existed for centuries, they note a pervasive tendency to focus on the benign nature of technology ('techno-optimism'); they prefer to draw attention to a need to recognise the ways in which technology is targeted towards particular goals, narratives or markets by those with power. That recognition of how elites shape the direction, use and progress of technology is fundamental to this volume and every contribution addresses it.

The chapters in Section Three identify a need for more deliberate and practical consideration of public sector innovation within the broader NSI at both national and sub-national levels. Chapter 10's critique of the narrow NSI policy framework considers it inadequate for counteracting the geopolitical imbalances faced by developing countries. It contends that a different approach to innovation and development should be adopted, one that is based on a broad framing of the NSI approach and takes account of the political economy. This was raised in several of the other chapters as well. In Chapter 3, however, emphasis was placed on the need to foster an inclusive and transformative focus for new technologies, especially those developed by public agencies. Related to that is a need to stimulate and incentivise researchers and programmes in public agencies for technologies with public value outcomes. Greater funding would assist such policies, and allow for more resources to flow towards technology transfer processes that emphasise public value inputs and outcomes.

A more developmental, human-centred public sector innovation policy is required to increase the impact of South Africa's technologies on the country's socioeconomic needs. Such policy would impact on the challenges being addressed by the technologies as well as on the ways in which innovators are enabled to address such challenges. Policy initiatives could include the formation of a public sector innovation 'living lab' that fosters collaborative arrangements and includes state and non-state actors. As previously mentioned, these types of policies are related to other efforts, including public interest technology, which seeks to prioritise historically disinvested populations while leveraging resources to generate better socioeconomic outcomes. Consideration of the socioeconomic impacts of technology should not be limited to public agencies only. Both chapters 7 and 8 described technologies that were developed for commercialisation by institutional structures. It is, however, important to interrogate the development of such technologies to consider the social costs and benefits of commercialisation for all sectors of society. Such an interrogation addresses the legacies of the unequal distribution of the benefits associated with the technologies' journeys, and facilitates the development of policies that realise, where needed, the transformation of existing technological domains.

A final policy implication of techno-optimism is its potential to simplify approaches to technology policy such that broader capabilities and the socioeconomic costs and benefits of new technologies are not considered. This issue is central to the South African debate around the innovation chasm and the extensive critique of that notion that was provided in Chapter 11. It was also illustrated in the Joule EV case study, which was described in Chapter 1 and in Appendix 1 of that chapter. The innovation chasm paradigm does not offer insight into whether any aspect of the innovation system is failing to support the commercialisation of technologies. In fact, its implication of viable South African technologies waiting to be commercialised seems dangerously misleading about the importance of the actual features that need to be addressed to enable the South African innovation system to realise its development goals. Therefore, actively curtailing the existing innovation chasm paradigm in South African innovation policy is an important step towards developing more impactful and aligned technology policy.

Decrease silos of responsibilities across and within agents

A movement towards technology policies aimed at wider social benefits requires innovators to reframe the missions of their technologies, with greater orientation to the outcomes of technological resources. Change of this kind involves significant reframing of science, technology and innovation policies in order to provide enhanced directionality and coordination. It seems that policy interventions such as demand-side mechanisms focused on building opportunity niches are needed to foster greater efficiency in the system.

Also clear from several contributions to this volume is the need to better understand what can be done to foster a connected, joined-up state working across various departments and geographic levels of government to advance South Africa's development goals. This entails moving beyond a traditional focus on binary distinctions (e.g., between product and process innovation, or between a scientific and technologically based innovation and learning-by-doing, by-using and by-interacting-based innovation), which provide limited policy direction and can lead to misalignment and gaps.

The disconnect between what is produced through the NSI in a narrow sense and decision-makers and public officials at the coalface of service delivery seems to result in many failures or unscaled innovations. That issue was examined in Chapter 9 where the role of local systems of innovation in cities was highlighted. These systems were identified as important vehicles for the provision of 'the basics' of local governance and development. In that context, the role of national government becomes a supportive one, in which it better enables the role of cities through funding, alignment and scaling of innovations that work.

Building a more integrated approach also seems to require

mechanisms to manage dynamic innovation 'life and death' cycles, including how to prevent failure, bridge chasms in funding and capacity and protect new niches whilst retiring innovations that have played their course. This relates to broader concepts of integrated and coordinated government such as 'joined-up' and 'whole-of-government',[5] but it represents a distinct change in and reconceptualisation of current technology policy. Importantly, it also requires active and purposeful management of technology failures, so that the lessons and capabilities generated become systemic contributions to a process of further discovery rather than isolated and abandoned investments.

This altered policy perspective relates to fundamental features of technologies' developmental processes. It assumes the technologies that are commercialised create a skeleton on which the economy rests. It also assumes an associated transformation in the state's role in fostering technologies: the focus shifts from specific projects and technologies to a broader and more systemic approach. In this context, emphasis is on stewardship of investment more akin to planting, watering and weeding of emerging technologies (Arthur, 2009: 163), rather than on the pursuit of science for a particular commercial aim.

RECOMMENDATION FOR FURTHER RESEARCH AND ANALYSIS

In this examination of issues associated with technologies achieving commercial viability, several areas requiring better understanding were identified. In closing we return to three issues that we believe are particularly important:

1. Advancing our knowledge of where new South African technologies originate and how they are commercialised;
2. Reframing our understanding of the socioeconomic costs and benefits of technologies' commercialisation and of institutional interests supporting and opposing commercialisation; and
3. Enhancing awareness and understanding of our capabilities to commercialise.

5　For more on these concepts, see Bogdanor (2005) and OECD (2006).

Technology origins, utilisation and commercialisation processes

Recently, Beinert and Dubow (2022) brought attention to the centrality of South Africa's science and technology system in understanding its journey to modernity. Their summary of national socio-technological imaginaries, or 'technological domains' as we refer to them within the Arthur (2009) conceptualisation, highlights themes similar to the focus of the book *The Emergence of Systems of Innovation in South(ern) Africa: Long Histories and Current Debates* by MISTRA (Scerri, 2016). Despite these important contributions, a lot remains unexamined in South Africa's and Africa's innovation history. In this volume we endeavoured to build on previous analyses as we explored the commercialisation of technology in South Africa and its ramifications for the evolution of the broad NSI. The need to develop a deeper historical perspective on South Africa's technological evolution is apparent from the chapters in this volume. This history matters in the development of a better understanding of existing technological domains and the forces influencing their direction and structure. Chapter 8 offers an analysis of technological commercialisation in South Africa's mineral resource finance network. The influence of historical context on technologies' contributions to a society's development goals or the creation of barriers to their realisation was apparent. Since the advent of democracy in South Africa, science and technology have largely been seen as advancing socioeconomic development, but it is important to recognise and increase understanding of technological legacies. The chapters in this volume suggest that identifying the historic and contemporary roles of these technological domains is an underdeveloped area. The history of the ways in which a technology has been directed matters, and understanding the structure of its influence over that direction is necessary for meaningful discussion of the social costs and benefits of a technology's commercialisation.

Similarly, this volume brought attention to the need to develop our understanding of technology utilisation, not just in expanding existing commercialisation opportunities but also in creating new ones. Despite South Africa conducting and publishing a National Survey of Innovation R&D for nearly two decades, integrating and applying the insights of that initiative are underdeveloped. Chapter 2 illustrates the value of the information contained in the Survey's analyses, suggesting a need to reframe our thinking about innovative activities in South Africa and move away from concepts that frame innovation as primarily occurring when based on early-stage, big-idea creation. While evidence suggests that the majority of new technologies in South Africa are adaptations and applications from other markets rather than novel creations, the scale of this divide remains crudely quantified, and the qualitative difference is underappreciated in many conversations about innovation and commercialisation. Such a change could shift focus towards developing capabilities that support technology's translation into practice rather than an emphasis just on novel solutions.

Further consideration of the technology development process also needs to recognise the amount of change and technological transformation that has already occurred and continues to be created in South Africa. In addition to enhancing awareness of what has worked and learning from these successes, there are considerable lessons to be had from examining neglected areas of economic and innovation activities such as the informal economy. Deepening understanding of these processes should include developing insights into the very long duration of many processes of technology commercialisation. The decades of investment in electric vehicle technology described in the Optimal Energy case study in Appendix 1 of Chapter 1 is but one example.

Research and analysis in these areas will assist in addressing key gaps in our understanding of where new technologies originate and how they are commercialised. Several contributions to this volume have already made important contributions to these areas. However, there is a need for further research into the viability of different channels for transmitting and utilising technology, which goes beyond the focus of the present analysis. Further research would be valuable to advance our understanding of how technologies are used and their impacts on the economy.[6]

---

6 For examples of this type of analysis in other developing economies, see Cirera et al. (2002). For a discussion of this approach to the study of technologies associated with the Fourth Industrial Revolution, see Lorenz and Kraemer-Mbula (2021) as well as Lorenz and Kraemer-Mbula (2020).

Reframing the total social costs and benefits of a technology's commercialisation

The case studies in this book suggest that it's necessary to further research and analyse the socioeconomic impacts of technology commercialisation, in addition to developing policies that emphasise the socioeconomic impacts of new technologies. In Chapter 1 technological domains were described as encompassing broader relationships between technology and society. While these domains establish the relationships through which solutions to health, education needs and other social challenges may be developed, they also determine the power and distribution of the costs and benefits associated with technology.

A better understanding of technology's social costs and benefits is also necessary to address factors promoting or impeding the commercialisation of technologies focused on addressing South Africa's socioeconomic challenges. In this context, Chapter 3 pointed to the need for a closer analysis of public research institutions' Offices of Technology Transfer (OTTs). Building an understanding of where these efforts are occurring and where they are lacking is an important step to improving policy and incentives that address these needs. This systemic assessment of outcomes related to investments will also assist in understanding why envisioned outcomes in the NSI are not being realised despite significant investments. Further, tracking the performance of these focused efforts could help facilitate the identification of lower-cost, better need-aligned technologies.

Many of the chapters described technologies' paths to commercialisation as complex and evolving processes that reflect what is happening in the economy. Therefore, developing additional knowledge about economic relationships, and about the relationship between technological innovation and economic development, is necessary for managing the direction of technology and ensuring its economic consequences are inclusively considered. Consideration of the influences on a technology's direction should not be construed as a pretext for rejecting technological change. Rather it's a recognition that technological change differentially benefits some more than others and that the organisation of technology can empower some while disempowering others.[7] In this context, a case can be made that several technological journeys described in this volume reflect a narrow targeting of aims in existing science and technology policy. See, for example, Chapter 5's description of frugal and reverse innovation in medical devices. A better understanding of the reality of these limitations should also provide insights into how the direction of technological innovation is currently being defined.

Better orientating technology towards supporting South Africa's developmental goals may require reflection on the inclusivity of the country's current technological vision. Several of the analyses in this volume raised questions about the extent to which the national system of innovation is supporting its socioeconomic aspirations and suggest that there is a need to reflect on what drives that vision. Such a vision should draw on African humanist perspectives (Mphahlele and Scerri, 2016). Muchie (2016) has also expressed the need for the innovation system to change to reflect South African and broader African, socioeconomic and environmental values. Such a (re)conceptualisation of human and social goals could create a foundation for the socio-political will to realise the interconnectedness of the broad NSI and national development. Some of the failures described in these pages could assist in building future successes, and provide insights that would facilitate the delivery of the promise that technology holds for addressing South Africa's socioeconomic needs.

Building an understanding of commercialisation capabilities

Lastly, the contributions to this volume also suggest that if South African technology is going to play a greater role in addressing South Africa's socioeconomic development, there needs to be considerable development of capabilities across the broad NSI. While it is necessary to understand how technologies are transferred and used, and their costs and benefits, it is also essential to understand what capacity exists for the utilisation and commercialisation of the technologies. A better understanding of varied types of capabilities is also necessary to

---

7   This feature of technological change is discussed at length by Acemoglu and Johnson (2023).

create effective technology policies.

Several socio-political capabilities have been identified as significantly influencing and defining the direction of technologies' developments. These range in nature from coercion capabilities, where command and direction are realised because of a real or perceived physical threat that an agent exerts over another, to more subtle persuasion capabilities associated with the power of ideas and agenda setting (Acemoglu and Johnson, 2023: 67–99). Nonetheless, the role of these capabilities in South Africa's technology adoption has not been extensively examined.

The issues analysed in this book lay the foundation for consideration of several other capabilities. Among these is the capacity to aid transition in South Africa, including minimising harm to the environment and leveraging the benefits of new technologies, as in the case of the wood industry described in Chapter 4 and the mining industry in Chapter 8. In addition, several chapters suggested the importance of financial capabilities to obtain the resources for the investment necessary in a technology's commercialisation. Finance capabilities also include the capacity to identify and manage over-optimism about technology. This is particularly important when social welfare may suffer because investments in less popular technological areas are ignored in favour of more popular ones (Lerner, 2009: 417).

This volume is the first to bring together a diverse range of experiences about the commercialisation of technologies in South Africa. Various chapters have sought to highlight policy recommendations to facilitate socioeconomic development. Nonetheless, we recognise that this contribution to the debate is only the beginning of important conversations around the commercialisation of technology that have previously been neglected.

REFERENCES

Acemoglu, D. and Johnson, S. 2023. *Power and Progress: Our Thousand-Year Struggle over Technology and Prosperity*. New York: Public Affairs.

Arthur, W.B. 2009. *The Nature of Technology: What It Is and How It Evolves*. New York: Allen Lane.

Arthur, W.B. 2021. 'Foundations of complexity economics'. *Nature Reviews*

Physics, 3, 136–145. https://doi.org/10.1038/S42254-020-00273-3, accessed 13 March 2023.

Beinart, W. and Dubow, S. 2022. *The Scientific Imagination in South Africa: 1700 to the Present*. Cambridge: Cambridge University Press.

Bogdanor, V. (ed.). 2005. *Joined-Up Government*. Oxford: Oxford University Press.

Boudreau, J. 2012. 'Tesla Motors begins delivering Model S electric cars in a Silicon Valley milestone'. *The Mercury News*, 22 June, https://www.mercurynews.com/2012/06/22/tesla-motors-begins-delivering-model-s-electric-cars-in-a-silicon-valley-milestone-2/, accessed April 2023.

Cassiolato, J.E. and Lastres, H.M.M. 2008. 'Discussing innovation and development: Converging points between the Latin American school and the innovation systems perspective?'. *GLOBELICS Working Paper Series* (08-02).

Cirera, X., Comin, D. and Cruz, M. 2022. *Bridging the Technological Divide: Technology Adoption by Firms in Developing Countries*. Washington, DC: The World Bank.

Fine, B. and Rustomjee, Z. 1996. *The Political Economy of South Africa: From Minerals-Energy Complex to Industrialisation*. London: Hurst.

Freund, B. 2010. 'The significance of the minerals-energy complex in the light of South African economic historiography framework'. *Transformation*, 71, 3–25. https://transformationjournal.org.za/71-2/, accessed 14 April 2023.

HESTIIL Ministerial Committee. 2020. 'A New Pathway 2030: Catalysing South Africa's NSI for Urgent Scaled Social and Economic Impact: A Review of South Africa's Higher Education, Science, Technology and Innovation Institutional Landscape (HESTIIL)'. September 2020. https://www.dst.gov.za/images/2021/Higher%20Education,%20Science,%20Technology%20and%20Innovation%20Institutional%20Landscape%20Review%20Report.pdf, accessed 1 April 2023.

Hilsenrath, P. and Pogue, T. 2017. 'Distributed dynamic capabilities in South Africa's mineral resource-finance network'. *Technology in Society*, 49(C), 57–67.

Hussain, M. 2019. 'How South Africa lost its electric Joule'. *City Press*, 18 October 2019. https://www.news24.com/citypress/business/how-south-africa-lost-its-electric-joule-20191011, accessed 1 April 2023.

Kruss, G., McGrath, S., Petersen, I. and Gastrow, M. 2015. 'Higher education and economic development: The importance of building technological capabilities'. *International Journal of Educational Development*, 43, 22–31.

Leih, S., Linden, G. and Teece, D.J. 2015. 'Business model innovation and organizational design: A dynamic capabilities perspective', in N.J. Foss, and T. Saebi (eds). *Business Model Innovation: The Organizational Dimension*. Oxford: Oxford University Press, pp. 24–42.

Lerner, J. 2009. 'The governance of new firms: A functional perspective', in Lamoreaux, N. and Sokoloff, K. (eds). *Financing Innovation in the United States 1870 to the Present*. Cambridge, Massachusetts: Massachusetts Institute of Technology.

Lorenz, E. and Kraemer-Mbula, E. 2020. 'The impacts of adopting 4IR-related technologies on employment and skills: The case of the automotive and mining equipment manufacturers in South Africa', in Kraemer-Mbula, E. and Mazibuko-Makena, Z. (eds). *LEAP 4.0: African Perspectives of the 4th IR*. Johannesburg: Mapungubwe Institute for Strategic Reflection (MISTRA).

Lorenz, E. and Kraemer-Mbula, E. 2021. 'Firm-level survey on frontier technology adoption in developing countries: A questionnaire proposal'. UNCTAD Information Document, https://unctad.org/system/files/information-document/unda1819L_firm-level-survey_en.pdf, accessed July 2023.

Mapungubwe Institute for Strategic Reflection (MISTRA). 2013. *The Concept and Application of Transdisciplinarity in Intellectual Discourse and Research*. Johannesburg: MISTRA.

Mazzucato, M., Qobo, M. and Kattel, R. 2021. 'Building state capacities and dynamic capabilities to drive social and economic development: The case of South Africa'. UCL Institute for Innovation and Public Purpose (WP 2021/09).

Mphahlele, L. and Scerri, M. 2016. 'The human factor in the evolution of systems of innovation', in Scerri, M. (ed). *The Emergence of Systems of Innovation in South(ern) Africa: Long Histories and Current Debates*. Johannesburg: Mapungubwe Institute for Strategic Reflection (MISTRA), pp. 227–255.

Muchie, M. 2016. 'Towards a unified theory of pan-African innovation systems and integrated development', in Adesida, O., Karuri-Sebina, G. and Resende-Santos J. (eds). *Innovation Africa: Emerging Hubs of Excellence*. Bingley, UK: Emerald, pp. 13–34.

Organisation for Economic Co-operation and Development (OECD). 2006. *Whole-of-Government Approaches to Fragile States*. Paris: Organization for Economic Cooperation and Development.

Perkins, G. and J.P. Murmann. 2018. 'What does the success of Tesla mean for the future dynamics in the global automobile sector?'. *Management and Organization Review*, 14(3), September 2018, 471–480. https://doi.org/10.1017/mor.2018.31, accessed April 2023.

Scerri, M. (ed.) 2016. *The Emergence of Systems of Innovation in South(ern) Africa: Long Histories and Current Debates*, Johannesburg: Mapungubwe Institute for Strategic Reflection (MISTRA).

Swart, G. 2015. 'Innovation lessons learned from the Joule EV development'. *IAMOT 2015 Conference Proceedings*, International Association for Management of Technology. https://www.researchgate.net/publication/280221310, accessed April 2023.

Teece, D. 2018. 'Tesla and the reshaping of the auto industry'. *Management and Organization Review*, 14(3), 501–512. https://doi.org/10.1017/mor.2018.33, accessed April 2023.

Teece, D., Peteraf, M. and Leih, S. 2016. 'Dynamic capabilities and organizational agility: Risk, uncertainty, and strategy in the innovation economy'. *California Management Review*, 58(4), 13–35.

Tesla, 2010. 'Tesla Motors begins regular production of 2008 Tesla Roadster'. *Tesla Blog*. 20 April 2010. https://www.tesla.com/blog/tesla-motors-begins-regular-production-2008-tesla-roadster, accessed April 2023.

U.S. Department of Energy. 2023. 'Energy Saver 101 History Timeline: The electric car'. United States Department of Energy website, https://www.energy.gov/energysaver/energy-saver-101-history-timeline-electric-car, accessed 22 April 2023.

Weber, K.M. and Rohracher, H. 2012. 'Legitimizing research, technology and innovation policies for transformative change: Combining insights from innovation systems and multi-level perspective in a comprehensive 'failures' framework'. *Research Policy*, 41(6), 1037–1047. https://doi.org/10.1016/j.respol.2011.10.015.

INDEX

Page numbers in *italics* indicate figures and tables.

A

active pharmaceutical ingredient *see* APIs
activity and citation ratio 333–334
African Explosives and Chemical Industries (AECI) 324–325
African National Congress (ANC) 80, 300
AIDS (acquired immuno-deficiency syndrome) 143, 283–285, 350
Alphawave *see also* EMSS Group 328–330
Anglo American Corporation 220, 222, 224
antiretroviral *see* ARV
antiretroviral treatment *see* ART
APIs 282–284, 286–290, 298–303, 307, 337
ART 21–22, 283–286, 288, 290, 301
Arthur, William Brian 7–8, 10, 217, 238, 356

ARV 21–22, 282–290, 298–303, 307
Astronomy Advantage Area (AAA) 195

B

Bacha, Edmar 316
barriers
    to innovation 54, 56, 170, 351
    to public sector innovation 168–169, 180
Black Economic Empowerment (BEE) *92*, *104*, 234–235
Bretton Woods international monetary system 228

C

CalAfrica 315–317, 335
centralisation 160, 244, 261–262, 265, 270
Centre for Public Service Innovation (CPSI) 164, 173, 175
Chamber of Mines of South Africa (COMSA) 222, 230
Chamber of Mines Research

Organisation *see* COMRO
chasms of understanding 315, *342*
chest drainage system *see also*
    Sinapi chest drains 18, 146
City of Tshwane 21, 249–250,
    263–276, 349
city-driven innovation systems
    244, 342
classification system 37, 42, 45
Cloete, Paul 126
collective efficiencies 113, 116,
    120, 129
commercialisation 1–2, 10–11,
    13–14, 17–19, 26–27, 29–30, 39,
    98–99, 103–104
    organisation 91
    policy 7
    processes 13
    of technology 23–24, 35, 233,
        237, 320, 341–351, 353–358,
        360
competency centres (CC) 197,
    205, 207
complexity economics 7
COMRO 221, 228, 230–232, 236
conceptualisation of technology
    10, 341, 348
constellation of technologies 9,
    221, 349
Council for Mineral Technology
    see MINTEK
Council for Scientific and
    Industrial Research *see* CSIR
Covid-19
    antigen test 18, 147–148, 152
    pandemic 78, 140, 142, 147–

    148, 157, 166, 247, 271, 283
    vaccines 288, 337
crossing the chasm 317–318
CSIR 125, 222, 224, 232, 236, 259,
    260, 288–289, 298, 318–320,
    323–324, 335

D
De Beers 149, 152, 325–328
Decadal Plan (DP) 39, 61, 76, 164
decentralisation 225, 245, 261
decoloniality 82–84
decolonisation 82–84
decolonisation of knowledge 82,
    98, 101–102, 104
DEFF 113, 129, 134
Department of Arts, Culture,
    Science and Technology
    (DACST) 3–5
Department of Environment,
    Forestry and Fisheries *see*
    DEFF
Department of Public Service
    Administration *see* DPSA
Department of Science and
    Innovation *see also* DSI 6–7,
    21, 76, 93, 250, 256, 269, 307
Department of Science and
    Technology *see* DST
Department of Trade and
    Industry (DTI) 28, 300
Department of Trade, Industry
    and Competition (DTIC)
    61–62, 113, 152–153, 303
disaster management 271
doing, using and interacting

(DUI) 16, 42, 63, 116, 163, 290

dolutegravir 286, 288

DPSA 171, 173–174

DSI 7, 61–62, 197, 205–207, 210–211, 270, 274

DST 5–7, 80, 163–164, 319–321, 336

dynamic innovation ecosystems 244, 255

E

economic development 2, 23, 40, 43, 103, 114, 211, 217, 245, 251, 261–262, 291, 307, 358
  initiatives 256
  local 256, 267

economic transition 298, 303

efavirenz (EFV) *286*, 301

electric vehicle (EV) *see* Joule electric vehicle

EMSS Antennas 203, 328–329

EMSS Group 328–330

emtricitabine (FTC) 286

EPWP 129, 132–133

ESIs 333–334

Eskom 188–189, 191–192, 207, 226, 302, 331–332

Essential Science Indicator *see* ESIs

European Statistics (EUROSTAT) 71

European Union (EU) 45, 71, 147, 326

Expanded Public Works Programme *see* EPWP

experience-based learning 115–

116, 163

export coal industry 219, 222–224, 226, 348

F

FEKO 328–330

firm innovation capabilities 37, 42, 46, 48

firm-level innovation 34, 36–37, 40–41, 62, 163, 291, 295, 304

fourth industrial revolution (4IR) 6, 271, 321

Framing 3 thinking 83–84

frugal innovation 18, 139–142, 145, 147, 149–150, 155, 168, *342*, 345, 359

frugal medical devices 18, 345

Fuel Research Institute of South Africa 219, 221, 224

furniture industry 112, 117, 119–122, 129, 132

Furniture Technology Centre Trust (Furntech) 113–114, 123–128, 134

G

Government Agency or State-Owned Enterprise (GOV) *86–87*

government-led technological missions 189, 342

Groote Schuur Hospital 152, 326

gross domestic product (GDP) 6, 122, 281

gross expenditure on research and development (GERD) 6, 336

H

health innovation systems 141–143, 153

healthcare systems 18, 139, 142–144, 151–152, 155, 345

High temperature Reactor *see also* HTR 187–188, 208, 331

High-Temperature Gas-Cooled Modular Pebble Bed (HTR-PM) 190, 202, 208

historically black and disadvantaged institutions (HBDIs) 77, 84, *86*, 87, 99, 100

historically white and privileged institutions *see also* HWPIs 77, 84, *86*, 87

HIV (human immunodeficiency virus) 94, *96–97*, 143, 148, 283–285, 288, 316, 336, 350

HIV/AIDS 143, 310, 350

HTR 188, 190, 202, 208

human capital development (HCD) 5, 187, 204, 235

Human Sciences Research Council (HSRC) 82, 259–*260*

HWPIs 92, 98, 100

hydraulic equipment 227–228

hydraulic mining technologies 217, 226, 228–232

hydraulic technologies 20, 226–232, 234

Hydrogen South Africa (HySA) 20, 186, 197–199, 203–205, 207, 211, 347

  programme 61, 197, 200, 209–210

  projects 186–187, 207, 209

  systems 197

I

ICT 176, 192, 208, 257, 316, 331, 333

IDC 26, 28, 149, 152–153, 189, 222–223, *260*, 316, 326–327

industrial development 28, 223, 282–283, 290, 292, 297–298, 300, 303, 306

Industrial Development Corporation *see* IDC

industrial policy 120, 124, 127, 135, 291, 293, 295, 299, *296*, 301, 303, 335

Industrial Technology (IT) 36

informal economy 21, 245, 357

informal sector 68, 254, 269, 272, 304

information, computing and telecommunication *see* ICT

innovation chasm 10, 14, 26, 28, 226, 315, 317–322, 324, 328, 342, 350

  concept 15, 22, 27

  construct 315

  paradigm 15, 30, 333, 337, 353–354

innovation ecosystems 18, 167, 180, 209, 232, 236, 244, 255–256, 270, 272, 275, 279

innovation enabler 165, 167

innovation funding 26, 268, 271, 273, 326, 336

innovation policy 161, 163,

251, 282–283, 290, 293, 295,
303–304, 315, 321, 343
development of 21–22
mix 39, 56
public sector 353
Institute of Electrical and
Electronic Engineers (IEEE)
329
Integrated Development Plan
(IDP) 267, 270–271
Integrated Systems Technology
(IST) 188
intellectual property and
technology transfer (IP&TT)
survey 85–86, 93
intellectual property rights 75,
165, 289, 295, 343
Intellectual Property *see* IP
intergovernmental organisation
(IGO) 194–195, 207
intermediation 71, 112–114, 118,
120, 128–129, 134–135, 298
invasive alien plant (IAP) 128, 130
IP 99, 322
    products 92, 103
    protection 99, 103–104
IT technologies 36
iThemba Pharmaceuticals 298,
300

J
Joule electric vehicle (EV) 2, 15,
26–30, 331–333, 336, 353
K
Karoo Array Telescope (KAT)
194–195, 329–330

Ketlaphela 300–303
key technology and innovation
concepts 2, 8

L
lamivudine 285–286, *288*, 299
large-scale export coal industry
218–219, 223, 226
linear model of innovation 40,
317–319, 322
local innovation systems 6, 21,
127, 246, 255, 349
local systems of innovation *see*
LSI
Lodox scanner 18, 149–152, 155,
327, 345
Lonza 301–302
low- and middle-income
countries 139, 141, 147, 153,
345
LSI 244–247, 249–252, 265–268,
270, 272–275, 325, 349
Lundvall, Bengt-Åke 81, 115, 163,
255, 308

M
managerialism 55, 58, 81, 99, 206
Maponya Mall Urban Thusong
Centre (MMUTSC) 171, 173,
346
market system failures 11, 19, *342*
    exploitation of public
        resources 11, *342*
    externalisation of costs 11, *342*
    knowledge spillovers 11, *342*
medical devices industry 139–140,

144, 155
Medical Diagnostech (Pty) Ltd
    147–149, 151–154
Medical Research Council (MRC)
    259, *260*, 289
MeerKAT array, 64-dish 194
MeerKAT radio telescope 195,
    203–204, 329–330
membrane electrode assembly
    (MEA) 198–199
MeMeZA Community Alarm
    System 174–176, 346
mineral resource finance network
    see MRFN
MINTEK 197–198, 259–*260*
MLP 10, 22, 296–*298*, 305–307,
    350
modes of innovation 34–37,
    40–45, 48–51, 53–57, 59–61, 72
MRFN 20, 216–217, 221–223,
    226, 229–230, 232–236, 348,
    356, 358
multi-dimensional analytical
    framework 10, 161–162, 217
multi-level perspective *see* MLP
Municipal Innovation Maturity
    Index (MIMI) 250, 259, 263
Mustapha, Nazeem 17, 93, 95, 344

N
National Advisory Council on
    Innovation (NACI) 5, 61, 260,
    321
national development plan (NDP)
    78, 104, 140, 152245, 266
National Environment

Management Biodiversity Act
    (NEMBA) 130
National Intellectual Property
    Management Office (NIPMO)
    10, 76, 85, *260*, 344
National Research and
    Development Strategy 5, 289,
    322
National Research Foundation
    (NRF) 321, 329–330
national system of innovation 2,
    23–24, 34, 39, 42, 48, 59, 63, 76,
    84, 162, 246, *260*, 359
    approach 21–22
    broad 14, 16, 237, 343
    narrow 14, 17
national system of innovation *see*
    NSI
National Treasury 174, 176, 299,
    301–302
NDP
NGOs 118, *169*, 249, 253, 255
non-government organisations *see*
    NGOs
novel technologies 8, 298, 351
NSI 4, 6–7, 78, 112–115, 160–164,
    180, 244, 249–251, 254, 265–
    267, 274–275, 343, 358–359
    approach 5, 283, 290, 293, 295,
        300, 303–305, 307, 341, 352
    concept 161, 179, 294
    definition 5
    framework 80, 259, 282–283, 290,
        293–295, 307
    functional 245–246, 252
    studies 119

Nuclear Energy Corporation of South Africa (NECSA) 205, 260, 332

O

OECD 6, 39, 44, 252, 256, 322
Offices of Technology Transfer *see* OTTs
opportunity niches 2, 9–10, 13, 16–20, 345, 354
Optimal Energy 2, 26–30, 332, 357
Organisation for Economic Co-operation and Development *see* OECD
OTTs 76–77, 79, 85, 90, 93, 95, 105, 344, 358

P

partnerships 18, 27, 58–60, 152–154, 156, 164, 167, 195, 205–210, 230, 271–272, 347
patenting and commercialisation 10, 91–92
Pebble Bed Modular Reactor (PBMR) 19, 186–192, 201–203, 205, 207–208, 210–211, 331–332, 335, 347
Pelchem 301–302
PEM 198–200
pharmaceutical production 290–291
phases in transition 297
Platinum Group Metal (PGM) 187, 197–199, 203, 208
PLHIV (People Living with HIV) 283–285, 299

pneumatic equipment 227
policy recommendations 23, 315, 341, 350, 360
post-apartheid national system of innovation 2–3
pressurised water reactor (PWR) 187, 191
procurement 59, 165–166, 176–177, 180, 299, 331, 346
Proton Exchange Membrane *see* PEM
public administration theory 81
public research organisation (PRO) 289, 315–316
public sector innovation (PSI) 19, 160–162, 165–166, 168–169, 177, 179–180, 253, 259, *342*, 352–353
public technology transfer system 76, 84, 95, 101–102, 105
public value 17, 75, 77, 84–85, 92, 93, 95–97, 100–102, 104–105, 166, 344, 353
inputs 104, 344, 353
outcomes 75, 77, 85, 92–93, 95–97, 100–102, 104–105, 344, 353
publicly supported research 2, 17, 21

Q

quadruple helix 81, 162, 248–249

R

R&D 35, 39, 75, 104–105, 121, 162, 165, 252, 290, 317–318,

327, 335–336

expenditure 77, 86–87, *96*, 100, 144, 327, 330, 334

funding 93, 101, 256

institutions 88–89, 91–92, 99, 103, 115, 275

military 326, 328

performance 87–89, 91–92, 99, 256

policy *298*

stages 153–155

strategy 80, 320–321

survey 85–86, 344

Ralphs, Gerard 17, 95, 344

Ramaphosa, Matamela Cyril 76, 78

rapid antigen test 148–149, 151–153

Reconstruction and Development Programme (RDP) 3

reorienting technology transfer 75, *342*

research and development *see also* R&D 5, 11, 29, 35, 75, 121, 140, 162, 165, 236, 252, 290, 344

research and innovation management 81, 84, 100

reverse innovation 18, 139, 141–142, 147, 149–150, 154, *342*, 345, 359

Richards Bay 219, 224–225

Rohracher, Harald 10, 217

role of intermediaries 112

S

SAMERDI 236–237

SANParks 113, 129, 131, 134

SARS-CoV-2 Antigen Device *see also* rapid antigen test 148

Scannex X-ray detectors 326

Schmitz, Hubert 116–117

School Desks and Conservation Initiative *see* SDCI

science and innovation policy 75, 77, 79, 83

science, engineering and technology (SET) 19, 163

science, technology and innovation *see also* STI 8, 80, 198, 201, 208, 281–282, 289, 335, 354

policy 35, 281, 289

policy and strategy 201

strategy 198, 208

SDCI 113–114, 128–133

Sinapi chest drains 18, 145–147, 151–152, 345

SKA 19, 186, 192, 196, 208–209, 211, 330, 347

project 187, 193–195, 202–204, 206–207

SKA Organisation Board 194

Slabber, Johan 188

socio-economic development 23, 254, 356, 359–360

socio-technical systems 83, 291, 295–297, 306

socioeconomic impacts of technologies 352–353, 358

Soudien, Crain 82

South African Business Innovation Survey 47, 49, 51, 72

South African Medical Research
Council (SAMRC) 144, 147,
152
South African Mining Extraction
Research, Development &
Innovation *see* SAMERDI
spatial development framework
(SDF) 270–271
Spatial Planning and Land Use
Management Act (SPLUMA)
271
Square Kilometre Array
Observatory (SKAO) 193–195
Square Kilometre Array *see* SKA
stavudine 285–*286*, 289, 298–299
STI 5–6, 40, 155
STI policy 23, 35, 39, 43–44,
48–49, 57, 59, 63, 80, 162, 256,
294, 317, 346
structural change 63, 216, *342*
in the economy 56
processes of 235
structural system failures 11, *342*
capabilities failure 11, *342*
infrastructural failure 11, 19,
342
institutional failures 11, 18, 21,
342
network failures 11, *342*
Support Programme for Industrial
Innovation (SPII) 326, 329
Sustainable Development Goals
(SDGs) 163, 211, 283, 334
systemic failure 112

T
techno-economics 291, 295, 297
technology and innovation policy
201, 281, 289, 348–349, 354
technology colony 318–319
technology domains 12, 14, 17, 40,
221, 230, 344, 349
Technology Innovation Agency
(TIA) 10, 28, *94*, 153, 259, *260*,
298, 300, 320–321
technology transfer 79, 84–86, 90,
96–97, 98, 101, *318–319*
capacity 85
enablers of 89
functions 17, 88, 90–91, 99–100
operations 87–89
processes 17, 91, 93, 95,
99–100, 104–105, 353
systems 76–77, 103, 344
tenofovir 285–286, *288*–289,
299–300
tenofovir, lamivudine and
dolutegravir (TLD) 285–286
Tesla 15, 28–30
Model S 28
Roadster 28
Thackeray, Michael 323–324, 335
The Innovation Hub (TIH) 175,
268
Trade-Related Aspects of
Intellectual Property (TRIPS)
289
transformation 12, 16, 20, 232–
234, 237–238, 247, *248*, 256,
342, 352–353, 355
economic 244, 254–255

healthcare 142
policies 23, 235
structural 37–38, 50, 57
transformational innovation
policy 84, 170, 305, 308
transformational system failures
12, 20, *342*
demand articulation failures
12, 20, *342*
directionality failure 12, 16,
342
policy coordination failures 12,
18, 21, *342*
reflexivity failure 12, 20, *342*
transformative innovation 102,
104
transformative innovation policy
84, 170, 305, 308
Transformative Innovation Policy
Consortium (TIPC) 83, 178,
180
transition theory 295
Transvaal Coal Owners'
Association (TCOA) 222, 224
triple helix model of innovation
81, 99, 118, 251, *257*
Tshabala-Msimang, Manto 299
Tshwane *see* City of Tshwane

W
Wakanda 268, 274
water-based hydraulic mining
technology 217
water-based hydraulic technology
20
Watkins, Andrew 119
Weber, Karl Matthias 10, 217
White Paper on Local
Government 247, 253, 261
White Paper on Science and
Technology 4–5, 80, 102, 259,
282, 289, 293, 295, 316
White Paper on Science,
Technology and Innovation 6,
39, 76, 80, 163, 261, 270, 282,
335
whole-body rapid scanner *see also*
Lodox scanner 18

X
X-ray body scanner 149–150
X-ray technology 325–328

Z
zidovudine (AZT) 284–*286*,
288–289, 298–299